Almanach '96

International IIHF Yearbook '96

Publisher: Horst Eckert

COPRESS

Fotos/Photographs: Eckert Archiv
Titelfoto/Cover Picture: Michael Sauer

Herausgeber/Publisher: Horst Eckert
Redaktionsleitung/Editorial Management: Horst Eckert
Mitarbeiter/Contributors: IIHF Zürich
Igor Kuperman (Winnipeg), Klaus Zaugg (Zürich), Ernst Martini (Darmstadt/GER),
Ivan Sajnoha (Switzerland), Birger Nordmark (Sweden), Michael Travnicek (CZE),
Dr. Andrei Stare (Ljubljana).

\

CIP-Titelaufnahme der Deutschen Bibliothek
Eishockey-Almanach ...: international icehockey annual ... –
München: Copress Verlag
erscheint jährlich. – Aufnahme nach 1990/91 (1990)
ISSN 0938-7722
1990/91. (1990). –
Erscheinungsbeginn mit diesem Bd.

© 1995 Copress Verlag GmbH, München
Alle Rechte vorbehalten/All Rights reserved
Satz/Typesetting: H. P. Werbung + Textverarbeitung, Aichach
Gesamtherstellung: Bruckmann, München
Printed in Germany
ISSN 0938-7722
ISBN 3-7679-0475-6

INDEX | # NATIONS

Foreword

René Fasel
President IIHF

Teamwork is the name of the game, especially in ice hockey, the game we love so much. Last season produced once again great results. The IIHF Championships all over the world proved to be a great success. The hosting organizations together with officials, referees, teams, coaches, players and trainers prepared unforgettable tournaments for the spectators. The efforts needed a lot of teamwork to make them happen and the results were excellent. But it also needed a lot of co-operation with the municipalities to have the support in order to be successful with the travelling plans, security measures, accommodation and even the financial support that was granted to the tournament. The people in ice hockey call it teamwork.

This coming season the IIHF will celebrate two major tournaments. The history of the World Junior Championship dates back a long time. This year's games in Massachussets, USA, will be the 20th championship games in the history of the IIHF. During this period, a vast number of top players have participated in this tournament. As a matter of fact, these games have always been open to all best players of the world. The tournaments have seen players like Wayne Gretzky, Mario Lemieux, Mats Sundin, Sergei Fedorov, Jari Kurri and many, many other great athletes to play their way to the hearts of the fans. There is no doubt that some players taking part in this year's event will be the shining stars of the future and we will enjoy their talents for years to come.

The IIHF 60th World Championship will be held in April and May in the beautiful city of Vienne. The first ever games took part as early as 1920. These games have earned their position among the fans as well. The history of these games was thrilling. Throughout the years, the organizers have been able to prepare the championships to the standard they represent today: a high quality tournament for teams to participate and memorable possibility for the fans to get together to cheer for their own National Teams. The tournament in Vienna will again represent an unforgettable IIHF Championship with games to remember. The history of both of these great Championships has taken a lot of efforts from everybody to make it happen. Again the secret behind these successful efforts has been teamwork.

InLine Hockey is the fastest growing team sport of today. The International Ice Hockey Federation has started to take steps to organize this great sport worldwide. InLine Hockey offers to the players the possibility to participate in the fastest team sport in summertime and also allows the people managing the rinks to see action all year round in their building. Most of the IIHF member associations are getting involved with InLine Hockey, and first official national championships will be organized next summer. The IIHF official World Championship will be organized in 1996, as well. The year 1996 means to the IIHF that the InLine Hockey will become the official sport of our Federation. For this we need the support from the people among our Federation, our member associations, people already in the sport, manufactures, municipalities and the players of course. We can all put this together to a great sport. But only with teamwork.

As the President of the International Ice Hockey Federation I wish to express my thanks to everyone who made the last season as one of the most unforgettable through the history of ice hockey. And I would also like to send my best wishes to all of you involved with the Championships to come in this season. Let us celebrate together especially these 20th and 60th anniversaries. Let us turn both Championships into the best ever held. We can all lend our assistance to be organizations in charge. We just have to use one tool: teamwork.

Abkürzungen – Statistik-Erklärung

Player		Spieler
G	Goals	Tore
A	Assists (A1 / A2)	Beihilfen 1 + 2
P	Points	Punkte
PIM	Penalty in minutes	Strafminuten
GP	Games played	Spiele absolviert
GK	Goalkeeper	Torhüter
D	Defenseman	Verteidiger
F	Forward	Stürmer
LW	Left wing	Linksaußen
RW	Right wing	Rechtsaußen
C	Center	Mittelstürmer

Goalkeeper Statistic		(Torhüter)
MIN	Minutes played	Minuten gespielt
GA	Goal against	Tore erhalten
SOG	Shots on goal	Schüsse auf Tor
SVS	Saves	Abwehraktionen

Teams		Mannschaften
promoted to Pool ... (into)		Aufsteiger in ...
relegated to Pool ... (into)		Absteiger in ...
Tournament		Turnier
Awards		Preise/Pokale
Best player		Bester Spieler
The three best player of each team		Die drei besten Spieler jeder Mannschaft
W	**Won games**	Gewonnene Spiele
T	**Tied games**	Unentschieden
L	**Lost games**	Verlorene Spiele

Championship
Meisterschaft

All Time
Alle Zeiten

Total medalcount
Medaillenspiegel

Top Scorer
Tore + Assists je 1 P.

World Championship
Weltmeisterschaft

Member = Mitglied

Chairmen = Vorsitzender

Referee = Schiedsrichter

Rules = Regeln

Oldtimer = Alte Herren

Honorary President
Ehrenpräsident

Council = Vorstand

Index = Inhalt

Federation = Verband

Medal winners
Medaillengewinner

Most Assists ... Goals
Meiste Beihilfen/Tore

Group = Gruppe

Abkürzungen der Länder siehe Seite 9

INTERNATIONAL
ICE HOCKEY FEDERATION

COUNCIL

René Fasel	**Ing. Miroslav Subrt**	**Shoichi Tomita**	**Walter Bush**
President	Vice President	Vice President	Vice President
President 1994	Vice President 1966	Vice President 1994	Vice President 1994
Council 1986	Council 1959	Council 1978	Council 1986

Kai Hietarinta	**Dr. Hans Dobida**	**Yuri Korolev**	**Rickard Fagerlund**
Finland	Austria	Russia	Sweden
Treasurer/Schatzmeister	1986	1990	1994
1990			

Philippe Lacarrière	**Frederick Meredith**	**Bogdan Tyszkiewicz**	**Dr. Günther Sabetzki**
France	Great Britain	Poland	Germany
1994	1994	1986	Honorary President 1994

Headquarters
International Ice Hockey Federation IIHF
Tödistrasse 23 · CH-8002 Zürich/Switzerland
Telephone (+41.1) 281 1430 · Fax (+41.1) 281 1433

Jan-Åke Edvinsson
General Secretary

Roman Neumayer
Technical Director

Kimmo Leinonen
PR and Marketing Manager

Renato Dall 'Oglio
Financial Manager

Dave Fitzpatrick
Sport Manager

Karin Pletscher
Secretary

Honorary Presidents
Ehrenpräsidenten

Paul Loicq †	1947
Dr. Fritz Kraatz †	1954
John F. Ahearne †	1975
Thayer Tutt †	1986
Dr. Günther Sabetzki	1994

Honorary Members / Ehrenmitglieder

Harry Lindblad †	1975
P. O. Wester	1975
Z. Wierbicki †	1975
Rudolf Eklöw †	1976
Gordon Juckes †	1977
Andrei Starovoitov	1986
Walter Wasservogel †	1986

S. E. M. Juan Antonio Samaranch	1987
Curt Berglund	1990
Marjan Luxa	1990
Gordon Renwick	1994
György Pasztor	1994

IIHF COMMITTEE MEMBERS
1994–1998

Asian/Oceania Committee
Sun-Kyu Lim (KOR), Ron O'Reilly (NZL), Pan Weimin (CHN).

Coaches Committee
Yuri Korolev (RUS) Chairman (IIHF-Council), Bob Nicholson (CAN), Jozef Dovalil (CZE), Conny Evensson (SWE), Dave Peterson (USA), Sakari Pietilä (FIN).

Development Committee
Shoichi Tomita (JPN) Chairman (IIHF-Council), Eduard Pana (ROM), Robert van Rijswijk (NED); Paul Shindman (ISR).

Disciplinary Committee
Dr. Hans Dobida (AUT), Chairman (IIHF-Council), Dr. Ernst Eichler (GER), Dusan Pasek (SVK), Janko Popovic (SLO), Frans Michael van Erp (NED).

Executive Committee
Rene Fasel (SUI) Chairman (IIHF-President), Ing. Miroslav Subrt (CZE) IIHF Vice-President, Walter Bush (USA), IIHF Vice-President, Shoichi Tomita (JPN) IIHF Vice-President, Kai Hietarinta (FIN) IIHF-Council, Jan-Ake Edvinsson (IIHF General Secretary) non voting member IIHF.

Junior Committee
Philippe Lacarriere (FRA) Chairman (IIHF-Council), Gino Merler (ITA), Juraj Okolicany (SVK), Jukka-Pekka Vuorinen (FIN), Claes-Göran Wallin (SWE), Erich Wüthrich (SUI).

Marketing Committee
Rickard Fagerlund (SWE) Chairman (IIHF-Council), Dr. Wolfgang Bonenkamp (GER), David Ogrean (USA), Alexander Steblin (RUS), Ron Robison (CAN).

Medical Committee
Frederick Meredith (GBR) Chairman (IIHF-Council), Dr. Wolf-Dieter Montag (GER), Prof. Paul Lereim (NOR), Dr. Mark Aubry (CAN), Dr. Pavel Jandik (CZE), Dr. Pietro Segantini (SUI)

Medical Sub Committee
Dr. Jan Nohejl (CZE), Dr. Frede Jensen (DEN), George Nagobads, M. D. (USA), Dr. Miroslav Klima (SVK), Dr. Jerzy Widuchowski (POL).

Oldtimer Committee
Dr. Hans Dobida (AUT) Chairman (IIHF-Council), Josef Linder (CZE), Bill MacGillivary (CAN), Jyrki Otila (FIN), Alexander Ragulin (RUS).

Referees Committee
Bogdan Tyskiewicz (POL) Chairman (IIHF-Council), Rob Nadin (CAN), Valentin Kozin (RUS), Dag Olsson (SWE), Josef Kompalla (GER), Jarmo Jalarvo (FIN).

Rules Committee
Philippe Lacariere (FRA) Chairman (IIHF-Council), Dr. Pietro Segantini (SUI), Slawa Bykov (RUS), Jon Haukeland (NOR).

Sports Committee
Ing. Miroslav Subrt (CZE) Chairman (IIHF Vice-President), Art Berglund (USA), Dr. Wolfgang Bonenkamp (GER), Dr. Dieter Kalt (AUT), Kalervo Kummola (FIN), Bo Tovland (SWE).

Statutes Committee
Frederick Meredith (GBR) Chairman (IIHF-Council), Murray Costello (CAN), Ing. Miroslav Subrt (CZE) IIHF Vice-President, Dr. Gerhard Mösslang (GER), Josef Brunner (SUI), Jan-Ake Edvinsson (IIHF General Secretary) non voting member IIHF.

Women's Committee
Walter Bush (USA) Chairman (IIHF-Vice President), Urpo Helkovaara (FIN), Herman Foss (NOR), Frank Libera (CAN), Sergej Samilov (RUS).

Arbitration Board
Robert Allen (USA), Per A. Flod (NOR), Othmar Heitmann (AUT), Martin Holmgren (SWE), Kalervo Kummola (FIN), Dr. Gerhard Mösslang (GER), James O'Grady (CAN).

IIHF-Members
IIHF Championships 1996

			Olympic Qualification	WC WM	Junior World U 20	Junior Continent. U18	Women European (E) World (W)
AND	Andorra	Andorra	–	–	–	–	–
AUS	Australia	Australien	–	D	–	–	–
AUT	Austria	Österreich	–	A	B	C	–
AZE	Azerbaijan	Aserbaidschan	–	–	–	–	–
BEL	Belgium	Belgien	–	D	–	D	–
BLR	Belarus	Weißrußland	–	B	B	A	–
BRA	Brazil	Brasilien	–	–	–	–	–
BUL	Bulgaria	Bulgarien	–	D	–	D	–
CAN	Cananda	Kanada	–	A	A	–	W
CHN	China	China	–	C	–	A/O	W
CRO	Croatia	Kroatien	–	C	D	C	–
CZE	Czech Republic	Czech Republik	–	A	A	A	E/B
DEN	Denmark	Dänemark	–	B	C	B	E/B
ESP	Spain	Spanien	–	D	C	C	–
EST	Estonia	Estland	–	C	D	C	–
FIN	Finland	Finnland	–	A	A	A	E-A/W
FRA	France	Frankreich	–	A	B	B	E/B
GBR	Great Britain	Großbritannien	–	B	C	C	E/B
GER	Germany	Deutschland	–	A	A	A	E/A/W
GRE	Greece	Griechenland	–	D	–	–	–
HKG	Hong Kong	Hong Kong	–	–	–	–	–
HUN	Hungary	Ungarn	–	C	B	B	–
IND	India	Indien	–	–	–	–	–
ISL	Iceland	Island	–	–	–	–	–
ISR	Israel	Israel	–	D	–	D	–
ITA	Italy	Italien	–	A	B	B	–
JPN	Japan	Japan	–	B	B	A/O	PAC
KOR	Korea	Korea	–	D	–	A/O	–
KAZ	Kazakhstan	Kasachstan	–	C	C	A/O	–
LAT	Latvia	Lettland	–	B	B	C	E/B
LTU	Lithuania	Litauen	–	D	D	C	–
LUX	Luxembourg	Luxemburg	–	–	–	–	–
MEX	Mexico	Mexiko	–	–	–	–	–
NED	Netherlands	Niederlande	–	B	C	D	E/B
NOR	Norway	Norwegen	–	A	B	B	E/A/W
NZL	New Zealand	Neuseeland	–	–	–	–	–
POL	Poland	Polen	–	B	B	B	–
PRK	PR Korea	Nord Korea	–	–	–	–	–
ROM	Rumania	Rumänien	–	C	C	B	–
RUS	Russia	Rußland	–	A	A	A	E/A
RSA	South Africa	Südafrika	–	D	–	–	–
SLO	Slovenia	Slowenien	–	C	C	C	–
SUI	Switzerland	Schweiz	–	B	A	A	E/A/W
SVK	Slovakia	Slowakei	–	A	A	A	E/B
SWE	Sweden	Schweden	–	A	A	A	E/A/W
THA	Thailand	Thailand	–	–	–	–	–
TPE	Chinese Taipei	Taiwan	–	–	–	–	–
TUR	Turkey	Türkei	–	D	–	D	–
UKR	Ukraine	Ukraine	–	C	A	B	E/B
USA	USA	USA	–	A	A	–	W
YUG	Yugoslavia	Jugoslawien	–	D	D	D	–

HIGH TECH HUMAN
COMMUNICATION.

Audio Visual Communication & Computer.

FUNAI ELECTRIC CO.,LTD.JAPAN.

IIHF-CALENDER INTERNATIONAL 1996

	Pool	Date/Venue	Teams
WORLD CHAMPIONSHIPS	**A**	**Austria,** April 21, – May 5, 1996 Vienna	**Group A:** CAN, USA, RUS, AUT, GER, SVK **Group B:** FIN, SWE, ITA, CZE, FRA, NOR
	B	**Netherlands,** April 10, – 20, 1996	SUI, LAT, POL, JPN DEN, NED, GBR, BLR
	C	**Slovenia,** March 22, – 31, 1996	ROM, KZK, UKR, EST CHN, HUN, SLO, CRO
	D	**Lithuania** 1996	YUG, BUL, LIT, ESP, KOR, BEL ISR, AUS, SAF, GRE, NZL, TUR
JUNIOR WORLD CHAMPIONSHIPS	**A**	**USA** – Boston December 26, 1995 – January 4, 1996	CAN, RUS, SWE, FIN, USA CZE, GER, UKR, SUI, SVK
	B	**Poland** December 27, 1995 – January 5, 1996	POL, FRA, NOR, AUT, JPN, ITA, LAT, HUN
	C	**Slovenia** December 27, 1995 – January 1996	DEN, BLR, ESP, ROM NED, GBR, KZK, SLO
	D	**Estonia** December 30, 1995 – January 4, 1996	EST, LIT, CRO, YUG, SAF
JUNIOR EUROPEAN CHAMPIONSHIPS	**A**	**Russia** – Ufa April 1996	FIN, GER, SWE, RUS CZE, SUI, BLR, SVK
	B	**Poland** March, 23 – 29, 1996	NOR, POL, DEN, HUN, ITA, FRA, ROM, UKR
	C	**Slovenia** March 20, – 22, 1996	AUT, LAT, SLO, GBR, EST, ESP, LIT, CRO
	D		NED, YUG, ISR, BUL, TUR, BEL
ASIAN/OCEANIA Junior Championships		**Kazakhstan** 1996	JPN, KZK, CHN, KOR
WOMEN'S EUROPEAN CHAM-PIONSHIPS	**A**	**Russia** March 20, – 26, 1996	FIN, SWE, SUI, NOR, GER, RUS
	B		LAT, DEN, CZE, SVK FRA, NED, GBR, UKR
PACIFIC WOMEN'S Championships		**Canada** 1996	USA, CAN, CHN, JPN, KZK

EUROPEAN CUP 1995-96

Quarter Finals – October 6–8

GROUP A (in Bulgaria)
Steaua Bucharest	ROM
Sokol Kiev	UKR
Partizan Belgrade	YUG
Levski Sofia	BUL

GROUP B (in Hungary)
Tivali Minsk	BLR
Ust Kamenogorsk	KZK
Ferencvarosi	HUN
Medvescak Zagreb	CRO

GROUP C (in Denmark)
Herning	DEN
Kreenholm	EST
Energija	LIT
Bat-Yam/ISR or Ankara/TUR	

GROUP D (in Netherlands)
Tilburg	NED
Sheffield	GBR
Olimpia	SLO
Urdin/ESP or Luxembourg/LUX	

Semi Finals, November 10–12

GROUP E (in Norway)
Jonköping	SWE
Storhamar	NOR
Kosice	SVK
Winner of Group A	

GROUP F (in Switzerland)
TPS Turku	FIN
VEU Feldkirch	AUT
ERC Kloten	SUI
Winner of Group B	

GROUP G (in Italy)
Dynamo Moscow	RUS
Bolzano	ITA
Pardaugava Riga	LAT
Winner of Group C	

GROUP H (Czech Rep.)
Dadak Vsetin	CZE
Rouen HC	FRA
Podhale Novy Targ	POL
Winner of Group D	

Finals Dec. 26, – 30, 1995 in Cologne/GER – Qualified Kölner EC and Jokerit Helsinki + Winners of Group E, F, G,H.

11

WORLD CHAMPIONSHIP 1996
POOL A
April 21 – May 5, 1996 · Vienna/Austria

EISHOCKEY
WM'96
Wien · Österreich

	Group A Stadthalle			Group B Albert-Schultz-Halle	
Sunday 21, April	14.30	Germany – Russia	16.00	Czech Republic – Sweden	
	18.30	Canada – Switzerland	20.00	Finland – Norway	
Monday 22, April	16.00	Austria – USA	16.00	France – Italy	
	20.00	Russia – Switzerland			
Tuesday 23, April	15.00	USA – Germany	16.00	Italy – Norway	
	19.00	Canada – Austria	20.00	Finland – Czech Republic	
Wednesday 24, April	15.00	Germany – Canada	16.00	Sweden – France	
			20.00	Norway – Czech Republic	
Thursday 25, April	16.00	Switzerland – Austria	16.00	France – Finland	
	20.00	USA – Russia	20.00	Sweden – Italy	
Friday 26, April	15.00	Austria – Germany			
	20.00	Russia – Canada	20.00	Italy – Finland	
Saturday 27, April	16.00	USA – Switzerland	16.00	Czech Republic – France	
			20.00	Sweden – Norway	
Sunday 28, April	16.00	Russia – Austria	16.00	Italy – Czech Republic	
	20.00	Canada – USA	20.00	Finland – Sweden	
Monday 29, April	15.00	Switzerland – Germany			
			20.00	Norway – France	

Play-offs Stadthalle

Quarter Finals	Tuesday April 30,	16.00 Game No 31 : A2 – B3
		20.00 Game No 32 : B2 – A3
	Wednesday May 1,	16.00 Game No 32 : A1 – B4
		20.00 Game No 35 : B1 – A4
Semi Finals	Friday May 3,	16.00 Game No 37 : W31 – W35
		20.00 Game No 38 : W32 – W33
Bronce medal	Saturday May 4,	20.00 Game No 40 : L38 – L37
Final	Sunday May 5,	15.00 Game No 41 : W38 – W37
Relegations games (best of 3)	Wednesday May 1, (Albert-Schultz-Halle)	16.00 Game No 34 : B6 – A6
	Thursday May 2	19.00 Game No 36 : A6 – B6
	Saturday May 4,	16.00 Game No 39 (if necessary) B6 – A6
World Championships POOL A	**1997:** April 19, – May 4,	in Finland
	1998: April – May	in Switzerland
	1999: April – May	in Norway (Oslo, Hamar, Lillehammer)

MEDAL WINNERS

European Championships 1910–1991

Land Country	Gold Gold	Silber Silver	Bronze Bronce
Soviet Union	27	5	2
TCH/Bohemia	15	22	16
Sweden	10	18	19
Switzerland	4	6	8
Great Britain	4	2	1
Germany	2	4	7
Austria	2	3	5
Belgium	1	1	4
France	1	1	–
Poland	–	2	–
Finland	–	1	4
FRG	–	1	–
Norway	–	–	2

World Championships 1920–1995

Land Country	Gold Gold	Silber Silver	Bronze Bronce
Soviet Union	22	7	5
Canada	20	9	9
Sweden	6	15	11
TCH	6	12	16
USA	2	9	3
Great Britain	1	2	2
Germany	–	1	2
Switzerland	–	1	8
Russia	1	–	–
Finland	1	2	–
FRG	–	1	–
Austria	–	–	2
Czech Republic	–	–	1

Olympics 1924–1994

	1924	1928	1932	1936	1948	1952	1956	1960	1964	1968	1972	1976	1980	1984	1988	1992	1994
Belgium	7	7	–	13	–	–	–	–	–	–	–	–	–	–	–	–	–
TCH/Bohemia	5	6	–	4	2	4	5	4	3	2	3	2	5	2	6	3	–
Germany	–	10	3	5	–	8	6	6	7	7	7	3	10	5	5	6	7
GDR	–	–	–	–	–	–	–	–	–	8	–	–	–	–	–	–	–
Finland	–	–	–	–	–	7	–	7	6	5	5	4	4	6	2	7	3
France	5	5	–	9	–	–	–	–	–	14	–	–	–	–	11	8	10
Great Britain	3	4	–	1	5	–	–	–	–	–	–	–	–	–	–	–	–
Netherlands	–	–	–	–	–	–	–	–	–	–	–	–	9	–	–	–	–
Italy	–	–	–	9	8	–	7	–	15	–	–	–	–	9	–	12	9
Canada	1	1	1	2	1	1	3	2	4	3	–	–	6	4	4	2	2
Latvia	–	–	–	13	–	–	–	–	–	–	–	–	–	–	–	–	–
Norway	–	–	–	–	–	9	–	–	10	11	8	11	9	–	11	9	11
Austria	–	7	–	7	7	–	10	9	13	13	–	8	–	11	12	–	12
Poland	–	9	4	9	6	6	8	–	9	–	6	6	7	8	10	11	–
Rumania	–	–	–	–	–	–	–	–	12	12	–	7	8	–	–	–	–
Sweden	4	2	–	5	4	3	4	5	2	4	4	–	3	3	3	5	1
Switzerland	7	3	–	13	3	5	9	–	8	–	10	11	–	–	8	10	–
Soviet Union	–	–	–	–	–	–	1	3	1	1	1	1	2	1	1	1	–
Hungary	–	11	–	7	–	–	–	–	16	–	–	–	–	–	–	–	–
USA	2	–	2	3	–	2	2	1	5	6	2	5	1	7	7	4	8
Yugoslavia	–	–	–	–	–	–	–	–	14	9	11	10	10	11	–	–	–
Japan	–	–	9	–	–	–	8	11	19	9	9	12	–	–	–	–	–
Bulgaria	–	–	–	–	–	–	–	–	–	12	–	–	–	–	–	–	–
Russia	–	–	–	–	–	–	–	–	–	–	–	–	–	–	–	–	4
Czech Republic	–	–	–	–	–	–	–	–	–	–	–	–	–	–	–	–	5
Slovakia	–	–	–	–	–	–	–	–	–	–	–	–	–	–	–	–	6

Olympic Medals

	Gold	Silver	Bronce
URS	8	1	1
CAN	5	4	2
USA	2	5	1
GBR	1	–	1
TCH	–	4	3
SWE	1	2	4
FIN	–	1	1
SUI	–	–	2
GER	–	–	2
FRG	–	–	1

World Championships 1920–1939

	1920	1924	1928	1930	1931	1932	1933	1934	1935	1936	1937	1938	1939
Canada	1	1	1	1	1	1	2	1	1	2	1	1	1
USA	2	2	–	–	2	2	1	2	–	3	–	7	2
TCH	3	5	5	6	4	–	3	5	4	4	6	3	4
Sweden	4	4	2	–	6	–	–	–	5	5	–	5	–
Switzerland	5	7	3	3	–	–	5	4	2	13	3	6	3
Belgium	6	7	8	10	–	–	11	12	14	13	–	–	11
France	6	5	5	6	9	–	–	11	7	9	7	–	–
Great Britain	–	3	4	10	8	–	–	8	3	1	2	2	6
Austria	–	–	5	4	3	–	4	7	6	7	–	10	–
Poland	–	–	8	5	4	4	9	–	10	9	8	7	6
Germany	–	–	8	2	–	3	5	3	9	5	4	4	5
Hungary	–	–	11	6	7	–	9	6	11	7	5	7	7
Japan	–	–	–	6	–	–	–	–	–	9	–	–	–
Italy	–	–	–	10	–	–	7	9	8	9	–	–	9
Rumania	–	–	–	–	10	–	6	10	11	–	–	13	–
Latvia	–	–	–	–	–	–	7	–	13	13	–	10	10
Netherlands	–	–	–	–	–	–	–	–	14	–	–	–	11
Lithuania	–	–	–	–	–	–	–	–	–	–	–	10	–
Norway	–	–	–	–	–	–	–	–	–	–	–	13	–
Yugoslavia	–	–	–	–	–	–	–	–	–	–	–	–	13
Finland	–	–	–	–	–	–	–	–	–	–	–	–	13

1947 – 1970

	1947	1948	1949	1950	1951	1952	1953	1954	1955	1956	1957	1958	1959	1960	1961	1962	1963	1964	1965	1966	1967	1968	1969	1970
Australia													A9		B5									
Belgium	A8		A8	A9	B4	B5			B5	B3					C6		C6							C7
Bulgaria																C4				C2			C5	B8
TCH	A1	A2	A1			A4	A4	A4	A3	A5	A3	A4	A3	A4	A2		A3	A3	A2	A2	A4	A2	A3	A3
Denmark		B1												B6	C3					C2	C3		C6	C5
Germany					A8	A2	A5	A6	A6			A7	A6	A8	A6	A7	A7	B3	B1	A8	A7		B4	B2
GDR									B1	A5		A9		A5		A6		A5	A5	A7	A8	B1		A5
Finland		B3		A7	A7		A6	A9		A4	A6	A6	A7		A7	A4	A5	A6	A7	A7	A6	A5	A5	A4
France			A7	B2	B6	B6									C2	B3	B6			C4	B6			C4
Great Britain		A5		A4	A5	B1	B2								B2	A8	B7		B6	B8				
Netherlands			A8	B3	B4	B5		B7							C4	B4	C5			C5			C4	C6
Italy		A8		B1	B3	B1		B1	A7			A10		B4			B7		C1	B5		B8		C2
Japan										A8				A8		B1		B3		C1	B2	C1		B5
Yugoslavia				B6					B4						C3		B5	B6	B7	B3	B4	B1	B3	B4
Canada		A1	A2	A1	A1	A1		A2	A1	A3		A1	A1	A2	A1	A2	A4	A4	A4	A3	A3	A3	A4	
Norway		B2	A6	A4	A9			A8			A7	A8		B1	A5	B1	B2	A8	B4	B3	B3	B5		B3
Austria	A3	A7	A6		B5	B2	B4			B2	A10	A7		A15		B6		C1	B5	B5	B5	B6	B5	B7
Poland	A7	A6					A6				A7	A8	A6	A8	A11	B5	B2	B4	B1	B1	A8	B1	B2	A6
Rumania	A7													A13		C1		B3	B4		B2	B2	B6	B7
Sweden	A2	A4	A4	A5	A2	A3	A1	A3	A5	A4	A1	A3	A5	A5	A4	A1	A2	A2	A3	A4	A2	A4	A2	A2
Switzerland	A4	A3	A5	A3	A3	A5	A3	A7	A8	A9			A12		B3	A7	B2	A8	B2	B6	B7		C2	B6
South Africa															C5						C3			
Soviet Union									A1	A2	A1	A2	A2	A2	A3	A3		A1	A1	A1	A1	A1	A1	A1
Hungary														A14		C2	B8		B4		B7	B8	C3	C3
USA	A5		A3	A2	A6	A2			A4	A2		A5	A4	A1	A6	A3	A8	A5	A6	A6	A5	A6	A6	B1

1971–1995

	1971	1972	1973	1974	1975	1976	1977	1978	1979	1981	1982	1983	1985	1986	1987	1989	1990	1991	1992	1993	1994	1995
Australia	–	–	–	C7	–	–	–	–	C8	–	–	–	–	C10	–	C8	D2	B5	C3	C7	C14	C16
Belgium	C8	–	–	–	C7	–	C6	C8	–	–	–	–	–	–	C8	D1	C8	C9	C5	C8	C13	C14
Bulgaria	C5	C4	C4	C3	C2	B8	C3	C5	C4	C6	C6	C6	C6	C3	C7	C5	C6	C4	B5	B8	C7	C9
China	–	C5	C5	C6	–	–	–	C4	B10	C2	B7	C3	C3	C2	B8	C3	C3	C2	B7	B7	B8	C5
TCH	A2	A1	A3	A2	A2	A1	A1	A2	A2	A3	A2	A2	A1	A5	A3	A3	A3	A6	A3	–	–	–
Denmark	C6	C7	C7	–	C6	C4	C2	C3	B8	C4	C3	C4	C5	C5	C2	B8	C2	C1	B4	B4	B5	B5
Germany	A5	A5	A6	B3	B2	A6	A7	A5	A6	A7	A6	A5	A7	A7	A6	A7	A7	A8	A6	A5	A9	A9
GDR/DDR	B3	B3	B1	A6	B1	A8	B1	A8	B2	B4	B1	A6	A8	B3	B5	B5	B5	–	–	–	–	–
Finland	A4	A4	A4	A4	A5	A5	A7	A5	A6	A5	A5	A7	A5	A4	A5	A5	A6	A5	A2	A7	A2	A1
France	C2	–	C6	C5	C5	C3	C4	C6	C3	C5	C6	C5	C1	B4	B4	B3	B4	B3	A11	A10	A10	A8
Great Britain	C4	–	C8	–	–	C5	C7	–	C6	C8	–	–	–	–	–	D3	D1	C5	C1	B1	A12	B7
Netherlands	C7	C6	C2	B5	B8	B6	B8	C1	B1	A8	B8	C1	B6	B5	B7	C1	B8	B7	B2	B3	B6	B4
Italy	B8	C2	B8	C2	B7	B7	C1	B7	C2	B1	A7	A8	B3	B2	B6	B2	B2	B1	A9	A8	A6	A7
Japan	B6	B5	B5	B4	B6	B2	B3	B2	B6	B8	C1	B5	B4	B6	C1	B7	B7	B8	B3	B5	B4	B6
Yugoslavia	B5	B6	B3	B2	B4	B5	B7	B8	C1	B7	C2	B8	C2	B7	C4	C2	C1	B6	B8	–	–	C8
Canada	–	–	–	–	–	–	A4	A3	A4	A4	A4	A3	A2	A3	A4	A2	A4	A2	A8	A4	A1	A3
PR Korea	–	–	–	C8	–	–	–	–	–	C7	–	C8	C7	C7	C6	C6	C5	C7	C2	C6	C8	–
Norway	B4	B7	C1	B7	C1	B3	B4	B6	B4	B6	B4	B4	B7	C1	B2	B1	A8	B2	A10	A11	A11	A10
Austria	B7	C1	B6	B8	C3	C1	B9	C2	B7	C1	B2	B3	B5	B6	B3	B6	B3	–	B1	A9	A8	A11
Poland	B2	B1	A5	A5	A5	A7	B2	B1	A8	B2	B3	B2	B1	A8	B1	A8	B6	B4	A12	B2	B3	B3
Rumania	C1	B4	B4	B6	B5	B1	A8	B4	B3	B5	B5	B7	C4	C4	C3	C2	C4	C3	B6	B6	B7	B8
Sweden	A3	A3	A2	A3	A3	A3	A2	A4	A3	A2	A3	A4	A6	A2	A1	A4	A2	A1	A1	A2	A3	A2
Switzerland	B1	A6	B7	C1	B3	B4	B5	B3	B5	B3	B6	B6	B2	B1	A8	B4	B1	A7	A4	A12	B1	A12
Spain	–	–	–	–	–	–	C5	C7	C5	–	C7	C7	C8	C8	–	D4	D3	–	C7	C10	C10	C12
Korea	–	–	–	–	–	–	–	–	C7	–	C8	–	–	C9	–	C7	C9	C8	C6	C9	C11	C13
Soviet Union	A1	A2	A1	A1	A1	A2	A3	A1	A1	A1	A1	A1	A3	A1	A2	A1	A1	A3	–	–	–	–
Hungary	C3	C3	C3	C4	C4	C2	B6	B5	B9	C3	C4	C2	B8	C6	C5	C4	C7	C8	C4	C5	C6	C6
USA	A6	B2	B2	B1	A6	A4	A6	A6	A7	A6	A8	B1	A4	A5	A7	A6	A5	A4	A7	A6	A4	A6
Russia	–	–	–	–	–	–	–	–	–	–	–	–	–	–	–	–	–	–	A5	A1	A5	A5
South Africa	–	–	–	–	–	–	–	–	–	–	–	–	–	–	–	–	–	–	C8	C12	C16	C17
Greece	–	–	–	–	–	–	–	–	–	–	–	–	–	–	–	–	–	–	C9	–	–	C18
Israel	–	–	–	–	–	–	–	–	–	–	–	–	–	–	–	–	–	–	C10	C11	C15	C15
Luxembourg	–	–	–	–	–	–	–	–	–	–	–	–	–	–	–	–	–	–	C11	–	–	–
Turkey	–	–	–	–	–	–	–	–	–	–	–	–	–	–	–	–	–	–	C12	–	–	–
Czech Republic	–	–	–	–	–	–	–	–	–	–	–	–	–	–	–	–	–	–	–	A3	A7	A4
Slovakia	–	–	–	–	–	–	–	–	–	–	–	–	–	–	–	–	–	–	–	–	C1	B1
Latvia	–	–	–	–	–	–	–	–	–	–	–	–	–	–	–	–	–	–	–	C1	B2	B2
Ukraine	–	–	–	–	–	–	–	–	–	–	–	–	–	–	–	–	–	–	–	C2	C3	C3
Kazakhstan	–	–	–	–	–	–	–	–	–	–	–	–	–	–	–	–	–	–	–	C3	C4	C2
Slovenia	–	–	–	–	–	–	–	–	–	–	–	–	–	–	–	–	–	–	–	C4	C5	C7
Belarus	–	–	–	–	–	–	–	–	–	–	–	–	–	–	–	–	–	–	–	–	C2	C1
Estonia	–	–	–	–	–	–	–	–	–	–	–	–	–	–	–	–	–	–	–	–	C9	C4
Croatia	–	–	–	–	–	–	–	–	–	–	–	–	–	–	–	–	–	–	–	–	C12	C10
Lithuania	–	–	–	–	–	–	–	–	–	–	–	–	–	–	–	–	–	–	–	–	–	C11
New Zealand	–	–	–	–	–	–	–	–	–	–	–	–	–	–	–	–	–	–	–	–	–	C19

IIHF DIRECTORATE AWARDS BEST PLAYERS

GOALKEEPER		DEFENCEMEN		FORWARD	
1954 Don Lockhardt	CAN	Lasse Björn	SWE	Vsevolod Bobrov	URS
1955 Don Rigazio	USA	Karel Gut	TCH	Bill Warwick	CAN
1956 Willard Ikola	USA	Nikolai Sologubov	URS	Jack McKenzie	CAN
1957 Karel Straka	TCH	Nikolai Sologubov	URS	Sven Tumba	SWE
1958 Vladimir Nadrchal	TCH	Ivan Tregubov	URS	Charlie Burns	CAN
1959 Nikolai Putskov	URS	Jean-Pierre Lamirande	CAN	Bill Cleary	USA
1960 Jack McCartan	USA	Nikolai Sologubov	URS	Nisse Nilsson	SWE
1961 Seth Martin	CAN	Ivan Tregubov	URS	Vlastimil Bubnik	TCH
1962 Lennart Häggroth	SWE	John Mayasich	USA	Sven Tumba	SWE
1963 Seth Martin	CAN	Roland Stoltz	SWE	Miroslav Vlach	TCH
1964 Seth Martin	CAN	Frantisek Tikal	TCH	Eduard Ivanov	URS
1965 Vladimir Dzurilla	TCH	Frantisek Tikal	TCH	Vjat. Starshinov	URS
1966 Seth Martin	CAN	Alexandr Ragulin	URS	Konstantin Loktev	URS
1967 Carl Wetzel	USA	Vitali Davydov	URS	Anatoli Firsov	URS
1968 Ken Broderick	CAN	Josef Horesovsky	TCH	Anatoli Firsov	URS
1969 Leif Holmqvist	SWE	Jan Suchy	TCH	Ulf Sterner	SWE
1970 Urpo Ylönen	FIN	Lennart Svedberg	SWE	Alexandr Maltsev	URS
1971 Jiri Holecek	TCH	Jan Suchy	TCH	Anatoli Firsov	URS
		Ilpo Koskela	FIN		
1972 Jorma Valtonen	FIN	Frantisek Pospisil	TCH	Alexandr Maltsev	URS
1973 Jiri Holecek	TCH	Valerij Vasiljev	URS	Boris Michailov	URS
1974 Vladislav Tretjak	URS	Lars-Erik Sjöberg	SWE	Vaclav Nedomansky	TCH
1975 Jiri Holecek	TCH	Pekka Marjamäki	FIN	Alexandr Jakushev	URS
1976 Jiri Holecek	TCH	Frantisek Pospisil	TCH	Vladimir Martinec	TCH
1977 Göran Högosta	SWE	Valerij Vasiljev	URS	Helmut Balderis	URS
1978 Jiri Holecek	TCH	Vyacheslav Fetisov	URS	Marcel Dionne	CAN
1979 Vladislav Tretjak	URS	Valerij Vasiljev	URS	Wilf Paiement	CAN
		Jiri Bubla	TCH	Boris Michailov	URS
				Sergej Makarov	URS
1981 Peter Lindmark	SWE	Larry Robinson	CAN	Alexandr Maltsev	URS
1982 Jiri Kralik	TCH	Vyacheslav Fetisov	URS	Viktor Shalimov	URS
1983 Vladislav Tretjak	URS	Aleksej Kasatonov	URS	Jiri Lala	TCH
1985 Jiri Kralik	TCH	Vyacheslav Fetisov	URS	Sergej Makarov	URS
1986 Peter Lindmark	SWE	Vyacheslav Fetisov	URS	Vladimir Krutov	URS
1987 Dominik Hasek	TCH	Craig Hartsburgh	CAN	Vladimir Krutov	URS
1989 Dominik Hasek	TCH	Vyacheslav Fetisov	URS	Brian Bellows	CAN
1990 Artur Irbe	URS	Mikhail Tatarinov	URS	Steve Yzerman	CAN
1991 Markus Ketterer	FIN	James Macoun	CAN	Valery Kamensky	URS
1992 Tommy Söderström	SWE	Robert Svehla	TCH	Mats Sundin	SWE
1993 Peter Briza	CZE	Dmitri Yushkewich	RUS	Eric Lindros	CAN
1994 Bill Ranford	CAN	Magnus Svensson	SWE	Paul Kariya	CAN
1995 Jarmo Myllys	FIN	Christer Olsson	SWE	Saku Koivu	FIN

LEADING SCORERS
World Championships 1956-1995

Year	WC	Name	Team	GP	G	A	P
1956	Cortina d'Ampezzo	Jim Logan	CAN	8	7	5	12*
1957	Moscow	Konstantin Loktev	URS	7	11	7	18*
1958	Dalo	Connie Broden	CAN	7	12	7	19*
1959	Praha, Brno	Red Berenson	CAN	8	9	2	11
1960	Squaw Valley	Fred Etcher	CAN	7	9	12	21*
1961	Geneve, Lausanne	Boris Majorow	URS	7	7	9	16
1962	Denver	Nisse Nilsson	SWE	7	12	6	18
1963	Stockholm	Harald Jones	CAN	7	7	5	12
1964	Innsbruck	Sven Tumba Johansson	SWE	7	8	3	11
1965	Tampere	Josef Golonka	TCH	7	6	8	14
1966	Ljubljana	Venjamin Alexandrov	URS	7	9	8	17
1967	Vienna	Anatoli Firsov	URS	7	11	11	22*
1968	Grenoble	Anatoli Firsov	URS	7	12	4	16
1969	Stockholm	Anatoli Firsov	URS	10	10	4	14
1970	Stockholm	Alexander Malzev	URS	10	15	6	21
1971	Bern, Geneve	Anatoli Firsov	URS	10	10	9	19
1972	Praha	Alexander Malzev	URS	10	10	12	22
1973	Moscow	Vladimir Petrov	URS	10	18	16	34*
1974	Helsinki	Boris Michailow	URS	10	9	8	17
1975	München, Düsseldorf	Viktor Shalimow	URS	10	11	8	19
1976	Katowice	Vladimir Martinec	TCH	10	9	11	20
1977	Vienna	Vladimir Petrov	URS	10	7	14	21
1978	Praha	Erich Kühnhackl	GER	10	8	8	16
1979	Moscow	Vladimir Petrov	URS	8	7	8	15
1981	Göteborg	Holger Meitinger	GER	8	8	12	20
1982	Helsinki, Tampere	Wayne Gretzky	CAN	10	6	8	14
1983	München, Dortmund	Sergej Makarov	URS	10	9	9	18
1985	Praha	Sergej Makarov	URS	10	8	6	14
1986	Moscow	Sergej Makarov	URS	10	4	14	18
1987	Vienna	Vladimir Krutov	URS	10	11	4	15
1989	Stockholm	Brian Bellows	CAN	10	8	6	14
1990	Bern, Fribourg	Steve Yzerman	CAN	10	10	10	20
1991	Turku, Tampere	Mats Sundin	SWE	10	7	5	12
1992	Praha, Bratislava	Jarkko Varvio	FIN	8	9	1	10
1993	Dortmund, München	Eric Lindros	CAN	8	11	6	17
1994	Bolzano, Milano	Mats Sundin	SWE	8	5	9	14
1995	Stockholm, Gävle	Andrew McKim	CAN	8	6	6	12

* = WC-Record

All Star Team A 1961–1995 World Championships

Year	GK	RD	LD	RW	CE	LW
1961	Martin (CAN)	Smith (CAN)	Sly (CAN)	B. Majorov (URS)	Lagarce (CAN)	Vlach (TCH)
1962	Häggroth (SWE)	Smith (CAN)	Douglas (CAN)	McLeod (CAN)	Nilsson (SWE)	Sterner (SWE)
1963	Svensson (SWE)	Smith (CAN)	Ragulin (URS)	Vlach (TCH)	Tambellini (CAN)	Mild (SWE)
1964	Martin (CAN)	Ragulin (URS)	Seiling (CAN)	Bourbonais (CAN)	V. Jakushev (URS)	Cerny (TCH)
1965	Dzurilla (TCH)	Ragulin (URS)	Tikal (TCH)	Loktev (URS)	Almetov (URS)	Jirik (TCH)
1966	Martin (CAN)	Ragulin (URS)	Begg (CAN)	Loktev (URS)	Huck (CAN)	Alexandrov (URS)
1967	Wetzel (CAN)	Ragulin (URS)	Brewer (CAN)	Firsov (URS)	Almetov (URS)	Alexandrov (URS)
1968	Broderick (CAN)	Suchy (TCH)	Svedberg (SWE)	Sevcik (TCH)	Huck (CAN)	Firsov (URS)
1969	Dzurilla (TCH)	Suchy (TCH)	Svedberg (SWE)	Firsov (URS)	Sterner (SWE)	Nedomansky (TCH)
1970	Konovalenko (URS)	Suchy (TCH)	Svedberg (SWE)	Maltsev (URS)	Nedomansky (TCH)	Firsov (URS)
1971	Holecek (TCH)	Suchy (TCH)	Koskela (FIN)	Maltsev (URS)	Vikulov (URS)	Charlamov (URS)
1972	Holecek (TCH)	Machac (TCH)	Pospisil (TCH)	Vikulov (URS)	Maltsev (URS)	Charlamov (URS)
1973	Holecek (TCH)	Salming (SWE)	Gusev (URS)	Michailov (URS)	Petrov (URS)	Charlamov (URS)
1974	Larsson (SWE)	Vasiljev (URS)	Sjöberg (SWE)	Martinec (TCH)	Nedomansky (TCH)	Jakushev (URS)
1975	Tretjak (URS)	Vasiljev (URS)	Vasiljev (URS)	Martinec (TCH)	Petrov (URS)	Jakushev (URS)
1976	Holecek (TCH)	Marjamäki (FIN)	Pospisil (TCH)	Martinec (TCH)	Novy (TCH)	Charlamov (URS)
1977	Högosta (SWE)	Waltin (SWE)	Vasiljev (URS)	Martinec (TCH)	Petrov (URS)	Balderis (URS)
1978	Holecek (TCH)	Pospisil (TCH)	Vasiljev (URS)	Maltsev (URS)	Hlinka (TCH)	Kapustin (URS)
1979	Tretjak (URS)	Bubla (TCH)	Fetisov (URS)	Michailov (URS)	Petrov (URS)	Makarov (URS)
1981	Lindmark (SWE)	Bubla (TCH)	Vasiljev (URS)	Makarov (URS)	Petrov (URS)	Kapustin (URS)
1982	Kralik (TCH)	Robinson (CAN)	Vasiljev (URS)	Makarov (URS)	Maltsev (URS)	Barber (CAN)
1983	Tretjak (URS)	Kasatonov (URS)	Fetisov (URS)	Makarov (URS)	Maltsev (URS)	Krutov (URS)
1985	Kralik (TCH)	Kasatonov (URS)	Fetisov (URS)	Makarov (URS)	Gretzky (CAN)	Krutov (URS)
1986	Lindmark (SWE)	Kasatonov (URS)	Fetisov (URS)	Makarov (URS)	Larionov (URS)	Krutov (URS)
1987	Hasek (TCH)	Kießling (GER)	Fetisov (URS)	Makarov (URS)	Ruzicka (CRS)	Krutov (URS)
1989	Hasek (TCH)	Eldebrink (SWE)	Fetisov (URS)	Makarov (URS)	Larionov (URS)	Krutov (URS)
1990	Hasek (TCH)	Tatarinov (URS)	Fetisov (URS)	Chomutov (URS)	Larionov (URS)	Kamensky (URS)
1991	Burke (CAN)	Kasatonov (URS)	Fetisov (URS)	Kurri (FIN)	Truntschka (GER)	Reichel (TCH)
1992	Ketterer (FIN)	Jutila (FIN)	Musil (TCH)	Varvio (FIN)	Bykov (URS)	Sundin (SWE)
1993	Briza (CZE)	Manson (CAN)	Biakin (RUS)	Renberg (SWE)	Yzerman (CAN)	U. Dahlen (SWE)
1994	Ranford (CAN)	Jutila (FIN)	Numminen (FIN)	Kurri (FIN)	Rundqvist (SWE)	Kariya (CAN)
1995	Myllys (FIN)	Sjödin (SWE)	Lidström (SWE)	Lehtinen (FIN)	Koivu (FIN)	Peltonen (FIN)

DM 6,80

Österreich 54 ÖS
Schweiz 6,80 sfr.
Italien 9.500 Lit.

Super
Gewinnspiele

Eishockey
NEWS

Spezial/I 95

Eishockey NEWS
Sondernummer
September,
Oktober, November

**Einzelfotos
aller
Spieler**

Alle Infos über die Saison 95/96

Im Blickpunkt: Die neuen Stars der DEL

Große Sonderteile: WM, Österreich, Schweiz, NHL

DEL - Sonderheft

Get ready
for
action

**Top informiert
mit den
Eishockey NEWS
Sonderheften!**

**Jetzt
beim
Zeitschriften-
händler!**

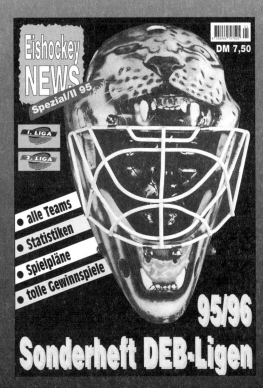

Eishockey
NEWS

Spezial/II 95

DM 7,50

1. LIGA

2. LIGA

● alle Teams
● Statistiken
● Spielpläne
● tolle Gewinnspiele

95/96

Sonderheft DEB-Ligen

Ihr Partner für Sportwerbung

CWL MARKETING AG   CWL TELESPORT AG
Internationale Sportagentur für Werbung und TV-Vermarktung

Offizieller Vertragspartner
des Internationalen
Eishockey-Verbandes

Offizieller Vertragspartner
des Deutschen
Fussballbundes

Offizieller Vertragspartner
der Internationalen
Handball Federation

Vertragspartner
Europäischer
Fussballclubs

Offizieller Vertragspartner
der Europäischen
Handball Föderation

Vertragspartner
Nationaler
Fussballverbände

CH-8280 Kreuzlingen Hauptstrasse 16 P.O. Box 260
Telefon (41) 72-71 22 41 Telefax (41) 72-72 31 02 Telex 882 299 CWL

WORLD CHAMPIONSCHIP 1995

Stockholm/Gävle – April 23 – May 7, 1995

Group A	RUS	ITA	FRA	CAN	GER	SUI	Goals	Pts
1. Russia	■	4:2	3:1	5:4	6:3	8:0	26:10	10
2. Italy	2:4	■	5:2	2:2	2:1	3:2	14:11	7
3. France	1:3	2:5	■	4:1	4:0	3:2	14:11	6
4. Canada	4:5	2:2	1:4	■	5:2	5:3	17:16	5
5. Germany	3:6	1:2	0:4	2:5	■	5:3	11:20	2
6. Switzerland	0:8	2:3	2:3	3:5	3:5	■	10:24	0

Group B	USA	FIN	SWE	CZE	NOR	AUT	Goals	Pts
1. USA	■	4:4	2:2	4:2	2:1	5:2	17:11	8
2. Finland	4:4	■	6:3	0:3	5:2	7:2	22:14	7
3. Sweden	2:2	3:6	■	2:1	5:0	5:0	17: 9	7
4. Czech Republic	2:4	3:0	1:2	■	3:1	5:2	14: 9	6
5. Norway	1:2	2:5	0:5	1:3	■	5:3	9:18	2
6. Austria	2:5	2:7	0:5	2:5	3:5	■	9:27	0

Play-off Quarterfinal

Italy	– Sweden	0:7
Finland	– France	5:0
Russia	– Czech Republic	0:2
USA	– Canada	1:4

Play-off Semifinal

Sweden	– Canada	3:2 ot.
Czech Republic	– Finland	0:3

Third place game

Canada	– Czech Republic	4:1

Final

Finland	– Sweden	4:1

Play-off Relegation

Austria	– Switzerland	4:0, 4:4

● Switzerland relegated into POOL B 1996

IIHF Awards to the three best players

Goalkeeper:	Jarmo Myllys	FIN
Defenseman:	Christer Olsson	SWE
Forward:	Saku Koivu	FIN

ALL STAR TEAM
(voted by the media)

	Turek (CZE)	
Sjödin (SWE)		Jutila (FIN)
Lehtinen (FIN)	Koivu (FIN)	Peltonen (FIN)

Goalkeeper Statistic

	Name	Team	GP	MIP	SOG	GA	SVS%	GAA	PIM
1	Michael Rosati	ITA	5	132.43	108	3	97,22	1,00	0,00
2	Roman Turek	CZE	7	359.23	148	9	93.92	1.50	0.00
3	Bruno Campese	ITA	3	60.00	3	2	93,33	2,00	0,00
4	Alexei Cherviakov	RUS	6	180.00	65	5	92,31	1,67	0,00
5	Pat Jablonski	USA	6	360.00	195	15	92,31	2,50	0,00
6	Petri Ylönen	FRA	5	300.00	140	11	92,14	2,20	0,00
7	Jarmo Myllys	FIN	7	420.00	145	12	91,72	1,71	2,00
8	Corey Hirsch	CAN	8	488.17	247	21	91,50	2,63	0,00
9	Claus Dalpiaz	AUT	6	214.09	141	12	91,49	3,00	0,00
10	Thomas Östlund	SWE	8	368.17	105	9	91,43	1,50	0,00
11	Jim Marthinsen	NOR	5	121.15	53	5	90,57	1,67	0,00
12	Petr Briza	CZE	7	60.00	21	2	90,48	2,00	0,00
13	Mario Brunetta	ITA	4	167.17	129	13	89,92	4,33	2,00
14	Sergei Abramov	RUS	6	180.00	66	7	89,39	2,33	0,00
15	Renato Tosio	SUI	7	300.00	176	21	88,07	4,20	0,00
16	Roger Nordström	SWE	8	120.00	49	6	87,76	3,00	0,00
17	Klaus Merk	GER	4	180.00	79	10	87,34	3,33	0,00
18	Robert Schistad	NOR	5	178.45	96	13	86,46	4,33	0,00
19	Reto Pavoni	SUI	7	120.00	81	11	86,42	5,50	0,00
20	Josef Heiss	GER	5	60.00	28	4	85,71	4,00	0,00
21	Marc Seliger	GER	1	60.00	40	6	85,00	6,00	0,00
22	Michael Suttnig	AUT	5	25.51	23	4	82,61	4,00	0,00
23	Antoine Mindjimba	FRA	5	60.00	23	5	78,26	5,00	2,00

Top Scorer

	Name	Team	GP	G	A1	A2	Pts
1	Andrew McKim	CAN	8	6	6	1	13
2	Ville Peltonen	FIN	8	6	5	0	11
3	Saku Koivu	FIN	8	5	3	2	10
4	Mikael Johansson	SWE	8	3	4	2	9
5	Andreas Johansson	SWE	8	3	4	2	9
6	Iain Fraser	CAN	8	2	5	2	9
7	Sergei Berezin	RUS	6	7	1	0	8
8	Jon Morris	USA	6	3	3	2	8
9	Christian Pouget	FRA	6	2	5	1	8
10	Raimo Helminen	FIN	8	1	4	3	8
11	Timo Jutila	FIN	8	5	0	2	7
12	Mika Nieminen	FIN	8	4	2	1	7
13	Andreas Dackell	SWE	8	3	3	1	7
14	Jere Lehtinen	FIN	8	2	4	1	7
15	Thomas Brandl	GER	5	5	1	0	6
16	Raffaele Intranuovo	CAN	8	5	0	1	6
17	Werner Kerth	AUT	7	4	1	1	6
18	Esa Keskinen	FIN	8	1	4	1	6
19	Andy Ton	SUI	7	5	0	0	5
20	Dieter Kalt	AUT	7	4	1	0	5

FINLAND

Name	POS	Club	GP	G	A1	A2	Pts	PIM
Jukka Tammi	GK	Ilves Tampere	6	0	0	0	0	0
Ari Sulander	GK	Jokerit Helsinki	3	0	0	0	0	0
Jarmo Myllys	GK	Luleå HF	7	0	0	0	0	2
Marko Kiprusoff	D	TPS Turku	8	0	2	1	3	0
Petteri Nummelin	D	TPS Turku	5	0	0	0	0	6
Erik Hämäläinen	D	Jokerit Helsinki	8	0	0	0	0	8
Timo Jutila	D	Tappara Tampere	8	5	0	2	7	10
Janne Niinimaa	D	Jokerit Helsinki	8	1	1	1	3	10
Mika Strömberg	D	Jokerit Helsinki	8	2	2	1	5	12
Hannu Virta	D	Grasshopper Zürich	7	1	1	0	2	8
Janne Ojanen	F	Tappara Tampere	8	0	2	2	4	4
Esa Keskinen	F	HV 71 Jönköping	8	1	4	1	6	6
Saku Koivu	F	TPS Turku	8	5	3	2	10	18
Marko Palo	F	HV 71 Jönköping	8	1	0	0	1	2
Raimo Helminen	F	Malmö IF	8	1	4	3	8	2
Antti Törmänen	F	Jokerit Helsinki	5	0	0	0	0	2
Ville Peltonen	F	IFK Helsinki	8	6	5	0	11	4
Jere Lehtinen	F	TPS Turku	8	2	4	1	7	4
Juha Ylönen	F	Jokerit Helsinki	8	1	1	2	4	2
Sami Kapanen	F	IFK Helsinki	8	2	1	1	4	6
Tero Lehterä	F	Malmö IF	8	1	0	0	1	0
Mika Nieminen	F	Luleå HF	8	4	2	1	7	6
Raimo Summanen	F	TPS Turku	8	1	1	0	2	0

Coach: Curt Lindström

SWEDEN

Name	POS	Club	GP	G	A1	A2	Pts	PIM
Thomas Östlund	GK	Djurgårdens Stockholm	8	0	0	0	0	0
Roger Nordström	GK	Malmö IF	8	0	0	0	0	0
Boo Ahl	GK	HV 71 Jönköping	0	0	0	0	0	0
Tomas Jonsson	D	Leksands IF	8	0	2	0	2	12
Marcus Ragnarsson	D	Djurgardens Stockholm	4	0	0	0	0	4
Leif Rohlin	D	Västerås IK	8	0	2	1	3	0
Fredrik Stillman	D	HV 71 Jönköping	8	2	1	0	3	4
Christer Olsson	D	Brynäs IF Gävle	8	2	0	1	3	4
Robert Nordmark	D	Djurgardens Stockholm	8	1	1	0	2	4
Tommy Sjödin	D	HC Lugano	8	2	1	2	5	6
Erik Huusko	F	Djurgardens Stockholm	8	2	2	0	4	6
Stefan Nilsson	F	Luleå HF	6	1	0	0	1	2
Per-Erik Eklund	F	Leksands IF	8	1	0	2	3	0
Andreas Johansson	F	Färjestads Karlstad	8	3	4	2	9	8
Roger Hansson	F	Malmö IF	8	0	2	0	2	0
Andreas Dackell	F	Brynäs IF Gävle	8	3	3	1	7	4
Stefan Örnskog	F	HV 71 Jönköping	8	1	1	2	4	2
Jonas Bergqvist	F	Leksands IF	5	1	0	0	1	0
Charles Berglund	F	Djurgardens Stockholm	8	0	1	1	2	2
Daniel Alfredsson	F	Västra Frölunda HC	8	3	1	0	4	4
Mikael Johansson	F	EHC Kloten	8	3	4	2	9	4
Tomas Forslund	F	Leksands IF	8	2	0	0	2	10
Jonas Johnson	F	Brynäs IF Gävle	8	1	1	0	2	0

Coach: Curt Lundmark

CANADA

Name	POS	Club	GP	G	A1	A2	Pts	PIM
Corey Hirsch	GK	Binghampton Rangers	8	0	0	0	0	0
Andrew Verner	GK	Canada National Team	3	0	0	0	0	0
Dwayne Roloson	GK	Saint John Flames	0	0	0	0	0	0
Leonard Esau	D	Saint John Flames	7	0	1	0	1	2
Brian Tutt	D	Ilves Tampere	7	0	0	0	0	6
Jamie Heward	D	Canada National Team	8	0	1	4	5	6
Greg Andrusak	D	Pittsburgh Penguins	7	0	0	0	0	12
Dale DeGray	D	Cleveland Lumberjacks	6	1	0	1	2	6
Peter Allen	D	Canada National Team	8	0	0	0	0	4
Brad Schlegel	D	Villacher SV	8	0	1	2	3	12
Todd Hlushko	F	Saint John Flames	8	4	0	0	4	4
Iain Fraser	F	Edmonton Oilers	8	2	5	2	9	8
Ralph Intranuovo	F	Cape Breton Oilers	8	5	0	1	6	6
Luciano Borsato	F	Springfield Falcons	8	3	1	0	4	18
Brandon Convery	F	St. John Maple Leafs	8	0	0	1	1	0
Andrew McKim	F	Adirondack Red Wings	8	6	6	1	13	4
Mark Freer	F	Houston Aeros	6	1	0	0	1	2
Rick Chernomaz	F	St. John Maple Leafs	8	0	3	0	3	10
Chris Govedaris	F	Adirondack Red Wings	8	1	0	0	1	6
Chris Bright	F	Canada National Team	8	0	3	0	3	8
Jean-Fr. Jomphe	F	Canada National Team	8	4	0	0	4	6
Michael Maneluk	F	Canada National Team	8	0	2	0	2	0
Tom Tilley	F	Indianapolis Ice	8	0	0	0	0	14

Coach: Tom Renney

CZECH REPUBLIC

Name	POS	Club	GP	G	A1	A2	Pts	PIM
Petr Briza	GK	EV Landshut	7	0	0	0	0	0
Roman Turek	GK	HC Ceske Budejovice	7	0	0	0	0	0
Roman Cechmanek	GK	HC Vsetin	2	0	0	0	0	0
Jiri Vykoukal	D	MoDo HK, Örnsköldsv.	8	2	1	0	3	4
Bedrich Scerban	D	Brynäs IF, Gävle	8	0	2	0	2	8
Antonin Stavjana	D	HC Vsetin	8	1	0	0	1	8
Ivan Vicek	D	HC Skoda Plzen	8	0	0	0	0	4
Petr Kuchny	D	HC Dukla Jihlava	8	0	1	0	1	4
Frantisek Kaberle	D	HC Kladno	0	0	0	0	0	0
Jan Vopat	D	HC CHP Litvinov	8	0	0	1	1	6
Pavel Patera	F	HC Kladno	7	0	0	0	0	2
Martin Hostak	F	MoDo HK, Örnsköldsv.	8	0	0	0	0	2
Richard Zemlicka	F	EHC Eisbären Berlin	8	1	1	0	2	6
Jiri Kucera	F	Luleå HF	8	1	0	0	1	2
Jiri Dopita	F	EHC Eisbären Berlin	8	1	1	0	2	4
Tomas Srsen	F	HC Vsetin	8	1	1	0	2	6
Radek Belohlav	F	HC Ceske Budejovice	8	2	1	0	3	2
Martin Prochazka	F	HC Kladno	8	2	1	0	3	2
Roman Horak	F	HC Ceske Budejovice	8	1	0	0	1	4
Otokar Vejvoda	F	HC Kladno	8	2	1	0	3	6
Pavel Janku	F	AC ZPS Zlin	8	1	0	0	1	2
Pavel Geffert	F	HC Sparta Praha	8	1	1	0	2	2
Roman Meluzin	F	AC ZPS Zlin	8	1	1	0	2	2

Coach: Dr. Ludek Bukac

RUSSIA

Name	POS	Club	GP	G	A1	A2	Pts	PIM
Andrei Zuev	GK	Traktor Chelyabinsk	0	0	0	0	0	0
Alexei Cherviakov	GK	Torpedo Yaroslavl	6	0	0	0	0	0
Sergei Abramov	GK	Itil Kazan	6	0	0	0	0	0
Sergei Sorokin	D	HC Fassa	6	1	1	1	3	6
Evgeni Gribko	D	Dynamo Moscow	6	0	0	0	0	2
Alexander Smirnov	D	TPS Turku	6	0	2	1	3	4
Sergei Fokin	D	Färjestads BK Karlstad	6	0	1	0	1	6
Dmitri Krasotkin	D	Torpedo Yaroslavl	6	0	0	0	0	0
Andrei Skopintsev	D	Krilya Moscow	6	1	1	0	2	0
Sergei Shendelev	D	Frankfurt Lions	6	1	2	1	4	2
Dmitri Frolov	D	Devils Hockey Milano	6	0	2	2	4	6
Alexei Salomatin	F	Västerås IK	6	2	0	1	3	2
Ravil Yakubov	F	Dynamo Moscow	6	0	1	0	1	2
Igor Fedolov	F	HC Ambri-Piotta	6	2	1	1	4	2
Andrei Tarasenko	F	Torpedo Yaroslavl	6	1	3	0	4	2
Andrei Khomutov	F	HC Fribourg	6	1	2	1	4	0
Stanislav Romanov	F	CSKA Moscow	6	4	0	1	5	4
Alexander Prokopiev	F	Dynamo Moscow	6	2	0	0	2	4
Vladimir Vorobiov	F	Dynamo Moscow	6	0	1	1	2	6
Pavel Torgaev	F	Jyp HT Jyväskylä	6	0	2	0	2	4
Vjacheslav Bykov	F	HC Fribourg	6	2	1	1	4	4
Sergei Berezin	F	Kölner EC Haie	6	7	1	0	8	4
Oleg Belov	F	CSKA Moscow	6	2	1	0	3	2

Coach: Boris Michailov

USA

Name	POS	Club	GP	G	A1	A2	Pts	PIM
Ray LeBlanc	GK	Chicago Wolves/IHL	4	0	0	0	0	0
Tim Thomas	GK	Univ. of Vermont/NCAA	2	0	0	0	0	0
Pat Jablonski	GK	Toronto Maple Leafs/NHL	6	0	0	0	0	0
Keith Aldridge	D	Lake Sup. State/NCAA	6	0	0	0	0	2
Christopher Imes	D	Minnesota Moose/IHL	6	1	0	0	1	0
Brett Hauer	D	AIK Stockholm/SWE	6	2	1	1	4	4
Jason McBain	D	Springfield Falcons/AHL	6	0	1	1	2	4
Brian Rafalski	D	Univ. of Wisconsin/NCAA	6	0	0	0	0	2
Tom O'Regan	D	Berliner SC Preussen/GER	6	0	2	0	2	2
Paul Stanton	D	New Yersey Islanders/NHL	6	2	1	0	3	4
Patrick Neaton	D	San Diego Gulls/IHL	4	1	0	0	1	8
Craig Charron	F	Dayton Bombers/ECHL	6	1	1	0	2	18
Brad Jones	F	Springfield Falcons/AHL	5	0	1	1	2	2
Jacques Joubert	F	Boston Univ./NCAA	6	1	1	0	2	2
Mike Knuble	F	Univ. of Michigan/NCAA	6	1	1	1	3	2
Joe Frederik	F	Adirondack Red W./AHL	6	1	0	1	2	2
Cal McGowan	F	Worcester Icecats/AHL	6	1	2	1	4	6
Jon Morris	F	HC Gardena/ITA	6	3	3	2	8	4
Chris O'Sullivan	F	Boston Univ./NCAA	6	0	0	0	0	10
Mike Pomichter	F	Indianapolis Ice/IHL	6	1	1	1	3	2
Tdd Harkins	F	Houston Aeros/IHL	6	1	3	0	4	28
James Spencer	F	Univ. of Wisconsin/NCAA	6	0	0	0	0	2
Timothy Bergland	F	Chicago Wolves/IHL	5	2	0	1	3	2

Coach: Jeff Sauer

FRANCE

Name	POS	Club	GP	G	A1	A2	Pts	PIM
Petri Ylonen	GK	Rouen HC	5	0	0	0	0	0
Antoine Mindjimba	GK	AC Amiens	5	0	0	0	0	2
Michel Valliere	GK	HsG Brest	2	0	0	0	0	0
Jean-Marc Soghomonian	G	Chamonix HC	6	1	0	0	1	2
Serge Djelloul	D	LBdL Grenoble	6	0	0	0	0	2
Steven Woodburn	D	Rouen HC	6	0	0	0	0	8
Tarras Zytynsky	D	Rouen HC	6	0	2	0	2	6
Jean-Philipe Lemoine	D	Rouen HC	6	1	0	0	1	6
Denis Perez	D	Rouen HC	6	0	0	0	0	4
Serge Poudrier	D	Rouen HC	6	4	0	0	4	2
Lionel Orsolini	F	Chamonix HC	5	0	0	0	0	0
Stephane Barin	F	Chamonix HC	6	2	0	0	2	0
Pierre Pousse	F	HC Amiens	6	0	0	0	0	4
Philipe Bozon	F	LBdL Grenoble	6	2	3	0	5	0
André Vittenberg	F	HsG Brest	6	0	0	0	0	0
Eric Lemarque	F	Rouen HC	6	0	0	1	1	4
Franck Pajonkowski	F	Rouen HC	6	1	0	1	2	6
Christophe Ville	F	Chamonix HC	6	1	1	0	2	2
Michel Galarneau	F	HsG Brest	6	1	1	0	2	2
Antoine Richer	F	HC Amiens	6	0	0	0	0	4
Christian Pouget	F	Chamonix HC	6	2	5	1	8	4
Roger Dubé	F	HsG Brest	6	0	0	0	0	0
Patrick Dunn	F	Rouen HC	6	0	0	0	0	0

Coach: Juhani Tamminen

ITALY

Name	POS	Club	GP	G	A1	A2	Pts	PIM
Bruno Campese	GK	HC Asiago	3	0	0	0	0	0
Mario Brunetta	GK	Devils Hockey Milano	4	0	0	0	0	2
Michael Rosati	GK	HC Bolzano	5	0	0	0	0	0
Robert Oberrauch	D	HC Bolzano	6	0	0	2	2	6
Leo Insam	D	HC Gardena	6	0	0	0	0	2
Giorgio Comploi	D	SG Saima Milano	6	2	0	0	2	14
Giovanni Marchetti	D	HC Fassa	4	0	0	0	0	0
Anthony Circelli	D	Varese Hockey	6	0	0	0	0	6
Christopher Bartolone	D	SG Saima Milano	6	0	1	0	1	6
Robert Nardella	D	Chicago Wolves	5	0	1	0	1	8
Michael de Angelis	F	Devils Hockey Milano	6	0	0	0	0	0
Armando Chelodi	F	Devils Hockey Milano	6	0	0	1	1	2
John Massara	F	Varese Hockey	3	1	0	1	2	0
Lino de Toni	F	HC Alleghe	6	0	1	0	1	2
Roland Ramoser	F	HC Bolzano	6	1	1	0	2	4
Maurizio Mansi	F	Varese Hockey	6	3	0	1	4	8
Bruno Zarrillo	F	HC Bolzano	2	0	0	0	0	0
Gaetano Orlando	F	SC Bern	6	1	2	0	3	12
Mario Chitarroni	F	Houston Aeros	5	1	1	0	2	14
Giuseppe Busillo	F	HC Alleghe	6	1	1	0	2	10
Lucio Topatigh	F	Devils Hockey Milano	4	0	1	0	1	2
Martin Pavlu	F	HC Bolzano	6	2	0	0	2	0
Stefano Figliuzzi	F	Varese Hockey	6	2	3	0	5	2

Coach: Brian Lefley

23

GERMANY

Name	POS	Club	GP	G	A1	A2	Pts	PIM
Klaus Merk	GK	Berliner SC Preussen	4	0	0	0	0	0
Josef Heiss	GK	Kölner EC Haie	5	0	0	0	0	0
Marc Seliger	GK	Star Bulls Rosenheim	1	0	0	0	0	0
Michael Bresagk	D	EV Landshut	5	0	0	0	0	2
Torsten Kienass	D	Düsseldorfer EG	5	1	0	0	1	4
Mirco Lüdemann	D	Kölner EC Haie	5	0	3	0	3	0
Andreas Niederberger	D	Düsseldorfer EG	5	1	0	0	1	0
Ulrich Hiemer	D	Düsseldorfer EG	5	0	1	1	2	2
Daniel Nowak	D	Schwenninger W. W.	5	0	0	0	0	6
Marcus Wieland	D	Star Bulls Rosenheim	5	0	1	0	1	0
Jayson Meyer	D	Krefelder EV	5	1	0	1	2	4
Thomas Brandl	F	Kölner EC Haie	5	5	1	0	6	6
Reemt Pyka	F	Krefelder EV	5	0	1	0	1	6
Georg Holzmann	F	Berliner SC Preussen	5	0	0	0	0	20
Leo Stefan	F	Kölner EC Haie	5	0	1	1	2	0
Raimond Hilger	F	Star Bulls Rosenheim	5	0	1	0	1	2
Benoit Doucet	F	Düsseldorfer EG	5	3	0	0	3	6
Andreas Lupzig	F	Kölner EC Haie	5	0	1	1	2	10
Sven Zywitza	F	Augsburger Panthers	5	0	0	0	0	2
Georg Franz	F	EV Landshut	3	0	0	0	0	0
Günther Oswald	F	Krefelder EV	5	0	0	0	0	16
Martin Reichel	F	Star Bulls Rosenheim	5	0	0	0	0	2
Alexander Serikow	F	Mannheimer ERC Adler	5	0	0	0	0	0

Coach: George Kingston; Erich Kühnhackl

SWITZERLAND

Name	POS	Club	GP	G	A1	A2	Pts	PIM
Reto Pavoni	GK	EHC Kloten	7	0	0	0	0	0
Renato Tosio	GK	SC Bern	7	0	0	0	0	0
Lars Weibel	GK	HC Lugano	0	0	0	0	0	0
Martin Brich	D	HC Davos	7	0	1	0	1	6
Andreas Zehnder	D	Zürcher SC	7	1	1	0	2	4
Sandro Bertaggia	D	HC Lugano	7	1	0	1	2	8
Martin Bruderer	D	EHC Kloten	7	1	0	1	2	29
Samuel Balmer	D	HC Davos	7	0	2	0	2	2
Marco Bayer	D	EHC Kloten	7	0	1	0	1	14
Patrick Howald	F	SC Bern	7	2	1	0	3	2
Felix Hollenstein	F	EHC Kloten	7	0	0	0	0	4
Roberto Triulzi	F	SC Bern	7	0	1	0	1	10
Theo Wittmann	F	HC Ambri-Piotta	7	0	0	0	0	4
Bruno Erni	F	EHC Kloten	7	0	1	0	1	6
Jean-Jacques Aeschlimann	F	HC Lugano	7	1	0	0	1	4
Andy Ton	F	HC Lugano	7	5	0	0	5	2
Roman Wäger	F	EHC Kloten	7	0	0	0	0	4
Thomas Heldner	F	HC Ambri-Piotta	6	0	0	0	0	2
Harry Rogenmoser	F	SC Rapperswil	7	0	2	0	2	2
Marcel Jenni	F	HC Lugano	7	1	0	0	1	8
Vjeran Ivankovic	F	Zürcher SC	7	2	1	0	3	4
Christian Weber	F	HC Davos	7	0	1	2	3	2

Coach: Mats Waltin

AUSTRIA

Name	POS	Club	GP	G	A1	A2	Pts	PIM
Michael Suttnig	GK	Klagenfurter AC	5	0	0	0	0	0
Michael Puschacher	GK	Klagenfurter AC	3	0	0	0	0	0
Claus Dalpiaz	GK	VEU Feldkirch	6	0	0	0	0	0
Karl Heinzle	D	VEU Feldkirch	7	0	1	0	1	6
James Burton	D	Klagenfurter AC	7	1	2	2	5	10
Gerhard Unterluggauer	D	Villacher SV	7	0	0	0	0	2
Engelbert Linder	D	Villacher SV	7	0	0	0	0	2
Michael Shea	D	Durham Wasps	7	0	0	0	0	4
Herbert Hohenberger	D	Kölner EC Haie	7	0	4	1	5	10
Michael Günter	D	EC Graz	3	0	0	0	0	2
Martin Ulrich	D	EC Graz	7	0	1	0	1	6
Andreas Pusnik	F	Klagenfurter AC	7	3	1	0	4	10
Gerald Rauchenwald	F	Villacher SV	7	0	0	0	0	8
Gerald Ressmann	F	Villacher SV	7	1	0	0	1	0
Gerhard Puschnik	F	VEU Feldkirch	7	0	0	1	1	8
Manfred Mühr	F	Villacher SV	7	0	0	0	0	4
Richard Nasheim	F	CE Wien	7	3	0	0	3	4
Patrick Pilloni	F	Klagenfurter AC	7	0	0	0	0	2
Kenneth Strong	F	HC Gardena	7	0	1	0	1	4
Werner Kerth	F	EC Graz	7	4	1	1	6	4
Robin Doyle	F	EC Graz	6	1	3	1	5	2
Helmut Karel	F	EC Graz	7	0	0	0	0	0
Dieter Kalt	F	Klagenfurter AC	7	4	1	0	5	4

Coach: Ken Tyler

NORWAY

Name	POS	Club	GP	G	A1	A2	Pts	PIM
Robert Schistad	GK	Viking IHK Stavanger	5	0	0	0	0	0
Jim Martinsen	GK	Storhamar IL	5	0	0	0	0	0
Mattis Haakensen	GK	Lillehammer IK	0	0	0	0	0	0
Petter Salsten	D	Storhamar IL	5	0	0	0	0	0
René Hansen	D	IL Stjernen Fredrikstad	5	0	0	0	0	4
Tommy Jakobsen	D	Spektrum Flyers Oslo	5	0	2	0	2	8
Johnny Nilsen	D	Lillehammer IK	4	0	0	0	0	0
Svein Enok Nörstebö	D	Lillehammer IK	5	0	0	0	0	4
Carl Oscar Andersen	D	Storhamar IL	5	0	0	0	0	6
Öystein Olsen	D	VIF Ishockey Oslo	5	1	1	0	2	4
Henrik Aaby	F	Spektrum Flyers Oslo	5	1	0	0	1	4
Geir Hoff	F	Spektrum Flyers Oslo	4	0	0	0	0	0
Örjan Lövdal	F	IL Stjernen Fredrikstad	5	0	1	0	1	2
Trond Magnussen	F	Lillehammer IK	5	3	0	3	3	2
Petter Thoresen	F	Storhamar IL	5	0	2	0	2	2
Eirik Paulsen	F	Viking IHK Stavanger	5	0	0	0	0	2
Erik Tveten	F	VIF Ishockey Oslo	5	0	0	0	0	2
Björn Anders Dahl	F	Trondheim IK	5	0	0	0	0	0
Rune Fjeldstad	F	VIF Ishockey Oslo	5	1	0	1	2	2
Tom Johansen	F	VIF Ishockey Oslo	1	0	0	0	0	0
Sjur Robert Nilsen	F	Lillehammer IK	5	0	0	1	1	4
Marius Rath	F	VIF Ishockey Oslo	5	1	0	0	1	4
Espen Knutsen	F	Djurgardens IF Stockh.	5	2	1	0	3	0

Coach: Geir Tore Myhre

The name of the game.

WORLD CHAMPIONSHIPS 1995

MJ´95

Bratislava (SVK) April 3. – 21., 1995

POOL B

	SVK	LAT	POL	NED	DEN	JPN	GBR	ROM	Goals	Pts
1. Slovakia		4:3	10:0	13:4	6:2	9:3	7:3	11:0	60:15	14
2. Latvia	3:4		6:2	6:1	9:2	15:2	8:4	18:1	65:16	12
3. Poland	0:10	2:6		8:1	3:1	7:5	3:4	6:3	29:30	8
4. Netherlands	4:13	1:6	1:8		3:2	4:3	2:3	5:3	20:38	6
5. Denmark	2:6	2:9	1:3	2:3		5:1	9:2	9:4	30:28	6
6. Japan	3:9	2:15	5:7	3:4	1:5		4:3	8:2	26:45	4
7. Great Britain	3:7	4:8	4:3	3:2	2:9	3:4		0:2	19:35	4
8. Rumania	0:11	1:18	3:6	3:5	4:9	2:8	2:0		15:57	2

Slovakia promoted to POOL A 1996 · **Rumania** relegated to POOL C 1996

Thee best players by teams

SVK	Jaromir Dragan	GK
	Peter Stastny	CE
	Zdeno Ciger	LW
LAT	Sergejs Naumovs	GK
	Serguei Cudinovs	RD
	Leonids Tambijevs	RW
POL	Sebastian Gonera	RD
	Jacek Zamojski	RD
	Miroslaw Copija	CE
NED	David Bouckaert	LD
	Tommy Speel	CE
	Christiaan Eimers	LW
DEN	Jan Jensen	GK
	Jesper Duus	RD
	Sören True	RW
JPN	Yasuhiro Honma	RD
	Norio Suzuki	CE
	Yuji Iga	CE
GBR	Stephen Foster	GK
	Jeffrey Lindsay	RD
	David Longstaff	CE
ROM	Daniel Herlea	RD
	Marius Gliga	CE
	Ioan Timaru	RW

Directorate prices best player

Best goalkeeper:	Sergejs Naumovs	LAT
Best defender:	Lubomir Sekeras	SVK
Best forward:	Peter Stastny	SVK

Winner of the Fair Play Cup
Japan

All Star Team

S. Naumovs
LAT

L. Sekeras	R. Svehla
SVK	SVK
M. Satan	P. Stastny	R. Petrovicky
SVK	SVK	SVK

Top scorers

Name	Team	GP	G	A	P
1. P. Stastny	SVK	6	8	8	16
2. A. Beliavskis	LAT	7	9	6	15
3. V. Fandoul	LAT	7	6	9	15
4. M. Satan	SVK	7	7	6	13
5. L. Tambijevs	LAT	7	6	6	12

Top defenseman

Name	Team	GP	G	A	P
1. S. Cudinovs	LAT	7	4	3	7
2. L. Sekeras	SVK	7	3	4	7
3. G. Ceplis	LAT	7	2	4	6
4. S. Medrik	SVK	7	1	5	6
5. C. D. Jensen	DEN	7	3	2	5

SLOVAKIA

Name	Pos	GP	G	A1	A2	Pts	PIM
Peter Stastny	CE	6	8	6	2	16	0
Miroslav Satan	LW	7	7	3	3	13	4
Zdeno Ciger	LW	7	7	3	1	11	4
Lubomir Kolnik	RW	7	6	3	2	11	0
Robert Petrovicky	RW	6	4	6	1	11	8
Oto Hascak	CE	7	1	6	2	9	10
Miroslav Ihnacak	RW	7	7	0	1	8	2
Lubomir Sekeras	LD	7	3	3	1	7	22
Jozef Dano	CE	7	1	5	1	7	4
Vlastimil Plavucha	RW	7	6	0	0	6	0
René Pucher	LW	7	3	3	0	6	2
Branislav Janos	LW	7	2	2	2	6	6
Stanislav Medrik	RD	7	1	3	2	6	4
Robert Svehla	RD	4	0	4	2	6	10
Marian Smerciak	LD	7	3	0	2	5	6
Miroslav Marcinko	RD	7	1	0	3	4	6
Stanislav Jasecko	RD	7	0	1	2	3	6
Jan Varholik	LD	7	0	2	1	3	6
Richard Sechny	CE	7	0	1	0	1	6
Slavomir Vorobel	LD	7	0	0	0	0	2

Goalkeepers

Name	GP	MIN	GA	SOG	SVS%	GAA
Jaromir Dragan	7	403.39	13	113	88.50	1.93
Roman Cunderlik	7	16.21	2	8	75.00	7.40

LATVIA

Name	Pos	GP	G	A1	A2	Pts	PIM
Alexandre Beliavskis	RW	7	9	3	3	15	12
Viatcheslav Fandoul	CE	7	6	7	2	15	8
Sergejs Senins	CE	7	6	5	1	12	4
Leonids Tambijevs	RW	7	6	6	0	12	8
Janis Tomans	RW	7	8	2	0	10	6
Sergejs Boldavesko	LW	7	3	5	2	10	0
Oleg Znaroks	LW	6	4	3	1	8	18
Andrei Ignatovitcs	LW	7	5	0	2	7	2
Serguei Cudinovs	RD	7	4	1	2	7	4
Harijs Vitolins	RW	7	3	3	1	7	16
Evgueni Semerjaks	CE	7	3	2	1	6	12
Gatis Ceplis	LD	7	2	2	2	6	2
Andrei Hatitsyn	RD	7	1	2	1	4	2
Normunds Sejejs	LD	7	1	1	2	4	4
Igors Bondarevs	RD	7	1	1	2	4	0
Alexandre Semjonovs	CE	7	1	2	0	3	0
Alexandre Nijivijs	LW	5	0	2	1	3	2
Karlis Skrastins	LD	7	1	1	0	2	4
Juris Opulskis	LD	7	0	1	1	2	4
Martins Grundmanis	RD	5	1	0	0	1	4

Goalkeepers

Name	GP	MIN	GA	SOG	SVS%	GAA
Sergejs Naumovs	7	358.42	11	119	90.76	1.84
Juris Klodans	0	0.00	0	0	0.00	0.00

POLAND

Name	Pos	GP	G	A1	A2	Pts	PIM
Waldemar Klisiak	RW	7	5	2	0	7	14
Roman Steblecki	RW	7	3	3	0	6	4
Miroslav Copija	CE	7	4	1	0	5	4
Andrzej Kadziolka	LD	7	2	2	0	4	6
Miroslaw Tomasik	LW	7	2	2	0	4	4
Wojciech Tkacz	CE	7	1	2	1	4	2
Janusz Hajnos	RW	7	3	0	0	3	0
Slawomir Wieloch	LW	7	2	1	0	3	0
Jacek Zamojski	RD	7	1	1	1	3	2
Sebastian Gonera	RD	7	1	2	0	3	4
Piotr Podlipni	LW	7	1	1	1	3	16
Czeslaw Niedzwiedz	LD	7	0	2	1	3	2
Michal Garbocz	CE	7	2	0	0	2	0
Rafal Sroka	LD	7	1	1	0	2	16
Mariusz Puzio	LW	7	1	1	0	2	0
Jacek Szopinski	CE	5	0	1	1	2	4
Zbigniew Koziel	LD	7	0	1	0	1	18
Ludwik Czapka	RW	7	0	0	1	1	8
Zbidniew Podlipni	LW	7	0	1	0	1	6
Janusz Syposz	RD	5	0	0	0	0	2

Goalkeepers

Name	GP	MIN	GA	SOG	SVS%	GAA
Marek Batkiewicz	7	298.17	15	135	88.89	3.02
Mariusz Kieca	2	0.00	0	0	0.00	0.00
Tomasz Jaworski	5	121.43	15	69	76.20	7.41

NETHERLANDS

Name	Pos	GP	G	A1	A2	Pts	PIM
Tommie Hartogs	RW	7	2	3	1	6	4
Dave Livingston	CE	5	4	1	0	5	12
Tommy Speel	CE	7	2	1	1	4	12
Leo van den Thillart	LD	7	3	0	0	3	10
Patrick van Eijk	LW	7	2	1	0	3	2
Christian Eimers	LW	7	1	2	0	3	8
Theo Kruger	RW	7	1	1	1	3	4
Marcel Houben	RD	7	2	0	0	2	6
Brian de Leeuw	LW	7	1	1	0	2	0
John Versteeg	CE	7	1	0	0	1	2
Danny Thie	RD	7	1	0	0	1	0
Tino Rison	CE	7	0	1	0	1	4
Lester Arts	LD	7	0	0	0	0	6
Jacco Landman	RD	7	0	0	0	0	6
David Bouckaert	LD	7	0	0	0	0	6
Henry Marty Goeree	LD	7	0	0	0	0	12
Henri de Kort	RW	7	0	0	0	0	2
Jordy Geesink	RW	6	0	0	0	0	4
Frank Versteeg	LW	4	0	0	0	0	0
Eric Lambooij	RD	7	0	0	0	0	2

Goalkeepers

Name	GP	MIN	GA	SOG	SVS%	GAA
Martin Trommelen	6	300.00	19	171	88.89	3.80
Boele Bregman	2	0.00	0	0	0.00	0.00
Honore M. Loos	6	120.00	19	106	62.41	9.50

DENMARK

Name	Pos	GP	G	A1	A2	Pts	PIM
Michael Widenborg	LW	7	1	5	3	9	0
Sören True	RW	7	6	1	1	8	10
Jens Christian Nielsen	CE	7	3	4	1	8	6
Struwe Ronny Larsen	LW	7	3	1	2	6	6
Christian Daniel Jensen	RD	7	3	2	0	5	8
Mads True	CE	7	2	3	0	5	0
Broeng Jesper Duus	RD	7	2	2	0	4	20
Michael F. Akesson	LD	7	1	2	0	3	10
Thomas Englund	CE	7	1	1	1	3	4
Jesper Damgaard	RD	7	2	0	0	2	8
Sören Gerber	LW	7	2	0	0	2	8
Ulrich Hansen	RW	7	1	1	0	2	6
Thomas Bjerrum	RW	7	0	2	0	2	4
Lars Oxholm	LD	7	1	0	0	1	8
Munk A. Erik Petersen	LD	7	1	0	0	1	8
Molbäk Th. Hansen	RW	7	1	0	0	1	0
Morten Hille	LD	7	0	1	0	1	0
Binne Morton Ovesen	CE	7	0	0	0	0	0
Emil von Bulow	RW	7	0	0	0	0	2
Karsten Arvidsen	LW	7	0	0	0	0	0

Goalkeepers

Name	GP	MIN	GA	SOG	SVS%	GAA
G. Jan Jensen	7	360.00	19	205	90.73	3.17
Lars Pagh	0	0.00	0	0	0.00	0.00
M. E. Anderson	7	60.00	9	49	81.63	9.00

JAPAN

Name	Pos	GP	G	A1	A2	Pts	PIM
Norio Suzuki	CE	7	5	3	1	9	2
Hiroshi Matsuura	LW	7	4	3	2	9	4
Yasuhiro Honma	RD	7	3	0	1	4	4
Taku Takahashi	RW	7	2	1	1	4	2
Akihito Sugisawa	RW	7	1	3	0	4	4
Yuji Iga	CE	7	2	0	1	3	14
Taro Nihei	RW	7	2	0	1	3	4
Takayuki Kobori	LD	7	1	1	1	3	8
Hidesato Takahashi	RW	7	1	2	0	3	2
Hidekatsu Takagi	LD	7	1	1	1	3	2
Kunio Takagi	LD	7	1	1	0	2	2
Ryuji Saito	CE	7	1	1	0	2	0
Atsuo Kudo	LD	7	1	1	0	2	2
Shin Yahata	LW	7	0	2	0	2	0
Tatsuki Katayama	RD	7	1	0	0	1	2
Koshi Kiyoe	LW	7	0	1	0	1	0
Takayuki Miura	RD	7	0	1	0	1	2
Yujiro Nakajimaya	RD	7	0	0	0	0	4
Toshiyuki Sakai	CE	7	0	0	0	0	10
Tomohito Kobayashi	LW	7	0	0	0	0	8

Goalkeepers

Name	GP	MIN	GA	SOG	SVS%	GAA
Shinichi Iwasaki	6	204.06	14	103	86.41	4.12
Katsunori Hirano	6	175.54	23	73	68.49	7.86
Jiro Nihei	2	40.00	7	30	76.67	10.5

GREAT BRITAIN

Name	Pos	GP	G	A1	A2	Pts	PIM
David Longstaff	Ce	7	6	0	1	7	8
Scott Morrison	RW	7	4	2	0	6	10
Terry Kurtenbach	LD	7	0	2	2	4	2
Nicholas Chinn	LW	4	1	1	1	3	4
Neil Morgan	RW	7	1	2	0	3	2
Shannon Hope	LD	6	1	1	0	2	14
Frank Morris	CE	7	1	0	1	2	20
Paul Dixon	RD	5	1	1	0	2	2
Iain Robertson	CE	7	1	0	0	1	0
Anthony Payne	CE	7	1	0	0	1	0
Ian Cooper	Rw	2	1	0	0	1	2
David Smith	LW	7	1	0	0	1	0
Lee Saunders	RD	7	0	1	0	1	0
Damian Smith	LW	7	0	0	1	1	10
Matthew Cote	LD	7	0	1	0	1	4
Michael Kindred	LW	5	0	1	0	1	2
Jeffrey Lindsay	RD	7	0	0	0	0	10
Richard Strachan	LD	7	0	0	0	0	2
Ian Pound	RD	7	0	0	0	0	10
Ashley Tait	RW	2	0	0	0	0	4

Goalkeepers

Name	GP	MIN	GA	SOG	SVS%	GAA
Stephen Foster	7	320.00	28	201	86.07	5.25
William Morrison	6	60.00	2	25	92.00	2.00
Richard Grubb	1	40.00	5	30	83.33	7.50

RUMANIA

Name	Pos	GP	G	A1	A2	Pts	PIM
Zsolt Antal	CE	6	4	0	0	4	32
Csaba Gal	LW	7	2	1	1	4	14
Karoly Antal	RW	7	1	3	0	4	4
Ioan Timaru	RW	7	1	0	0	3	4
Jeno Salamon	LD	7	0	2	1	3	22
Cristian Daia	LD	6	2	0	0	2	4
Daniel Heliea	RD	7	1	1	0	2	6
Iulian Popovici	LD	7	1	0	1	2	8
Marius-C. Gliga	Ce	7	1	1	0	2	0
Marian Dospin	RD	7	1	0	0	1	2
Laszlo Vargyas	RD	7	0	0	1	1	8
Ion Zaharia	LW	7	0	0	1	1	6
Catalin-Gabriel Geru	RW	7	0	1	0	1	0
Roberto Cazacu	CE	7	0	1	0	1	4
Levente Elekes	RW	7	0	1	0	1	2
Ion Dimache	LD	7	0	0	0	0	2
Attila Nagy	RD	7	0	0	0	0	2
Gergecy Lukacs	CE	7	0	0	0	0	0
Arpad Sofron	LW	7	0	0	0	0	0
Viorel Nicolescu	LW	7	0	0	0	0	2

Goalkeepers

Name	GP	MIN	GA	SOG	SVS%	GAA
Viorel Radu	7	321.55	40	222	81.98	7.46
Szabolcs Molnar	0	0.00	0	0	0.00	0.00
Vasilica Zaharia	7	98.05	17	81	79.01	10.4

Seiko Kinetic – you are the power

...ko Kinetic®. The first and only quartz watch that generates power from your every ...vement. Perpetual accuracy. Ultimate quartz reliability. Naturally, without a battery. ...usively by Seiko. Built to last. **Someday all watches will be made this way.**

SEIKO
KINETIC

WORLD CHAMPIONSHIP 1995

Sofia (BUL) · March 20. – 26., 1995

POOL C

Group 1

Group A	KAZ	CHN	BUL	Goals	P
1. Kazakhstan		12:0	8:1	20:1	4
2. China	0:12		4:2	4:14	2
3. Bulgaria	1:8	2:4		3:12	0

Group B	BLR	EST	SLO	Goals	P
1. Belarus		6:1	5:4	11: 5	4
2. Estonia	1:6		6:3	7: 9	2
3. Slovenia	4:5	3:6		7:11	0

Group C	UKR	HUN	YUG	Goals	P
1. Ukraine		9:1	15:3	24: 4	4
2. Hungary	1:9		9:1	10:10	2
3. Yugoslavia	3:15	1:9		4:24	0

Final Round

Group A	BLR	KAZ	UKR	Goals	P
1. Belarus		3:1	5:2	5:2	4
2. Kazakhstan	1:2		2:2	3:4	1
3. Ukraine	1:3	2:2		3:5	1

Group B	EST	CHN	HUN	Goals	P
4. Estonia		9:5	6:2	15:7	4
5. China	5:9		4:3	9:12	2
6. Hungary	2:6	3:4		5:10	0

Group C	SLO	YUG	BUL	Goals	P
7. Slovenia		7:3	14:1	21: 4	4
8. Yugoslavia	3:7		6:0	9: 7	2
9. Bulgaria	1:14	0:6		1:20	0

Belarus promoted to Pool B 1996 – **Yugoslavia** and **Bulgaria** relegated to Pool D 1996

Most goals

1. Jan Ivo — SLO 5
   Tomaz Vnuk — SLO 5
   Ivan Prokic — YUG 5
4. Eduard Valiullin — ESt 4
   Andrej Ptcheliakov — KZK 4

Most assists

1. A. Stepanichtchev — UKR 6
   Valentin Oletskii — UKR 6
3. Igor Beliaevski — KZK 5
   Valeri Chiriaev — UKR 5
5. Sergej Antipor — KZK 4

Top defensemen

		G	A	P
1. Andrej Brodnik	SLO	3	4	7
2. Valeri Chiriaev	UKR	1	5	6
3. Mikail Fadeev	UKR	2	2	4
4. Tom Jug	SLO	1	3	4

Leading scorers

Name	Team	Pos	GP	G	A1	A2	Pts
1. Tomaz Vnuk	SLO	CE	4	5	1	2	8
2. Igor Beliaevski	KZK	CE	4	3	3	2	8
3. Valentin Oletskii	UKR	RW	4	2	3	3	8
4. Jan Ivo	SLO	LW	4	5	2	0	7
5. Ivan Rokic	YUG	LW	4	5	2	0	7
6. Eduard Valiullin	EST	CE	4	4	2	1	7
7. Andrei Ptcheliakov	KZK	CE	4	4	2	1	7
8. Andrej Brodnik	SLO	LD	4	3	2	2	7
9. Sergei Antipov	KZK	RW	4	3	3	1	7
10. Anatoli Stepanichtchev	UKR	RW	4	1	6	0	7
11. Vasily Pankov	BLS	CE	4	4	2	0	6
12. Ivan Loginov	EST	LW	4	3	3	0	6
13. Andrei Raiski	KZK	RW	4	2	2	2	6
14. Mikhail Zakharov	BLS	LW	4	2	3	1	6
15. Valeri Chiriaev	UKR	RD	4	1	3	2	6
16. Ranil Iouldachev	UKR	LW	4	4	1	0	5
17. Nik Zupancic	SLO	CE	4	3	2	0	5
18. Vitali Litvinenko	UKR	RW	4	3	0	2	5
19. Anatoli Maida	UKR	CE	4	3	1	1	5
20. Alexander Filippov	KZK	LW	4	2	3	0	5
21. Boris Alexandrov	KZK	LW	4	2	1	2	5
22. Andrej Razinger	SLO	RW	4	2	2	1	5
23. Zoran Kozic	YUG	RW	4	2	3	0	5
24. Victor Gontcharenko	UKR	LW	4	1	4	0	5
25. Saso Pretnar	SLO	LW	4	1	3	1	5

BELARUS

Name	Pos	GP	G	A1	A2	Pts	PIM
Vasily Pankov	CE	4	4	2	0	6	4
Mikhail Zakharov	LW	4	2	3	1	6	12
Andrei Kavaliov	RW	4	2	1	1	4	2
Sergei Shitkovsky	RW	4	2	1	1	4	2
Andrei Skabelka	RW	4	0	1	2	3	0
Oleg Khmyl	LD	4	0	1	2	3	2
Alexandr Andreievsky	LW	4	1	0	1	2	6
Edurad Zankovets	RW	4	1	0	1	2	6
Alexandre Alexeev	CE	4	1	1	0	2	2
Andrei Gusov	CE	4	1	0	0	1	2
Oleg Romanov	LD	4	0	1	0	1	4
Ruslan Saley	RD	4	0	1	0	1	4
Vladimir Kopat	RD	4	0	1	0	1	6
Alexandr Pstyga	CE	4	0	1	0	1	0
Sergei Tcherniavsky	LW	4	0	0	0	0	0
Dmitry Ovsiannikov	LW	4	0	0	0	0	0
Sergei Fedotov	RD	2	0	0	0	0	2
Alexandr Makritsky	LD	4	0	0	0	0	0

Goalkeepers

Name	GP	MIP	GA	SOG	GAA	PIM
Alexei Emelianov	4	240.00	7	217	1.75	0
Alexandr Gavrilionok	4	0.00	0	0	0.00	0

KAZAKHSTAN

Name	Pos	GP	G	A1	A2	Pts	PIM
Igor Beliaevski	CE	4	3	3	2	8	2
Andrei Ptcheliakov	CE	4	4	2	1	7	2
Serguei Antipov	RW	4	3	3	1	7	8
Andrei Raiski	RW	4	2	2	2	6	35
Boris Alexandrov	LW	4	2	1	2	5	4
Alexander Filippov	LW	4	2	3	0	5	0
Pavel Kametsev	CE	4	2	2	0	4	0
Andrei Samokhvalov	RW	4	1	1	2	4	0
Roman Zavodov	LW	4	1	1	1	3	2
Andrei Savenkov	LD	4	2	0	0	2	0
Vitali Tregoubov	LD	4	0	2	0	2	18
Valeri Touchentsov	CE	4	0	2	0	2	0
Oleg Kovalenko	RD	4	1	0	0	1	4
Vladimir Antipine	RD	4	0	0	1	1	20
Vadim Tounikov	RD	4	0	0	0	0	0
Igor Zemlianoi	LD	4	0	0	0	0	2
Igor Mervedev	LD	4	0	0	0	0	6
Andrei Tsiba	LW	4	0	0	0	0	4

Goalkeepers

Name	GP	MIP	GA	SOG	GAA	PIM
Alexander Chimine	4	80.00	1	43	0.75	0
Vitali Eremeev	4	160.00	4	142	1.50	0

UKRAINE

Name	Pos	GP	G	A1	A2	Pts	PIM
Valentin Oletskii	RW	4	2	3	3	8	2
Anatoli Stepanichtchev	RW	4	1	6	0	7	2
Valeri Chiriaev	RD	4	1	3	2	6	4
Ranil Iouldachev	LW	4	4	1	0	5	0
Anatoli Maida	CE	4	3	1	1	5	0
Vitali Litvinenko	RW	4	3	0	2	5	2
Victor Gontcharenko	LW	4	1	4	0	5	2
Vadim Chakhraitchouk	CE	4	3	1	0	4	8
Andrei Nikolaev	LW	4	3	1	0	4	6
Mikhail Fadeev	RD	4	2	2	0	4	2
Alexandre Savitskii	RD	4	2	1	0	3	0
Vadim Koulaboukhov	RW	4	2	0	0	2	2
Evgueni Mlintchenko	LW	4	0	2	0	2	0
Iouri Gounko	LD	4	0	0	1	1	0
Vassili Bobrovnikov	CE	4	0	1	0	1	0
Serguei Loubnine	LD	4	0	0	0	0	6
Oleg Polkovnikov	RD	4	0	0	0	0	8
Anatoli Khomenko	LD	4	0	0	0	0	0

Goalkeepers

Name	GP	MIP	GA	SOG	GAA	PIM
Iouri Choundrov	4	118.51	4	54	2.03	0
Igor Karpenko	4	121.09	5	80	2.48	2

ESTONIA

Name	Pos	GP	G	A1	A2	Pts	PIM
Eduard Valiullin	CE	4	4	2	1	7	0
Ivan Loginov	LW	4	3	3	0	6	0
Mihail Korsunov	LW	4	3	0	1	4	6
Oleg Puzanov	RW	4	1	3	0	4	2
Igor Osipenkov	RW	4	2	0	1	3	0
Sergei Boikov	LW	4	2	1	0	3	2
Vjatseslav Kulpin	LD	4	2	0	0	2	6
Dmitri Rodin	LD	4	1	1	0	2	4
Aleksandr Agnevstsiko	RD	4	1	1	0	2	4
Mihail Kozlov	CE	4	1	1	0	2	4
Georgi Kozlov	LW	4	1	1	0	2	6
Gennadi Ryzkov	RD	4	1	0	0	1	4
Oleg Trubatsov	LD	4	0	0	1	1	6
Valeri Lebedev	CE	4	0	0	0	0	4
Roman Potsinok	RD	4	0	0	0	0	0
Mati Parvoja	CE	4	0	0	0	0	0
Aleksandr Dmitrijev	RW	4	0	0	0	0	2
Sergei Morkovnikov	RW	4	0	0	0	0	0

Goalkeepers

Name	GP	MIP	GA	SOG	GAA	PIM
Vjatseslav Skvortsov	4	120.00	9	140	4.50	0
Andrus Ahi	4	120.00	7	67	3.50	0

CHINA

Name	Pos	GP	G	A1	A2	Pts	PIM
Guang-Hua Chen	CE	4	2	2	0	4	0
Xiao-Fang Guan	RD	4	2	1	1	4	4
Zhang-Yong Wang	RW	4	2	1	1	4	4
Xiao-Bo Guan	RW	4	2	0	1	3	29
Yuqiang Pan	LW	4	2	0	0	2	4
Shou-Sheng Zhang	CE	4	2	0	0	2	2
Xue Liu	LD	3	1	0	0	1	16
Jiu-Ming Liu	LD	4	0	1	0	1	4
Ling-Yuan Wei	LW	4	0	1	0	1	0
Wen-Wu Liu	CE	4	0	1	0	1	2
Hong-Lei Sun	CE	4	0	1	0	1	0
Ke Tan	RW	4	0	1	0	1	2
Meng-Yuan Zhai	RW	4	0	0	0	0	6
Lei Luo	LW	4	0	0	0	0	0
Hong-Qun Gao	LD	4	0	0	0	0	4
Feng Liu	RD	4	0	0	0	0	0
Zhi-Feng Zhamg	LD	4	0	0	0	0	6
Ning Yin	RD	3	0	0	0	0	0

Goalkeepers

Name	GP	MIP	GA	SOG	GAA	PIM
Hua Geng	4	173.14	24	288	8.32	0
Li-Qun Zhang	3	66.46	2	53	1.81	0

HUNGARY

Name	Pos	GP	G	A1	A2	Pts	PIM
Csaba Simon	RW	4	4	0	0	4	4
Gabor Ocskay	CE	4	1	2	1	4	2
Janos Ancsin	LW	4	3	0	0	3	0
Tamas Dobos	CE	4	2	0	0	2	2
Balazs Kangyal	LD	4	2	0	0	2	0
Lajos Tokesi	RD	4	1	1	0	2	4
Peter Erdosi	CE	4	1	1	0	2	0
Laszlo Pindak	RW	4	0	2	0	2	0
Krisztian Palkovics	RW	4	1	0	0	1	4
Viktor Szelig	LD	4	0	1	0	1	6
Laszlo Ancsin	RD	4	0	1	0	1	2
Balazs Ladanyi	LW	4	0	1	0	1	2
Kristof Kovago	CE	4	0	0	1	1	0
Zoltan Hegyi	LD	4	0	1	0	1	0
Andras Horvath	RD	4	0	0	0	0	6
Viktor Tokaji	LD	4	0	0	0	0	0
Zsolt Bali	LW	4	0	0	0	0	2
Szilard Sandor	LW	4	0	0	0	0	0

Goalkeepers

Name	GP	MIP	GA	SOG	GAA	PIM
Norbert Berenyi	4	235.18	18	232	4.59	0
Karoly Ban	4	4.42	2	8	27.2	0

SLOVENIA

Name	Pos	GP	G	A1	A2	Pts	PIM
Tomaz Vnuk	CE	4	5	1	2	8	0
Ivo Jan	LW	4	5	2	0	7	0
Andrej Brodnik	LD	4	3	2	2	7	2
Nik Zupancic	CE	4	3	2	0	5	4
Andrej Razinger	RW	4	2	2	1	5	47
Saso Pretnar	LW	4	1	3	1	5	2
Dejan Kontrec	LW	4	0	4	1	5	2
Borut Potocnik	RD	4	2	1	1	4	0
Jure Vnuk	RW	4	2	1	1	4	2
Tom Jug	RD	4	1	2	1	4	6
Rok Rojsek	RW	4	0	3	0	3	4
Borut Vukcevic	LD	4	2	0	0	2	4
Elvis Beslagic	LD	4	1	1	0	2	8
Dejan Varl	CE	4	1	1	0	2	6
Samo Kumar	LD	4	0	0	1	1	2
Boris Kuncic	RD	4	0	0	0	0	0
Jure Smolej	LW	4	0	0	0	0	0
Dragutin Mlinarec	CE	3	0	0	0	0	0

Goalkeepers

Name	GP	MIP	GA	SOG	GAA	PIM
Luka Simsic	4	212.55	14	171	3.95	25
Zvone Bolta	4	27.50	1	25	2.22	0

YUGOSLAVIA

Name	Pos	GP	G	A1	A2	Pts	PIM
Ivan Rokic	LW	4	5	2	0	7	18
Zoran Kozic	RW	4	2	3	0	5	8
Aleksandr Kosic	CE	4	2	0	0	2	14
Dejan Tatic	RW	4	1	0	1	2	0
Mirko Karaica	LD	4	0	2	0	2	4
Milos Nikolic	LW	4	1	0	0	1	0
Aleksandr Ramadanovic	LW	4	1	0	0	1	2
Tivadar Gabric	RW	4	1	0	0	1	0
Kolja Lazarevic	LW	4	0	1	0	1	6
Igor Trifunovic	LD	4	0	0	0	0	4
Nenad Milinkovic	RD	4	0	0	0	0	8
Goran Radovic	RD	4	0	0	0	0	4
Darko Rudan	LD	4	0	0	0	0	8
Zoran Lazic	CE	4	0	0	0	0	4
Dragan Stojic	RW	3	0	0	0	0	2
Boris Semsedinovic	D	4	0	0	0	0	0
Aleksandar Pesic	CE	4	0	0	0	0	2
Goran Ristic	RD	4	0	0	0	0	0

Goalkeepers

Name	GP	MIP	GA	SOG	GAA	PIM
Miroslav Radak	4	140.00	9	128	3.86	0
Petar Mihailovic	4	100.00	22	154	13.2	0

BULGARIA

Name	Pos	GP	G	A1	A2	Pts	PIM
Gueorqui Banqueev	LW	4	2	0	0	2	4
Zlatko Zinoviev	CE	4	0	2	0	2	2
Gueorgui Dimitrov	RW	4	0	0	2	2	0
Boris Mihaylov	CE	4	1	0	0	1	0
Stoyan Batchvarov	RW	4	1	0	0	1	4
Plamen Vesselinov	LW	4	0	1	0	1	6
Emil Damev	LW	4	0	1	0	1	0
Tzvetan Mihaylov	CE	4	0	0	0	0	0
Kiril Petrov	LD	4	0	0	0	0	2
Alexander Panev	RD	4	0	0	0	0	6
Gueorgui Simeonov	RW	4	0	0	0	0	0
Stefan Gueorguiev	LD	4	0	0	0	0	2
Istalian Zarev	RD	4	0	0	0	0	2
Ventzislav Venev	LD	4	0	0	0	0	2
Iovko Terziev	RW	3	0	0	0	0	2
Martin Gurov	RD	4	0	0	0	0	4
Dimitar Stoitchkov	LW	3	0	0	0	0	0
Anton Bratanov	CE	3	0	0	0	0	0

Goalkeepers

Name	GP	MIP	GA	SOG	GAA	PIM
Konstantin Mihailov	4	102.57	9	143	5.26	0
Ivaylo Assenov	4	137.03	23	241	10.1	0

MAJOR SPORTS EVENTS IN TIVOLI HALL, LJUBLJANA-SLOVENIA

1965
World Table Tennis Championship

1966
World Ice Hockey Championship (Pool A)

1967
European Figure Skating Championship

1969
World Ice Hockey Championship (Pool B)

1970
World Figure Skating Championship
World Basketball Championship (Men)
World Gymnastics Championship

1974
World Ice Hockey Championship (Pool B)

1982
World Weightlifting Championship

1984
World Bowling Championship (ninepins)

1991
World Ice Hockey Championship (Pool B)

1992
European Pool Billiards Championship

1993
World Ice Hockey Championships (Pool C)
European Junior Table Tennis Championship

1994
European Basketball Championship for Men
"22" and Under

WORLD CHAMPIONSHIP 1995

Elektrenai (LIT) · March 11. – 17., 1995

POOL

C

Group 2

Group A	LTU	ESP	BEL	AUS	GRE	Goals	P
1. Lithuania		4:3	8:2	8:2	20:1	40: 8	8
2. Spain	3:4		4:1	4:2	21:1	32: 8	6
3. Belgium	2:8	1:4		10:2	5:5	18:19	3
4. Australia	2:8	2:4	2:10		10:2	16:24	2
5. Greece	1:20	1:21	5:5	2:10		9:56	1

Group B	CRO	KOR	ISR	RSA	NZL	Goals	P
1. Croatia		4:3	7:2	11:1	19:5	41:11	8
2. Korea	3:4		7:1	8:2	19:0	37: 7	6
3. Isreal	2:7	1:7		8:1	12:0	23:15	4
4. South Africa	1:11	2:8	1:8		3:2	7:29	2
5. New Zealand	5:19	0:19	0:12	2:3		7:53	0

The results of the games A1-A2, A3-A4, B1-B2, B3-B4 in the first four rounds are also counted in deciding the place in the two final divisions. A4-B5 ist a play-off game.

Final Round

Group A

CRO – ESP 6:3   ESP – KOR 7:5
LTU – KOR 5:2   LTU – CRO 3:3

1. Croatia	13: 9	5
2. Lithuania	12: 8	5
3. Spain	13:15	2
4. Korea	10:16	0

Group C

Greece – New Zealand   10:7

Group B

BEL – RSA 10:1   AUS – ISR 5:1
AUS – RSA 10:6   BEL – ISR 2:7

1. Belgium	22:10	4
2. Israel	18: 8	4
3. Australia	17:17	4
4. South Africa	8:28	0

Final standing

1. Croatia
2. Lithuania
3. Spain
4. Korea
5. Belgium
6. Israel
7. Australia
8. South Africa
9. Greece
10. New Zealand

Croatia promoted to POOL C 1996

CROATIA

Name	Pos	GP	G	A1	A2	Pts	PIM
Gennadij Gorbacev	RW	6	12	5	0	17	8
Igor Zajev	CE	6	4	8	2	14	8
Hovoje Appelt	LW	6	6	5	2	13	4
Goran Jelinek	RW	6	4	5	0	9	8
Ivan Muslim	CE	6	2	6	1	9	8
Marko Belinic	LW	6	6	0	1	7	16
Hrvoje Lukic	RW	6	1	3	1	5	4
Zvonko Tkalcec	RD	6	4	0	0	4	4
Ivo Ratej	LD	6	3	1	0	4	37
Mazen Kire	LW	6	3	0	0	3	8
Marin Latkovic	LD	6	2	0	1	3	12
Dubravko Orlic	CE	6	2	0	1	3	0
Martin Pancirov	RD	6	0	2	1	3	0
Zoran Almer	RD	6	1	0	0	1	0
Zarko Trumbetas	LD	6	0	0	1	1	8
Mario Kocijancic	RD	6	0	1	0	1	0
Danijel Kolombo	CE	6	0	1	0	1	8
Swen Skrgatic	LW	6	0	1	0	1	0

Goalkeepers

Name	GP	MIN	GA	SOG	SVS%	GAA
Dragutin Ljubic	6	390.26	15	2	35.98	2.73
Jura Sinanovic	6	29.34	2	2	3.00	4.09

LITHUANIA

Name	Pos	GP	G	A1	A2	Pts	PIM
Jainius Bauba	CE	6	13	5	3	21	12
Egidijus Bauba	LW	6	5	6	1	12	8
Jurij Merkltov	RW	6	3	6	2	11	6
Erikas Stepovaitis	CE	6	7	1	1	9	0
Audrius Zusrus	LD	6	2	2	4	8	0
Jaurius Zevelskis	RD	6	2	3	2	7	6
Vadimas Jakuta	RW	6	3	1	2	6	12
Sergej Krumkac	LD	6	1	4	1	6	0
Antanas Daugirdas	CE	6	2	3	0	5	4
Andrejus Jadkauskas	LD	6	1	2	2	5	10
Audrius Rimkus	RW	6	2	2	0	4	0
Ervinas Verenis	CE	6	3	0	0	3	0
Andrej Simankov	RW	6	1	2	0	3	6
Rolandas Bucys	RD	6	0	2	1	3	6
Dangyras Rimkus	RD	6	0	1	1	2	2
Edmundas Micevicius	LW	6	0	1	1	2	10
Valdas Skadauskas	LW	6	0	0	2	2	6
Dmitrij Piazenko	LW	6	0	1	0	1	0

Goalkeepers

Name	GP	MIN	GA	SOG	SVS%	GAA
Vytentas Parazinskas	3	390.00	10	63	84.13	2.00
Arunas Aleinikova	6	60.00	3	18	83.33	3.00

SPAIN

Name	Pos	GP	G	A1	A2	Pts	PIM
Ignacio Salegui	CE	6	6	5	0	11	2
Ignacio Izaguirre	RW	9	5	3	1	9	2
Miguel Baldris	LD	6	2	3	3	8	16
Alejandro Calvo	LW	6	3	2	2	7	2
Juan Maria Izquierdo	RW	6	2	1	3	6	4
Gonzalo Eguiluz	RD	6	2	3	0	5	2
Ignacio Noguerol	CE	6	0	3	2	5	0
Igor Santamaria	LD	6	1	2	1	4	12
Jorge Pous	LW	6	1	3	0	4	6
Alayn Iturralde	CE	6	0	4	0	4	0
Juan Jose Palacin	RW	6	0	1	2	3	4
Enrique Zapata	RW	6	0	0	3	3	0
Inigo Arangoya	LW	6	0	3	0	3	8
Eugsnio Arbesu	LD	6	0	0	2	2	6
Jose Ruiz de Galarreta	RD	6	0	1	1	2	8
Roman Jimenez	LD	6	0	0	1	1	10
Unai Arizcorreta	RD	6	0	0	1	1	2
Gabriel Maso	LW	6	0	0	1	1	0

Goalkeepers

Name	GP	MIN	GA	SOG	SVS%	GAA
Gregorio Martin	6	360.00	18	73	75.34	3.00

KOREA

Name	Pos	GP	G	A1	A2	Pts	PIM
Sang-Won Seo	LW	6	7	3	1	11	18
Chang-Gun An	RW	6	5	3	2	10	8
Eui-Sik Shim	CE	6	5	3	1	9	20
Woo-Sam Shin	CE	6	6	0	1	7	41
Hyun-Mo Sung	LW	6	5	1	0	6	6
Young-Ho Bae	LW	6	3	2	1	6	2
Kwang-Hee Lee	LW	6	3	2	1	6	20
Youn-Sung Kim	RD	6	1	2	3	6	16
Jong-Ok Park	CE	6	1	3	2	6	4
Sung-Bok Kim	RW	6	1	4	1	6	2
Yong-Nam Kim	RW	6	2	2	1	5	0
Yong-Seung Lee	LD	6	1	1	3	5	6
Kook-Chan Han	CE	6	1	2	2	5	2
Do.Sik Park	RD	6	1	2	1	4	2
Sung-Min Cho	RW	6	1	1	2	4	4
Chang-Bum Kim	LD	6	0	2	2	4	14
Hyun-Suk Song	LD	6	1	2	0	3	4
Shi-Won Kim	Rd	6	0	0	0	0	2

Goalkeepers

Name	GP	MIN	GA	SOG	SVS%	GAA
Dong-Ho Lee	6	190.13	8	42	80.95	2.52
Jae-Yong Choi	6	169.47	10	50	80.00	3.54

BELGIUM

Name	Pos	GP	G	A1	A2	Pts	PIM
Bob Moris	RW	6	7	4	2	13	10
Walter Stappaerts	CE	6	3	2	4	9	2
Yourie Steijlen	RW	6	2	4	0	6	26
Tim Vos	RD	6	1	4	1	6	16
Ivan Reyntjens	LD	6	3	0	2	5	2
Danny Gyesberghs	LD	6	2	2	0	4	4
Kristoff van den Broeck	CE	6	2	2	0	4	6
Koen Hermans	LW	6	1	2	1	4	14
Philippe Cools	LW	6	2	1	0	3	4
Alain Scheltjens	RW	6	2	1	0	3	2
Gunther Guylaerts	RD	6	1	0	2	3	12
Jesse Raekelboom	CE	6	1	1	0	2	2
Ward Szarzynski	CE	6	1	0	1	2	0
Buck Rombouts	LW	6	0	1	1	2	2
Tom Matthe	LD	6	1	0	0	1	16
Bart Leten	RD	6	0	1	0	1	0
Joris Peusens	RW	6	0	0	1	1	0
Stefan Casteels	LW	6	0	0	0	0	4

Goalkeepers

Name	GP	MIN	GA	SOG	SVS%	GAA
Luc van Walle	6	234.06	15	54	72.22	3.85
Steven Raeymaekers	6	125.54	12	22	45.45	5.74

ISRAEL

Name	Pos	GP	G	A1	A2	Pts	PIM
MironSchacham	CE	6	3	10	1	14	2
Evgeny Fekdman	RW	6	5	7	1	13	4
Oleg Agapov	RW	6	7	3	0	10	8
Benjamin Shapiro	RW	6	6	1	2	9	6
Sergey Gudzik	LW	6	5	2	1	8	48
Boris Paessel	LW	6	2	2	2	6	0
Sergei Matin	CE	6	1	1	1	3	8
Alexander Stotyar	LD	6	1	0	2	3	12
Assaf Eukon	RW	6	1	0	1	2	2
Ran Oz	LD	6	0	1	1	2	34
Odeo Orgil	LD	6	0	1	0	1	6
Michael Rubin	CE	6	0	1	0	1	0
Mladem Mlademov	LW	6	0	0	1	1	6
Michael Blumberg	RD	6	0	1	0	1	33
Maryus Lazar	LW	6	0	0	0	0	2
Lev Genin	LD	6	0	0	0	0	0

Goalkeepers

Name	GP	MIN	GA	SOG	SVS%	GAA
Boris Amomin	6	182.40	5	67	92.54	1.64
Yevgeny Gusin	6	177.20	16	83	80.72	5.42

AUSTRALIA

Name	Pos	GP	G	A1	A2	Pts	PIM
Charles Tracey Cooper	LW	6	9	6	0	15	20
Christopher Corey Rurak	CE	6	4	5	1	10	14
IGlen Foll	LD	6	1	3	3	7	0
Anthony John Wilson	RD	6	3	1	1	5	4
Howard Peter Jones	RD	6	1	3	1	5	0
Andrew Kirkham	RW	6	4	0	0	4	6
Nigel Chandler	CE	6	3	1	0	4	0
Andrew James Brunt	RW	6	3	1	0	4	6
Murray James Wand	CE	6	1	1	0	2	4
Glann Alan Neal Grandy	LW	6	1	1	0	2	0
Douglas Stevenson	LD	6	1	1	0	2	4
Arto Kalevi Malste	LD	6	0	1	0	1	0
David Andrew Mann	RD	6	0	1	0	1	12
Paul Michael Shumak	LW	6	0	0	0	0	0
Trevor Banks	LW	6	0	0	0	0	28
Paul Adam Nesterczuk	RW	6	0	0	0	0	4

Goalkeepers

Name	GP	MIN	GA	SOG	SVS%	GAA
Damian C. Holland	5	300.00	15	143	89.51	3.00
David Andrew Mann	6	60.00	15	10	0.00	10.0

NEW ZEALAND

Name	Pos	GP	G	A1	A2	Pts	PIM
John Philip Dowman	RW	5	4	1	1	6	14
Eirik John Hoglund	CE	5	3	2	0	5	6
Michael B. Luggen	RW	5	2	1	1	4	0
Darren Ernest Blong	CE	5	2	0	1	3	4
Graeme Allen Scott	LD	5	2	1	0	3	4
Matthew Ch. Wilcock	LW	5	0	2	1	3	8
Davis Andrew le Comte	LD	5	1	1	0	2	20
Christopher H. Blong	RD	5	0	2	0	2	20
Mark Kenneth Symons	CE	5	0	1	0	1	10
Ramon Jay Thackwell	LW	5	0	0	1	1	2
Daniel Christian Seth	LD	5	0	0	0	0	2
Daniel John Ainsworth	RW	5	0	0	0	0	2
Peter Alan Oliver	RW	5	0	0	0	0	10
Rene Michael Aish	CE	5	0	0	0	0	6
Paul Donald Dixon	RD	5	0	0	0	0	10
Graham William Green	LW	5	0	0	0	0	0
Jeffrey David Price	LW	5	0	0	0	0	2

Goalkeepers

Name	GP	MIN	GA	SOG	SVS%	GAA
Neale Duncan Glass	5	263.48	58	106	45.28	13.2
Craig R. Andrewartha	4	36.12	5	5	0.00	8.31

SOUTH AFRICA

Name	Pos	GP	G	A1	A2	Pts	PIM
Chad Jayson Lawrence	CE	6	3	5	1	9	2
Ronald Crichton	RW	6	3	1	1	5	0
Andrew Wallace Milne	LW	6	1	2	1	4	0
Alan William Verwey	LD	6	3	0	0	3	4
Jacques Booysen	RW	6	2	1	0	3	4
Peter Miles Strydom	RD	6	1	1	0	2	2
Dan M. van Hemmert	LW	6	0	0	2	2	6
Glen Lazarus	CE	6	0	2	0	2	0
Arn Wayne Potter	RD	6	1	0	0	1	0
Cornelius Otto le Roux	LD	6	0	1	0	1	2
Nicholas Thornton	RD	6	0	0	0	0	12
Andre Loubser	RW	6	0	0	0	0	16
Errol Michael Saffy	LW	6	0	0	0	0	2
Pereira Edgar E. Lopes	CE	6	0	0	0	0	0
Michael Hanekom	LD	6	0	0	0	0	0
Riaan Booysen	LW	6	0	0	0	0	0
Pedro Miguel S. Santos	RW	6	0	0	0	0	0

Goalkeepers

Name	GP	MIN	GA	SOG	SVS%	GAA
Geoffrey Pelger	6	284.56	40	119	66.39	8.43
Angelo Coppola	6	75.04	9	45	80.00	7.20

GREECE

Name	Pos	GP	G	A1	A2	Pts	PIM
Georgios Adamidis	RW	5	0	5	4	9	0
Dimitris Malamas	LW	5	6	2	0	8	0
Pavlos Kapagianidis	RD	5	1	2	1	4	0
Konstantinos Papistas	CE	5	1	2	1	4	0
Marius Konstantinidis	CE	5	2	1	0	3	4
Dimitrios Kalyvas	LD	5	0	2	1	3	0
Ioannis Giatagantzidis	LW	5	2	0	0	2	6
Nikolas Alexandronakis	LW	5	0	1	1	2	0
Alexandros Apostolidis	RW	5	0	1	1	2	8
Christian Vassiou	RW	5	0	1	0	1	0
Klimis Efkarpidis	LD	5	0	0	1	1	8
Michalis Grigoriadis	RD	5	0	0	0	0	0
Ioannis Ziakas	LD	5	0	0	0	0	2
Panagiotis Efkarpidis	RD	5	0	0	0	0	0
Vasilios Oumperal	LW	5	0	0	0	0	2
Ioannis Tilios	RW	5	0	0	0	0	0
Gian Noutsos	CE	5	0	0	0	0	4
Orestis Tillios	CE	5	0	0	0	0	0

Goalkeepers

Name	GP	MIN	GA	SOG	SVS%	GAA
Savas Adamidis	5	252.18	45	137	67.15	10.71
Georgios Katsandris	5	47.42	18	28	35.71	22.78

  *Prešernova 44*
64260 Bled
tel. (064)741-144
fax (064) 77-850

 *Kidričeva 1, 64260 Bled*
tel. (064) 741-608

ASIAN CUP 1995
Jan. 27. – 30. 1995 Seoul (KOR)

	KZK	JPN	CHN	KOR	Goals	Pts
1. Kazakhstan		3:2	4:0	5:1	12: 3	6
2. Japan	2:3		7:4	6:2	15: 9	4
3. China	0:4	4:7		3:3	7:14	1
4. Korea	1:5	2:6	3:3		6:14	1

Kazakhstan Winner of the Asian Cup 1995
Kazakhstan Winner of the Fair Play Cup

Best player of the Tournament	GK:	Dong-ho Lee	KOR
	D:	Dmitri Dubrovsky	KAZ
	F:	Norio Suzuki	JPN

KAZAKHSTAN

Name	Pos	GP	Pts	G	A	PIM
Vladimir Balandin	GK	2	0	0	0	0
Nikolai Kolioglov	GK	1	0	0	0	0
Alexander Kharitonov	FW	3	1	1	0	0
Alexander Filippov	FW	3	1	1	0	2
Alexei Murzin	FW	3	1	1	0	0
Dmitri Dubrovsky	DF	3	4	3	1	4
Alexander Gasnikov	DF	3	0	0	0	0
Sergei Kuksov	FW	3	1	0	1	4
Andrei Zalipyatskikh	FW	2	1	0	1	0
Yury Petrushin	DF	3	0	0	0	2
Vladislav Kern	DF	3	1	0	1	2
Ildus Gabdrakhmanov	FW	3	1	1	0	8
Oleg Bolyakin	DF	3	1	0	1	2
Galym Mambetaliev	FW	3	0	0	0	2
Pavel Tsukalov	FW	3	2	0	2	2
Evgeny Avdeev	FW	2	1	1	0	0
VladimirZhabunin	FW	3	3	1	2	0
Vitaly Kats	DF	2	0	0	0	0
Leonid Zavitaev	FW	3	0	0	0	0
Valery Tushentsov	FW	3	3	3	0	0

JAPAN

Name	Pos	GP	Pts	G	A	PIM
Shinichi Iwasaki	GK	2	0	0	0	0
Katsunori Hirano	GK	1	0	0	0	0
Kunio Takagi	DF	3	1	0	1	0
Atsuo Kudoh	DF	3	1	0	1	0
Tatsuki Katayama	DF	3	1	0	1	4
Yujiro Nakajimaya	DF	3	1	0	1	0
Hidekatsu Takagi	DF	3	3	2	1	0
Yasuhiro Honma	DF	3	0	0	0	2
Takayuki Kobori	DF	3	1	0	1	4
Toshiyuki Sakai	FW	3	2	1	1	0
Yuji Iga	FW	3	1	1	0	7
Junji Sakata	FW	1	0	0	0	2
Taro Nihei	FW	3	4	1	3	2
Hidesato Takahashi	FW	3	1	1	0	4
Isao Sujuki	FW	3	1	1	0	2
Norio Suzuki	FW	3	6	1	5	2
Toshiyuki Yajima	FW	3	2	1	1	4
Akihito Sugisawa	FW	3	3	1	2	0
Hiroshi Matsuura	FW	3	2	2	0	0
Takayuki Seto	FW	3	3	3	0	0

CHINA						
Name	**Pos**	**GP**	**Pts**	**G**	**A**	**PIM**
Liqun Zhang	GK	2	0	0	0	0
Ning Yin	DF	3	1	1	0	0
Lingyuan Wei	FW	3	1	1	0	0
Xue Liu	DF	3	1	1	0	4
Feng Liu	DF	3	0	0	0	0
Hongqun Gao	DF	3	1	0	1	0
Zhanyong Wang	FW	3	1	0	1	2
Guanghua Chen	FW	3	0	0	0	0
Xiaobo Guan	FW	2	0	0	0	8
Jiuming Liu	DF	3	1	0	1	4
Mengyuan Zhai	FW	3	1	1	0	4
Shousheng Zhang	FW	3	2	2	0	4
Yuqiang Pan	FW	3	0	0	0	0
Lei Luo	FW	3	0	0	0	2
Honglei Sun	FW	3	1	1	0	4
Ke Tan	FW	3	0	0	0	2
Lanfeng Wu	FW	0	0	0	0	0
Zhifeng Zhang	DF	3	0	0	0	2
Hua Geng	GK	1	0	0	0	0

KOREA						
Name	**Pos**	**GP**	**Pts**	**G**	**A**	**PIM**
Dong-Ho Lee	GK	3	0	0	0	0
Jae-Yong Choi	GK	0	0	0	0	0
Eui-Sik Shim	CF	3	0	0	0	2
Sung-Min Cho	RW	2	0	0	0	0
Kook-Chan Han	CF	3	0	0	0	0
Hyun-Mo Sung	LD	3	0	0	0	0
Woo-Sam Shin	LW	3	3	3	0	2
Youn-Sung Kim	RD	3	0	0	0	4
Sang-Won Seo	LW	3	2	1	1	0
Chang-Gun An	RW	3	0	0	0	4
Yong-Seung Lee	LD	3	0	0	0	2
Yong-Nam Kim	RW	3	0	0	0	4
Do-Sik Park	RD	3	1	0	1	0
Hyun-Suk Song	LD	3	1	1	0	2
Chang-Bum Kim	LD	3	0	0	0	4
Sung-Bok Kim	RW	3	0	0	0	0
Young-Ho Bae	CF	3	0	0	0	2
Sang-Hyun Han	RD	3	0	0	0	8
Jong-Ok Park	CF	3	1	1	0	2
Shi-Won Kim	LD	3	0	0	0	0

IIHF WORLD CUP FOR OLDTIMER
Slovenia 19-22 March, 1995

Tournament	Group over 35		Group over 45	
1th	Cesky Veteranov	CZE	Trim Team 45 +	SLO
2nd	Ruskoe Zoloto	RUS	St. Petersburg	RUS
3rd	Rus Saratov	RUS	Oslo Oilers	NOR
Fair Play Cup	UK Kometsot	FIN	Oslo Oilers	NOR
Best player	Jiri Hrdina	CZE	Franc Mirnik	SLO

WORLD JUNIOR CHAMPIONSHIP 1995

Red Deer, Alberta (Canada) · Dec. 26, 1994 – Jan. 4, 1995

Pool A

Team	CAN	RUS	SWE	FIN	USA	CZE	GER	UKR	Goals	Pts.
1. Canada		8:5	4:3	8:4	8:3	7:5	9:1	7:1	49:22	14
2. Russia	5:8		6:4	8:2	3:4	4:3	8:1	4:2	36:24	10
3. Sweden	3:4	4:6		3:3	4:2	4:3	10:2	7:1	35:21	9
4. Finland	4:8	2:8	3:3		7:5	0:3	7:1	6:2	29:26	7
5. USA	3:8	4:3	2:4	5:7		7:5	5:3	2:3	28:33	6
6. Czech Republic	5:7	3:4	3:4	3:0	5:7		14:3	10:1	43:26	6
7. Germany	1:9	1:8	2:10	1:7	3:5	3:14		6:2	17:55	2
8. Ukraine	1:7	2:4	1:7	2:6	3:2	1:10	2:6		12:42	2

Kein Absteiger – there is no relegation – 1996 Pool A 10 Teams

Top Scorers

Name	Team	GP	G	A	P
1. M. Murray	CAN	7	6	9	15
2. J. Allison	CAN	7	3	12	15
3. B. McCabe	CAN	7	3	9	12
4. A. Serikov	GER	7	2	9	11
5. E. Daze	CAN	7	8	2	10
A. Koroliuk	RUS	7	8	2	10
7. A. Deadmarsh	USA	7	6	4	10
V. Varada	CZE	7	6	4	10
9. J. Marha	CZE	7	5	5	10
10. A. Daigle	CAN	7	2	8	10

Most Goals

Name	Team	GP	G
1. E. Daze	CAN	7	8
A. Koroliuk	RUS	7	8
3. M. Murray	CAN	7	6
A. Deadmarsh	USA	7	6
V. Varada	CZE	7	6
A. Söderberg	SWE	7	6
I. Malyakov	RUS	7	6
V. P. Nutikka	FIN	7	6
T. Harvay	CAN	7	6

Top Defensemen

Name	Team	GP	G	A	P
1. B. McCabe	CAN	7	3	9	12
2. A. Eriksson	SWE	7	3	7	10
3. K. Timonen	FIN	7	2	6	8
4. M. Malik	CZE	7	2	5	7
5. Vychedkevitch	RUS	7	1	6	7

Most Assists

Name	Team	GP	G
1. J. Allison	CAN	7	12
2. A. Serikov	GER	7	9
B. McCabe	CAN	7	9
M. Murphy	CAN	7	9
5. A. Daigle	CAN	7	8

Directorate-Awards

Best Player

Goalkeeper:	Yevgeny Tarasov	RUS
Defenseman:	Brian McCabe	CAN
Forward:	Marty Murray	CAN

All Star Team

I. Karpenko
(UKR)

B. McCabe	A. Eriksson
(CAN)	(SWE)
M. Murray	J. Allison	E. Daze
(CAN)	(CAN)	(CAN)

CANADA

Player	GP	G	A	Pts	PIM
Marty Murray	7	6	9	15	0
Jason Allison	7	3	12	15	6
Bryan McCabe	7	3	9	12	4
Eric Daze	7	8	2	10	0
Alexandre Daigle	7	2	8	10	4
Jeff Friesen	7	5	2	7	4
Ryan Smyth	7	2	5	7	4
Jamie Rivers	7	3	3	6	2
Jeff O'Neill	7	2	4	6	2
Todd Harvey	7	6	0	6	4
Larry Courville	7	2	3	5	6
Wade Redden	7	3	2	5	0
Darcy Tucker	7	0	4	4	0
Denis Pederson	7	2	2	4	0
Jason Botterill	7	0	4	4	6
Ed Jovanovski	7	2	0	2	4
Nolan Baumgartner	7	0	1	1	4
Lee Sorochan	7	0	1	1	6
Chad Allan	7	0	0	0	4
Dan Cloutier	7	0	0	0	0
Jamie Storr	7	0	0	0	2
Shean Donovan	7	0	0	0	6

Goaltending

	GP	MIN	W	L	T	GAA	%
Dan Cloutier	3	180	3	0	0	.905	2.67
Jamie Storr	4	240	4	0	0	.852	3.50
Totals	**7**	**420**	**7**	**0**	**0**	**.867**	**3.14**

SWEDEN

Player	GP	G	A	Pts	PIM
Anders Eriksson	7	3	7	10	10
Anders Söderberg	7	6	2	8	2
Niklas Sundström	7	4	4	8	8
Per Svartvadet	7	2	6	8	2
Johan Davidsson	7	4	2	6	2
Johan Finnström	7	1	5	6	8
Per-Johan Axelsson	7	2	3	5	2
Peter Ström	7	2	4	6	2
Jesper Mattsson	7	0	6	6	22
Fredrik Johansson	7	3	1	4	2
Jonas Andersson-Junkka	7	2	4	6	8
Dick Tarnström	7	2	2	4	4
Andreas Karlsson	7	2	2	4	0
Mathais Pihlström	7	1	1	2	0
Daniel Back	7	0	2	2	0
Mattias Öhlund	7	1	0	1	4
Daniel Tjärmquist	7	0	0	0	2
Peter Nylander	7	0	0	0	0
Anders Burström	7	0	0	0	0
Jonas Forsberg	7	0	0	0	4
Henrik Smangs	7	0	0	0	0
Kristoffer Ottosson	7	0	0	0	0

Goaltending

	GP	MIN	W	L	T	GAA	%
Henrik Smangs	2	120	1	0	1	.922	2.00
Jonas Forsberg	5	300	3	2	0	.864	3.20
Totals	**7**	**420**	**4**	**2**	**1**	**.879**	**2.86**

CZECH REPUBLIC

Player	GP	G	A	Pts	PIM
Vaclav Varada	7	6	4	10	25
Josef Marha	7	5	5	10	0
Vaclav Prospal	7	3	7	10	2
Jaroslav Kudrna	7	4	4	8	6
Zdenek Nedved	7	4	4	8	10
Petr Cajanek	7	3	5	8	68
Tomas Blazek	7	3	4	7	2
Marek Malik	7	2	5	7	12
Vlastimil Kroupa	7	4	2	6	10
Jan Hlavac	7	2	3	5	4
Petr Buzek	7	2	2	4	10
Milan Hejduk	7	1	3	4	14
Ladislav Kohn	7	0	4	4	8
Jan Hrdina	7	2	1	3	4
Marek Zidlicky	7	0	2	2	36
Frantisek Ptacek	7	1	0	1	8
Angel Nikolov	7	1	0	1	6
Pavel Nestak	7	0	0	0	0
Miloslav Guren	7	0	0	0	4
Michal Marik	7	0	0	0	2
Pavel Trnka	7	0	0	0	8
Petr Sykora	7	0	0	0	0

Goaltending

	GP	MIN	W	L	T	GAA	%
Michal Marik	4	207	2	2	0	.841	4.06
Pavel Nestak	4	212	1	2	0	.897	5.94
Totals	**7**	**419**	**0**	**4**	**0**	**.680**	**5.01**

RUSSIA

Player	GP	G	A	Pts	PIM
Alexandre Koroliuk	7	8	2	10	47
Vadim Charifianov	7	4	6	10	6
Igor Melyakov	7	6	1	7	2
Valentin Morozov	7	3	4	7	4
Vitali Yachmenev	7	3	4	7	2
Serguei Vychedekevitch	7	1	6	7	4
Nikolai Zavarukhine	7	2	4	6	4
Ruslan Batyrchine	7	1	4	5	10
Alexander Charlamov	7	2	2	4	2
Vadim Epantchinsev	7	1	2	3	24
Serguei Gussev	7	1	2	3	4
Dmitri Klevakin	7	2	0	2	2
Pavel Boichenko	7	0	2	2	2
Vladimir Tchebaturkin	7	0	2	2	2
Anvar Gatiatulline	7	1	0	1	4
Ilja Vorobiev	7	1	0	1	4
Ramil Saiulline	7	0	1	1	0
Mikhail Okhotnikov	7	0	0	0	4
Artem Anisimov	7	0	0	0	0
Yevgeny Tarasov	7	0	0	0	0
Denis Kuzmenko	7	0	0	0	0
Alexander Boikov	7	0	0	0	0

Goaltending

	GP	MIN	W	L	T	GAA	%
Yevgeny Tarasov	5	244	4	0	0	.931	2.47
Denis Kuzmenko	3	177	1	2	0	.829	4.74
Totals	**7**	**420**	**5**	**3**	**0**	**.894**	**3.43**

FINLAND

Player	GP	G	A	Pts	PIM
Kimmo Timonen	7	2	6	8	4
Veli-Pekka Nutikka	7	6	1	7	12
Tommi Miettinen	7	2	5	7	2
Jere Karalahti	7	2	4	6	8
Antti Aalto	7	2	3	5	18
Janne Niinimaa	7	2	3	5	6
Jussi Tarvainen	7	3	1	4	32
Timo Salonen	7	3	1	4	10
Niko Halttunen	7	1	3	4	8
Tommi Rajamäki	7	1	2	3	8
Tommi Sova	7	1	1	2	4
Martti Järventie	7	1	1	2	6
Tommi Hämäläinen	7	1	1	2	4
Petri Kokko	7	1	0	1	22
Mikko Helisten	7	1	0	1	0
Miika Elomo	7	0	1	1	6
Jani Hassinen	7	0	1	1	2
Toni Mäkiaho	7	0	1	1	2
Jussi Markkanen	7	0	0	0	18
Miska Kangasniemi	7	0	0	0	2
Juha Vuorivirta	7	0	0	0	2
Miikka Kiprusoff	7	0	0	0	2

Goaltending

	GP	MIN	W	L	T	GAA	%
Miikka Kiprusoff	2	116	1	1	0	.900	2,58
Jussi Markkanen	5	296	2	2	1	.901	3.65
Totals	**7**	**412**	**3**	**3**	**1**	**.901**	**3.35**

UKRAINE

Player	GP	G	A	Pts	PIM
Alexey Lazarenko	7	3	1	4	34
Andrey Kuzminski	7	1	3	4	2
Igor Yankovitch	7	3	0	3	12
Sergey Chubenko	7	2	1	3	6
Boris Tchursin	7	0	3	3	2
Roman Salnikov	7	1	1	2	31
Alexandre Mukhanov	7	1	0	1	8
Oleg Tsirkunov	7	1	0	1	0
Sergey Kartchenko	7	0	1	1	8
Sergey Karnaukh	7	0	1	1	6
Alexey Bernatsky	7	0	1	1	14
Vitaly Tretjakov	7	0	1	1	2
Alexander Fyodorov	7	0	0	0	0
Igor Drifan	7	0	0	0	2
Vladislav Shevtchenko	7	0	0	0	8
Yuri Ljaskovsky	7	0	0	0	0
Dmitry Mozheiko	7	0	0	0	2
Audrey Kurilko	7	0	0	0	4
Igor Karpenko	7	0	0	0	2
Alexandre Govorun	7	0	0	0	0
Denis Lobanovsky	7	0	0	0	0
Daniel Didkovsky	7	0	0	0	4

Goaltending

	GP	PIM	W	L	T	GAA	%
Igor Karpenko	7	420	1	6	0	.869	6.00
Totals	**7**	**420**	**1**	**6**	**0**	**.869**	**6.00**

GERMANY

Player	GP	G	A	Pts	PIM
Alexander Serikow	7	2	9	11	4
Jochen Hecht	7	5	3	8	18
Sven Valenta	7	4	2	6	2
Stefan Mann	7	1	0	1	12
Martin Williams	7	1	0	1	2
Stephan Retzer	7	1	0	1	4
Erich Goldmann	7	1	0	1	18
Markus Weiland	7	1	0	1	4
Lars Brüggermann	7	1	0	1	20
Oliver Häusler	7	0	1	1	2
Florian Keller	7	0	1	1	6
Stephan Lahn	7	0	0	0	2
Kai Fischer	7	0	0	0	0
Tino Boos	7	0	0	0	14
Hubert Buchwieser	7	0	0	0	4
Florian Schneider	7	0	0	0	4
Thorsten Fendt	7	0	0	0	4
Stefan Tillert	7	0	0	0	2
Andreas Renz	7	0	0	0	6
Matthias Sänger	7	0	0	0	0
Marco Eltner	7	0	0	0	12
Marco Sturm	7	0	0	0	6
Eric Dylla	7	0	0	0	2

Goaltending

	GP	MIN	W	L	T	GAA	%
Oliver Häusler	7	376	1	6	0	.851	7.02
Stephen Lahn	1	14	0	0	0	.786	12.86
Kai Fischer	1	31	0	0	0	.714	16.12
Totals	**7**	**420**	**1**	**6**	**0**	**.837**	**7.86**

USA

Player	GP	G	A	Pts	PIM
Adam Deadmarsh	7	6	4	10	10
Richard Park	7	1	7	8	29
Sean Haggerty	7	1	6	7	8
Shawn Bates	7	5	1	6	2
Deron Quint	7	3	3	6	6
Jon Battaglia	7	3	2	5	2
Landon Wilson	7	3	2	5	37
Jason Bonsignore	7	2	2	4	6
Mike Crowley	7	0	3	3	8
Kevin Hilton	7	2	0	2	0
Jamie Langenbrunner	7	1	1	2	6
Rory Fitzpatrick	7	0	2	2	8
Ashlin Halfnight	7	0	2	2	4
Mike Grier	7	0	2	2	12
Chris Kelleher	7	1	0	1	0
Reg Berg	7	0	1	1	0
Dan Tompkins	7	0	1	1	4
Bryan Berard	7	0	1	1	36
John Grahame	7	0	0	0	4
Doug Bonner	7	0	0	0	0
Brian LaFleur	7	0	0	0	4
Jeff Mitchell	7	0	0	0	4

Goaltending

	GP	MIN	W	L	T	GAA	%
John Grahame	5	280	2	3	0	.856	4.07
Doug Bonner	3	140	1	1	0	.875	5.59
Totals	**7**	**420**	**3**	**4**	**0**	**.857**	**4.57**

World Junior Championships 1977–1995

	19 77	19 78	19 79	19 80	19 81	19 82	19 83	19 84	19 85	19 86	19 87	19 88	19 89	19 90	19 91	19 92	19 93	19 94	19 95
TCH	3	4	2	4	4	2	2	3	2	5	2	4	3	3	3	5	3	–	–
URS	1	1	1	1	3	4	1	1	3	1	d	2	1	2	2	1	–	–	–
Canada	2	3	5	5	7	1	3	4	1	2	d	1	4	1	1	6	1	1	1
Finland	4	6	4	2	2	3	6	2	4	6	1	3	6	4	5	4	5	4	4
Sweden	5	2	3	3	1	5	4	5	5	4	3	5	2	5	6	2	2	2	3
USA	7	5	6	7	6	6	5	6	6	3	4	6	5	7	4	3	4	6	5
Germany	6	7	7	6	5	7	7	7	7	8	–	7	8	–	–	7	7	7	7
Poland	8	–	–	–	–	–	–	–	8	–	5	8	–	8	–	–	–	–	–
Switzerland	–	8	–	8	–	8	–	8	–	7	6	–	–	–	7	8	–	8	–
Norway	–	–	8	–	–	–	8	–	–	–	–	–	7	6	8	–	–	–	–
Austria	–	–	–	–	8	–	–	–	–	–	–	–	–	–	–	–	–	–	–
Japan	–	–	–	–	–	–	–	–	–	–	–	–	–	–	–	–	8	–	–
Russia	–	–	–	–	–	–	–	–	–	–	–	–	–	–	–	–	6	3	2
Czech Republic	–	–	–	–	–	–	–	–	–	–	–	–	–	–	–	–	–	5	6
Ukraine	–	–	–	–	–	–	–	–	–	–	–	–	–	–	–	–	–	–	8

Total Medal Count
Medaillenspiegel
Pool A 1977–1995
Gold · Silver · Bronce

	G	S	B
URS	9	3	2
CAN	8	2	2
SWE	1	5	4
FIN	1	3	2
TCH	–	5	6
USA	–	–	2
RUS	–	1	1

All Time Statistic 1977–1995

	Years	GP	Goals	Pts
1. Canada	19	129	642:378	193
2. URS	16	108	687:262	174
3. Sweden	19	129	638:382	164
4. Finland	19	129	615:455	150
5. TCH	17	115	619:365	144
6. USA	19	129	361:691	105
7. Germany	16	108	242:652	38
8. Russia	3	21	85: 61	27
9. Czech Republic	2	14	74: 55	12
10. Switzerland	9	68	124:512	7
11. Norway	5	34	67:304	6
12. Poland	5	35	62:315	4
13. Ukraine	1	7	12: 42	2
14. Austria	1	6	10: 78	0
15. Japan	1	7	9: 83	0

Top Scorer

WC	Name		GP	G	A	P
1974	R. Eriksson	SWE	5	5	4	9
1975	Boris Churchin	URS	5	4	4	8
+	Dag Bredberg	SWE	5	4	4	8
1976	Valerj Estifeyev	URS	4	4	4	8
1977	Dale McCourt	CAN	7	10	8	18
1978	Wayne Gretzky	CAN	6	8	9	17
1979	Vladimir Krutov	URS	6	8	6	14
1980	Vladimir Krutov	URS	5	7	4	11
1981	Dieter Hegen	GER	5	8	1	9
1982	Raimo Summanen	FIN	7	7	9	16
1983	Vladimir Ruzicka	TCH	7	12	8	20
1984	Raimo Helminen	FIN	7	11	13	24
1985	Esa Keskinen	FIN	7	6	14	20
1986	Shayne Corson	CAN	7	7	7	14
1987	Ulf Dahlen	SWE	7	7	8	15
1988	Alexander Mogilny	URS	7	9	9	18
1989	Jeremy Roenick	CAN	7	8	8	16
1990	Robert Reichel	TCH	7	11	10	21
1991	Doug Weight	USA	7	5	13	18
1992	Mikael Nylander	SWE	7	8	9	17
1993	Peter Forsberg	SWE	7	7	24	31
1994	Niklas Sundström	SWE	7	4	7	11
1995	Marty Murray	CAN	7	6	9	15

Junior World Championships 1977–1995 · Pool A

Year Jahr	Place Platz		First Erster	Second Zweiter	Third Dritter
1977	Banska-Bystriza	TCH	USSR	Canada	CSSR
1978	Montreal	CAN	USSR	Sweden	Canada
1979	Karlstad	SWE	USSR	CSSR	Sweden
1980	Helsinki	FIN	USSR	Finland	Sweden
1981	Füssen/Augsburg	GER	Sweden	Finland	USSR
1982	Minnesota	USA	Canada	CSSR	Finland
1983	Leningrad	URS	USSR	CSSR	Canada
1984	Norköping/Nyköping	SWE	USSR	Finland	CSSR
1985	Helsinki/Turku	FIN	Canada	CSSR	USSR
1986	Hamilton	CAN	USSR	Canada	USA
1987	Trencin/Nitra	TCH	Finland	CSSR	Sweden
1988	Moscow	URS	Canada	USSR	Finland
1989	Anchorage	USA	USSR	Sweden	CSSR
1990	Helsinki	FIN	Canada	USSR	CSSR
1991	Saskatchewan	CAN	Canada	USSR	CSSR
1992	Füssen/Kaufbeuren	GER	GUS	Sweden	USA
1993	Gävle/Falun	SWE	Canada	Sweden	CFSR
1994	Ostrava/F. Mistek	CZE	Canada	Sweden	Russia
1995	Red Deer	CAN	Canada	Russia	Sweden

Directorate awards / Beste Spieler · JUN-WC · Pool A

Year	Goalkeeper/Torhüter		Defenseman/Verteidiger		Forward/Stürmer	
1977	Jan Hrabak	TCH	Vyacheslav Fetisov	URS	Dale McCourt	CAN
1978	Alexander Tyzhnyk	URS	Vyacheslav Fetisov	URS	Wayne Gretzky	CAN
1979	Pelle Lindbergh	SWE	Alexej Kasatonov	URS	Vladimir Krutov	URS
1980	Jari Paavola	FIN	Reijo Ruotsalainen	FIN	Vladimir Krutov	URS
1981	Lars Eriksson	SWE	Miloslav Horava	TCH	Patrick Sundström	SWE
1982	Mike Moffat	CAN	Gord Kluzak	CAN	Petri Skriko	FIN
1983	Dominik Hasek	TCH	Ilija Byakin	URS	Tomas Sandström	SWE
1984	Allan Perry	USA	Alexej Gusarov	URS	Raimo Helminen	FIN
1985	Craig Billington	CAN	Vesa Salo	FIN	Michail Pivonka	TCH
1986	Evgeny Belosheikin	URS	Mikhail Tatarinov	URS	Jim Sandlak	CAN
1987	Markus Ketterer	FIN	Calle Johansson	SWE	Robert Kron	TCH
1988	Jimmy Waite	CAN	Teppo Numminen	FIN	Alexander Mogilny	URS
1989	Alexej Ivashkin	URS	Richard Persson	SWE	Pavel Bure	URS
1990	Stephane Fiset	CAN	Alexej Godynyuk	URS	Robert Reichel	TCH
1991	Pauli Jaks	SUI	Jiri Slegr	TCH	Eric Lindros	CAN
1992	Mike Dunhan	USA	Darius Kasparaitis	GUS	Michael Nylander	SWE
1993	Manny Legace	CAN	Janne Grönvall	FIN	Peter Forsberg	SWE
1994	Jamie Storr	CAN	Kenny Jönsson	SWE	Niklas Sundström	SWE
1995	Igor Karpenko	UKR	Bryan McCabe	CAN	Marty Murray	CAN

WORLD JUNIOR CHAMPIONSHIP 1995

Rouen, Caen, Le Havre, Louviers (FRA)
Dec. 27. 1994 – Jan. 5., 1995

POOL B

	SUI	SVK	POL	FRA	NOR	AUT	JPN	ITA	Goals	Pts
1. Switzerland		3:1	4:4	4:1	4:4	6:1	11:1	8:0	40:12	12
2. Slovakia	1:3		4:2	6:1	4:1	8:2	7:3	3:4	33:16	10
3. Poland	4:4	2:4		0:6	5:4	4:1	6:0	5:3	26:22	9
4. France	1:4	1:6	6:0		2:1	3:0	6:3	6:0	24:15	8
5. Norway	4:4	1:4	4:5	1:2		2:7	9:1	5:4	27:26	7
6. Austria	1:6	2:8	1:4	0:3	7:2		4:4	5:4	20:31	5
7. Japan	1:11	3:7	0:6	3:6	1:9	4:4		5:1	17:44	3
8. Italy	0:8	4:3	3:5	0:6	4:5	4:5	1:5		16:37	2

Switzerland and **Slovakia** promoted to POOL A 1996; there ist no relegation

Three best players by teams

SUI	30	Thomas Papp	GK
	14	Jerry Zuurmond	LD
	21	Sandy Jeannin	CE
SVK	12	Juraj Stefanka	F
	16	Rudolf Vercik	F
	23	Radoslav Kropac	F
POL	30	Pavel Kuszaj	GK
	9	Dariusz Lyszczarczyk	LW
	17	Rafal Selega	CE
FRA	1	Cristobal Huet	GK
	4	Gregory Dubois	LD
	9	Maurice Rozenthal	CE
NOR	20	Anders Myrvold	RD
	16	André Hansen	RW
	19	Morten Fjeld	CE
AUT	24	Reinhard Divis	GK
	6	Gerhard Unterluggauer	RD
	25	Christoph Brandner	CE
JPN	21	Naoto Ohno	CE
	19	Tsutsumi Otomo	LW
	22	Takahito Suzuki	RW
ITA	6	Michele Strazzabosco	LD
	7	Leo Giuseppe Insam	LD
	9	Roberto Bortot	LW

The three best players of each team received a SEIKO watch

Best goalkeeper	Thomas Papp	SUI
Best defender	Anders Myrvold	NOR
Best forward	Radoslav Kropac	SVK
Best scorer	Vjeran Ivankovic	SUI

ALL STAR TEAM

C. Huet
FRA

L. Visnovsky **R. Ziegler**
SVK SUI

R. Kropac
SVK

D. Lyszczarczyk **V. Ivankovic**
POL SUI

Winner of the FAIR PLAY CUP
JAPAN

SWITZERLAND

Name	Pos	GP	G	A1	A2	Pts	PIM
Vjeran Ivankovic	LW	7	8	1	1	10	6
Lars Leuenberger	RW	7	4	4	0	8	4
Sandy Jeannin	CE	7	4	3	0	7	6
Matthias Baechler	CE	7	3	4	0	7	0
Patrick Fischer	LW	7	4	2	0	6	12
Frederic Rothen	RW	7	4	1	0	5	6
Reto von Arx	CE	7	3	1	0	4	17
Thierry Paterlini	LW	7	2	2	0	4	10
Bruno Habisreutinger	RD	7	0	4	0	4	4
Marco Koeppel	LW	7	3	0	0	3	0
Rolf Ziegler	LD	7	1	0	2	3	0
Daniel Aegerter	RD	7	1	1	0	2	4
Philipp Lueber	RW	7	1	1	0	2	8
Jerry Zuurmond	LD	7	1	0	0	1	6
Fabian Guignard	RD	7	1	0	0	1	47
Benoit Pont	CE	7	0	1	0	1	12
Patric della Rossa	RW	7	0	1	0	1	8
Marco Kloett	LD	7	0	0	0	0	0
Stefan Schneider	RD	7	0	0	0	0	6
Ivo Ruethimann	RW	7	0	0	0	0	2

Goalkeepers

Name	GP	MIN	GA	SOG	SVS%	GAA	PIM
Thomas Papp	7	270.35	8	108	92.59	1.78	0
Claudio Bayer	4	120.00	1	18	94.44	0.50	0
Stephane Rosset	3	29.25	2	7	71.43	4.10	0

SLOVAKIA

Name	Pos	GP	G	A1	A2	Pts	PIM
Radoslav Kropac	F	7	6	2	1	9	6
Lubomir Visnovsky	D	7	1	5	1	7	4
Rudolf Vercik	F	7	4	1	1	6	8
Jozef Kohut	F	7	4	2	0	6	14
Juraj Stefanka	F	7	4	2	0	6	22
Miroslav Pazak	F	7	4	0	0	4	2
Radovan Somik	F	7	3	0	0	3	2
Martin Opatovsky	F	7	2	1	0	3	30
Vladimir Orszagh	F	7	1	1	1	3	8
Rastislav Palov	F	7	1	2	0	3	4
Martin Kivon	D	7	1	1	0	2	4
Rastislav Pavlikovsky	F	7	1	1	0	2	4
Martin Strbak	D	7	0	1	1	2	4
Oliver Pastinsky	D	7	0	2	0	2	8
Patrik Scibran	D	7	0	1	0	1	8
Daniel Socha	D	7	0	0	1	1	4
Peter Klepac	D	7	0	0	0	0	2
Michal Kudzia	D	7	0	0	0	0	0
Andrej Farkasovsky	F	7	0	0	0	0	6
Mario Kazda	F	7	0	0	0	0	0

Goalkeepers

Name	GP	MIN	GA	SOG	SVS%	GAA	PIM
Branislav Fatul	7	300.00	10	90	88.89	2.00	0
Patrik Nemcak	7	120.00	4	26	84.62	2.00	0

POLAND

Name	Pos	GP	G	A1	A2	Pts	PIM
Bartosz Orzel	RW	6	1	2	6	9	2
Dariusz Lyszczarczyk	LW	7	5	1	1	7	14
Grzegorz Lowas	RW	7	2	4	1	7	0
Robert Kwiatkowski	CE	7	2	4	0	6	36
Rafal Selega	CE	7	2	3	1	6	0
Sebastian Pajerski	LW	7	4	0	1	5	14
Stanislaw Urban	LW	7	2	1	1	4	0
Dariusz Zabawa	RD	7	3	0	0	3	0
Jaroslaw Rozanski	LW	7	1	1	0	2	4
Dariusz Siemieniec	LD	7	1	0	1	2	18
Patryk Pysz	CE	4	1	1	0	2	6
Robert Biela	CE	7	1	0	1	2	4
Krzysztof Smielowski	RW	7	0	2	0	2	4
Tomasz Podlipni	LD	7	1	0	0	1	4
Rafal Piekarski	RD	7	0	0	1	1	2
Adam Witek	LD	7	0	0	0	0	8
Tomasz Piatek	RD	7	0	0	0	0	14
Piotr Korczak	LD	7	0	0	0	0	2
Adam Borzecki	RD	7	0	0	0	0	4
Tomasz Rysz	RW	7	0	0	0	0	2

Goalkeepers

Name	GP	MIN	GA	SOG	SVS%	GAA	PIM
Pawel Kuszaj	7	471.47	22	146	84.93	2.80	0
Lukasz Kiedewicz	7	8.13	0	0	0.00	0.00	0

FRANCE

Name	Pos	GP	G	A1	A2	Pts	PIM
Paul Mottiet	RW	7	3	2	1	6	14
Steve Michou	LW	7	2	3	1	6	4
Laurent Jeandet	CE	7	3	2	0	5	16
Maurice Rozenthal	CE	6	2	0	5	5	2
Franck Guillemard	CE	7	3	0	2	5	2
Jonathan Zwikel	LW	7	3	0	0	3	4
Laurent Gras	CE	7	2	1	0	3	2
Mathieu Guidoux	RD	7	1	0	2	3	4
Luc Chauvel	LW	7	1	1	1	3	6
Allan Carriou	RD	7	2	0	0	2	4
Christophe Negro	LW	7	1	1	0	2	18
Jerome Veret	RW	7	0	0	2	2	6
Fabrice Aumenier	RW	7	0	2	0	2	2
Frederick Brodin	RD	7	1	0	0	1	8
Sebastian Oprandi	RW	6	1	0	0	1	4
Patrice Bellier	RD	7	0	0	1	1	20
Stephane Balmat	LD	7	0	1	0	1	8
Christopher Lepers	LD	7	0	0	0	0	2
Gregory Dubois	LD	7	0	0	0	0	6
Gael Chauvin	LD	6	0	0	0	0	8

Goalkeepers

Name	GP	MIN	GA	SOG	SVS%	GAA	PIM
Cristobal Huet	7	420.00	15	148	89.86	2.14	2
Damien Laurent	7	0.00	0	0	0.00	0.00	0

NORWAY

Name	Pos	GP	G	A1	A2	Pts	PIM
Andre Manskow Hansen	RW	7	5	2	0	7	6
Morten Fjeld	LW	7	4	3	0	7	10
Pal Johnson	CE	7	4	1	1	6	0
Henrik Aaby	CE	7	3	2	0	5	4
Tore Vikingstad	RW	7	3	1	0	4	4
Jonny Nilsen	LD	7	1	1	1	3	16
Thomas Fjeld	CE	7	1	2	0	3	14
Anders Myrvold	RD	7	0	1	2	3	36
Marius Trygg	CE	5	2	0	0	2	2
Tom Cato Myhre	RW	7	1	1	0	2	12
Morten Svendsen	LW	7	1	1	0	2	2
Mats Trygg	RD	7	1	0	0	1	2
Stig Vesterheim	RW	7	1	0	0	1	2
Glenn Arne Jessesen	RD	7	0	1	0	1	2
Per Marius Thorbjörnsen	LW	7	0	0	1	1	16
Bard Sörlie	LD	7	0	0	0	0	2
Morten Johansen	LD	7	0	0	0	0	2
Anders Skaslien	Rd	7	0	0	0	0	0
Krister Sätre	LW	7	0	0	0	0	2
Daniel Geving Östbye	LD	7	0	0	0	0	0

Goalkeepers

Name	GP	MIN	GA	SOG	SVS%	GAA	PIM
Lars Christian Beck	7	420.00	25	160	84.38	3.57	0
E. Ström-Normann	7	0.00	0	0	0.00	0.00	0

AUSTRIA

Name	Pos	GP	G	A1	A2	Pts	PIM
Christoph Brandner	CE	7	5	0	1	6	30
Markus Melcher	LW	7	2	2	0	4	18
Ulrich Lanz	RW	6	2	2	0	4	0
Jürgen Leittner	LD	7	2	1	0	3	32
Christian Sintschnig	LD	7	0	2	1	3	16
Stefan Hofer	RW	7	2	0	0	2	4
Kurt Burkhart	RW	7	2	0	0	2	22
Gerhard Unterluggauer	RD	7	1	1	0	2	16
Josef Sulzbacher	RD	7	0	1	1	2	12
Klaus Spelbrink	RW	7	1	0	0	1	8
Christian Widauer	LW	7	1	0	0	1	0
Christoph Gesson	LW	7	1	0	0	1	6
Christian Csontala	LW	7	0	1	0	1	18
Roland Schurian	CE	6	0	1	0	1	29
Alexander Tomanek	CE	7	0	0	0	0	0
Björn Kraiger	RD	7	0	0	0	0	2
Andreas Hausner	LD	7	0	0	0	0	2
Peter Klumpp	CE	7	0	0	0	0	4
Patrick Michel	RD	7	0	0	0	0	10
Enrico Schramm	LD	7	0	0	0	0	0

Goalkeepers

Name	GP	MIN	GA	SOG	SVS%	GAA	PIM
Reinhard Divis	7	348.26	22	262	91.60	3.79	2
M. Kerschbaumer	7	71.34	9	59	84.75	7.57	0

JAPAN

Name	Pos	GP	G	A1	A2	Pts	PIM
Takahito Suzuki	RW	7	5	1	0	6	2
Naoto Ohno	CE	7	2	2	1	5	4
Yoshifumi Fujisawa	CE	7	3	1	0	4	10
Tsutsumi Otomo	LW	7	1	1	1	3	8
Takayoshi Shiratori	RD	5	2	0	0	2	10
Isamu Ishiguro	LD	7	1	0	1	2	2
Shinjiro Tsuji	LW	7	1	1	0	2	2
Shiro Ishiguro	RW	7	1	1	0	2	2
Gen Ishioka	CE	7	1	1	0	2	0
Kouichi Yamazaki	RD	7	0	1	0	1	4
Tomohito Okhubo	RD	7	0	0	1	1	6
Shinichi Takizawa	LD	7	0	1	0	1	6
Tsutomu Takahashi	CE	5	0	1	0	1	4
Kenichiro Ike	RW	7	0	0	1	1	2
Toru Takahashi	RD	6	0	0	0	0	6
Nobuhiro Sugawara	LD	7	0	0	0	0	6
Jun Hanzawa	RW	7	0	0	0	0	8
Youhai Masuko	LD	7	0	0	0	0	0
Junya Shirono	LW	7	0	0	0	0	0
Satoru Iwai	LW	7	0	0	0	0	8

Goalkeepers

Name	GP	MIN	GA	SOG	SVS%	GAA	PIM
Yuji Sasaki	7	326.29	32	208	84.62	5.88	2
Hirokazu Takahashi	7	93.31	12	50	76.00	7.72	0

ITALY

Name	Pos	GP	G	A1	A2	Pts	PIM
Giuliano Panciera	LW	7	3	1	0	4	8
Roberto Bortot	LW	7	2	0	2	4	10
Luca Rigoni	CE	7	1	3	0	4	16
Christian Timpone	RW	7	2	1	0	3	18
Harald Oberrauch	CE	7	1	1	1	3	10
Leo Pitscheider	LD	7	0	3	0	3	8
Michele Strazzabosco	LD	7	2	0	0	2	20
Leo Giuseppe Insam	LD	7	1	0	1	2	8
Martin Götsch	LW	7	0	2	0	2	2
Stefano Margoni	RW	7	1	0	0	1	2
Manuel Bergamo	RD	7	1	0	0	1	6
Giovanni Carlo Volante	RW	7	1	0	0	1	8
Paatric Lochi	LW	7	1	0	0	1	2
Martin Rainer	RD	7	0	1	0	1	14
Ruggero de mio Rossi	RW	7	0	1	0	1	8
Ingemar Gruber	LD	7	0	0	0	0	14
Milos de Toni	LW	7	0	0	0	0	6
Niki Cadorin	RD	7	0	0	0	0	0
Marco Vaccani	CE	7	0	0	0	0	0
Gary Delladio	LD	7	0	0	0	0	0

Goalkeepers

Name	GP	MIN	GA	SOG	SVS%	GAA	PIM
Gianfranco Basso	7	169.44	12	115	89.57	4.25	0
Andrea Carpano	7	250.16	25	90	72.22	6.00	0

Qualification for the World Junior Championship 1995
Pool C · Group 1
Minsk (BLR) · September 3 – 5, 1994

Belarus – Slovenia	5:1	1. Belarus	13: 5 4	**Belarus qualified for the**

Belarus – Slovenia   5:1   1. Belarus   13: 5 4   **Belarus qualified for the**
Slovenia – Kazakhstan 0:11   2. Kazakhstan 15: 8 2   **World Championship**
Belarus – Kazakhstan 8:4   3. Slovenia   1:16 0   **Pool C · Group 1 1995**

WORLD JUNIOR CHAMPIONSHIP 1995
Puigcerda (ESP) · Dec. 29, 1994 – Jan. 3, 1995

POOL **C**
Group 2

Group A	HUN	BLR	ROM	GBR	Goals	P
1. Hungary		5:2	11:0	6:1	22: 3	6
2. Belarus	2:5		3:2	8:2	13: 9	4
3. Rumania	0:11	2:3		4:3	8:17	2
4. Great Britain	1:6	2:8	3:4		6:18	0

Group A	LAT	DEN	ESP	NED	Goals	P
1. Latvia		7:5	9:0	13:1	29: 6	6
2. Denmark	5:7		5:2	5:2	15:11	4
3. Spain	0:9	2:5		4:3	6:17	2
4. Netherlands	1:13	2:5	3:4		6:22	0

Final round

Great Britain	– Netherlands	3:4
Spain	– Rumania	3:2
Belarus	– Denmark	2:3
Hungary	– Latvia	2:5

Latvia and **Hungary** promoted to POOL B 1996.
There is no relegation.

Winner of the FAIR PLAY CUP:
Spain

Final standing

1. Latvia
2. Hungary
3. Denmark
4. Belarus
5. Spain
6. Rumania
7. Netherlands
8. Great Britain

Best player by teams

LAT	17	Aleksandrs Nizivijs	F
HUN	20	Krisztian Palkovics	RW
DEN	19	Jan Jensen	LW
BLR	9	Viatcheslav Sokol	RD
ESP	13	Juan José Palacin	F
ROM	12	Laszlo Kovacs	LW
NED	3	Ronald Spijkers	LD
GBR	3	James Manson	LD

The best player of each team received a **SEIKO** watch.

LATVIA

Name	Pos	GP	G	A1	A2	Pts	PIM
Aleksandr Macijevskis	F	4	6	5	0	11	2
Pavels Parhomenko	F	4	8	1	0	9	12
Aleksandrs Nizivijs	F	4	4	3	0	7	0
Atvars Tribuncovs	RD	4	5	0	0	5	6
Sergejs Cubars	F	4	2	2	0	4	2
Valerius Kulibaba	F	4	2	2	0	4	2
Guntars Pals	F	4	2	2	0	4	4
Edgars Rozentals	F	4	1	2	0	3	6
Sandijs Girvics	D	4	0	3	0	3	4
Girts Ankipans	CE	4	2	0	0	2	4
Mareks Jass	RW	4	1	1	0	2	16
Voktors Cimbaliuks	F	4	0	2	0	2	6
Aigars Mironovics	LD	4	0	2	0	2	6
Sergejs Visegorodcevs	RD	4	1	0	0	1	6
Mihails Salijenko	F	4	0	1	0	1	6
Atis Silavnieks	LD	4	0	0	0	0	2
Edmunds Pivaruns	F	4	0	0	0	0	2
Kaspars Astasenko	RD	4	0	0	0	0	18

Goalkeepers	GP	MIP	GA	SOG	GAA	PIM
Edgars Eihvalds	4	237.32	7	7	1.77	0
Uldis Kierpe	4	2.28	1	1	26.32	0

HUNGARY

Name	Pos	GP	G	A1	A2	Pts	PIM
Krisztian Palkovics	RW	4	5	4	1	10	0
Balazs Ladanyi	LW	4	6	1	2	9	2
Gabor Ocskay	CE	4	6	2	1	9	6
Zoltan Szilassy	LW	4	1	3	1	5	0
Viktor Tokaji	LD	4	0	3	0	3	2
Lajos Tokesi	RD	4	0	1	2	3	16
Istvan Hollo	RW	4	2	0	0	2	2
Peter Erdosi	LW	4	1	1	0	2	0
Laszlo Orso	CE	4	1	1	0	2	0
Zsolt Bali	RW	4	1	1	0	2	4
Kristof Kovago	CE	4	0	0	2	2	4
Gyula Farago	CE	4	1	0	0	1	6
Pal Merenyi	LW	4	0	0	1	1	0
Viktor Szelig	LD	4	0	1	0	1	6
Miklos Zalavari	LW	6	0	0	0	0	2
Balasz Horvath	RD	4	0	0	0	0	2
Attila Rajz	LW	4	0	0	0	0	4
Andras Horvath	RD	2	0	0	0	0	4

Goalkeepers	GP	MIP	GA	SOG	GAA	PIM
Miklos Meszaros	4	120.00	2	2	1.00	0
Norbert Bertenyi	4	120.00	6	6	3.00	4

DENMARK

Name	Pos	GP	G	A1	A2	Pts	PIM
Jan Jensen	LW	4	6	3	0	9	22
Ulrik S. Olsen	LW	4	3	1	1	5	26
Becker Christensen	RW	4	2	2	0	4	8
Andreas Mattson	CE	4	3	0	0	3	4
Kasper Kristensen	CE	4	1	2	0	3	6
Johan M. Jensen	RW	4	0	3	0	3	8
Jesper M. Nielsen	RW	4	1	0	0	1	2
Lasse Degn	LW	4	1	0	0	1	2
Jesper Damgaard	LD	4	1	0	0	1	6
Rasmus Edmund	CE	4	0	1	0	1	0
Andreas Andreasen	RD	4	0	1	0	1	2
Morten Dahlmann	RD	4	0	1	0	1	4
Jesper Gaarde	Rd	4	0	1	0	1	6
Martin Skygge	RD	4	0	1	0	1	10
Rasmus Jakobsen	LD	4	0	0	0	0	2
Kim Staal	LW	4	0	0	0	0	4
Andreas Christensen	LD	4	0	0	0	0	6
Soren Pedersen	RW	4	0	0	0	0	16

Goalkeepers

Name	GP	MIP	GA	SOG	GAA	PIM
Dan Jensen	4	120.37	4	4	1.99	0
Peter Therkildsen	4	119.23	9	9	4.53	10

BELARUS

Name	Pos	GP	G	A1	A2	Pts	PIM
Dmitri Choulga	RW	4	3	0	0	3	12
Vitali Kiselev	RW	4	2	0	1	3	0
Vladimir Khailak	LW	4	2	1	0	3	2
Alexei Vinokourov	RW	4	2	1	0	3	4
Guennadi Savilov	LW	4	2	0	0	2	4
Alexei Strakhov	RW	4	1	1	0	2	2
Alexandre Rymcha	RW	4	0	2	0	2	6
Alexandre Zapolski	CE	4	0	1	1	2	12
Vladimir Pereverzev	RD	4	1	0	0	1	0
Iouri Karpenko	CE	4	1	0	0	1	0
Victor Oprichko	CE	4	1	0	0	1	6
Vladimir Naiduon	LD	4	0	0	1	1	0
Serguri Glouchinsky	LD	4	0	1	0	1	2
Viatcheslav Sokol	RD	4	0	1	0	1	4
Alexandre Zhurik	LD	4	0	0	1	1	6
Oleg Teterev	RD	4	0	1	0	1	14
Vitali Kouznetsov	RD	4	0	0	0	0	0
Dmitri Doudik	LW	4	0	0	0	0	2

Goalkeepers

Name	GP	MIP	GA	SOG	GAA	PIM
A. Proudnikovitch	4	239.52	12	12	3.01	0
Kirill Kashevsky	4	0.08	0	0	0.00	0

SPAIN

Name	Pos	GP	G	A1	A2	Pts	PIM
Juan J. Palacin	F	4	5	0	0	5	0
Jorge Calvo	CE	4	1	3	0	4	2
Alejandro Calvo	F	4	0	2	0	2	4
Antonio Roig	LD	4	1	0	0	1	2
Huc Codina	F	4	1	0	0	1	2
Jaume Castell	F	4	1	0	0	1	6
Juan A. Artero	RD	4	0	1	0	1	10
Marti Masdeu	RD	4	0	0	0	0	0
Ernesto Ubieto	F	4	0	0	0	0	0
Salvador Barnola	CE	4	0	0	0	0	0
Ivan Codina	F	4	0	0	0	0	0
Xavier Pous	LD	4	0	0	0	0	0
Javier Lahoz	F	4	0	0	0	0	2
Joseba Garcia	LD	4	0	0	0	0	2
Alvaro Andino	RD	4	0	0	0	0	4
Jose A. Biec	F	4	0	0	0	0	4
Jordi Bernet	F	4	0	0	0	0	4
Javier Cuadrado	LD	4	0	0	0	0	4

Goalkeepers

Name	GP	MIP	GA	SOG	GAA	PIM
Guillermo Alvarez	4	101.25	8	8	4.74	0
Jose L. Alonso	4	138.35	11	11	4.77	0

RUMANIA

Name	Pos	GP	G	A1	A2	Pts	PIM
Laszlo Kovacs	LW	4	2	2	1	5	0
Levente Hozo	CE	4	2	2	0	4	14
Jozsef Adorjan	LD	4	0	2	1	3	4
Endre Kosa	RW	4	2	0	0	2	4
Razvan Lupascu	RW	4	1	0	0	1	0
Robert Rusu	CE	4	1	0	0	1	4
Levente Tofan	RD	4	0	1	0	1	0
Adrian Popa	RD	4	0	1	0	1	4
Ferencz Domokos	LD	4	0	0	1	1	25
Nicolae Stoiculescu	RD	4	0	0	0	0	0
IulianCacenschi	RW	4	0	0	0	0	0
Attila Benedek	RD	4	0	0	0	0	0
Tibor Koos	CE	4	0	0	0	0	0
Jozsef Petres	LW	4	0	0	0	0	0
Marian Bocioanca	LW	4	0	0	0	0	4
Iustin Musca	CE	4	0	0	0	0	8
Victor Corduban	LD	4	0	0	0	0	12
Emilian Banesanu	RD	4	0	0	0	0	12

Goalkeepers

Name	GP	MIP	GA	SOG	GAA	PIM
Attila Nagy	4	209.01	14	14	4.02	0
Szabolcs Molnar	4	30.59	6	6	11.77	0

NETHERLANDS

Name	Pos	GP	G	A1	A2	Pts	PIM
Ronald Spijkers	LD	4	3	1	0	4	2
Denmis Gosselin	CE	4	2	1	1	4	12
Erik Landman	LW	4	2	2	0	4	14
Don Galjaard	LW	4	1	0	0	1	8
Hes Roelofs	CE	4	1	0	0	1	14
Robert Delcliseur	RW	4	1	0	0	1	14
Addie Kroeze	CE	4	0	1	0	1	0
Marc von Ranzow	LW	4	0	1	0	1	18
Rene Kronenburg	RD	4	0	1	0	1	18
Hans van Nunen	LD	4	0	0	0	0	0
Maarten Polkamp	LW	4	0	0	0	0	2
Mark van de Heuvel	RW	4	0	0	0	0	2
Robert van Laarhoven	RD	4	0	0	0	0	2
Oswin Bomius	CE	4	0	0	0	0	6
Corme Koenen	LW	4	0	0	0	0	6
Casper Oosterman	RW	4	0	0	0	0	6
Pascal Keus	LD	4	0	0	0	0	12
Rody Jacobs	RD	4	0	0	0	0	16

Goalkeepers

Name	GP	MIP	GA	SOG	GAA	PIM
Homore Loos	4	150.12	19	16	6.39	0
Jair van der Meer	4	29.48	6	6	12.21	0

GREAT BRITAIN

Name	Pos	GP	G	A1	A2	Pts	PIM
Ashley Tait	CE	4	2	2	0	4	22
Neil Francis	RW	4	2	0	1	3	2
Simon Keating	CE	4	1	0	1	2	4
James Manson	LD	4	0	2	0	2	4
Garry Dowd	RD	4	1	0	0	1	0
Andrew Carter	CE	4	1	0	0	1	4
Andrew Holmes	RW	4	1	0	0	1	8
Elliot Andrews	RW	4	1	0	0	1	8
Jonathan Weaver	LW	4	0	1	0	1	8
Jake French	RD	4	0	1	0	1	22
Daniel Boome	LW	4	0	0	0	0	0
Russell Plant	LW	4	0	0	0	0	2
Michael Knights	LD	4	0	0	0	0	2
Andrew Port	LD	4	0	0	0	0	4
Alan Armour	LW	4	0	0	0	0	4
Jack Waghorn	LD	4	0	0	0	0	4
Stuart J. Heasman	RD	4	0	0	0	0	4
Nick Cross	CE	4	0	0	0	0	6

Goalkeepers

Name	GP	MIP	GA	SOG	GAA	PIM
Simon D. Wren	4	180.00	18	18	6.00	0
Paul Cast	4	0.00	4	0	0.00	20

WORLD JUNIOR CHAMPIONSHIP 1995

Tallinn (EST) · Dec. 31, 1994 – Jan. 6, 1995

POOL C

Group 2

	KAZ	SLO	EST	LTU	CRO	YUG	Goals	Pts
1. Kazakhstan		3:3	13:1	11:2	2:2	18:2	47:10	8
2. Slovenia	3:3		3:3	9:3	8:2	17:4	40:15	8
3. Estonia	1:13	3:3		6:4	2:2	12:3	24:25	6
4. Lithuania	2:11	3:9	4:6		7:2	13:2	29:30	4
5. Croatia	2:2	2:8	2:2	2:7		2:2	10:21	3
6. Yugoslavia	2:18	4:17	3:12	2:13	2:2		13:62	1

Kazakhstan and **Slovenia** promoted to **POOL C, Group 1 1996**

Winner of the FAIR PLAY CUP: Lithuania

Best player by teams

KAZ	23	Andrei Prutchovsky	D
SLO	11	Matjaz Mahrovic	F
EST	30	Igor Tshernosov	GK
LTU	29	Irmantas Bosac	GK
CRO	16	Mario Kocijancic	D
YUG	10	Iwan Prokic	F

The best player of each team received a **SEIKO** watch.

Best goalkeeper	Robin Keller	CRO
Best defender	Dmitri Rodin	EST
Best forward	Dmitri Dudarev	KAZ

LITHUANIA

Name	GP	G	A	Pts	PIM
Andrej Kibickij	2	0	0	0	0
Aleksey Kondratjev	5	0	0	0	0
Dangiras Rimkus	5	1	2	3	8
Aurelijus Krishiunas	5	1	0	1	8
Saulius Limontas	5	6	3	9	4
Audrius Zubrus	5	0	2	2	8
Egidius Bauba	5	7	2	9	8
Andrej Klimovec	5	3	3	6	0
Tomas Kaminskas	5	0	1	1	0
Andrius Jankauskas	4	0	0	0	0
Darius Janusonis	2	0	0	0	0
Andrei Simankov	5	3	2	5	8
Sergej Jakuta	3	0	1	1	0
Vitalij Zencenko	5	3	0	3	0
Timur Suponev	2	1	0	1	0
Andrius Navickas	5	0	1	1	6
Tomas Vishniauskas	5	0	0	0	2
Martinas Shlikas	5	2	2	4	8
Aleksandr Zaicev	5	1	1	2	2
Sarunas Kuliesius	4	1	0	1	2

Goalkeepers

Name	GP	MIN	GA	PIM
Arunas Aleinikovas	5	87	10	2
Irmantas Bosas	5	213	20	0

KAZAKHSTAN

Name	GP	G	A	Pts	PIM
Alexander Balitchougouv	5	0	0	0	18
Evgueni Kozlov	5	0	0	0	2
Serguei Jakovenko	5	1	1	2	4
Salim Prmanov	5	4	4	8	4
Alexandre Golovatiouk	5	1	4	5	6
Evgueni Liapounov	5	3	3	6	2
Igor Kamensky	5	4	5	9	8
Serguei Aleksandrov	5	2	1	3	2
Roman Fadin	5	4	7	11	6
Alexandre Oboukhov	5	4	1	5	4
Dmitry Dudarev	5	5	9	14	6
Andrei Singuileev	5	6	5	11	4
Andrei Proutchkovski	5	6	6	12	8
Alexandre Pokladov	5	2	0	2	2
Victor Chilov	5	5	2	7	4

Goalkeepers

Name	GP	MIN	GA	PIM
Sergei Ogureshnikov	5	246	8	0
Viatcheslav Tregoubov	5	54	2	2

ESTONIA

Name	GP	G	A	Pts	PIM
Aleksei Sibalov	3	0	0	0	4
Aleksandr Obodennoi	5	1	0	1	0
Andrei Orletski	5	0	0	0	0
Stanislav Pankov	2	0	0	0	0
Vadim Vesselov	3	0	0	0	0
Dmitri Rodin	5	1	1	2	14
Sergei Sein	5	1	0	1	2
Vadim Vogulkin	2	0	1	1	2
Roman Potsinok	5	1	1	2	8
Veiko Suvaoja	5	2	1	3	0
Andrus Pihlak	5	1	2	3	0
Jevgeni Varlamov	4	1	2	3	31
Mihail Kozlov	5	6	4	10	18
Ivar Sander	1	0	0	0	0
Dmitri Raskidajev	5	2	1	3	0
Vassill Makrov	5	1	0	1	0
Aleksandr Dmitrijev	5	3	5	8	20
Andrei Griskun	5	4	2	6	0
Pelle Sildre	4	0	0	0	2
Märt Mägi	1	0	0	0	0

Goalkeepers

Name	GP	MIN	GA	PIM
Alar Tooming	5	12	5	0
Igor Tsemysov	5	228	20	0

CROATIA

Name	GP	G	A	Pts	PIM
Domagoj Kucis	0	0	0	0	0
Sven Skrgatic	4	0	0	0	0
Silvio Erakovic	5	0	0	0	2
Hrvoje Brletic	0	0	0	0	0
Marin Latkovic	5	0	0	0	10
Borko Cvitan	5	0	0	0	4
Dean Volic	5	0	1	1	0
Marijo Brcic	4	0	0	0	2
Igor Grosic	5	3	1	4	8
Ivan Muslim	5	1	2	3	2
Vejko Zibret	0	0	0	0	0
Goran Jelinek	5	2	1	3	0
Mario Kocijancic	5	2	0	2	14
Vanja Keller	4	0	0	0	0
Mihael Babic	5	0	0	0	6
Tomislav Grahor	4	0	0	0	4
Mato Mladenovic	3	0	0	0	0
Davor Safar	5	0	0	0	2
Domagoj Radin	5	0	0	0	2
Danijel Kolombo	5	2	0	2	29

Goalkeepers

Name	GP	MIN	GA	PIM
Robin Keller	5	275	18	2
Damir Glad	5	25	3	0

YUGOSLAVIA

Name	GP	G	A	Pts	PIM
Milan Vladimirovic	3	0	0	0	8
Goran Pavlovic	4	0	0	0	8
Nenad Brkic	5	1	0	1	12
Uros Banovic	5	0	0	0	4
Ognjen Ivanovic	5	0	1	1	2
Igor Obrovski	3	0	0	0	8
Jovica Rus	5	2	0	2	14
Ivan Prokic	5	2	4	6	14
Relja Budisavljevic	2	0	0	0	0
Nenad Zikic	5	1	0	1	10
Misa Ramadan	2	0	0	0	0
Ivan Temunovic	1	0	0	0	0
Igor Polkovnikov	4	0	0	0	0
Filip Sovljanski	5	0	1	1	36
Ivan Jovanovic	5	0	0	0	4
Vojin Jaukovic	5	5	1	6	2
Boris Danon	5	0	0	0	2
Aleksandar Ramadanovic	5	2	1	3	8
Nenad Kecojevic	5	0	1	1	0
Damir Rudinski	3	0	0	0	2

Goalkeepers

Name	GP	MIN	GA	PIM
Tihomir Zecevic	5	247	46	2
Goran Knezevic	5	53	16	0

SLOVENIA

Name	GP	G	A	Pts	PIM
Tielen Zugwitz	5	1	3	4	8
Klemen Kelgar	5	1	2	3	14
Bostjan Kranjc	2	2	0	2	8
David Macek	4	1	1	2	16
Ales Wagner	4	0	0	0	2
Miha Soba	3	0	1	1	2
Grega Trojak	4	0	0	0	2
Matjaz Mahkovic	5	6	5	11	4
Edvin Karahodzic	5	6	5	11	2
Matej Poljansek	5	5	0	5	4
Dragan Mrdjenovic	5	2	5	7	6
Andrej Kolar	5	5	4	9	4
Boris Pretnar	5	3	1	4	0
Tomaz Razinger	4	1	0	1	0
Bostjan Kos	5	0	2	2	2
Milan Hafner	5	6	2	8	12
Gregor Por	5	1	1	2	4
Miha Rebolj	5	0	1	1	6

Goalkeepers

Name	GP	MIN	GA	PIM
Ales Petronijevic	5	220	10	0
Gaber Glavic	5	80	5	0

Die komplette Eishockey-Saison ausführlich in einem Band!

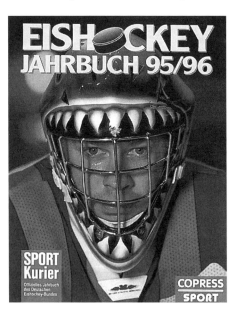

EISH CKEY
JAHRBUCH 95/96

SPORT
Kurier
Offizielles Jahrbuch
des Deutschen
Eishockey-Bundes

COPRESS
SPORT

Das erfolgreiche COPRESS-Eishockey-Jahrbuch jetzt in neuem Outfit: erstmals komplett in Farbe und in attraktivem, modernem Layout.
Gewohnt ausführlich und informativ die Beiträge zu DEL, NHL und WM, Bundesliga und Eishockey allgemein. Neben Features zu den einzelnen Spielern und Mannschaften sind natürlich die üblichen Jahres-Chroniken und der ausführliche Tabellenteil enthalten.

DM 39,80

COPRESS VERLAG GMBH
Postfach 2003 53, 80003 München

EUROPEAN JUNIOR CHAMPIONSHIP 1995
Berlin (GER) · April 9. – 16., 1995

POOL A

Group A	SWE	FIN	SUI	BLR	Goals	P
1. Sweden		3:2	4:3	10:3	17: 8	6
2. Finland	2:3		6:1	7:2	15: 6	4
3. Switzerland	3:4	1:6		4:1	8:11	2
4. Belarus	3:10	2:7	1:4		6:21	0

Group B	GER	RUS	CZE	NOR	Goals	P
1. Germany		3:2	4:4	4:1	11: 7	5
2. Russia	2:3		4:3	6:1	12: 7	4
3. Czech Republic	4:4	3:4		16:0	23: 8	3
4. Norway	1:4	1:6	0:16		2:26	0

Final round

	FIN	GER	SWE	RUS	Goals	Pts
1. Finland		5:3	2:3*	4:2	11: 8	4:2
2. Germany	3:5		3:3	3:2*	9:10	3:3
3. Sweden	3:2*	3:3		2:6	8:11	3:3
4. Russia	2:4	2:3*	6:2		10: 9	2:4

* = Results 1th round

Relegation

	CZE	SUI	BLR	NOR	Goals	Pts
1. Czech Republic		3:2	11:1	16:0*	30: 3	6:0
2. Switzerland	2:3		4:1*	5:2	10: 6	4:2
3. Belarus	1:11	1:4*		4:4	6:19	1:5
4. Norway	0:16*	2:5	4:4		6:24	1:5

Norway relegated into POOL B 1996

Three best players by teams

BEL	Dmitri Dudik	LW
	Vitali Gegania	RD
	Iouri Kouzmenkov	RD
CZE	Ladislav Kudrna	GK
	Petr Buzek	LD
	Marek Melenovsky	LD
FIN	Miika Elomo	LW
	Tomi Hirvonen	CE
	Vesa Toskala	GK
GER	Andreas Renz	RD
	Kai Fischer	GK
	Jochen Hecht	CE
NOR	Arne-Villy Skrøder	GK
	Bård Sørlie	LD
	Stian Berntsen	CE
RUS	Oleg Orekhovsky	LD
	Alexei Permiakov	CE
	Sergei Samsonov	LW
SWE	Robert Borgqvist	GK
	Per-Anton Lundström	LD
	Niklas Anger	RW
SUI	Paolo della Bella	GK
	Mattia Baldi	LW
	Mathias Seger	RD

Top scorers

Name	Team	Pos	GP	G	A1	A2	Pts
Pavel Rosa	CZE	RW	5	8	2	1	11
Josef Straka	CZE	CE	5	3	3	2	8
Niklas Anger	SWE	RW	5	4	3	1	8
Marcus Nilsson	SWE	LW	5	4	3	1	8
Mikko Markkanen	FIN	LW	5	3	2	2	7
Michal Horak	CZE	LW	5	2	3	2	7
Radek Dvorak	CZE	LW	5	1	1	2	7
Jochen Hecht	GER	CE	5	3	3	0	6
Dmitri Dudik	BLR	LW	5	1	1	1	6
Jaako Niskavaara	FIN	LD	5	3	3	0	6

Best players of the championship

Goalkeeper	Kai Fischer	GER
Defense	Jaako Niskavaara	FIN
Forward	Sergei Samsonov	RUS

ALL STAR TEAM

K. Fischer
GER

P. Buzek   **A.-P. Berg**
CZE/Jihlava   FIN/Turku

A. Morozov   **J. Hecht**   **S. Samsonov**
RUS/Krylija   GER/Mannheim   RUS/CSKA

53

FINLAND

Name	Pos	GP	G	A1	A2	Pts	PIM
Mikko Markkanen	LW	5	3	2	2	7	0
Toni Kallio	LW	5	4	2	0	6	6
Jaako Niskavaara	LD	5	3	3	0	6	2
Miika Elono	LW	5	3	1	2	6	10
Toni Lydman	LD	5	2	2	1	5	2
Tuomas Reijonen	LW	5	4	1	0	5	4
Tino Hakanen	CE	5	2	0	2	4	0
Toni Hirvonen	CE	5	1	2	1	4	6
Pekka Kangasalusta	RW	5	1	1	0	2	4
Teenu Riihijärvi	RW	4	0	1	1	2	10
Sami Salonen	CE	5	0	1	1	2	0
Juha Viinikainen	CE	5	0	2	0	2	2
Sami-Ville Salomaa	LD	5	0	1	0	1	0
Antti-Jussi Niemi	RD	5	0	0	1	1	7
Janne Lehtinen	CE	5	0	0	1	1	2
Jussi Salminen	RD	5	0	1	0	1	2
Aki-Petteri Berg	LD	5	0	1	0	1	10
Marko Mäkinen	RW	5	1	0	0	1	4
Pasi Petrilainen	RD	5	0	0	0	0	2
Jussi Tie	RW	5	0	0	0	0	0

Goalkeeper Name	GP	MIN	GA	SOG	SVS	GAA
Juha Kauhanen	0	0	0	0	0.00	0.00
Jani Riihinen	5	120	1	17	94.12	0.50
Vesa Toskala	5	180	10	85	88.24	3.33

GERMANY

Name	Pos	GP	G	A1	A2	Pts	PIM
Jochen Hecht	CE	5	3	3	0	6	18
Marco Sturm	CE	5	2	2	1	5	2
Sven Gerike	CE	5	2	2	0	4	4
Klaus Kathan	LW	5	2	1	1	4	2
Nico Pyka	LD	5	0	1	2	3	10
Boris Lingemann	LW	5	1	2	0	3	2
Markus Draxler	RW	5	2	1	0	3	4
Denny Böttger	RW	5	1	1	1	3	4
Robert Francz	LW	2	2	0	0	2	2
Marco Flügel	RW	5	1	1	0	2	0
Torsten Fendt	RD	5	0	1	0	1	0
Andreas Renz	RD	5	1	0	0	1	2
Andreas Morczinietz	RW	5	0	1	0	1	0
Thomas Vogel	LD	5	0	0	1	1	4
Niki Mondt	CE	5	0	0	0	0	0
Sebastian Pech	RD	5	0	0	0	0	0
Werner Schaeffler	LW	2	0	0	0	0	0
Alexander Erdmann	RD	5	0	0	0	0	0
Markus Poettinger	LD	5	0	0	0	0	0
Gordon Borberg	RD	5	0	0	0	0	0

Goalkeeper Name	GP	MIN	GA	SOG	SVS	GAA
Ingo Schwarz	0	0	0	0	0.00	0.00
David Berge	5	0	0	0	0.00	0.00
Kai Fischer	5	300	15	158	90.51	3.00

SWEDEN

Name	Pos	GP	G	A1	A2	Pts	PIM
Niklas Anger	RW	5	4	3	1	8	2
Marcus Nilsson	LW	5	4	3	1	8	0
Patrik Kallenberg	RW	5	2	2	2	6	4
Fredrik Loven	CE	5	1	4	1	6	12
Samuel Phalsson	CE	5	1	3	1	5	2
Jan Labraaten	LW	5	4	0	0	4	0
Peter Wallin	LW	5	1	1	0	4	0
Björn Danielsson	CE	5	1	2	0	3	0
Per-Anton Lundström	LD	5	0	1	2	3	2
Andreas Sjölund	LW	5	0	0	2	2	8
Erik Nilsen	RD	5	1	0	1	2	0
Henrik Rehnberg	RD	5	1	0	1	2	8
Per Gustavsson	RW	5	1	0	0	1	4
Johan Ranstedt	RW	5	1	0	0	1	0
Henrik Andersson	CE	5	0	0	1	1	2
Jonas Göthberg	LD	5	0	1	0	1	4
Per Hallberg	LD	5	0	0	1	1	2
Ted Christensen	RD	5	0	0	0	0	18
Timmy Petterson	RD	5	0	0	0	0	0
Daniel Carlsson	LD	5	0	0	0	0	2

Goalkeeper Name	GP	MIN	GA	SOG	SVS	GAA
Johan Holmqvist	0	0	0	0	0.00	0.00
Robert Borgqvist	5	270	14	114	87.72	3.11
Marten Engren	5	10	3	13	76.92	6.00

RUSSIA

Name	Pos	GP	G	A1	A2	Pts	PIM
Sergei Samsonov	LW	5	2	3	1	6	0
Alexei Morozov	RW	5	3	1	1	5	6
Dmitry Nabokov	LW	5	1	3	1	5	4
Andrei Petrunin	RW	5	4	0	0	4	2
Vadim Gusev	RD	5	1	0	3	4	0
Eduard Pershin	RW	5	1	2	0	3	4
Dmitry Subbotin	LW	5	0	1	1	2	4
Rustem Gabdullin	LW	5	0	2	0	2	2
Sergei Pedotov	RD	5	1	1	0	2	4
Alexei Permiakov	CE	5	2	0	0	2	4
Oleg Orekhovsky	LD	5	2	0	0	2	0
Alexei Kolkunov	CE	5	1	1	0	2	4
Dmitry Evdokinov	LD	5	0	1	0	1	2
Pavel Smirnov	CE	5	1	0	0	1	2
Alexei Vasiljev	RD	5	0	0	1	1	2
Alexei Makarov	RW	5	0	1	0	1	0
K. Golokhvastov	LW	5	0	0	1	1	0
Dmitry Emeljantsev	CE	5	1	0	0	1	2
Andrei Zyuzin	LD	5	0	0	0	0	1
Alexander Zhmaev	RD	5	0	0	0	0	0

Goalkeeper Name	GP	MIN	GA	SOG	SVS	GAA
Denis Aralin	5	0	0	0	0.01	0.00
Denis Khlopotnov	5	300	13	94	86.17	2.60

CZECH REPUBLIC

Name	Pos	GP	G	A1	A2	Pts	PIM
Pavel Rosa	RW	5	8	2	1	11	0
Josef Straka	CE	5	3	3	2	8	2
Michal Horak	LW	5	2	3	2	7	0
Radek Dvorak	LW	5	4	1	2	7	6
Marek Melenovsky	CE	5	2	3	1	6	2
David Hruska	RW	5	2	4	0	6	4
Martin Streit	LW	5	1	1	3	5	0
Marek Vorel	CE	5	2	2	1	5	2
Tomas Kaberle	LD	5	0	3	2	5	0
Ondrej Kratena	RW	4	3	1	0	4	0
Martin Spanhel	LW	5	1	0	1	4	0
Petr Buzek	LD	5	2	1	1	4	10
Kamil Glabazna	LW	5	3	0	0	3	0
Jiri Burger	LW	5	0	3	0	3	0
Libor Pavlis	CE	5	1	1	0	2	0
Lukas Zib	LD	5	1	1	0	2	4
Jiri Polak	RD	5	0	0	1	1	2
Ales Pisa	RD	5	0	1	0	1	2
Robert Kantor	RD	4	0	0	0	0	2
Jakub Ficenec	LD	5	0	0	0	0	0

Goalkeeper

Name	GP	MIN	GA	SOG	SVS	GAA
Robert Hamrla	5	0	0	0	0.00	0.00
Ladislav Polacek	0	0	0	0	0.00	0.00
Ladislav Kudrna	5	300	11	99	88.89	2.20

SWITZERLAND

Name	Pos	GP	G	A1	A2	Pts	PIM
Michel Riesen	RW	5	3	1	0	4	2
Mattia Baldi	LW	5	0	2	1	3	2
Fabio Obrist	RW	5	2	1	0	3	2
Christian Wohlwend	RW	5	3	0	0	3	10
Mark Streit	RD	5	1	0	2	3	6
Martin Pluess	CE	5	0	1	1	2	0
Mario Schocher	CE	5	1	1	0	2	0
Laurent Mueller	CE	5	1	1	0	2	2
Sascha Schneider	LW	5	1	1	0	2	2
Mathias Seger	RD	5	0	1	0	1	10
Andre Baumann	RW	5	1	0	0	1	0
Rolf Badertscher	CE	5	0	0	1	1	0
Stefan Grauwiler	LD	5	0	1	0	1	0
Sandro Rizzi	CE	5	0	1	0	1	2
Benjamin Winkler	LW	5	0	1	0	1	6
Michel Faeh	LD	5	1	0	0	1	6
Daniel Mares	LW	5	0	0	0	0	0
Jan von Arx	LD	5	0	0	0	0	4
Marcel Mueller	LD	5	0	0	0	0	0
Philipp Portner	RD	5	0	0	0	0	4

Goalkeeper

Name	GP	MIN	GA	SOG	SVS	GAA
Flavio Streit	0	0	0	0	0.00	0.00
Paolo della Bella	5	260	12	126	90.18	2.77
Matthias Lauber	5	40	4	23	82.61	6.00

BELARUS

Name	Pos	GP	G	A1	A2	Pts	PIM
Dmitri Dudik	LW	5	4	1	1	6	6
Viatcheslav Sokol	RD	5	0	3	0	3	8
Dmitri Shabunevitch	RW	5	2	0	1	3	2
Sergei Zmitrovich	LW	5	2	1	0	3	0
Alexander Zelenko	LD	5	1	0	0	1	0
Anatoli Volodkevitch	CE	5	0	1	0	1	8
Vladislav Sosedkov	CE	5	1	0	0	1	2
Victor Shariton	CE	5	0	0	1	1	0
Pavel Tolstik	LD	5	0	1	0	1	4
Dmitri Belko	RW	5	1	0	0	1	4
Andrei Mikhailov	RW	5	0	1	0	1	0
Eugeni Esaulov	CE	5	0	0	0	0	2
Vitali Gegania	RD	5	0	0	0	0	6
Sergei Radko	LD	5	0	0	0	0	14
Andrei Sharkevitch	LD	5	0	0	0	0	2
Denis Matiukhin	CE	5	0	0	0	0	2
Victor Lobynko	RD	5	0	0	0	0	0
Pavel Merzliakov	CE	5	0	0	0	0	4
Iouri Kouzmenkov	RD	5	0	0	0	0	6
Andrei Rashchinsky	RW	5	0	0	0	0	2

Goalkeeper

Name	GP	MIN	GA	SOG	SVS	GAA
Sergei Kutchinsky	5	214	20	130	84:62	5:61
Pavel Titol	5	86	16	80	80.00	11.16

NORWAY

Name	Pos	GP	G	A1	A2	Pts	PIM
Joakin Saether	CE	5	1	1	2	4	2
Per-Age Skroder	LW	5	1	2	0	3	4
Per Olav Skarpiordet	LW	5	1	1	0	2	0
Marius Koldre	LD	5	1	1	0	2	6
Jan Robert Flatekval	LD	5	1	0	1	2	2
Torkil Brustad	LW	5	0	2	0	2	8
Dan Remy Tangnes	CE	5	2	0	0	2	0
Bard Sorlie	LD	5	0	1	0	1	2
Ronny Tajet	LW	5	1	0	0	1	2
Thomas Mervik	LW	5	0	0	0	0	2
Kristian M. Lingson	RW	5	0	0	0	0	2
Jarle Haessel	RD	5	0	0	0	0	2
Truls Andersen	RD	5	0	0	0	0	2
Stian Berntsen	CE	5	0	0	0	0	0
Marius Asle	RW	5	0	0	0	0	10
Magnus Osteraas	RD	5	0	0	0	0	4
O. C. Tangen-Andersen	RD	5	0	0	0	0	0
Kjell Richard Hygard	CE	5	0	0	0	0	4
Jarl Espen Ygranes	LD	5	0	0	0	0	2
Truls Lindahl	LW	4	0	0	0	0	0

Goalkeeper

Name	GP	MIN	GA	SOG	SVS	GAA
Jarle Kristoffersen	0	0	0	0	0.00	0.00
Arne-Villy Skroder	5	185	19	129	85.27	6.16
Kare Olsen	5	115	15	82	81.71	7.83

EUROPEAN JUNIOR CHAMPIONSHIPS 1968-1995

EC	YEAR	PLACE	FIRST	SECOND	THIRD
1	1968	Tampere/Helsinki	Czechoslowakia	Soviet Union	Sweden
2	1969	Garmisch-Partenkirchen	Soviet Union	Sweden	Czechoslowakia
3	1970	Geneve	Soviet Union	Czechoslowakia	Sweden
4	1971	Presov	Soviet Union	Sweden	Czechoslowakia
5	1972	Lulea/Skelleftea	Sweden	Soviet Union	Czechoslowakia
6	1973	Leningrad	Soviet Union	Sweden	Czechoslowakia
7	1974	Herisau/St. Gallen	Sweden	Soviet Union	Finland
8	1975	Grenoble/Gap	Soviet Union	Czechoslowakia	Sweden
9	1976	Opava	Soviet Union	Sweden	Finland
10	1977	Bremerhaven	Sweden	Czechoslowakia	Soviet Union
11	1978	Helsinki	Finland	Soviet Union	Sweden
12	1979	Tichy/Katowice	Czechoslowakia	Finland	Soviet Union
13	1980	Hrusdec/Kralowec	Soviet Union	Czechoslowakia	Sweden
14	1981	Minsk	Soviet Union	Czechoslowakia	Sweden
15	1982	Angelholm/Tyringe	Sweden	Czechoslowakia	Soviet Union
16	1983	Oslo	Soviet Union	Finland	Czechoslowakia
17	1984	Germisch-Partenkirchen	Soviet Union	Czechoslowakia	Finland
18	1985	Anglet	Sweden	Soviet Union	Czechoslowakia
19	1986	Düsseldorf	Finland	Sweden	Czechoslowakia
20	1987	Tampere/Kouvola	Sweden	Czechoslowakia	Soviet Union
21	1988	Frydek-Mistek	Czechoslowakia	Finland	Soviet Union
22	1989	Kiev	Soviet Union	Czechoslowakia	Finland
23	1990	Ömsköldsvik	Sweden	Soviet Union	Czechoslowakia
24	1991	Presov/Spisska/Nova	Czechoslowakia	Soviet Union	Finland
25	1992	Lillehammer/Hamar	Czechoslowakia	Sweden	Russia
26	1993	Nowy Targ	Sweden	Russia	Czechoslowakia
27	1994	Jyväskylä	Sweden	Russia	Czech Republic
28	1995	Berlin	Finland	Germany	Sweden

TOTAL MEDAL COUNT

Team	G	S	B
URS	11	7	5
Sweden	9	6	7
Czechoslowakia	5	9	9
Finland	3	3	5
Russia	–	2	1
Czech Republic	–	–	1
Germany	–	1	–

EUROPEAN JUNIOR CHAMPIONSHIP 1995

Senica, Skalica (SVK) · March 25 – 31, 1995

POOL B

Group A	SVK	POL	ITA	AUT	Goals	P
1. Slovakia	■	9:1	7:0	10:1	26: 2	6
2. Poland	1:9	■	9:1	7:5	17:15	4
3. Italy	0:7	1:9	■	5:3	6:19	2
4. Austria	1:10	5:7	3:5	■	9:22	0

Group B	DEN	HUN	FRA	ROM	Goals	P
1. Denmark	■	7:4	6:1	9:3	22: 8	6
2. Hungary	4:7	■	4:4	5:1	13:12	3
3. France	1:6	4:4	■	3:1	8:11	3
4. Rumania	3:9	1:5	1:3	■	5:17	0

The results of the games A1 - A2, A3 - A4, B1 - B2, B3 - B4 in the first three rounds are also counted in deciding the places in the two final divisions.*

Final round

Group A	SVK	POL	DEN	HUN	Goals	P
1. Slovakia	■	9:1*	13:1	19:0	41: 2	6
2. Poland	1:9*	■	6:3	7:3	14:15	4
3. Denmark	1:13	3:6	■	7:4*	11:23	2
4. Hungary	0:19	3:7	4:7*	■	7:33	0

Group A	ITA	FRA	ROM	AUT	Goals	P
5. Italy	■	6:5	9:1	5:3*	20: 9	6
6. France	5:6	■	3:1*	6:2	14: 9	4
7. Rumania	1:9	1:3*	■	5:2	7:14	2
8. Austria	3:5*	2:6	2:5	■	7:16	0

Slovakia promoted to POOL A 1996

Austria relegated to POOL C 1996

SLOVAKIA

Name	Pos	GP	G	A1	A2	Pts	PIM
Denis Buzinkay	D	5	1	0	1	2	4
Andrej Podkonicky	F	5	0	1	0	1	0
Juraj Durco	D	5	3	1	2	6	4
Boris Zabka	D	5	0	2	2	4	6
Peter Barinka	F	5	1	0	1	2	2
Erik Marinov	D	5	0	2	0	2	0
Michal Barto	D	5	1	1	0	2	0
Robert Dome	F	5	7	7	3	17	2
Lubomir Vaic	F	5	6	10	0	16	4
Jiri Bicek	F	5	6	0	1	7	0
Marian Cisar	F	5	8	7	0	15	2
Robert Bucko	D	5	2	2	4	8	0
Martin Cerven	F	5	1	1	1	3	0
Martin Misak	D	5	2	0	0	2	0
Rastislav Pavlikovsky	F	5	8	5	3	16	18
Richard Lintner	D	5	0	0	4	4	2
Rudolf Haluza	F	5	2	3	0	5	6
Michal Handzus	F	5	5	2	1	8	4
Radovan Somik	F	5	0	0	1	1	25
Peter Slamiar	F	5	5	7	1	13	6

Goalkeepers

Name	GP	MIP	GA	GAA	SVS	SVS%
Peter Miksa	5	251	2	0.478	46	95.83
Tomas Kordiak	5	49	1	1.224	4	80.00

POLAND

Name	Pos	GP	G	A1	A2	Pts	PIM
Rafal Piekarski	D	5	0	0	0	0	4
Jaroslav Klys	D	5	1	2	2	5	10
Oktawiusz Marcinczak	D	5	0	0	0	0	0
Mariusz Trzopek	D	5	0	3	0	3	6
Artur Slusarczyk	F	5	1	1	0	2	2
Rafal Selega	F	5	8	3	2	13	0
Robert Suchomski	F	5	0	0	0	0	0
Rafal Twardy	F	5	1	1	0	2	0
Lukasz Gil	F	5	3	4	0	7	8
Pawel Zwolinski	F	5	0	0	0	0	2
Piotor Sermik	F	5	0	1	0	1	0
Bartolomiej Wrobel	F	5	1	0	1	2	2
Jaroslaw Kuc	D	5	0	0	2	2	2
Slawomir Krzak	F	5	2	1	0	3	0
Leszek Laszkiewicz	F	5	2	1	1	4	0
Sebastian Pajerski	F	5	7	5	2	14	4
Rafal Skrtekowski	D	5	0	0	1	1	0
Adam Borzecki	D	5	1	3	0	4	6
Damian Slabon	F	5	0	1	0	1	0
Wojciech Heltman	F	5	3	1	1	5	2

Goalkeepers

Name	GP	MIP	GA	GAA	SVS	SVS%
Lukasz Kiedewicz	5	252	20	4.762	87	81.31
Tomasz Wawrzkiewicz	5	48	1	1.250	22	95.65

AUSTRIA

Name	Pos	GP	G	A1	A2	Pts	PIM
Mark Brabant	D	5	0	0	0	0	0
Andreas Hausner	D	5	0	0	0	0	6
Robert Lukas	D	5	0	0	1	1	2
Roland Steinberger	D	5	1	1	0	2	8
Gerald Penker	D	5	0	0	0	0	2
Michael Bacher	F	5	1	1	0	2	4
Bernhard Austerer	F	5	0	2	1	3	12
Thomas Alfare	D	5	0	0	0	0	2
Jürgen Leitner	D	5	0	0	0	0	12
Andreas Drexler	D	5	0	0	0	0	0
Christof Kothgasser	F	5	0	0	0	0	0
Heimo Lindner	F	5	2	0	0	2	4
Karim Allouche	F	5	1	1	0	2	0
Christoph Gesson	F	5	2	1	0	3	8
Rene Zerlauth	F	5	0	0	0	0	18
Dietmar Reiner	F	5	2	0	0	2	4
Helmut Schlögl	F	5	0	1	1	2	0
Christoph Wutte	F	5	3	0	0	3	8
Martin Pewal	F	5	1	1	0	2	0
Martin Hohenberger	F	5	0	0	0	0	0

Goalkeepers

Name	GP	MIP	GA	GAA	SVS	SVS%
Markus Seidl	5	239	26	6.527	180	87.38
Joerg Strasser	5	60	6	6.000	31	83.78

DENMARK

Name	Pos	GP	G	A1	A2	Pts	PIM
Soren Lykke Jorgensen	D	5	0	0	0	0	10
Rene Henriksen	D	5	0	1	0	1	2
Sascha Ch. Hilfred	D	5	0	0	1	1	2
Nicolai Soegaard	D	5	2	1	1	4	4
Rene Eller	F	5	2	1	1	4	10
Martin Lopdrup	F	5	2	1	1	4	8
Claus Damgaard	F	5	1	1	2	4	4
Kartsen R. Andersen	F	5	1	1	0	2	4
Christian Mourier	F	5	5	1	1	7	8
Morten Skibsted	F	5	3	1	0	4	4
Lasse Degn	F	5	5	1	0	6	0
Mikkel Schmidt	F	5	1	2	1	4	4
Soren Nielsen	F	5	0	1	0	1	0
Michael Thomsen	F	5	2	3	1	6	4
Henrik Borner	F	5	1	5	1	7	8
Mathies Steengaard	F	5	0	0	0	0	6
Kim Staal	F	4	3	3	3	9	0
Erik Johnsen	F	5	0	0	1	1	2

Goalkeepers

Name	GP	MIP	GA	GAA	SVS	SVS%
Mikkel Q. Lund	5	20	6	18	14	70.00
Michael Senderovitz	5	280	21	4.5	177	89.39

FRANCE

Name	Pos	GP	G	A1	A2	Pts	PIM
Christophe Ribanelli	F	5	2	1	0	3	0
Julien Garoux	F	5	0	0	0	0	0
Sebastian Berges	D	5	0	0	0	0	6
Romain Moussier	F	5	1	2	1	4	6
Maxime Boschetti	F	5	1	0	0	1	0
Samuel Laurens	D	5	0	0	0	0	6
Stephen Dugas	F	5	2	1	1	4	0
Romain Carry	F	5	0	1	1	2	6
Brice Bornbal	D	5	1	2	0	3	0
Stephane Hohnadel	F	5	1	2	1	4	2
Thomas Berruex	D	5	0	0	0	0	2
Patrice Tollet	F	5	2	1	0	3	0
Frederic Leveque	F	5	0	0	0	0	4
Loic Sadoun	F	5	1	1	0	2	4
Laurent Fraty	D	5	1	1	0	2	12
Romain Guibet	D	5	0	1	1	2	4
Emmanuel Giusti	F	5	0	1	1	2	4
Christophe Meunier	D	5	0	0	0	0	6
Stephane Ravoire	F	5	2	2	0	4	6
Simon Bachelet	F	5	2	1	0	3	2

Goalkeepers

Name	GP	MIP	GA	GAA	SVS	SVS%
Remy Caillou	5	300	19	3.8	167	89.78
Damien Laurent	5	0	0	0	0	

HUNGARY

Name	Pos	GP	G	A1	A2	Pts	PIM
Zoltan Keszhelyi	D	5	0	0	0	0	4
Bama Czvikovski	D	5	0	0	0	0	14
Botond Gergely	D	5	0	1	0	1	16
Viktor Tokaji	D	5	0	0	0	0	6
Tamas Hegedus	D	5	0	0	0	0	4
Gyorgy Kovacs	F	5	2	0	1	3	2
Attila Hoffmann	F	5	2	1	0	3	4
Adam Tozser	D	5	0	0	0	0	0
Nandor Kocsis	F	5	1	2	0	3	0
Kornel Kovacs	F	5	0	0	2	2	2
Tamas Groschl	F	5	1	1	1	3	4
Miklos Szabo	F	5	0	0	0	0	0
Janos Kaszala	F	5	3	2	0	5	4
Robert Wilcsek	F	5	0	0	0	0	0
Tibor Kiss	F	5	3	0	0	3	0
Gabor Deak	F	5	2	3	0	5	8
Balazs Svab	D	5	1	0	0	1	6
Csaba Gergely	F	5	1	2	1	4	26
Gabor Haluska	F	5	0	0	0	0	0
Zsolt Lajko	D	5	0	0	0	0	0

Goalkeepers

Name	GP	MIP	GA	GAA	SVS	SVS%
Tamas Halmosi	5	260	26	6	210	88.98
Gyula Halsz	5	40	12	18	218	70.00

ITALY

Name	Pos	GP	G	A1	A2	Pts	PIM
Maurizio Schivo	D	5	0	0	0	0	10
Christian Palmosi	D	5	0	0	0	0	0
Roland Pircher	D	5	0	1	0	1	2
Daniele Vegiato	F	5	2	5	0	7	6
Ingemar Gruber	D	5	1	1	0	2	6
Sascha Meneghetti	F	5	0	0	0	0	0
Marco Pellizari	F	5	0	0	0	0	2
Manuel de Toni	F	5	0	2	2	4	4
Martin Gotsch	F	5	0	3	1	4	6
Manuel Demetz	F	5	3	1	0	4	4
Sergio Rigoni	F	5	3	0	0	3	2
Giovanni Volante	F	5	2	2	0	4	8
Davide Mella	F	5	0	1	0	1	4
Andreas Huber	D	5	0	0	0	0	0
Andrea Ralse	F	5	3	0	0	3	2
Patric Lochi	F	5	4	1	0	5	2
Giovanni dal Sasso	F	5	0	0	0	0	2
Omar Pra Floriani	D	5	0	0	0	0	8
Fabrizio Fontanive	F	5	2	1	2	5	4
Niki Cadorin	D	5	1	0	0	1	6

Goalkeepers

Name	GP	MIP	GA	GAA	SVS	SVS%
Daniele Moretti	5	269	24	5.353	165	87.30
David Gislimberti	5	31	1	1.935	15	9375

ROMANIA

Name	Pos	GP	G	A1	A2	Pts	PIM
Robert Antal	D	5	0	1	0	1	2
Laszio Szabo	D	5	0	0	0	1	2
Csaba Miklos	D	5	0	0	0	1	10
Levente Tofan	D	5	1	1	0	2	14
Robert Rusu	F	5	2	0	1	3	2
Lucian Filip	F	5	0	1	0	1	4
Ervin Moldovan	F	5	1	0	1	2	4
Zoltan Bazilides	F	5	0	0	0	0	0
Attila Kovacs	F	5	0	2	0	2	0
Valentin Gherebe	F	4	0	0	0	0	0
Jan A. Palanga	F	5	0	0	0	0	0
Nicolae B. Stoiculescu	D	5	0	1	0	0	2
Jozsef Petres	F	5	2	0	0	2	0
Razvan Lupascu	F	5	0	0	0	0	4
Ferenc Domokos	D	5	0	1	0	1	0
Robert Benedek	F	5	3	1	0	4	2
Tibor Koos	F	5	1	0	0	1	0
Laszio Lazar	D	5	0	0	0	0	0
Tudor Marinescu	F	5	0	0	0	0	0
Csaba Farkas	F	5	1	1	1	3	2

Goalkeepers

Name	GP	MIP	GA	GAA	SVS	SVS%
Szabolcz Molnar	5	267	22	4.943	157	87.70
Horatiu Gurau	5	33	6	10.90	26	81.25

HOCKEY PRODUCTS

production and sale of
hockey jerseys
hockey socks
hockey products / materials
hockey badges
hockey flags
hockey labels
hockey advertisement

Address: Vajnorská 89, 831 04 Bratislava, Slovakia
tel. (+42.7) 271 218 or 272 430 · fax (+42.7) 272 690

EUROPEAN JUNIOR CHAMPIONSHIP 1995

Kiev (UKR) · March 24. – 30., 1995

POOL C
Group 1

	UKR	LAT	SLO	GBR	EST	ESP	Goals	Pts
1. Ukraine		5:2	3:4	8:3	19:2	16:1	51:12	8
2. Latvia	2:5		6:1	5:0	8:0	12:1	33: 7	8
3. Slovenia	4:3	1:6		7:1	9:1	17:0	38:11	8
4. Great Britain	3:8	0:5	1:7		2:1	16:0	22:21	4
5. Estonia	2:19	0:8	1:9	1:2		5:0	9:38	2
6. Spain	1:16	1:12	0:17	0:16	0:5		2:66	0

Ukraine promoted to POOL B 1996

Winner of the FAIR PLAY CUP:
Estonia

Best player by teams

UKR	Oleg Krikuonenko	F
LAT	Igors Novoselcev	F
SLO	Milan Hafner	CE
GBR	Richard Grubb	GK
EST	Alar Tooming	GK
ESP	Salvador Barnola	CE

The best player of each team received a **SEIKO** watch.

UKRAINE

Name	Pos	GP	G	A	Pts	PIM
Vasil Polonitskiy	RD	5	4	6	10	2
Dmitri Tolkounov	RD	4	0	0	0	6
Mikhail Grichin	RD	4	1	1	2	2
Sergei Revenko	D	5	2	3	5	0
Andrei Grichtchenko	LD	4	0	1	1	0
Sergei Dechevyi	RD	5	0	1	1	2
Hipolit Gorokhov	LW	4	3	1	4	0
Ivan Benevelski	RW	4	4	1	5	2
Serguei Radchenko	C	5	1	4	5	14
Andrei Bakoumenko	C	5	4	7	11	2
Oleg Krikunenko	RW	5	7	6	13	10
Vladislav Lisovenko	LD	5	1	1	2	6
Pavel Gomeniouk	RW	5	2	6	8	14
Jouri Gorulko	C	5	1	1	2	6
Alexandre Zinevitch	LW	5	5	2	7	12
Andrei Lupandin	RW	5	3	1	4	16
Andrei Scherbakov	F	5	6	2	8	4
Oleg Tsirkounov	RW	5	4	2	6	0
Alexandr Jakovenko	C	5	2	2	4	2
Serguei Sadii	LD	5	1	1	2	2

Goalkeeper

Name	GP	MIN	GA	PIM
Alexandre Fedorov	5	155	10	0
Oleg Martynov	5	137	2	0

LATVIA

Name	Pos	GP	G	A	Pts	PIM
Vents Feldmanis	LD	5	4	2	6	2
Dmitrijs Derjabins	LW	4	0	1	1	0
Vjaceslav Klujevskijs	F	5	0	2	2	12
Juris Drilins	F	5	3	0	3	0
Janis Vegners	F	4	1	1	2	0
Konstantin Kovanskijs	F	5	1	1	2	0
Igors Novoselcev	F	5	6	2	8	14
Vadims Romanovskijs	F	5	2	2	4	12
Romans Nikitins	F	5	3	3	6	6
Aleksejs Maslenko	D	5	1	2	3	10
Martins Lans	RD	5	1	2	3	6
Vadims Teluskins	LD	5	0	0	0	0
Arvids Rekis	LD	5	3	2	5	8
Vadim Korneev	RW	2	0	2	2	0
Ilgvars Broks	LW	3	0	1	1	0
Karlis Zirnis	LD	3	2	2	4	10
Vitalij Galuzo	F	5	4	5	9	4
Andrejs Utans	RD	5	0	0	0	10
Sergei Kocetov	C	3	1	2	3	0
Rihards Augstkalns	LW	5	1	2	3	0

Goalkeeper

Name	GP	MIN	GA	PIM
Edvins Silavnieks	5	160	5	0
Helmuts Eglitis	5	140	2	0

SLOVENIA

Name	Pos	GP	G	A	Pts	PIM
Goran Petronijevic	RD	5	1	1	2	4
Anze Obersnel	RD	5	1	1	2	6
Gasper Sekelj	RD	5	0	0	0	6
Ziga Mirtic	LD	5	1	3	4	0
Jaka Adlesic	LD	3	0	1	1	4
Miha Rebolj	LD	5	4	1	5	22
Milan Hafner	C	5	3	1	4	8
Matija Lepsa	LW	5	2	0	2	2
Gregor Por	LW	5	3	4	7	22
Dejan Kalan	LW	5	3	1	4	6
Mitja Brgant	C	5	1	1	2	6
Luka Zagar	RW	4	4	2	6	2
Boris Pretnar	LW	5	3	1	4	2
Uros Jakopic	LW	5	1	3	4	4
Gorazd Rekelj	LD	3	0	0	0	0
Urban Lajevec	C	5	3	2	5	4
Gregor Branc	RD	5	0	0	0	0
Miha Vesel	RW	4	0	0	0	12
Denis Marincic	C	3	4	2	6	2
Saso Divjak	RW	5	4	4	8	6

Goalkeeper

Name	GP	MIN	GA	PIM
Gaber Glavic	5	60	1	4
Ales Petronijevic	5	240	10	0

UNITED KINGDOM

Name	Pos	GP	G	A	Pts	PIM
Lee Brathwaite	D	5	0	0	0	14
Jack Waghorn	D	5	1	3	4	6
Michael Knights	D	5	1	2	3	6
Wayne Maxwell	D	5	0	0	0	8
Neil Liddiard	D	5	1	1	2	24
Laurie Dunbar	F	5	0	0	0	4
James Manson	D	5	0	2	2	12
Scott Heaton	D	3	0	0	0	2
John Robertson	D	5	0	0	0	20
Gary Clarke	F	3	0	0	0	4
William Downes	F	5	2	2	4	6
Jonathan Weaver	F	5	7	3	10	10
Grant Bailey	F	5	0	0	0	2
Andrew Holmes	F	5	4	1	5	2
Paul Miller	F	3	0	0	0	2
Thomas Watkins	F	5	0	1	1	6
Richard Plant	F	5	1	0	1	6
Mark Galazzi	F	3	3	3	6	2
Andrew Finlay	F	3	2	0	2	2
Fraser Gilfillan	F	3	0	1	1	0

Goalkeeper

Name	GP	MIN	GA	PIM
Joseph Watkins	5	60	7	0
Richard Grubb	5	240	14	2

ESTONIA

Name	Pos	GP	G	A	Pts	PIM
Dmitri Rumjantsev	D	5	0	0	0	20
Stanislav Pankov	D	5	0	0	0	2
Vassill Makrov	F	5	0	0	0	18
Urmas Valge	D	1	0	0	0	0
Sergei Tulzakov	F	5	0	0	0	6
Aleksei Harkov	F	5	1	0	1	2
Rene Valge	D	4	0	2	2	0
Leonid Senjuk	D	5	0	0	0	2
Deniss Soldatenko	F	4	0	0	0	0
Veiko Syvaoja	F	4	1	0	1	4
Andrus Pihlak	F	5	2	0	2	0
Andrei Makrov	F	5	2	0	2	2
Andrei Heitkov	F	4	0	0	0	0
Ilja Sevelilov	F	5	0	1	1	0
Dmitri Raskidajev	F	4	3	0	3	10
Vladimir Tsernetsov	D	5	0	0	0	2
Vitali Kirtjanov	D	5	0	1	1	6
Lauri Lahesalu	F	5	0	0	0	2

Goalkeeper

Name	GP	MIN	GA	PIM
Alar Tooming	5	197	28	0
Aleksandr Sustov	5	103	10	0

SPAIN

Name	Pos	GP	G	A	Pts	PIM
Fernandez J. Perellon	CE	5	0	0	0	6
Yon Arbizu	D	4	0	0	0	4
Jose Antonio Biec	W	5	0	0	0	24
Alain Arteaga	D	5	0	0	0	2
Salvador Barnola	CE	5	0	0	0	0
Nicolas Sanchez-Osorio	D	5	0	0	0	2
Inigo Aranzabal	W	4	0	0	0	2
Ivan Codina	CE	5	1	0	1	22
Marc Codina	CE	5	0	0	0	35
Martinez Jaime Castell	C	5	0	0	0	6
Valdeano Aitor de Garcia	CE	5	1	0	1	4
Ivan Anglada	CE	5	0	0	0	2
Jordi Bernet	W	5	0	0	0	2
Guillermo Lope	W	5	0	1	1	6
Sergio Valles	D	3	0	0	0	2
Patricio Aspero	D	5	0	0	0	6
Daniel Hilario	D	5	0	0	0	10

Goalkeeper

Name	GP	MIN	GA	PIM
Roger Navales	5	80	23	0
Angel Javier Marin	5	220	43	2

EUROPEAN JUNIOR CHAMPIONSHIP 1995

Elektrenai (LIT) · March 11. – 17., 1995

POOL C

Group 2

Group A	NED	YUG	BUL	Goals	P
1. Netherlands		6:4	7:2	13: 6	4
2. Yugoslavia	4:6		6:3	10: 9	2
3. Bulgaria	2:7	3:6		5:13	0

Group A	LIT	CRO	NED	YUG	Goals	P
1. Lithuania		4:3*	4:2	8:3	16: 8	6
2. Croatia	3:4*		4:1	8:4	15: 9	4
3. Netherlands	2:4	1:4		6:4*	9:12	2
4. Yugoslavia	3:8	4:8	4:6*		11:22	0

Lithuania and Croatia promoted to Pool C 1996

Group B	LIT	CRO	ISR	TUR	Goals	P
1. Lithuania		4:3	14:2	39:0	57: 5	6
2. Croatia	3:4		9:0	37:0	49: 4	4
3. Israel	2:14	0:9		15:1	17:24	2
4. Turkey	0:39	0:37	1:15		1:19	0

	ISR	BUL	TUR	Goals	P
5. Israel		5:2	15:1*	20: 3	4
6. Bulgaria	2:5		20:2	22: 7	2
7. Turkey	1:15*	2:20		3:35	0

The results of the games A1-A2, B1-B2, B3-B4 in the first 2 resp. 3 rounds are also counted in deciding the places in the two final divisions.*

Winner of the FAIR PLAY CUP
Bulgaria

Best player by teams

LTU	Egidijus Bauba	F
CRO	Mato Mladenovic	LW
NED	Robert van Laarhoven	D
YUG	Jovica Rus	F
ISR	Ran Oz	D
BUL	Atanas Masliankov	F
TUR	Koray Bakir	RW

The best player
of each team received a **SEIKO** watch.

Best player of the tournament

Best goalkeeper	Miran Spiljak	CRO
Best defender	Ran Oz	ISR
Best forward	Mato Mladenovic	CRO
Best scorer	Egidijus Bauba	LTU

LITHUANIA

Name	Pos	GP	G	A	Pts	PIM
Andrei Kibickij	D	3	0	0	0	0
Aleksey Kondratjev	D	5	0	1	1	0
Titas Bertasius	F	5	1	0	1	2
Raimondas Strimaitis	F	3	1	1	2	0
Darius Pliskauskas	F	5	3	0	3	8
Sergej Drozdov	D	3	0	1	1	2
Egidijus Bauba	F	5	15	13	28	14
Andrej Klimovec	F	5	3	5	8	0
Andrius Jankauskas	F	5	0	0	0	0
Darius Janusonis	D	4	0	0	0	4
Oleg Sibaev	F	5	3	0	3	4
Sergej Jakuta	D	5	3	2	5	12
Vitalij Zencenko	F	4	3	3	6	0
Sergej Kovalenko	D	4	0	1	1	0
Tomas Jasinevicius	F	4	0	1	1	0
Tomas Vysniauskas	D	5	0	1	1	9
Martinas Slikas	F	5	13	8	21	10
Aleksandr Zaicev	F	5	5	5	10	4
Sarunas Kuliesius	F	5	10	8	18	12
Tomas Kaminskas	F	5	9	1	10	4

Goalkeeper Name	GP	MIN	GA	PIM
Arunas Aleinikovas	5	240	10	4
Aleksej Budvitis	5	60	0	0

BULGARIA

Name	Pos	GP	G	A	Pts	PIM
Gueorgui Kehayov	D	2	0	0	0	2
Vesselin Karaivanov	F	4	1	2	3	4
Martin Milanov	F	4	8	3	11	0
Stanish Stoichkov	D	4	0	0	0	0
Svetoslav Sotirov	D	3	2	0	2	0
Kiril Makaveev	F	4	1	1	2	0
Ilian Tzvetanov	F	4	6	5	11	2
Detelin Spassov	F	4	1	0	1	0
Atanas Masliankov	F	4	2	5	7	4
Anton Tzltzelkov	F	3	1	0	1	0
Tzvetan Tzvetanov	D	4	1	1	2	14
Kalin Mihailov	D	4	1	0	1	4
Pavlin Kostadinov	F	4	1	2	3	0
Dimitar Dimitrov	F	1	2	1	3	0

Goalkeeper

Name	GP	MIN	GA	PIM
Iovo Stefanov	4	210	18	0
Boyko Shalganov	4	30	2	0

NETHERLANDS

Name	Pos	GP	G	A	Pts	PIM
Robert van der Linden	D	3	0	0	0	0
Carl van Neer	D	2	0	0	0	0
Martien van den Berg	D	4	1	0	1	8
Wesley M. de Bruijn	F	4	1	1	2	2
Patrick Engels	D	3	0	0	0	0
Addy Kroeze	F	4	1	1	2	0
Nico Harmes	D	4	1	0	1	2
Peter Hennekens	F	4	0	0	0	0
Dennis ten Bokkel	F	3	2	0	2	4
Rob Delcliseur	F	4	1	1	2	0
Casper Oosterman		4	0	1	1	2
Jean-P. van der Weide	F	4	4	0	4	2
Maarten Polkamp	F	3	1	1	2	8
Dennis Fredriks	F	3	1	2	3	2
Alf Phillippen	F	0	0	0	0	0
Dennis van Dijk	D	4	1	0	1	2
Robin P. de Vroede	F	3	2	0	2	2
Arjan Peters	D	3	0	0	0	0
Robert van Laarhoven	D	4	0	0	0	2

Goalkeeper

Name	GP	MIN	GA	PIM
Jan Kiers	4	60	4	0
Dennis van Gool	4	180	10	0

YUGOSLAVIA

Name	Pos	GP	G	A	Pts	PIM
Viktor Mirnic	D	4	0	0	0	4
Goran Pavlovic	D	4	0	1	1	8
Jovica Rus	F	4	4	3	7	6
Marko Karanfilov	D	1	0	0	0	0
Igor Polkovnikov	F	4	2	0	2	6
Matija Kurek	D	2	0	0	0	2
Ivan Temunovic	D	4	0	0	0	0
Goran Durutovic	F	4	0	1	1	0
Uros Banovic	D	4	0	0	0	4
Ivan Brkic	D	2	0	0	0	2
Dejan Pavicevic	F	4	4	1	5	2
Misa Ramadan	F	3	0	0	0	6
Damir Rudinski	F	4	0	1	1	0
Predrag Jokovic	F	2	0	0	0	0
Uros Brestovac	F	4	2	2	4	10
Svetozar Mijin	F	2	1	0	1	0
Srdjan Ristic	F	4	0	1	1	0
Blagoje Veljkovic	D	4	1	1	2	4
Ivan Jovanovic	F	3	0	0	0	25
Boris Danon	F	4	3	0	3	4

Goalkeeper

Name	GP	MIN	GA	PIM
Tihomir Zecevic	4	98	14	0
Marko Nicolic	4	142	11	0

ISRAEL

Name	Pos	GP	G	A	Pts	PIM
Nadan Evan	D	4	0	0	0	6
Simon Levine	D	4	0	0	0	4
Eitan Adler	F	2	0	0	0	2
Eran Gilvarg	D	3	0	0	0	0
Ran Oz	D	4	4	0	4	6
Mark Josef	F	4	2	1	3	10
Guy Peled	F	4	0	1	1	0
Roy Cohen	F	4	0	0	0	2
Bryan Freidman	F	4	5	1	6	8
Jason Goldberg	D	4	0	0	0	12
Omri Lamm	F	4	3	0	3	4
Uriel Haran	D	4	0	0	0	2
Jason Elliot Shiff	F	4	4	3	7	10
Eli Oosterhuis	F	4	2	1	3	12
Yaron Orgil	F	4	1	3	4	0
Saai Luxemburg	F	3	0	0	0	0
Dotan Lamm	F	2	0	0	0	0
Assaf Evron	F	4	1	1	2	27
Idan Levin	D	2	0	0	0	0

Goalkeeper

Name	GP	MIN	GA	PIM
Aviv Gleeck	4	240	26	2
Sergei Ostrovski	4	0	0	0

CROATIA

Name	Pos	GP	G	A	Pts	PIM
Drazen Svetina	RW	5	2	2	4	0
Marko Sertic	LD	2	0	0	0	2
Silvio Erakovic	LD	5	2	0	2	6
Danijel Grubjesic	LD	5	2	0	2	4
Kresimir Svigir	LW	3	1	1	2	0
Ivan Spajic	RD	3	0	0	0	0
Marko Bujanovic	RD	1	1	3	4	2
Dean Volic	CE	5	8	5	13	2
Marijo Brcic	RW	5	10	3	13	8
Luka Zuk	LW	3	2	0	2	2
Veljko Zibret	RW	5	4	2	6	6
Vedran Zidanic	RD	4	0	3	3	2
Jurica Marinovic	LD	0	0	0	0	0
Ozren Jelenek	RD	4	0	0	0	2
Vedran Celegin	LW	3	2	5	7	0
Mato Mladenovic	LW	5	15	5	20	4
Dalibor Franjkovic	LW	1	0	0	0	0
Domagoj Radin	CE	5	5	3	8	4
Marko Lasic	CE	3	2	0	2	4
Ozren Kaic	RW	5	5	3	8	0

Goalkeeper

Name	GP	MIN	GA	PIM
Miran Spiljak	5	280	9	0
Nader Kire	5	20	0	0

TURKEY

Name	Pos	GP	G	A	Pts	PIM
Rizatur Gut Gencer	D	4	0	0	0	10
Memet Tekmen	RD	4	1	0	1	12
Ali Sezgin	RW	4	0	0	0	0
Onur Ozmen	FW	4	0	0	0	2
Yucel Citak	FW	4	0	0	0	0
Cem Bursali	LD	4	0	0	0	14
Onur Yuncu	FW	4	0	0	0	2
Ogan Kokgil	FW	4	1	0	1	0
Selim Gursan	D	4	0	0	0	0
Coskun Olcer	D	4	0	0	0	16
Ekin Niksarli	FW	4	0	0	0	0
Koray Bakir	RW	4	1	0	1	31
Serhat Altinci	D	4	0	0	0	2
Batuhan Tufan	RW	4	0	0	0	2
Kutay Aldanmaz	FW	4	0	0	0	0
Gorhan Basan	PW	4	0	0	0	4
Ahmet Sesigurgil	C	4	0	0	0	2

Goalkeeper

Name	GP	MIN	GA	PIM
Cem Tuncel	4	144	48	2
Omer Aybers	4	96	63	0

Ich bi zfride mit der WAADT

Generalagentur Zürich-Ost
Stampfenbachstr. 40, 8023 Zürich
Tel. 01/365 31 11
Fax 01/365 32 33
Meinrad Mader, Generalagent

WAADT VERSICHERUNGEN

sichert Zufriedenheit

ASIAN/OCEANIA JUNIOR CHAMPIONSHIP 1995
March 20. – 23., 1995 · Obihiro (JPN)

	JPN	KAZ	CHN	KOR	Goals	Pts
1. Japan		5:2	7:0	2:5	14: 7	4
2. Kazakhstan	2:5		6:1	7:4	15:10	4
3. China	0:7	1:6		5:3	6:16	2
4. Korea	5:2	4:7	3:5		12:14	2

JAPAN

Name	Pos	GP	G	A	Pts	PIM
Kiyohide Chiba	GK	3	0	0	0	0
Michio Hashimoto	GK	3	0	0	0	0
Kazuyoshi Yamaguchi	DF	3	1	1	2	8
Yasuhito Minobe	DF	3	0	0	0	2
Shinji Kishibe	DF	3	0	2	2	2
Masahisa Nishiguchi	DF	3	0	0	0	4
Takayuki Yoshimoto	DF	3	0	0	0	0
Masaya Kyouzuka	DF	3	0	1	1	2
Sakae Kawaguchi	DF	3	0	0	0	4
Ryouhei Sasoya	FW	3	2	4	6	2
Manabu Kitamura	FW	3	0	0	0	0
Masanori Kaneko	FW	3	0	1	1	0
Tomohiro Miura	FW	3	0	0	0	2
Yuu Yamano	FW	3	4	1	5	2
Yuu Yamamoto	FW	3	1	3	4	0
Keiji Sasaki	FW	3	0	1	1	2
Naoto Yoshida	FW	3	1	2	3	0
Norihiko Odaira	FW	3	0	0	0	0
Koutaro Kanou	FW	3	2	0	2	4
Shuhei Tadamura	FW	3	3	2	5	2

CHINA

Name	Pos	GP	G	A	Pts	PIM
Guicheng Wang	GK	3	0	0	0	2
Ligang Wang	GK	3	0	0	0	0
Feng Zheng	DF	3	0	0	0	2
Lei Liu	DF	3	1	0	1	8
Dahai Wang	DF	3	0	0	0	2
Yu Wang	DF	3	0	0	0	4
Lei Zhang	FW	3	3	0	3	4
Nan Wang	FW	3	0	0	0	0
Yao Xu	FW	3	1	1	2	2
Dong Mao	FW	3	0	0	0	0
Dahai Xu	FW	3	1	0	1	6
Chuanxing Jia	FW	3	0	0	0	2
Bingyue Chen	DF	3	0	0	0	0
Chunlei Zhao	DF	3	0	0	0	2
Liang Zhao	FW	3	0	0	0	2
Lei Yang	DF	3	0	0	0	2
Xiaowu Guo	FW	3	0	0	0	2
Hongtao Shi	FW	3	0	0	0	2
Haiyu Wang	FW	3	0	0	0	0

KAZAKHSTAN

Name	Pos	GP	G	A	Pts	PIM
Serguei Ogourechnikov	GK	3	0	0	0	0
Viatcheslav Tregoubov	GK	3	0	0	0	0
Roman Chekhtman	DF	3	0	0	0	4
Evgueni Kozlov	FW	3	0	0	0	8
Maxim Polkovnikov	DF	3	0	0	0	0
Serguei Aleksandrov	FW	3	2	1	3	0
Roman Fadine	FW	3	2	2	4	10
Salim Prmanov	FW	3	2	1	3	2
Igor Kamenski	DF	3	2	0	2	0
Alexandre Pokladov	FW	3	2	2	4	0
Evgueni Liapounov	FW	3	0	0	0	2
Ivan Peltek	DF	3	0	0	0	10
Viatcheslav Zemskov	FW	3	2	2	4	4
Denis Leonov	FW	3	0	0	0	0
Serik Toussoupbekov	FW	3	2	0	2	4
Nikolai Deviatkin	DF	3	0	2	2	2
Evgueni Ivanov	FW	3	0	2	2	2

KOREA

Name	Pos	GP	G	A	Pts	PIM
Dae-Gun Oh	GK	3	0	0	0	0
Sung-Min Kim	GK	3	0	0	0	2
Young-Ho Choi	FW	3	0	0	0	0
Tae-Hee Kim	DF	3	0	0	0	6
Sang-Woo Song	FW	3	1	1	2	2
Young-Tae Kwon	FW	3	0	1	1	0
Seung-Jae Lee	FW	3	1	2	3	10
Kwang-Suk Seo	FW	3	0	0	0	4
Young-Bae Park	DF	3	1	0	1	4
Ho-Jung Lee	FW	3	6	0	6	4
Seung-Ik Shin	DF	3	1	0	1	0
Sung-Ho Park	DF	3	0	0	0	0
Shin-Il Choi	DF	3	0	4	4	2
Tae-Wan Kim	FW	3	1	0	1	4
Young-Do Kim	FW	3	0	0	0	0
Jong-Moon Chang	DF	3	1	1	2	0
Tae-Hyun Kim	DF	3	0	0	0	0
Se-Hwan Park	DF	3	0	0	0	0
Seung-Hoon Baek	FW	3	0	0	0	2
Wan-Sub Kim	FW	3	0	0	0	0

EUROPEAN WOMEN'S CHAMPIONSHIP 1995

POOL A

Riga (LAT) · March 20. – 25, 1995

	FIN	SWE	SUI	NOR	GER	LAT	Goals	Pts
1. Finland		9:0	10:0	12:0	13:2	17:0	61: 2	10
2. Sweden	0:9		7:0	5:0	7:1	8:0	27:10	8
3. Switzerland	0:10	0:7		2:0	6:2	3:1	11:20	6
4. Norway	0:12	0:5	0:2		5:1	2:0	7:20	4
5. Germany	2:13	1:7	2:6	1:5		5:4	11:35	2
6. Latvia	0:17	0:8	1:3	0:2	4:5		5:35	0

Latvia relegated to POOL B 1996

Top scorers

	Name	Team	GP	G	A	Pts
1.	Nieminen	FIN	5	8	13	21
2.	Reima	FIN	5	7	7	14
3.	Krooks	FIN	5	6	8	14
4.	Ihalainen	FIN	5	6	6	12
5.	Lehtimäki	FIN	5	7	3	10
6.	Hänninen	FIN	5	3	7	10
7.	Vaarakallio	FIN	5	6	3	9
8.	Fisk	FIN	5	6	3	9
9.	Valenti	GER	5	5	3	8
10.	Almblad	SWE	5	5	2	7

FINLAND

Pos	Name	GP	G	A	Pts	PIM
GK	Tuula Puputti	2	0	0	0	0
GK	Kati Ahonen	3	0	0	0	0
D	Katri-Helena Luomajoki	5	0	0	0	2
D	Päivi Halonen	5	2	1	1	2
D	Katja Lehto	3	0	1	1	2
D	Satu Huotari	5	1	3	4	8
D	Kirsi Hänninen	5	3	7	10	4
D	Anne Haanpää	5	3	3	6	0
D	Niina Siren	5	0	1	1	0
F	Marianne Ihalainen	5	6	6	12	0
F	Sanna Kanerva	5	1	0	1	0
F	Rose Matilainen	5	2	5	7	4
F	Riikka Nieminen	5	8	13	21	2
F	Sari Fisk	5	6	3	9	2
F	Tiia Reima	5	7	7	14	6
F	Marika Lehtimäki	5	7	3	10	0
F	Sari Krooks	5	6	8	14	2
F	Petra Vaarakallio	5	6	3	9	0
F	Anna Aaltomaa	4	1	0	1	0
F	Kati Kovalainen	5	3	4	7	2

SWEDEN

Pos	Name	GP	G	A	Pts	PIM
GK	Lotta Gothesson	3	0	0	0	0
GK	Annica Ahlen	3	0	0	0	0
D	Asa Lidstrom	5	0	0	0	16
D	Pia Morelius	5	1	1	2	4
D	Ann-Sofie Gustafsson	5	2	0	2	4
D	Minna Dunder	5	0	1	1	6
D	Pernilla Burholm	5	0	0	0	8
D	Anne Ferm	5	3	1	4	0
D	Gunilla Andersson	5	1	1	2	0
F	Annika Eriksson	5	1	1	2	2
F	Erika Holst	5	2	0	2	4
F	Malin Persson	4	1	0	1	0
F	Marie Nordgren	4	0	1	1	0
F	Yilva Lindberg	5	1	0	1	0
F	Kristina Bergstrand	5	1	1	2	0
F	Lotta Almblad	5	5	2	7	4
F	Camilla Kempe	5	3	2	5	2
F	Äsa Elfving	5	1	4	5	2
F	Tina Mänsson	5	5	1	6	0
F	Ann-Louise Edstrand	4	0	0	0	2

LATVIA

Pos	Name	GP	G	A	Pts	PIM
GK	Lolita Andrisevska	5	0	0	0	0
GK	Amanda Apsite	2	0	0	0	0
D	Inese Geca	5	0	0	0	6
D	Zane Valdmane	5	0	0	0	10
D	Eva Dinsberga	5	0	0	0	2
D	Sintija Rukmane	1	0	0	0	0
D	Aija Balode	5	2	0	2	8
D	Ingrida Zambare	1	0	0	0	2
D	Aija Sakne	5	0	0	0	8
F	Laila Dekmeijere	5	0	1	1	2
F	Iveta Koks	5	0	1	1	0
F	Adrija Radzina	5	0	0	0	2
F	Anna Verhoustinska	5	0	0	0	0
F	Baiba Liepina	5	0	1	1	4
F	Liene Letinska	3	0	0	0	0
F	Solvita Melne	5	0	1	1	4
F	Inguna Lukasevica	5	2	0	2	2
F	Jelena Lavrenova	4	0	0	0	4
F	Linda Kalnina	3	0	0	0	2
F	Jana Gerkena	5	1	0	1	2

SWITZERLAND

Pos	Name	GP	G	A	Pts	PIM
GK	Sabine Schumacher	2	0	0	0	0
GK	Patricia Sautter	5	0	0	0	0
D	Jacqueline Mischler	4	0	0	0	2
D	Mireille Nöthiger	5	0	1	1	6
D	Prisca Mosimann	5	0	0	0	4
D	Mirjam Baechler	5	0	0	0	4
D	Gillian Jeannottat	5	0	0	0	4
D	Monika Leuenberger	5	0	1	1	8
F	Ruth Künzle	5	2	0	2	4
F	Rachel Wild	4	0	0	0	2
F	Jeanette Marty	5	0	3	3	10
F	Ramona Fuhrer	5	0	1	1	2
F	Ursula Walther	5	0	0	0	4
F	Doris Wyss	5	1	2	3	6
F	Michaela Keusch	4	0	0	0	2
F	Kathrin Lehmann	5	1	1	2	0
F	Sandra Cattaneo	5	3	1	4	0
F	Regula Müller	5	1	0	1	0
F	Edith Enzler	5	3	2	5	6

NORWAY

Pos	Name	GP	G	A	Pts	PIM
GK	Hege Moe	5	0	0	0	0
GK	Linda Brunborg	4	0	1	1	0
D	Sissel Bruvik	5	0	0	0	2
D	Vibeke Lærum	4	0	0	0	0
D	Hege Haugen	5	0	0	0	4
D	Jeanette Giørtz	5	0	2	2	2
D	Birgitte Lersbryggen	5	1	0	1	0
D	Anne Meisingset	5	0	0	0	6
F	Kari-Ann Nilsen	4	0	0	0	0
F	Ingvild Øversveen	3	0	0	0	2
F	Inger Lise Fagernes	5	1	2	3	2
F	Marianne Dahlstrøm	5	1	1	2	2
F	Christin Smerud	4	0	0	0	4
F	Heidi Flølo	3	0	0	0	0
F	Jeanette Hansen	5	0	0	0	8
F	Lena Bergersen	5	0	0	0	6
F	Tonje Larsen	5	2	0	2	6
F	Camilla Hille	5	1	0	1	6
F	Unn Haugen	5	0	0	0	8
F	Aina Høve	5	1	0	1	2

GERMANY

Pos	Name	GP	G	A	Pts	PIM
GK	Stephanie Kürten	4	0	0	0	0
GK	Aurelia Vonderstraß	3	0	0	0	0
RD	Anja Merkel	5	0	0	0	12
RD	Nicole Schmitten	5	0	0	0	0
LD	Bettina Aumüller	5	0	1	1	4
LD	Nina Linde	5	0	0	0	2
RD	Sabine Kürten	5	2	0	2	4
LD	Sonja Kuisle	5	0	0	0	4
LW	Patricia Austin	5	0	0	0	0
C	Sandra Kürten	5	0	0	0	2
C	Silvia Schneegans	5	0	0	0	2
LW	Nadine Kirchner	4	0	0	0	0
RW	Natascha Schaffrik	5	1	2	3	0
LW	Alexandra Schulz	5	0	0	0	8
RW	Maritta Becker	5	1	2	3	2
RW	Stefanie Pütz	5	1	0	1	2
C	Iris Heußen	5	0	0	0	4
C	Christine Oswald	5	1	3	4	6
RW	Corinna Pelant	5	0	0	0	2
LW	Maren Valenti	5	5	3	8	10

EUROPEAN WOMEN'S CHAMPIONSHIP 1995

Odense and Esbjerg (DEN) · March 27. – 31., 1995

POOL B

Group A	DEN	SVK	NED	GBR	Goals	P
1. Denmark	■	3:1	6:0	14:1	23: 2	6
2. Slovakia	1:3	■	4:4	4:1	9: 8	3
3. Netherlands	0:6	4:4	■	7:2	11:12	3
4. Great Britain	1:14	1:4	2:7	■	4:25	0

Group B	RUS	CZE	FRA	UKR	Goals	P
1. Russia	■	8:1	15:0	14:0	37: 1	6
2. Czech Republic	1:8	■	7:2	7:1	15:11	4
3. France	0:15	2:7	■	7:1	9:23	2
4. Ukraine	0:14	1:7	1:7	■	2:28	0

Finals

Place 7/8	Great Britain	– Ukraine	2:0
Place 5/6	France	– Netherlands	4:3
Place 3/4	Czech Republic	– Slovakia	7:1
Place 1/2	Russia	– Denmark	4:0

Russia promoted to POOL A 1996

Winner of the FAIR PLAY CUP: Finland

Best players of the tournament

Best goalkeeper	Patricia Sautter	SUI
Best defender	Gunilla Andersson	SWE
Best forward	Sari Krooks	FIN
Best scorer	Hanna-Riikka Nieminen	FIN

Top scorer

	Name	Team	G	A	P
1.	Ekaterina Pashkevich	RUS	5	14	19
2.	Tatiana Tsareva	RUS	8	4	12
3.	Zuzanne Kralova	CZE	8	2	10
4.	Tine Perry	DEN	4	6	10
5.	Larisa Mishina	RUS	6	2	8
6.	Svetlana Gavrilova	RUS	5	3	8
7.	Katja Moesgaard	DEN	4	4	8
8.	Lyudmila Yurlova	RUS	3	4	7
9.	Milena Trckova	CZE	3	3	6
10.	Saskia Admiraal	NED	2	3	5

DENMARK

Name	G	A	Pts	PIM
Jannie Madsen	1	2	3	2
Sussi Hansen	2	0	2	0
Susanne Hougaard	3	1	4	0
Christina Palsmar	0	0	0	2
Anne Mette Nedergaard	0	0	0	2
Betina Johnsen	0	0	0	2
Sofie Lund	0	2	2	0
Julie Hansen	0	1	1	0
Susan Gregersen	0	1	1	8
Linda Jensen	0	0	0	6
Lene Christensen	1	1	2	6
Tine Perry	4	6	10	2
Katja Moesgaard	4	4	8	2
Annie Dahlmann	0	1	1	0
Dorte Schäffer	2	2	4	0
Henriette Jensen	4	0	4	0
Connie Jørgensen	0	0	0	0
Lene Rasmussen	0	0	0	0
Helle Ejstrup	1	0	1	0
Lise Christensen	0	0	0	0

RUSSIA

Name	G	A	Pts	PIM
Irena Votintseva	0	0	0	0
Maria Misropian	1	0	1	4
Lyudmila Krechetnikova	1	1	2	6
Elena Osipova	0	3	3	2
Yulia Perova	3	0	3	2
Elena Rodikova	0	0	0	2
Natalia Kozlova	1	1	2	4
Svetlana Makukhina	1	1	2	2
Yulia Voronina	1	0	1	2
Svevtlana Trefilova	1	2	3	2
Zhanna Scelchkova	3	1	4	2
Svetlana Nikolaeva	0	1	1	0
Larisa Mishina	6	2	8	0
Elena Oreshkina	2	0	2	6
Svetlana Gavrilova	5	3	8	2
Tatiana Tsareva	8	4	12	2
Lyudmila Yurlova	3	4	7	0
Irena Gahennikova	0	0	0	0
Irena Shumskaya	0	0	0	0
Ekaterina Pashkevich	5	14	19	4

CZECH REPUBLIC

Name	G	A	Pts	PIM
Hana Tahlova	3	2	5	4
Martina Vankova	0	0	0	0
Marcela Mannova	1	0	1	0
Andrea Dedicova	0	0	0	0
Milena Trckova	3	3	6	0
Hana Fridrmucova	0	1	1	2
Iveta Zieglerova	0	0	0	0
Lenka Smidova	1	0	1	0
Gabriela Müllerova	1	0	1	6
Hana Hofrichtrova	0	0	0	0
Martina Zrala	0	0	0	0
Iva Mastalirova	1	2	3	0
Dagmar Danihelkova	0	0	0	0
Vera Sladkova	0	0	0	6
Klara Quagliatova	2	1	3	0
Jana Dubnova	0	0	0	0
Eva Sterbova	0	0	0	8
Zuzanne Kralova	8	2	10	4
Drahomira Fialova	1	2	3	0
Dagmar Adamcikova	1	1	2	0
Slavena Smetakova	0	0	0	0

SLOVAKIA

Name	G	A	Pts	PIM
Bernadetta Decova	0	0	0	0
Zuzana Zetkova	0	0	0	0
Lucia Petrovicova	0	1	1	10
Ivana Pjatakova	0	0	0	2
Andrea Prochazkova	1	0	1	6
Andrea Badikova	0	1	1	6
Nina Vondrakova	0	1	1	6
Bozena Kevesova	0	1	1	8
Nada Kotykova	1	0	1	6
Slavka Kollarova	0	0	0	4
Danica Zahradnikova	2	1	3	2
Marcela Lukacsova	2	0	2	6
Andrea Pribisova	0	0	0	0
Denisa Schimplova	0	1	1	2
Zuzana Malachova	0	1	1	4
Andrea Suchankova	1	1	2	2
Slavka Karolyova	2	1	3	4
Maria Zemiakova	1	1	2	4
Petra Borikova	0	0	0	4
Monoka Demitrova	0	0	0	4

FRANCE

Name	G	A	Pts	PIM
Aurore Caulet	0	0	0	0
Angela Lezziero	0	1	1	2
Carole Ounissi	0	1	1	6
Vanessa Parent	2	0	2	0
Karene Libermann	1	0	1	2
Doborah Iszaelewicz	2	2	4	0
Gwenola Personne	1	1	2	4
Lydie Breton	1	0	1	2
Cathy Deschaume	0	0	0	2
Marie Picavet	0	0	0	0
Noelle Roy	0	3	3	0
Laetitia Maguelle	0	0	0	0
Marjolaine Henry	0	1	1	0
Caroline Mougeolle	0	1	1	2
Celine Parmentier	1	1	2	2
Isabelle Savoye	0	1	1	0
Sophie Watteeuw	1	0	1	4
Christien Duchame	3	0	3	0
Catherine Laboureur	1	1	2	2
Veronique Gravier	0	0	0	0

NETHERLANDS

Name	G	A	Pts	PIM
Mandy Fonken	0	1	1	0
Chantal Koster	0	0	0	0
Kujtessa Taci	0	0	0	0
Sylvia Piket	3	1	4	4
Lieke Erades	1	1	2	2
Anna Koster	0	0	0	4
Natalie Elderhorst	0	0	0	4
Josje Tubbing	0	0	0	2
Marion Pepels	1	3	4	6
Saskia Admiraal	2	3	5	4
Suzette le Noble	0	0	0	0
Ile Robben	0	0	0	4
Nancy van der Linden	3	1	4	4
Irene Pepels	1	0	1	4
Desiree Jacobs	0	0	0	0
Esmee Beekhuis	3	1	4	0
Nenne Karlsson	0	0	0	4
Ronella van de Ven	0	0	0	2
Elly van Lieshout	0	2	2	0
Helena Kysela	0	0	0	0

GREAT BRITAIN

Name	G	A	Pts	PIM
Gillian Barton	0	0	0	0
Verity Moome	0	0	0	0
Louise Wheeler	0	1	1	2
Jane McClelland	0	0	0	10
Kim Strongman	2	1	3	8
Rachel Cotton	0	0	0	12
Julie Lossnitzer	0	0	0	4
Lynsey Emmerson	2	0	2	4
Kathryn Nike	0	0	0	0
Jeanett Montjoy	0	0	0	10
Lisa Davis	1	0	1	4
Sarah Musgrove	0	0	0	0
Teresa Lewis	0	1	1	0
Laura Urquhart	0	1	1	2
Laura Bugbee	0	0	0	6
Fiono King	0	0	0	0
Julie Biles	0	0	0	0
Fiona Johnstone	1	1	2	0
Sarah Burton	0	0	0	2

UKRAINE

Name	G	A	Pts	PIM
Inga Ghirlo	0	0	0	0
Yelena Vansovich	0	0	0	22
Viktoria Kapustian	0	0	0	0
Irina Didenko	0	0	0	4
Nataly Velikorod	0	0	0	6
Nataly Petrenko	0	0	0	0
Tatyana Kanonenko	2	0	2	4
Inna Vansovich	0	0	0	2
Olga Ninogradova	0	0	0	4
Anna Vainshtejn	0	0	0	4
Galina Zonova	0	0	0	0
Nataly Stus	0	0	0	0
Alla Ryabovol	0	0	0	0
Lina Banya	0	0	0	0
Viktoria Demishenko	0	0	0	2
A. Mokrenskaya	0	0	0	0
Nataly Zinevich	0	0	0	2
Yelena Migotina	0	0	0	0
Maiya Mikhailovich	0	0	0	0
Nataly Donchenko	0	0	0	0

PACIFIC WOMEN'S CHAMPIONSHIP 1995
San Jose (USA) · April 3. – 8., 1995

Preliminary round	USA	CAN	CHN	JPN	Goals	P
1. USA		5:2	3:2	14:0	22: 4	6
2. Canada	2:5		9:1	12:0	23: 6	4
3. China	2:3	1:9		3:1	6:13	2
4. Japan	0:14	0:12	1:3		1:29	0

Play-off

USA – Japan 12:0
Canada – China 3:2 OT, PEN

Final place 3/4
China – Japan 5:0

Final place 1/2
Canada – USA 2:1 OT, PEN

Top scorers

	Name	Team	GP	G	A	P
1.	Bye	USA	5	9	2	11
2.	Granato	USA	5	4	7	11
3.	Boyd	USA	5	1	10	11
4.	Goyette	CAN	5	6	4	10
5.	Looney	USA	5	6	3	9
6.	Wickenheiser	CAN	5	3	6	9
7.	Uljan	USA	5	2	7	9
8.	Brown	USA	5	4	4	8
9.	Liu	CHN	5	3	2	5
10.	Deschamps	CAN	5	2	3	5

CANADA

Name	GP	G	A	Pts	PIM
Danielle Goyette	5	6	4	10	2
Hayley Wickenheiser	5	3	6	9	8
Nancy Deschamps	5	2	3	5	0
Judy Diduck	5	2	3	5	4
Stacy Wilson	5	3	2	5	0
Laura Schuler	5	3	1	4	6
Martine Berube	5	2	1	3	0
Lori Dupuis	5	2	1	3	4
Melanie Haz	5	2	1	3	0
Marianne Grnak	5	1	1	2	4
Anne Rodrigue	5	1	1	2	0
Bobbi Auger	5	1	0	1	4
Cassie Campbell	5	0	1	1	2
Luce Letendre	5	0	1	1	4
Fiona Smith	5	0	1	1	2
Rebecca Fahey	5	0	0	0	0
Cindy Francoeur	5	0	0	0	4
Chantal Leclair	5	0	0	0	0
Lesley Reddon	3	0	0	0	2
Danielle Dube	3	0	0	0	0

Goaltending

Name	GP	MP	SH	SVS	GA	GAA
Danielle Dube	3	170.00	34	27	7	2.47
Lesley Reddon	3	150.00	49	47	2	0.80

USA

Name	GP	G	A	Pts	PIM
Cammi Granato	5	4	7	11	4
Karyn Bye	5	9	2	11	6
Stephanie Boyd	5	1	10	11	4
Shelley Looney	5	6	3	9	0
Gretchen Ulion	5	2	7	9	2
Lisa Brown	5	4	4	8	2
Jeanine Sobek	5	2	2	4	0
Wendy Tatarouns	5	2	2	4	2
Stephanie O'Sullivan	5	1	3	4	0
Cindy Curley	5	1	2	3	2
Vicki Movsessian	5	0	3	3	2
Sandra Whyte	5	2	0	2	2
Allison Mleczko	5	1	1	2	0
Colleen Coyne	5	0	2	2	0
Shawna Davidson	5	0	2	2	0
Suzanne Merz	5	0	2	2	0
Kelly O'Leary	5	0	1	1	0
Christina Bailey	5	0	0	0	2
Erin Whitten	3	0	0	0	0
Kelly Dyer	2	0	0	0	0

Goaltending

Name	GP	MP	SH	SVS	GA	GAA
Kelly Dyer	2	120.00	12	12	0	0.00
Erin Whitten	3	190.00	57	51	6	1.89

CHINA

Name	GP	G	A	Pts	PIM
Hongmei Liu	5	3	2	5	4
Jinping Ma	5	2	2	4	6
Wei Guo	5	1	2	3	2
Hong Dang	5	0	3	3	0
Lei Xu	5	3	0	3	4
Lan Zhang	5	3	0	3	2
Hong Sang	5	0	2	2	0
Wei Wang	5	0	2	2	4
Ming Gong	5	1	0	1	6
Xuan Li	5	0	1	1	12
Ying Diao	5	0	1	1	2
Yan Lu	5	0	0	0	4
Xioqing Yang	5	0	0	0	2
Jing Chen	5	0	0	0	2
Hongqiao	5	0	0	0	2
Jing Zhang	5	0	0	0	0
Xiaojun Ma	5	0	0	0	0
Hong Guo	5	0	0	0	2
Lina Huo	1	0	0	0	0

Goaltending

Name	GP	MP	SH	SVS	GA	GAA
Hong Guo	5	270.00	145	129	16	3.56
Lina Huo	1	40.00	6	6	0	0.00

JAPAN

Name	GP	G	A	Pts	PIM
Yoko Tamada	5	1	0	1	2
Aki Sudo	5	0	1	1	2
Mitsuko Igarashi	5	0	0	0	4
Yukari Ohno	5	0	0	0	0
Yuki Togawa	5	0	0	0	2
Mai Usami	5	0	0	0	0
Yuiko Satomi	5	0	0	0	4
Chie Sakuma	5	0	0	0	0
Akiko Naka	5	0	0	0	0
Yuka Takaya	5	0	0	0	2
Masako Sato	5	0	0	0	0
Rie Sato	5	0	0	0	0
Miharu Araki	5	0	0	0	0
Maiko Obikawa	5	0	0	0	4
Naho Yoshimi	5	0	0	0	4
Shiho Fujiwara	5	0	0	0	0
Akiko Iwase	5	0	0	0	0
Akiko Hatanaka	5	0	0	0	2
Yuka Oda	3	0	0	0	0
Tamae Satsu	2	0	0	0	0

Goaltending

Name	GP	MP	SH	SVS	GA	GAA
Yuka Oda	3	180.00	140	120	20	6.67
Tamae Satsu	2	120.00	145	119	26	13.0

Australia

Federation:
Australian Ice Hockey Federation
Suite 1 – 8th Floor
National Building 250 Pitt Street
Sydney, N.S.W. 2000
Australia
Telephone (+61.2) 261 3270
Fax   (+61.2) 261 3278
President: Phillip R. Ginsberg
Gen. Secretary: Norm McLeod

Phillip Ginsberg
President

Australian Championships 1994/95

Team	GP	Goals	Pts
1. New South Wales	3	22: 3	6
2. Queensland	3	10: 9	4
3. South Australia	3	10:17	2
4. Western Australia	3	8:21	0

Play-off

Semifinals

New South Wales	– Western Australia	13:10
Queensland	– South Australia	3:4

Final

New South Wales	– South Australia	9:1

All Star Team

Damien Holland
(QUE)

Arto Malste   **Fred Christen**
(SA)   (QUE)

Howie Jones   **Tim Kehler**   **Pavel Bohacik**
(NSW)   (NSW)   (SA)

Most valuable player: Howie Jones (New South Wales)

State leagues finals

Western Australia
Hawks – Devils 4:3

Victoria
Saints Monarchs Melbourne – Demonds 5:1

Australian Capital Territory
Winner: Canberra Knights
(best ACT team in Super League)

New South Wales
Warringah Bombers Sydney
                    – Canberra Knights   6:5

Queensland
Brisbane Panthers
                    – Southern Stars 7:3, 7:1

Andorra

Federation:
Federacio Andorrana de Patinatge
Casal de l'Esport
Baixada del Moli s/n
Andorra la Vella
Telephone (+37.6) 863 469
Contact person: Carles Puig

Azerbaijan

Federation:
**Ice Hockey Federation of
the Republic Azerbaijan**
Litemiy Pereulok 2
370603 Baku
Azerbaijan
Telephone (+789.2) 944 000
(+789.2) 954 000
President: Vagif D. Mussayev
Gen. Secretary: Valerj Lanukov

Vagif D. Mussayev
President

Austria

Federation:
Österreichischer Eishockey-Verband
Prinz-Eugen-Straße 12
A-1040 Wien
Austria
Telephone (+43.1) 505 7347
Fax (+43.1) 505 7347
President: Dr. Hans Dobida
Gen. Secretary: Mrs. Rita Hrbacek

Dr. Hans Dobida
President

Rita Hrbacek
Gen. Secretary

Clubs

Bundesliga

Klagenfurter AC
Postfach 170
A-9010 Klagenfurt

VSV Villach
Postfach 7
A-9500 Villach

VEU Feldkirch
Postfach 40
A-6806 Feldkirch

EC Graz
Zeisweg 1
A-8041 Graz

CE Wien
Brigittenauer Ländle 236
A-1200 Wien

EHC Lustenau
Postfach 26
A-6890 Lustenau

EC Ehrwald
Im Tale 14
A-6632 Ehrwald

SV Kapfenberg
Brandlgasse 23
A-8605 Kapfenberg

Eisbären Zell a. See
Steinergasse 3–5
A-5700 Zell a. See

Regular season

Team	GP	W	T	L	Goals	Pts
1. VSV Villach	18	15	1	2	91: 40	31
2. Klagenfurter AC	18	13	1	4	83: 43	27
3. EC Ottakringer Graz	18	12	1	5	104: 55	25
4. VEU Feldkirch	18	12	0	6	69: 42	24
5. EC Ehrwald	18	8	0	10	62: 68	16
6. EHC Lustenau	18	7	1	10	74:102	15
7. Puntigamer Wien CE	18	7	0	11	73: 84	14
8. Kapfenberger SV	18	7	0	11	64: 80	14
9. Pinzg. Eisbären Zell a. See	18	3	1	14	54: 93	7
10. Eishockeyverein Zeltweg	18	3	1	14	48:115	7

Qualification A

Team	GP	W	T	L	Goals	Pts
1. VEU Feldkirch	10	9	1	0	55:20	20
2. Klagenfurter AC	10	7	1	2	64:34	18
3. VSV Villach	10	5	1	4	45:31	15
4. EC Ottakringer Graz	10	5	1	4	42:33	13
5. EC Ehrwald	10	1	0	9	26:62	2
6. EHC Lustenau	10	1	0	9	21:73	2

Qualification B

Team	GP	W	T	L	Goals	Pts
1. Kapfenberger SV	12	6	1	5	60:51	14
2. Puntigamer Wien CE	12	5	2	5	65:62	14
3. Eishockeyverein Zeltweg	12	6	1	5	62:71	13
4. Pinzg. Eisbären Zell a. See	12	4	2	6	54:57	10

Play-off

Teams		GP	W – L	Goals
VSV Villach	– EHC Lustenau	3	3:0	22: 2
EC Graz	– EC Ehrwald	3	3:0	17: 0
VEU Feldkirch	– Wien EC	3	3:0	20: 5
Klagenfurter AC	– Kapfenberg SV	3	3:0	20:10

Semifinals

VSV Villach	– Klagenfurter AC	4	3:1	19:15
VEU Feldkirch	– EC Graz	5	3:2	15:18

Final

VEU Feldkirch	– VSV Villach	5	3:2	18:12

Austria players 1994/95 Top 50

Name	Team	GP	G	A	P
1. Penney	VSV Villach	38	48	27	75
2. Gregor	Zeltweg	34	38	17	55
3. Jiranek	Kapfenberger SV	33	37	38	75
4. Issel	Eisbären Zell a. See	32	34	25	69
5. Wheeldon	VEU Feldkirch	40	31	37	68
6. Burakovsky	Klagenfurter AC	31	30	38	68
7. Liba	EV Zeltweg	31	30	23	53
8. Lazaro	EC Graz	32	28	29	57
9. Nasheim	CE Wien	26	28	28	56
10. Puschnig A.	Klagenfurter AC	35	25	35	60
11. Derraugh	EC Graz	36	24	29	53
12. Viktorsson	EC Graz	36	24	26	50
13. Rymsha	CE Wien	32	24	21	45
14. Puschnig G.	VEU Feldkirch	41	23	35	58
15. Kalt	Klagenfurter AC	34	23	22	45
16. Huiatt	Kapfenberger SV	33	22	19	41
17. Sevcik	VSV Villach	40	21	52	73
18. Gustafsson	VEU Feldkirch	41	21	42	63
19. Messier	Klagenfurter AC	35	21	23	44
20. Podloski	EHC Lustenau	23	21	10	31
21. Schaden	Klagenfurter AC	35	20	8	28
22. Cijan	EC Graz	33	18	25	43
23. Haberl S.	VEU Feldkirch	38	18	13	31
24. Laylin	Eisbären Zell a. See	34	17	21	38
25. Kerth	EC Graz	31	16	21	37
26. Lavoie	VEU Feldkirch	41	16	19	36
27. Karel	EC Graz	35	16	16	32
28. Benes	EV Zeltweg	31	16	5	21
29. Burton	Klagenfurter AC	35	15	35	50
30. Schuler	Eisbären Zell a. See	34	15	24	39
31. Perthaler	Eisbären Zell a. See	34	15	15	30
32. Florianschitz	VSV Villach	40	15	15	30
33. Kromp	VSV Villach	34	15	10	25
34. Lundh	EC Ehrwald	27	15	9	24
35. Rossmann	VSV Villach	38	14	33	52
36. Gross	EC Ehrwald	25	14	9	23
37. Flynn	Eisbären Zell a. See	29	13	39	52
38. Sillinger	CE Wien	41	13	14	27
39. Robitaille	Kapfenberger SV	33	12	23	35
40. Rauchenwald	VSV Villach	36	12	22	34
41. Searle	VEU Feldkirch	41	12	19	31
42. Rundqvist	VEU Feldkirch	36	12	15	27
43. Smirnov	EC Graz	30	12	13	25
44. Brandnar	Kapfenberger SV	30	12	10	22
45. Gratton	EV Zeltweg	16	11	31	42
46. Winkler	Kapfenberger SV	33	11	26	37
47. Felix	Klagenfurter AC	33	11	25	36
48. Boriskov	CE Wien	8	11	11	22
49. Griffin	EHC Lustenau	28	10	21	31
50. Janisch	Kapfenberger SV	33	10	18	28

Brazil

Federation:
Brazil Ice Sport Union
Rua F – Lotes 65–79
Cep. 25.645 Bairro
Maua Petropolis – R. J.
Brazil
Telephone (+552.1) 3911263 or
(+552.1) 2424 31730

Das erste umfassende Nachschlagewerk zum Thema Eishockey

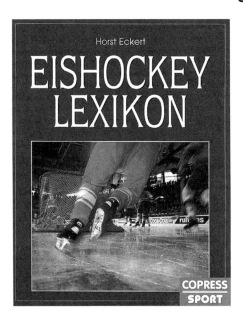

Horst Eckert

EISHOCKEY LEXIKON

Rund 2000 Stichwörter, etwa 500 Abbildungen auf 232 Seiten – geballte Information zum »schnellsten Mannschaftssport der Welt«. Neben einer Übersicht über die Entwicklung des Eishockey sind fundierte Daten zu allen Themenbereichen enthalten: EM und WM, Olympische Spiele und Europapokal, Profiliga NHL, Technik und Training, Taktik und Ausrüstung und vieles mehr.

DM 68,–

COPRESS VERLAG GMBH
Postfach 2003 53, 80003 München

Belgium

Federation:
Koninklijke Belgische Ijshockey Federatie
Stevennekens 111
B-2310 Rijkevorsel
Belgium
Telephone (+32.3) 312 1889
Fax (+32.3) 311 7716
President: Chris Clement

**Secretary
for international affairs:** Jan Bergman

Chris Clement
President

Jan Bergman
Secretary for
international affairs

First Division 1994/95

Team	GP	W	T	L	Goals	Pts
1. Olympia	20	16	4	0	163: 83	32
2. Herentals	20	14	5	1	188: 92	29
3. Griffoens	20	12	8	0	130:102	24
4. Phantoms	20	11	8	1	109: 93	23
5. Yeti Bears	20	4	16	0	116:216	8
6. Chiefs	20	2	18	0	90:210	4

No Play-offs were played. No champion was declared.

Second Division 1994/95

Team	GP	W	T	L	Goals	Pts
1. White Caps	24	22	2	0	307: 54	44
2. Buffalos	24	18	6	0	221: 83	36
3. Herentals	24	17	7	0	140: 79	34
4. Phantoms	24	14	8	2	169:130	30
5. Black Sheep	24	15	9	0	206:148	30
6. Hycat	24	14	9	1	191:109	29
7. Griffoens	24	11	11	2	110: 97	24
8. Olympia	24	12	12	0	148:177	24
9. Cosmos	24	9	12	3	89:103	21
10.Gullegem Jets	24	6	17	1	126:203	13
11.Chiefs	24	5	19	0	101:251	12
12.Yeti Bears	24	2	21	0	47:246	5
13.White Sharks	24	0	24	0	45:247	0

White Caps – Turnhout Champions

Belgian Champions 1994/95

Second division	White Caps-Turnhout
Juniors-B	Phantoms-Deurne
Juniors-C	Phantoms-Deurne
Juniors-D	Olympia-Heist op den Berg
Juniors-E	Phantoms-Deurne

Belgian Champion Since 1975

1975–1978	Brussels Icehockey and Skating Club
1979+1980	Olympia Icehockey Club Antwerp
1981	HIJC Herentals
1982	Brussels Icehockey and Skating Club
1983	Olympia Icehockey Antwerp
1984+1985	HIJC Herentals
1986–1992	Olympia Icehockey Club Heist/Berg
1993	HIJC Herentals
1994	HIJC Herentals
1995	Champion Pending

Belarus

Federation:
Ice Hockey Federation
of the Republic Belarus
4, Masherov av.
Rooms 34 and 36
220004 Minsk
Belarus
Telephone (+375.172) 223 6369
Fax (+375.172) 227 6484
President: Lev Kontarovitch
Gen. Secretary: Anatoly Beliaev

Lev Kontarowitsch
President

Anatoly Beliaev
Gen. Secretary

Adress of Clubs

Tivali Minsk
Korolya Str. 5
220000 Minsk
Belarus

Polymir Novopolotsk
Molodiozhnaya Str. 94a
211440 Novopolotsk
Belarus

Neman Grodno
Kommunalnya Str. 3a
230000 Grodno
Belarus

Belstal Zhlobyn
Shosseinnaya Str. 149
247210 Zhlobyn
Belarus

Junost Minsk
Peryomaiskaya Str. 3
220000 Minsk
Belarus

National Champions

1993: Dynamo Minsk
1994: Tivali Minsk
1995: Tivali Minsk

3rd National Championship 1994/95

Final standing

Team	GP	Goals	Pts
1. Tivali Minsk	10	88:13	20: 0
2. Polymir Novopolotsk	10	59:25	16: 4
3. Neman Grodno	10	53:30	10:10
4. Belstal Zhlobyn	10	31:50	9:11
5. Torpedo Minsk	10	28:83	5:15
6. Junost Minsk	10	19:77	0:20

Scoring leaders

Name	Team	GP	G	A	Pts
1. A. Skabelka	Tivali	9	12	11	23
2. O. Antonenko	Tivali	10	12	6	18
3. A. Andrievsky	Tivali	10	11	7	18
4. O. Malashkevitch	Neman	10	6	10	16
5. I. Kadyrov	Neman	10	10	4	14

All Star Team

Y. Ivashin
Tivali

R. Saley   **O. Khmyl**
Tivali   Tivali

A. Andrievsky   **V. Pankov**   **A. Prima**
Tivali   Tivali   Polymir

Bulgaria

Federation:
Bulgarian Ice Hockey Federation
75 »Vassil Levski« Blvd.
BG-1040 Sofia
Bulgaria
Telephone (+359.2) 662 550 or 654 328
Fax (+359.2) 879 670 or 800 520
President: Konstantin Popov

Ex. Director: Dimitar Lazarov

Konstantin Popov — President

Dimitar Lazarov — Ex. Director

Clubs

HC »Levski«
»11 August« Str. 21
Sofia/Bulgaria

HC »Slavia«
128 »Tzar Boris III« Blvd.
Sofia/Bulgaria

HC »TZSCA-AKADEMIK
Stadion, »Narodna Armia«
Sofia/Bulgaria

HC »Metalurg«
Pernik
Bulgaria

All Time Champions

CSKA Sofia	14
Levski-Spartak Sofia	11
Cherveno Zname Sofia	8
Slavia Sofia	5
Udarnik Sofia	2
Torpedo Sofia	1
Krakra Pernik	1
Metalurg Pernik	1

Championships 1994/95

Team	GP	W	T	L	Goals	Pts
1. HC Levski Sofia	12	10	0	2	155: 21	20
2. HC Slavia Sofia	12	10	0	2	94: 29	20
3. HC Metalurg Pernik	12	4	0	8	42: 89	8
4. HC TZSKA Sofia	12	0	0	12	35:187	0

Top scorers

Name	GP	G	A	P
1. Stoian Bachvarov	12	21	20	41
2. Emil Damev	12	21	9	30

National Cup 1994/95

Team	GP	W	T	L	Goals	Pts
1. HC Levski Sofia	3	3	0	0	38: 4	6
2. HC Slavia Sofia	3	2	0	1	33:13	4
3. Metalurg Pernik	3	1	0	2	15:25	2
4. HC Akademik Sofia	3	0	0	3	9:53	0

Junior Champion: HC Slavia Sofia
Children Champion: HC ETRO '92

Canada

Federation:
Canadian Hockey
1600 James Naismith Drive
Gloucester, Ontario K1B 5N4
Canada
Telephone (+1.613) 748 5613
Fax   (+1.613) 748 5709
President: J. Murray Costello
Vice President: Bob Nicholson
Vice President: Ron Robinson

J. Murray Costello
President

Bob Nicholson
Vice President

Competition
Allan Cup (men's senior)
Esso Women's Nationals (women's senior)
Memorial Cup (men's major junior A)
Centennial Cup (men's junior A)
Air Canada Cup (men's under-18)

Teams/Winners
Warroad Lakers (Hockey Manitoba)
Equipe Quebec
Kamloops Blazers (B.C.)
Calgary Canucks (Alberta)
Thunder Bay Kings (Ontario)

WHL
WESTERN HOCKEY LEAGUE
Final Standings
East Division

Team	GP	W	L	T	GF	GA	P
Brandon	72	45	22	5	315	235	95
Prince Albert	72	44	26	2	308	267	90
Saskatoon	72	41	23	8	324	254	90
Moose Jaw	72	39	32	1	315	275	79
Medicine Hat	72	38	32	2	244	229	78
Swift Current	72	31	34	7	274	284	69
Regina	72	26	43	3	269	306	55
Lethbridge	72	22	48	2	263	341	46
Red Deer	72	17	51	4	209	356	38

West Divison

Team	GP	W	L	T	GF	GA	P
Kamloops	72	52	14	6	375	202	110
Tacoma	72	43	27	2	294	246	88
Seattle	72	42	28	2	318	282	86
Tri-City	72	36	31	5	295	279	77
Spokane	72	32	36	4	244	261	68
Portland	72	23	43	6	240	308	52
Prince George	72	14	55	3	229	392	31

Scoring Leaders

Name	GP	G	A	P	PIM
Daymond Langkow, TC	72	67	73	140	142
Darcy Tucker, Kam (Mtl)	64	64	73	137	94
Marty Murray, Bran (Cgy)	65	40	88	128	53
Stacy Roest, MH	69	37	78	115	32
Darren Ritchie, Bran	69	62	52	114	12

Play-offs
Bye: Brandon

Regina	– Prince Albert	4:6, 3:4, 6:9, 2:5
Swift Current	– Saskatoon	1:4, 5:3, 3:4, 3:1, 0:3, 2:3
Medicine Hat	– Moose Jaw	2:3, 2:5, 4:6, 2:1, 4:5

First Round (Round Robin)

Division A	GP	W	L	P
Kamloops	4	3	1	6
Portland	4	3	1	6
Seattle	4	0	4	0

Divison B

	GP	W	L	P
Spokane	4	3	1	6
Tri City	4	2	2	4
Tacoma	4	1	3	2

Semifinals West

Portland	– Kamloops	5:3, 1:4, 2:3, 1:2, 2:7
Spokane	– Tri City	2:5, 9:1, 3:5, 5:6, 9:7, 4:2, 4:5

Semifinals East

Moose Jaw	– Brandon	5:6, 5:4, 6:7, 3:4, 3:4
Saskatoon	– Prince Albert	2:3, 4:6, 2:3, 2:5

Division Finals East
Prince Albert – Brandon   2:3, 4:1, 2:3, 4:3, 4:5, 5:4, 1:5

Division Finals West
Kamloops   – Tri City   4:2, 2:1, 6:7, 3:4, 6:2, 7:1

Championship Finals
Kamloops   – Brandon   0:3, 4:5, 4:1, 3:2, 5:4, 5:4

OHL
ONTARIO HOCKEY LEAGUE
Final Standings

East Division

Team	GP	W	L	T	GF	GA	P
Kingston	66	40	19	7	284	224	87
Oshawa	66	40	21	5	300	242	85
North Bay	66	35	27	4	272	247	74
Belleville	66	32	31	3	295	287	67
Peterborough	66	26	34	6	255	286	58
Ottawa	66	22	38	6	232	276	50

Central Divison

Guelph	66	47	14	5	330	200	94
Sudbury	66	43	17	6	314	208	92
Owen Sound	66	22	38	6	239	299	50
Niagara Falls	66	18	40	8	231	298	44
Kitchener	66	18	42	6	216	296	42

West Divison

Detroit	66	44	18	4	306	223	92
Windsor	66	41	22	3	303	232	85
Sarnia	66	24	37	5	250	292	53
London	66	18	44	4	210	309	40
Sault Saint Marie	66	17	45	4	228	346	38

Scoring Leaders

Name	GP	G	A	P	PIM
Marc Savard, Osh	66	43	96	139	78
David Ling, King (Que)	62	61	74	135	136
Bill Bowler, Wind	61	33	102	135	61
Jeff O'Neill, Guelph (Hfd)	57	43	81	124	56
Darryl Lafrance, Osh	57	55	67	122	10

Play-offs

Guelph, Kingston first Round bye

Peterborough	– Oshawa	6:4, 5:2, 3:4, 2:5, 5:8, 5:3, 7:5
North Bay	– Belleville	3:2, 5:6, 4:7, 7:8, 5:4, 3:5
Sudbury	– Kitchener	11:4, 10:2, 1:2, 4:3, 6:1
Niagara Falls	– Owen Sound	3:4, 2:3, 5:3, 3:2, 1:6, 3:4
Detroit	– London	11:0, 5:4, 3:2, 4:0
Windsor	– Samia	4:3, 4:3, 7:0, 7:4

Second Round

Guelph	– Owen Sound	5:2, 4:3, 5:2, 6:2
Detroit	– Peterborough	8:0, 4:3, 3:2, 4:3
Kingston	– Belleville	1:10, 2:3, 3:6, 6:3, 5:8
Sudbury	– Windsor	6:2, 1:6, 2:4, 5:1, 9:2, 6:5

Semifinals

Sudbury	– Detroit	4:5, 4:5, 4:3, 4:3, 2:1, 1:2, 4:11
Guelph	– Belleville	3:2, 3:1, 7:3, 7:4

Finals

Detroit	– Guelph	3:5, 5:2, 5:4, 7:4, 3:5, 5:4

QMJHL
QUEBEC MINOR JUNIOR HOCKEY LEAGUE
Final Standings

Robert Lebel Division

Team	GP	W	L	T	GF	GA	P
Laval	72	48	22	2	302	232	98
Hull	72	42	28	2	340	274	86
St. Jean	72	39	27	6	282	277	84
Granby	72	31	36	5	314	294	67
St. Hyacinthe	72	26	42	4	241	310	56
Val d'Or	72	21	49	2	232	341	44

Frank Dillio Division

Beauport	72	39	24	9	291	202	87
Shawinigan	72	40	28	4	325	270	84
Chicoutimi	72	38	29	5	290	259	81
Sherbrooke	72	37	30	5	297	261	79
Drummondville	72	31	38	3	272	302	65
Halifax	72	24	42	6	257	317	54
Victoriaville	72	24	45	3	266	371	51

Scoring Leaders

Name	GP	G	A	P	PIM
Patrick Carignan, Shaw	71	37	100	137	43
S. Bordeleau, Hull (Mtl)	68	52	76	128	142
Daniel Briere, Drum	72	51	72	123	54
Christian Matte, Granby (Que)	66	50	56	116	36
Alain Savage, Shaw	71	55	57	112	112

Play-offs

Victoriaville	– Laval	4:7, 3:8, 4:8, 2:9
Halifax	– Beauport	2:3, 3:4, 6:2, 2:1, 0:3, 2:0, 1:5
St. Hyacinthe	– Hull	1:3, 5:4, 1:3, 3:7, 0:2
Drummondville	– Shawinigan	1:6, 7:10, 2:3, 1:5
Granby	– St. Jean	2:4, 9:2, 3:6, 5:1, 2:9, 4:1, 2:0
Sherbrooke	– Chicoutini	6:1, 6:3, 3:4, 0:3, 3:4, 4:3, 1:4

Second Round (Round Robin)

Division A	GP	W	L	P
Beauport	6	5	1	10
Laval	6	5	1	10
Shawinigan	6	3	3	6
Chicoutimi	6	2	4	4
Granby	6	0	6	0

Semifinals

Shawinigan	– Laval	3:2, 3:4, 2:5, 4:5, 5:6
Hull	– Beauport	0:3, 5:3, 4:1, 5:2, 3:2

Finals

Hull	– Laval	4:3, 5:3, 3:6, 3:1, 4:3

Memorial Cup

Brandon	(WHL)	– Hull	(QMJHL)	9:2
Detroit	(OHL)	– Brandon	(WHL)	4:3
Kamloops	(WHL)	– Detroit	(OHL)	5:4
Detroit	(OHL)	– Hull	(QMJHL)	5:2
Kamloops	(WHL)	– Brandon	(WHL)	6:4

Semifinals

Detroit	(OHL)	– Brandon	(WHL)	2:1

Championship Final

Kamloops (WHL)	– Detroit (OHL)	8:2

81

China

Federation:
Chinese Ice Hockey Association
54, Baishiqiao Road
Haidian District
100044 Beijing
China
Telephone (+86.10) 833 2576
Fax   (+86.10) 835 8083
President: Dong Nianli
Gen. Secretary: Wang Yingfu

Dong Nianli
President

Championships 1994/95
Final standing
1. Qiqihar
2. Harbin „A"
3. Jiamusi
4. Daxing'anling
5. Harbin „B"

Last Champions
1991   Nei Menggol
1992   No Championship
1993   Qiqihar
1994   Qiqihar
1995   Qiqihar

Chinese Taipei

Federation:
Chinese Taipei Skating Association
Room 610, 6 Fl., 20 Chu Lun Str.
Taipei
Taiwan ROC
Telephone (+886.2) 775 8722 or 775 8723
Fax   (+886.2) 778 2778
President: John P. C. Chiang
Gen. Secretary: Rich K. H. Lee

Croatia

Federation:
Croatian Ice Hockey Association
Bogoviceva 7/III
41000 Zagreb
Croatia
Telephone (+385.1) 424 100
Fax   (+385.1) 157 886
President: Kresimir Uzelac
Secretary: Petar Stankovic
Int. Secretary: Ivan Hegedüs

Krezimir Uzelac
President

Ivan Hegedüs
Int. Secretary

Clubs

HK »INA«
44103 Sisak
A. Kovacica 1
Croatia

HK »Medvescak«
41000 Zagreb
Schlosserove stube 2
Croatia

HK »Mladost«
41000 Zagreb
Vlaska 81a
Croatia

HK »Zagreb«
41000 Zagreb
Remetinecka 77a
Croatia

Championships 1994/95
Regular Season

Team	Gp	W	T	L	Goals	Pts
1. HK »Zagreb«	11	10	0	1	88: 15	21
2. HK »Medvescak«	11	6	4	1	67: 25	13
3. HK »Mladost«	10	3	7	0	27: 47	6
4. HK »INA«	11	1	10	0	13:121	2

Play-off
Final

HK »Zagreb«	– HK »Medvescak«	3:2
HK »Medvescak«	– HK »Zagreb«	5:3
HK »Zagreb«	– HK »Medvescak«	2:3, 0:5
HK »Medvescak«	– HK »Zagreb«	1:2, 5:0
HK »Zagreb	– HK »Medvescak«	4:2, 0:5

3th place

HK »Mladost«	– HK »INA«	2:4, 0:5
HK »INA«	– HK »Mladost«	3:5, 0:5
HK »Mladost«	– HK »INA«	4:1, 5:0

Final standings
1. HK »Medvescak«
2. HK »Zagreb«
3. HK »Mladost«
4. HK »INA«

Czech Republic

Federation:
Czech Ice Hockey Association
Sportovni hala
Za eletrarnou 419
17000 Praha 7
Czech Republic
Telephone (+42.2) 377 218
Fax   (+42.2) 311 6096 or 372 853
President: Karel Gut
Gen. Secretary: Stanislav Sulc

Karel Gut
President

Stanislav Sulc
Gen. Secretary

Clubs

HC Olomouc
Hynaisova 9a, 77112 Olomouc

HC Pardubice
Sukovo nabr. 1735
53002 Pardubice

HC Kladno
Petra Bezruce 2531, 27280 Kladno

HC Sparta Praha
Sportovni hala
Za elektrarnou 419, 17000 Praha 7

HC Ceske Budejovice
F. A. Gerstnera 8
37001 Ceske Budejovice

HC Vitkovice
Sovova 16, 70300 Ostrava-Vitkovice

AC ZPS Zlin
Breznicka 4068, 76001 Zlin

HC Litvinov
S. K. Neumanna 1598, 43601 Litvinov

HC Skoda Plzen
Stefanikovo nam. 1, 30133 Plzen

HC Dukla Jihlava
Seifertova 26, 58601 Jihlava

HC Dadak Vsetin
Sportovni areal Lapac, 75501 Vsetin

HC Slavia Praha
Vladivostocka 1460/10
10005 Prah 10

Extraleague 1994/95

Team	GP	W	T	L	Goals	Pts
1. HC Vsetin	44	23	8	13	141:107	54
2. HC Kladno	44	24	6	14	178:142	54
3. HC Olomouc	44	19	10	15	130:124	48
4. AC ZPS Zlin	44	20	8	16	158:149	48
5. HC Skoda Plzen	44	16	14	14	118:112	46
6. HC Ceske Budejovice	44	20	6	18	142:124	46
7. HC Slavia Praha	44	18	7	19	133:164	43
8. HC CHP Litvinov	44	18	6	20	149:143	42
9. HC Sparta Praha	44	16	9	19	123:129	41
10. HC Vitkovice	44	18	5	21	144:156	41
11. HC Pardubice	44	13	11	20	134:151	37
12. HC Dukla Jihlava	44	12	4	28	117:166	28

Play-off

1th round		H	H	A	A	H
HC Vsetin	– HC Litvinov	3:0	4:2	3:6	5:1	–
HC Kladno	– Slavia Praha	7:4	4:2	3:2	–	–
HC Olomouc	– HC Budejovice	2:5	2:10	3:5	–	–
AC Zlin	– Skoda Plzen	2:1	3:1	4:3	–	–

Semifinals		H	H	A	A	H
HC Vsetin	– HC Budejovice	3:1	3:2	4:2	–	–
HC Kladno	– AC Zlin	3:7	3:2	3:8	4:3	1:5

Finals		H	H	A	A	H
HC Vsetin	– AC Zlin	3:6	2:1	4:2	2:1	–

Goalkeeper

Name	Team	MIN	GA	GØ	%
1. Ivo Pesat	HC Vsetin	320	10	1.8	92.9
2. Michal Marik	HC Skoda Plzen	694	28	2.4	92.5
3. Robert Slavik	HC Ceske Budejovice	133	7	3.1	92.4
4. Rudolf Pejchar	HC Skoda Plzen	1914	73	2.2	92.4
5. Roman Cechmanek	HC Vsetin	3032	121	2.3	92.3
6. Roman Turek	HC Ceske Budejovice	3988	143	2.7	92.0
7. Lukas Sablik	HC Dukla Jihlava	59	3	3.0	91.6
8. Zdenek Orct	HC CHP Litvinov	2242	107	2.8	91.6
9. Pavel Malac	AC ZPS Zlin	459	24	3.1	91.2
10. Martin Chlad	HC Kladno	1721	96	3.3	91.1

Top scorers

Name	Team	P	G	A
1. Pavel Patera	HC Kladno	87	31	56
2. Martin Prochazka	HC Kladno	70	33	37
3. Pavel Janku	AC ZPS Zlin	67	37	30
4. Roman Horak	HC C. Budejovice	67	26	41
5. Otakar Vejvoda	HC Kladno	62	26	36
6. Radek Belohlav	HC C. Budejovice	54	23	31
7. Vladimir Ruzicka	HC Slavia Praha	53	29	24
8. Jan Alinc	HC CHP Litvinov	53	19	34
9. Josef Straub	AC ZPS Zlin	53	17	36
10. Roman Meluzin	AC ZPS Zlin	49	24	25

Top defenseman

Name	Team	GP	P	G	A
1. Jaroslav Nedved	Spartak Praha	41	9	18	27
2. Jan Vopat	Litvinov	46	7	20	27
3. Frantizek Kaberle	Kladno	48	7	20	27
4. Jan Krulis	Kladno	38	9	17	26
5. Petr Kuda	Kladno	51	10	15	25
6. Ales Tomasek	Olomouc	45	7	18	25
7. Miroslav Horava	Slavia Praha	38	7	17	24
8. Antonin Stavjana	Vsetin	52	5	19	24
9. Libor Prohazka	Kladno	51	6	17	23
10. Rudolf Suchanek	Budejovice	53	5	15	20

Season Awards

Gold Star Award	Jaromir Jagr	Pittsburgh
Rude-Pravo Award (Goalie)	Roman Cechemanek	Vsetin
Prace Award (Top Rookie)	Lubos Jenacek	Vsetin
Best Defenseman	Antonin Stavjana	Vsetin
CTK Fair Play Award	Roman Meluzin	Zlin
Top Veteran	Antonin Stavjana	Vsetin
Lidov novini Award (Coach)	Horst Valesek	Vsetin
Sport Award (Shooter)	Pavel Janku	Zlin
Hockey-Press (Player of the year)	Martin Prochazka	Kladno

HC VSETIN

Goalkeepers	MIN	GA	SOG	Ø	SV%
Ivo Pesat	320	10	131	1.8	92.9
Roman Cechmanek	3032	121	1471	2.3	92.3

Defenseman	GP	G	A	Pts	+	-
Antonin Stavjana	52	5	19	24	43	55
Alexej Jaskin	55	6	8	14	52	48
Stanislav Pavelec	51	3	9	12	44	36
Marek Tichy	52	5	7	12	22	33
Daniel Vrla	45	4	4	8	32	36
Radek Mesicek	52	6	7	13	32	49
Pavel Augusta	40	1	6	7	33	34
Tomas Jakes	2	0	1	1	2	2
Jan Srdinko	1	0	0	0	0	2

Forward						
Zbynek Marak	54	22	27	49	17	46
Michal Tomek	53	24	18	42	18	43
Andrej Galkin	54	15	20	35	29	44
Tomas Srsen	35	15	21	36	10	36
Rostislav Vlach	55	11	27	38	28	61
Roman Stantien	55	12	16	28	19	33
Miroslav Stavjana	51	12	11	23	19	24
Martin Smetak	27	13	13	26	13	27
Lubos Jenacek	49	11	8	19	16	27
Josef Beranek	16	7	7	15	5	20
Libor Forch	26	2	1	3	10	13
Miroslav Barus	31	3	3	6	5	16
Radim Radevic	6	0	3	3	0	3
Pavel Rohlik	16	0	3	3	3	6
Josef Podlaha	7	0	2	2	1	4
Ivan Padelek	4	0	0	0	1	0

HC KLADNO

Goalkeepers	MIN	GA	SOG	Ø	SV%
Martin Chlad	1721	96	986	3.3	91.1
Tomas Vokoun	1635	91	890	3.3	90.7

Defenseman	GP	G	A	Pts	+	-
Jan Krulis	38	9	17	26	44	42
Frantisek Kaberle	48	7	20	27	70	69
Peter Kuda	51	10	15	25	31	64
Libor Prochazka	51	6	17	23	46	82
Jan Dlouhy	18	0	6	6	9	13
Pavel Trnka	28	0	5	5	26	27
Martin Ancicka	17	1	1	2	8	9
Jiri Petrus	2	0	0	0	3	1
Pavel Kolarik	1	0	0	0	1	0
Martin Stepanek	40	3	3	6	34	53
Tomas Kaberle	4	0	1	1	2	8
Otakar Cerny	14	0	3	3	6	17
Marek Zidlicky	41	3	3	6	21	51

Forward						
Pavel Patera	54	31	56	67	28	72
Martin Prochazka	52	33	37	70	41	57
Otakar Vejvoda	47	26	36	62	23	72
Miroslav Mach	49	17	11	28	16	29
Jan Blaha	54	19	24	43	14	69
Jaromir Jagr	11	8	14	22	3	15
David Cermak	55	10	17	27	28	65
Petr Ton	54	16	16	32	22	86
Milos Kajer	30	2	8	10	4	17
Jiri Burger	12	2	2	4	6	10
Tomas Placatka	26	2	2	4	6	11
Patrik Elias	35	5	5	10	12	33
Milan Ruchar	43	7	7	14	12	44
Tomas Mikolasek	9	0	2	2	1	3
Milan Petrzelka	1	0	0	0	1	2
Jiri Kuchler	1	0	0	0	0	1
Petr Tenkrat	1	0	0	0	0	1

HC OLOMOUC

Goalkeepers	MIN	GA	SOG	Ø	SV%
Pavel Cagas	2546	117	1210	2.7	91.1
Ladislav Blazek	331	26	187	4.7	87.7

Defenseman	GP	G	A	Pts	+	-
Jan Vavrecka	47	3	12	15	33	37
Ales Tomasek	45	7	18	25	30	60
Jiri Kuntos	47	3	11	14	38	56
Jaromir Latal	44	5	12	17	23	54
Petr Tejkl	46	4	9	13	27	50
Ales Flasar	43	5	7	12	24	51
Petr Bosnakov	1	0	0	0	0	0
Jiri Latal	2	0	0	0	0	1
Patrik Rimmel	21	0	1	1	3	17

Forward						
Ales Zima	43	22	20	42	9	34
Martin Smetak	27	10	13	23	11	26
Tomas Martinec	32	7	13	20	13	19
Pavel Nochel	47	8	9	17	35	43
Peter Fabian	45	13	19	32	11	58
Michal Slavik	45	10	11	21	24	50
Zdenek Eichenmann	41	15	8	23	13	50
Radim Radevic	14	1	7	8	4	5
Miroslav Chalanek	46	4	17	21	22	53
Milan Navratil	43	8	8	16	17	45
Richard Brancik	28	6	5	11	2	19
Ondrej Kratena	12	3	2	5	2	15
Petr Nemecek	14	1	2	3	3	10
Milan Ministr	2	1	0	1	0	3
Robert Holy	10	1	0	1	0	4
Ivo Hrstka	3	0	0	0	0	1
Jan Tomajko	1	0	0	0	0	1
Martin Janecek	7	0	0	0	0	5

AC ZPS ZLIN

Goalkeepers	MIN	GA	SOG	Ø	SV%
Pavel Malac	459	24	250	3.1	91.2
Jaroslav Kames	2644	131	1165	2.9	89.8
Richard Hrazdira	335	19	145	3.4	88.4

Defenseman	GP	G	A	Pts	+	-
Pavel Kowalczyk	51	6	13	19	39	52
Roman Kankovsky	47	8	7	15	41	48
Miloslav Guren	44	4	7	11	43	40
Martin Maskarinec	56	1	15	16	62	67
Radim Tesarik	54	3	15	18	45	65
Jan Krajicek	51	3	6	9	32	48
Roman Hamrlik	2	1	0	1	5	7
Jiri Marusak	1	0	0	0	1	0
Karel Beran	2	0	0	0	0	3
Pavel Rajnoha	29	0	6	6	18	38
Patrik Hucko	21	0	3	3	18	35

Forward						
Pavel Janku	54	37	30	67	19	60
Josef Straub	54	17	36	53	25	64
Roman Meluzin	49	24	25	49	15	60
Miroslav Okal	55	24	15	39	18	53
Petr Kankovsky	54	21	26	47	13	64
Juraj Jurik	51	11	12	23	24	45
Petr Cajanek	47	9	15	24	12	34
Jaroslav Hub	42	5	22	27	14	39
Roman Mezlik	47	5	19	24	19	45
Tomas Nemcicky	21	5	4	9	15	11
Zdenek Okal	31	7	7	14	12	23
Martin Kolasek	29	6	2	8	10	18
Zdenek Sedlak	35	4	4	8	9	22
Petr Klima	1	1	0	1	0	2
Martin Spanhel	1	0	0	0	0	0

HC SKODA PLZEN

Goalkeepers	MIN	GA	SOG	Ø	SV%
Michal Marik	694	28	349	2.4	92.5
Rudolf Pejchar	1914	73	889	2.2	92.4
Jiri Kucera	298	19	130	3.8	87.2

Defenseman	GP	G	A	Pts	+	−
Martin Kovarik	47	6	13	19	32	47
Karel Smid	46	9	7	16	32	45
Jaroslav Spacek	41	5	8	13	23	36
Ivan Vlcek	36	6	8	14	23	40
Jiri Hanzlik	23	1	5	6	14	19
Jiri Jonak	27	2	6	7	9	22
Vaclav Ruprecht	34	1	2	3	16	20
Pavel Trnka	6	0	0	0	4	3
Robert Jindrich	11	1	0	1	6	9
Alexandr Savitskij	4	0	0	0	0	1
Stanislav Benes	18	0	1	1	6	14

Forward						
Martin Straka	19	10	11	21	14	17
Milan Volak	46	16	11	27	17	44
Martin Zivny	44	10	12	22	10	24
Peter Veselovsky	44	7	22	29	12	44
Michal Straka	26	10	5	15	16	26
Josef Rybar	32	5	6	11	14	20
Tomas Kucharcik	43	14	4	18	11	43
Jiri Beranek	42	3	12	15	13	30
Jaroslav Kreuzman	41	5	10	15	21	44
Ondrej Steiner	23	3	5	8	3	15
Dusan Huml	21	3	4	7	3	14
Milan Cerny	36	3	2	5	17	28
Lubos Pazler	4	0	1	1	1	1
Pavel Metlicka	6	0	0	0	1	3
David Trachta	22	3	2	5	6	23

HC CESKE BUDEJOVICE

Goalkeepers	MIN	GA	SOG	Ø	SV%
Robert Slavik	133	7	86	3.1	92.4
Roman Turek	3088	143	1646	2.7	92.0

Defenseman	GP	G	A	Pts	+	−
Libor Zabransky	53	2	10	12	56	61
Milan Nedoma	29	5	6	11	30	39
Rudolf Suchanek	53	5	15	20	40	68
Petr Mainer	44	1	4	5	31	29
Petr Sedy	47	2	5	7	52	56
Jiri Hala	9	2	1	3	9	7
Michael Kubicek	47	2	6	8	25	35
Lukas Zib	22	3	0	3	19	23
Jaroslav Modry	19	1	3	4	21	30
Filip Vanecek	1	0	0	0	0	0
Petr Hodek	9	0	1	1	1	6

Forward						
Roman Horak	52	26	41	67	13	69
Radek Belohlav	53	23	31	54	19	67
Lubos Rob	50	17	26	43	32	57
Pavel Pycha	44	18	20	38	18	44
Radek Toupal	31	14	23	37	8	36
Ondrej Vosta	46	14	13	27	10	30
Filip Turek	53	14	17	31	9	41
Radek Dvorak	19	8	6	14	14	17
Roman Bozek	34	6	12	18	11	27
Arpad Gyori	52	5	13	18	12	29
Jaroslav Brabec	22	6	6	12	7	19
Frantisek Sevcik	19	5	1	6	9	15
Petr Sailer	19	1	3	4	3	11
Vaclav Kral	1	0	0	0	0	0
Martin Strba	1	0	0	0	0	0
Petr Paukner	3	0	0	0	0	0
Zdenek Sperger	8	0	2	2	4	9
Michal Horak	1	0	0	0	0	1

HC SLAVIA PRAHA

Goalkeepers	MIN	GA	SOG	Ø	SV%
Vladimir Hudacek	421	24	204	3.4	89.0
Martin Altrichter	1611	102	850	3.7	89.0
Radek Toth	795	47	373	3.5	88.0
Marek Riha	33	2	14	3.6	87.0

Defenseman	GP	G	A	Pts	+	−
Miloslav Horava	38	7	17	24	33	69
Andrej Jakovenko	30	3	13	16	36	58
Jiri Hes	40	5	10	15	27	53
Jan Horacek	2	0	0	0	2	1
Miroslav Hosek	22	0	2	2	9	20
Pavel Blaha	26	0	5	5	16	34
Radomir Brazda	36	2	7	9	23	54
Jan Penk	35	0	6	6	19	45
Petr Macek	35	0	1	1	23	47
Tomas Arnost	35	1	3	4	10	44

Forward						
Vladimir Ruzicka	44	29	24	53	11	73
Ladislav Svoboda	31	7	15	22	25	37
Roman Blazek	45	17	6	23	13	43
Vaclav Eiselt	28	11	2	13	4	10
Jaroslav Bednar	23	6	7	13	15	20
Milan Antos	44	7	18	25	8	43
Tomas Kupka	43	10	17	27	19	62
Tomas Jelinek	44	11	17	28	24	72
Anatolij Nadja	37	7	15	22	6	39
Vadim Kulabuchov	6	2	0	2	0	3
Lubos Pazler	16	2	3	5	2	12
Petr Nemecek	3	1	0	1	2	3
Jiri Hlinka	46	8	19	27	8	69
Ladislav Slizek	24	2	1	3	3	10
Tomas Hyka	8	0	0	0	2	1
Kamil Glabazna	1	0	0	0	0	0
Miroslav Tejral	9	0	2	2	0	6
Emil Snoblt	3	0	0	0	1	4
Lubos Dopita	24	3	3	6	5	24

HC CHP LITVINOV

Goalkeepers	MIN	GA	SOG	Ø	SV%
Zdenek Orct	2242	107	1174	2.8	91.6
Petr Franek	672	47	333	4.1	87.6

Defenseman	GP	G	A	Pts	+	−
Jan Vopat	46	7	20	27	44	66
Ondrej Zetek	48	2	10	12	57	56
Jiri Slegr	11	3	10	13	10	21
Angel Nikolov	45	1	4	5	26	34
Martin Stelcich	12	2	1	3	6	13
Petr Martinek	2	0	0	0	3	3
Petr Molnar	38	0	6	6	17	33
Petr Svoboda	8	2	0	2	3	13
Kamil Prachar	48	2	3	5	51	68
Radek Sulc	11	1	1	2	8	19
Radek Mrazek	27	3	1	4	12	34

Forward						
Jan Alinc	46	19	34	53	14	60
Vladimir Machulda	44	17	17	34	20	43
Ivo Prorok	45	18	20	38	17	56
Martin Rucinsky	13	12	10	22	8	15
Robert Kysela	46	18	15	33	23	71
Robert Lang	16	4	19	23	7	23
Martin Rouzek	46	12	15	27	13	48
Tomas Vlasak	39	6	14	20	7	32
Zdenek Skorepa	31	3	3	6	14	18
Radek Sip	29	6	9	15	11	37
David Balazs	29	6	7	13	4	26
Kamil Kolacek	17	4	4	8	3	18
Radim Piroutek	46	9	5	14	17	53
Stanislav Rosa	3	0	0	0	1	1
Pavel Rosa	1	0	0	0	0	0
Jindrich Kotrla	7	1	1	2	2	9

HC SPARTAK PRAHA

Goalkeepers	MIN	GA	SOG	Ø	SV%
Jaromir Sindel	1151	50	500	2.6	90.9
Ivo Capek	1870	91	807	2.9	89.8
Ivan Vasilev	34	3	7	5.2	70.0

Defenseman	GP	G	A	Pts	+	-
Jaroslav Nedved	41	9	18	27	29	46
Pavel Srek	43	3	12	15	37	53
Frantisek Musil	19	1	4	5	19	18
Frantisek Ptacek	45	1	12	13	33	50
Pavel Taborsky	41	3	9	12	28	49
Frantisek Kucera	16	1	2	3	12	15
Vaclav Benak	3	0	0	0	5	3
Zdenek Touzimsky	36	1	2	3	23	34
Jan Bohacek	13	0	1	1	5	17
Vaclav Burda	21	0	4	4	10	31
Jan Krulis	15	0	0	0	7	27
Forward						
Patrik Martinec	50	15	34	49	13	46
Andrej Potajcuk	39	17	13	30	10	23
David Bruk	50	18	11	29	9	39
Miroslav Hlinka	50	13	27	40	6	60
Jan Hlavac	43	7	8	15	22	22
Pavel Geffert	49	20	17	37	13	74
Jaromir Kverka	50	7	17	24	11	42
Jiri Zelenka	49	13	18	31	12	64
Zbynek Kukacka	43	6	9	15	13	34
Michal Sup	42	4	8	12	6	20
Vladimir Petrovka	9	3	4	7	5	8
Martin Simek	23	2	4	6	4	7
Jaroslav Hlinka	9	1	3	4	1	4
Milan Kastner	16	1	6	7	5	15
Martin Kodada	1	0	0	0	0	0
Jan Vasilev	3	0	0	0	0	0

HC PARDUBICE

Goalkeepers	MIN	GA	SOG	Ø	SV%
Dominik Hasek	125	6	62	2.8	91.1
Dusan Salficky	732	37	371	3.0	90.9
Radovan Biegl	1912	99	908	3.1	90.1
Libor Barta	301	21	156	4.1	88.1

Defenseman	GP	G	A	Pts	+	-
Robert Kostka	50	2	17	19	37	54
Petr Jancarik	43	7	9	16	40	59
Stanislav Meciar	28	5	9	14	27	45
Pavel Ricar	38	5	5	10	29	41
Kamil Toupal	22	1	6	7	14	23
Jan Filip	11	1	2	3	11	12
Lubomir Jandera	8	0	0	0	5	3
Tomas Pacal	32	0	1	1	20	27
Jiri Malinsky	36	0	7	7	25	45
Jan Bohacek	10	0	1	1	5	15
Jaroslav Spelda	12	0	0	0	5	14
Ales Pisa	24	0	0	0	6	16
Forward						
David Pospisil	47	21	25	46	22	60
Richard Kral	41	22	20	42	14	60
Jiri Sejba	36	16	16	32	15	45
Milan Hejduk	49	14	14	28	19	44
Josef Zajic	43	10	23	34	16	51
Milan Kastner	25	7	13	20	9	22
Tomas Blazek	38	9	11	19	10	33
Martin Sekera	32	4	8	12	8	18
Jiri Jantovsky	17	3	6	9	4	11
Stanislav Prochazka	43	8	8	16	13	40
Patrik Weber	21	4	2	6	10	15
Ladislav Lubina	14	7	0	7	3	17
Milan Filipi	5	1	2	3	0	3
Jiri Antonin -ob.	8	0	3	3	5	7
Richard Bauer ob.	8	0	1	1	7	5
Martin Koudelka	26	2	2	4	6	14
Pavel Kabrt	2	0	1	1	0	0
Marek Zadina	48	8	8	16	22	61
Jiri Provaznik	13	1	2	3	1	7
Martin Slaby	4	1	0	1	1	3

HC VITKOVICE

Goalkeepers	MIN	GA	SOG	Ø	SV%
Oldrich Svoboda	645	33	282	3.0	89.5
Vladimir Hudacek	1107	64	493	3.4	88.5
Michal Hlinka	231	16	115	4.1	87.7
Tomas Vasicek	831	54	366	3.8	87.1
Martin Prusek	232	18	86	4.6	82.6

Defenseman	GP	G	A	Pts	+	-
Miroslav Javin	49	9	10	19	37	56
Daniel Kysela	39	5	13	18	38	65
Vitezslav Skuta	50	5	10	15	33	57
Pavel Marecek	49	6	11	17	32	65
Richard Smehlik	13	5	2	7	17	30
Antonin Planovsky	4	0	1	1	4	2
Pavel Kubina	12	2	0	2	7	10
Rudolf Wolf	33	0	5	5	26	34
Rene Sevecek	8	2	2	4	4	13
Filip Kuba	4	0	0	0	5	4
Filip Konstacky	1	0	0	0	0	0
Tomas Kramny	26	1	4	5	16	32
Kamil Pribyla	34	1	0	1	18	38
Forward						
Roman Rysanek	50	18	23	41	27	70
Lumir Kotala	42	15	22	37	15	60
Jan Peterek	41	14	15	29	11	44
Roman Kadera	44	19	19	38	12	69
Roman Simicek	47	12	17	29	22	60
Michal Cerny	31	7	6	13	16	22
Tomas Chlubna	23	9	3	12	8	21
Pavel Sebesta	44	10	14	24	10	52
David Moravec	44	5	20	25	9	49
Michal Piskor	19	4	6	10	8	17
Vladimir Vujtek	18	5	7	12	11	29
Petr Folta	43	6	7	13	25	52
Ales Badal	9	2	1	3	2	6
Juris Opulskis	14	2	1	3	5	9
Radovan Glas	5	0	2	2	3	4
Radovan Fras	6	0	0	0	2	2
Jan Matejny	14	2	1	3	0	9
Pavel Zdrahal	5	0	0	0	3	0
Ales Pavlik	6	0	0	0	1	3
David Kostelnak	4	0	0	0	0	4

HC DUKLA JIHLAVA

Goalkeepers	MIN	GA	SOG	Ø	SV%
Lukas Sablik	59	3	33	3.0	91.6
Oldrich Svoboda	687	40	304	3.4	88.3
Marek Novotny	2102	136	1012	3.8	88.1
Pavel Falta	187	14	83	4.4	85.5

Defenseman	GP	G	A	Pts	+	-
Petr Kuchyna	48	5	12	17	45	69
Michael Vyhlidal	50	3	7	10	44	60
Marian Morava	12	1	0	1	8	16
Pavel Zmrhal	47	2	9	11	28	58
Roman Cech	47	3	4	7	31	58
Jaroslav Benak	36	3	8	11	25	70
Antonin Necas	21	1	4	5	5	40
Petr Buzek	45	2	5	7	23	69
Forward						
Viktor Ujcik	44	21	18	39	19	65
Libor Dolana	42	17	21	38	16	56
Jiri Poukar	50	17	19	46	13	81
Ladislav Prokupek	49	10	10	20	25	56
Petr Vlk	22	7	12	19	12	38
Jiri Cihlar	47	9	18	27	13	61
Patrik Fink	35	6	7	13	8	26
Ales Badal	10	1	4	5	1	10
Marek Melenovsky	8	1	3	4	5	12
Miroslav Bruna	2	0	1	1	2	2
Jiri Hradecky	5	0	1	1	1	3
Jiri Holik	2	0	1	1	0	2
Oldrich Valek	45	13	10	23	3	63
Josef Marha	35	3	7	10	11	35
Radek Sip	10	2	2	4	1	12
Zdenek Cely	16	4	1	5	2	21
Leos Pipa	47	8	10	18	14	70

Setzen Sie wie der IIHF auf blitzschnelle Kommunikation?

Dann spielen Sie uns den Puck zu!

eloc ag 994 11 11

Telefon- und EDV-Anlagen

Bankstrasse 36 · CH-8610 Uster · Telefon 01/994 11 11 · Telefax 01/994 11 12

Denmark

Federation:
Danmarks Ishockey Union
Bröndby-Stadion 20
DK-2605 Bröndby
Denmark
Telephone (+45.43) 262 626
Fax (+45.43) 262 123
President: Ejvind Olesen
Gen. Secretary: Bent H. Nielsen

Ejvind Olesen
President

Bent H. Nielsen
Gen. Secretary

Clubs

AAB Ishockey Aalborg
Boks 757
9100 Aalborg

EIK Esbjerg
Stormgade 14, 3
6700 Esbjerg

Fredrikshavn IK
Sondergade 222
9900 Frederikshavn

Herning IK
Holing Knuden 1
7400 Herning

Odense IK
Lollandsgade 40
5000 Odense

Rødovre Ishockey
Himmelkol 15
2610 Rødovre

Vojenns IK
Runebakken 90
6500 Vojens

Elite Serien 1994/95

Team	GP	W	T	L	Goals	Pts
1. Herning IK	36	31	3	2	281:104	49
2. EIK Esbjerg	36	26	4	6	218:109	42
3. Rungsted	36	21	5	10	207:139	34
4. AAB Aalborg	36	15	9	11	159:138	32
5. Frederikshavn	36	14	5	17	143:171	25
6. Vojens IK	36	15	1	20	183:198	23
7. Odense IK	36	13	4	19	157:169	23
8. HIK	36	11	8	17	110:134	22
9. Rødovre	36	7	7	22	109:225	22
10. Hvidovre	36	1	4	31	79:254	5

Super League

POOL A	GP	W	T	L	Goals	Pts
1. Herning IK	4	4	0	0	33: 9	8
2. Vojens IK	4	1	1	2	12:26	3
3. AAB Aalborg	4	0	1	3	12:22	1

POOL B	GP	W	T	L	Goals	Pts
1. EIK Esbjerg	4	4	0	0	31:10	8
2. Rungsted	4	1	0	3	15:22	2
3. Frederikshavn	4	1	0	3	11:25	2

Play-off
Gold/Silver: Herning IK – EIK Esbjerg 7:1, 6:1, 9:2
Bronce: Rungsted – Vojens IK 12:3, 7:5

All Time Champions

Kobenhavn SF	10	Esbjerg IK	3
Herning IK	7	Rungsted	2
Rødovre SIK	5	Frederikshavn IK	1
Gladsave SF	5	Aalborg BK	1
Vojens IK	3	Herlev	1

Estonia

Federation:
Estonian Ice Hockey Federation
Regati 1
EE 0019 Tallinn
Estonia
Telephone (+372.2) 238 321
Telex   173 236 Sport SU
Fax   (+372.2) 238 387
President: Rein Miller
Gen. Secretary: Jaan Ahi

Rein Miller
President

Jaan Ahi
Gen. Secretary

Estonian Championship 1994/95

Team	GP	W	T	L	Goals	Pts
1. Kreenholm Narva	8	8	0	0	60:17	16
2. Monstera Tallinn	8	5	1	2	74:30	11
3. THK-88 Tallinn	8	2	1	5	25:41	5
4. LNSK Narva	8	2	0	6	28:63	4
5. Keemik Kahtla-Järve	8	2	0	6	22:58	4

Play-off
Semifinals
Kreenholm Narva	– THK Tallinn	10:2, 2:1, 10:3
LNSK Narva	– Monstera Tallinn	7:5, 4:4, 5:0

Finals
Kreenholm Narva	– LNSK Narva	
		3:2, 11:3, 14:0, 11:2, 4:3

Relegation

Team	GP	W	T	L	Goals	Pts
1. LNSK Narva	6	5	1	0	39:15	11
2. THK-88 Tallinn	6	2	2	2	27:24	6
3. Keemik Kohtla-Järve	6	3	0	3	29:25	6
4. Kajakas Tartu	6	0	1	5	16:47	1
5. Keemik Kothla-Järve	4	3	0	1	29:15	6
6. Kajakas Tartu	4	2	0	2	14:16	4
7. Hokiklubi Jogeva	4	1	0	3	16:28	2

Awards
Goalkeeper: Andrus Ahi   THK-88
Defender: Aleksandr Kiritsenko   Kreenholm
Forward: Aleksandr Sljapnikov   Kreenholm
Leading Scorer: Igor Averkin (Kreenholm) 18 + 9 = 27 Pts

Champion Team
Kreenholm Narva
Vjatseslav Skvortsov
Vladimir Tsiprovski
Aleksandr Romantsov
Aleksandr Kolpakov
Aleksandr Bokov
Juri Panin
Aleksandr Kiritsenko
Igor Nazmetdinov
Anatoli Zaharov
Aleksandr Sljapnikov
Sergei Kuzmin
Igor Averkin
Vladimir Nazarenko
Aleksandr Guljajev
Vladimir Karatsov
German Dolzenkov
Mihail Tsetlin
Leonid Tsetlin

All Time Champion Title
1934 – 1995
Keemik Kohtala-Järve	13
Kreenholm Narva	9
Dünamo Tallinn	9
Kalev Tallinn	7

Finland

Federation:
Finnish Ice Hockey Association
Radiokatu 20
SF-00240 Helsinki
Finland
Telephone (+358.0) 1581
Fax   (+358.0) 147 342
President: Kai Hietarinta
Managing Director: Jukka-Pekka Vuorinen

Kai Hietarinta
President

Jukka-Pekka Vuorinen
Managing Director

1994/95

Final Standings

Team	GP	W	T	L	Goals	Pts
1. Jokerit Helsinki	50	34	10	6	202:122	74
2. Lukko Rauma	50	29	12	9	210:134	67
3. HIFK Helsinki	50	32	15	3	203:141	67
4. TPS Turku	50	30	17	3	219:149	63
5. JyP HT	50	22	20	8	164:181	52
6. Ässät Pori	50	20	19	11	164:166	51
7. Kiekko-Espoo	50	20	26	4	154:169	44
8. KalPa Kuopio	50	17	25	8	154:195	42
9. HPK Hämeenlinna	50	16	27	7	170:197	39
10. Tappara Tampere	50	16	30	4	154:221	36
11. TuTo Turku	50	18	32	0	152:227	36
12. Ilves Tampere	50	12	33	5	152:196	29

Play-off

Quarterfinals (Best of five)
Jokerit Helsinki	– Kalpa Kuopio	3:0	(6:3, 6:0, 5:1)
Lukko Rauma	– Kiekko-Espoo	3:1	(4:3 OT, 2:4, 2:1 OT, 4:3)
Ässät Pori	– HIFK Helsinki	3:0	(2:1, 3:0, 1:0)
TPS Turku	– JyP HT Jyvaskyla	3:1	(2:1 OT, 2:4, 4:3, 8:0)

Semifinals (Best of five)
Jokerit Helsinki	– Ässät Pori	3:0	(6:0, 4:3 OT, 7:0)
TPS Turku	– Lukko Rauma	3:1	(6:4, 3:4, 6:4, 4:3)

Finals (Best of five)
TPS Turku   – Jokerit Helsinki   3:2 (1:2, 3:1, 2:5, 5:2, 5:1)

Relegation/Promotion (Best of five)
Ilves Tampere   – SaiPa   3:0 (5:4, 6:3, 5:3)
Ilves remains in SM-Liiga

Third Place
Ässät Pori 3, Lukko Rauma 0 (One games only)

Regular Season

Leading Scorers

Name	Team	GP	G	A	P
1. Saku Koivu	TPS	45	27	47	74
2. Kai Nurminen	HPK	49	30	25	55
3. Janne Ojanen	Tappara	50	22	33	55
4. Jari Korpisalo	Ässät	50	21	32	53
5. Jukka-Pekka Seppo	TuTo	46	18	33	51
6. Otakar Janecky	Jokerit	50	12	38	50
7. Raimo Summanen	TPS	47	23	26	49
8. Petr Korinek	KalPa	50	14	34	48
9. Jari Hirsimäki	TuTo	47	19	28	47
10. Tero Arkiomaa	Lukko	45	22	23	45
11. Kalle Sahlstedt	Lukko	50	22	23	45
12. Risto Jalo	HPK	50	12	33	45
13. Jari Torkki	Lukko	33	14	30	44
14. Iiro Järvi	HIFK	50	14	29	43
15. Pasi Saarela	Lukko	39	23	19	42

Leading Goaltenders

Name	Team	GP	MINS	GA	GAA
1. Ari Sulander	Jokerit	49	2970	116	2.34
2. Boris Rousson	Lukko	42	2529	100	2.37
3. Fredrik Norrena	TPS	22	1328	60	2.71
4. Kimmo Kapanen	HIFK	8	417	19	2.74
5. Sakari Lindfors	HIFK	44	2597	119	2.75
6. Mika Rautio	Espoo	45	2525	131	3.11
7. Jouni Rokama	TPS	15	803	42	3.14
8. Kari Takko	Ässät	49	2963	157	3.18
9. Kimmo Lecklin	TPS	12	647	35	3.25
10. Ari-Pekka Siekkinen	JyP	46	2736	154	3.38
11. Kari Rosenberg	HPK	48	2835	1645	3.49
12. Jukka Tammi	Ilves	31	1804	106	3.53
13. Pasi Kuivalainen	KalPa	50	2955	181	3.68
14. Timo Lehkonen	TuTo	31	1771	112	3.79

Clubs SM League

IFK Helsinki Mäntytie 23 00270 Helsinki	**K-Espoo** Niittysillantie 2 02200 Espoo
HPK Hämeenlinna Raatihuoneenkatu 13A 13100 Hämeenlinna	**Lukko Rauma** Äijänsuo 26100 Rauma
Ilves Tampere Tursonkatu 3 33540 Tampere	**Tappara Tampere** Sammonkatu 50 33540 Tampere
Jokerit Helsinki Nordenskiöldinkatu 7 00250 Helsinki	**TPS Turku** Uudenmaankatu 19B 20700 Turku
JyP Jyväskylä Heikinkatu 4 B 18 40100 Jyväskylä	**Ässät Pori** Satakunnankatu 1B 28100 Pori
KalPa Kuopio Lapinlinnankatu 6 70100 Kuopio	**TuTo Turku** Eerikinkatu 30 20100 Turku

Play-off

Leading Scorers

Name	Team	GP	G	A	P	PIM
1. Saku Koivu	TPS	13	7	10	17	16
2. Otakar Janecky	Jokerit	11	2	13	15	8
3. Jere Lehtinen	TPS	13	8	6	14	4
4. Vjatscheslav Fandul	TPS	13	8	3	11	0
5. Raimo Summanen	TPS	12	7	4	11	29
6. Antti Törmänen	Jokerit	11	7	4	11	20
7. Juha Jokiharju	Jokerit	11	1	10	11	4
8. Mika Strömberg	Jokerit	11	5	5	10	10
9. Petri Varis	Jokerit	11	7	2	9	10
10. Mikko Peltola	Lukko	9	5	4	9	14

Leading Goaltenders

Name	Team	GP	MINS	GA	SO	GAA
1. Ari Sulander	Jokerit	11	662	22	3	1.99
2. Sakari Lindfors	HIFK	3	178	6	0	2.02
3. Fredrik Norrena	TPS	11	666	27	1	2.43
4. Kari Takko	Ässät	7	425	18	3	2.54
5. Mika Rautio	Espoo	4	264	12	0	2.73
6. Boris Rousson	Lukko	9	562	30	0	3.20
7. Miikka Kiprusov	TPS	2	120	7	0	3.50
8. Ari-Pekka Siekkinen	JyP	4	245	16	0	3.91
9. Pasi Kuivalainen	KalPa	3	178	17	0	5.72

All Time Champions 1928–1995

1928	Reipas Viipuri	1967	RU-38 Pori
1929	HJK Helsinki	1968	KooVee Tampere
1931	TaPa Tampere	1969/70	HIFK Helsinki
1932	HJK Helsinki	1971	Ässät Pori
1933/34	HSK Helsinki	1972	Ilves Tampere
1935	HJK Helsinki	1973	Jokerit Helsinki
1936–38	Ilves Tampere	1974	HIFK Helsinki
1939	KIF Helsinki	1975	Tappara Tampere
1941	KIF Helsinki	1976	TPS Turku
1943	KIF Helsinki	1977	Tappara Tampere
1945–47	Ilves Tampere	1978	Ässät Pori
1948/49	Tarmo Hämeenlinna	1979	Tappara Tampere
1950–52	Ilves Tampere	1980	HIFK Helsinki
1953–55	TBK Tampere	1981	Karpat Oulu
1956	TPS Turku	1982	Tappara Tampere
1957–58	Ilves Tampere	1983	HIFK Helsinki
1959	Tappara Tampere	1984	Tappara Tampere
1960	Ilves Tampere	1985	Ilves Tampere
1961	Tappara Tampere	1986–88	Tappara Tampere
1962	Ilves Tampere	1989–91	TPS Turku
1963	Lukko Rauma	1992	Jokerit Helsinki
1964	Tappara Tampere	1993	TPS Turku
1965	Karhut Pori	1994	Jokerit Helsinki
1966	Ilves Tampere	1995	TPS Turku

JOKERIT HELSINKI

Regular Season | Play-offs

Pos	Name	GP	G	A	P	PM	GP	G	A	P	PM
F	Otakar Janecky	50	12	38	50	26	11	2	13	15	8
F	Petri Varis	47	21	20	41	53	11	7	2	9	10
D	Mika Strömberg	50	15	25	40	52	11	5	5	10	10
F	Juha Jokiharju	43	18	17	35	26	11	1	10	11	4
F	Antti Törmänen	50	19	13	32	32	11	7	4	11	20
F	Timo Saarikoski	47	12	18	30	26	8	2	2	4	4
F	Juha Ylönen	50	13	15	28	10	11	3	2	5	0
D	Erik Hämäläinen	49	7	19	26	18	0	0	0	0	0
D	Waltteri Immonen	50	6	18	24	16	11	1	2	3	4
F	Sami Wahlsten	47	9	13	22	20	11	2	3	5	0
F	Teemu Selänne	20	7	12	19	6	0	0	0	0	0
F	Jari Kurri	20	10	9	19	10	0	0	0	0	0
D	Kari Martikainen	38	7	12	19	10	8	2	0	2	4
F	Juha Lind	50	10	8	18	12	11	1	2	3	6
D	Janne Niinimaa	42	7	10	17	36	10	1	4	5	35
D	Erik Hämäläinen	31	6	11	17	12	10	3	3	6	25
F	Timo Norppa	34	6	11	17	6	11	2	6	8	2
F	Keijo Säilynoja	20	6	7	13	4	8	2	1	3	0
F	Rami Koivisto	33	6	5	11	16	5	0	2	2	0
D	Ari Salo	49	4	6	10	20	9	1	2	3	2
D	Pasi Sormunen	41	4	2	6	22	11	2	4	6	6
F	Santeri Immonen	18	0	2	2	4	4	0	0	0	0
F	Mikko Konttila	33	2	0	2	2	10	1	2	3	0
F	Niko Halttunen	14	1	1	2	8	0	0	0	0	0
F	Tomi Sova	4	0	1	1	0	0	0	0	0	0
G	Ari Sulander	50	0	1	1	4	11	0	0	0	0
G	Marko Rantanen	0	0	0	0	0	0	0	0	0	0

LUKKO Rauma

Regular Season | Play-offs

Pos	Name	GP	G	A	P	PM	GP	G	A	P	PM
F	Kalle Sahlstedt	50	22	23	45	26	9	2	1	3	4
F	Tero Arkiomaa	45	22	23	45	54	9	2	3	5	4
F	Jari Torkki	33	14	30	44	48	9	2	0	2	4
F	Pasi Saarela	39	23	19	42	18	9	3	2	5	8
F	Harri Lönnberg	49	19	21	40	14	3	0	0	0	0
F	Juha Riihijärvi	32	14	26	40	20	9	2	6	8	4
F	Mikko Peltola	50	16	18	34	22	9	5	4	9	14
D	Jarmo Kuusisto	50	12	17	29	51	9	1	4	5	12
D	Mika Yli-Mäenpää	50	7	20	27	12	9	1	2	3	6
F	Mikko Luovi	50	15	10	25	18	9	2	3	5	0
D	Joni Lehto	49	8	15	23	81	4	2	0	2	4
D	Marko Tuulola	46	7	14	21	34	9	1	3	4	6
D	Vesa Salo	43	4	14	18	40	6	0	3	3	8
F	Tomas Kapusta	27	7	9	16	10	0	0	0	0	0
F	Petri Lätti	41	6	10	16	10	9	0	1	1	0
D	Toni Porkka	47	1	9	10	103	8	0	1	1	6
F	Sakari Palsola	47	5	5	10	4	8	0	2	2	2
F	Jussi Kiuru	25	1	7	8	2	9	1	1	2	6
F	Harri Suvanto	28	0	7	7	2	0	0	0	0	0
F	Toni Koivunen	16	4	3	7	8	9	2	4	6	0
D	Kari-Pekka Friman	49	1	4	5	12	9	1	2	3	0
G	Boris Rousson	42	0	4	4	12	9	0	0	0	8
F	Glenn Anderson	4	1	1	2	0	0	0	0	0	0
F	Veli-Pekka Ahonen	16	1	0	1	2	7	0	1	1	2
G	Kimmo Vesa	0	0	0	0	0	9	0	0	0	0

HIFK HELSINKI

		Regular Season				Play-offs				
Pos	Name	GP	G	A	P	PM	GP	G	A	P	PM
F	Iiro Järvi	50	14	29	43	50	3	0	0	0	2
F	Sami Kapanen	49	14	28	42	42	3	0	0	0	0
F	Mika Kortelainen	48	22	18	40	58	3	0	0	0	4
F	Pertti Lehtonen	46	15	21	36	34	3	0	0	0	4
F	Ville Peltonen	45	20	16	36	16	3	0	0	0	0
F	Darren Boyko	48	15	20	35	24	3	0	0	0	2
F	Jari Laukkanen	50	15	19	34	30	3	0	0	0	0
F	Pekka Peltola	49	15	18	33	26	3	0	1	1	0
F	Niklas Hede	49	17	12	29	8	3	0	0	0	2
D	Juri Kuznetsov	49	9	18	27	56	3	0	1	1	0
D	V. Kautonen	48	8	11	19	77	3	0	0	0	4
F	Juha Nurminen	26	6	10	16	8	0	0	0	0	0
F	Pekka Tuomisto	44	6	9	15	16	3	0	0	0	0
F	Simo Saarinen	42	7	7	14	40	3	0	0	0	2
F	Esa Tikkanen	19	2	11	13	16	0	0	0	0	0
F	Christian Ruuttu	20	4	8	12	24	0	0	0	0	0
D	Jere Karalahti	37	1	7	8	42	3	0	0	0	0
F	Kim Ahlroos	27	3	4	7	12	0	0	0	0	0
D	Roland Carlsson	26	3	3	6	18	3	0	0	0	2
F	Markku Hurme	26	1	3	4	8	3	1	0	1	0
F	Miro Haapaniemi	9	2	2	4	0	2	0	0	0	0
G	Sakari Lindfors	47	0	3	3	16	3	0	0	0	2
F	Marko Ojanen	16	2	1	3	0	3	0	0	0	0
F	Tony Arima	20	2	0	2	2	1	0	0	0	0
D	Jari Munck	30	0	1	1	16	0	0	0	0	0
G	Kimmo Kapanen	49	0	1	1	0	3	0	0	0	0
D	K. Fagerstrom	16	0	0	0	6	0	0	0	0	0
D	Kimmo Hyttinen	10	0	0	0	4	0	0	0	0	0

TPS TURKU

		Regular Season				Play-offs				
Pos	Name	GP	G	A	P	PM	GP	G	A	P	PM
F	Saku Koivu	45	27	47	74	73	13	7	10	17	16
F	Jere Lehtinen	39	19	23	42	33	13	8	6	14	4
F	Raimo Summanen	47	23	26	49	53	12	7	4	11	29
F	Mika Alatalo	44	23	13	36	79	13	2	5	7	8
F	Harri Sillgren	44	18	16	34	33	11	3	3	6	0
D	Marko Kiprusoff	50	10	21	31	16	13	0	9	9	2
F	Kimmo Rintanen	49	13	17	30	12	13	4	3	7	8
F	Vjatseslav Fandul	32	12	15	27	45	13	8	3	11	0
D	Petteri Nummelin	48	10	17	27	32	11	4	3	7	0
D	Tuomas Grönman	47	4	20	24	66	13	2	2	4	43
F	Lasse Pirjetä	49	7	13	20	64	8	0	1	1	29
F	Ari Vuori	40	6	13	19	41	6	0	1	1	0
F	Antti Aalto	44	11	7	18	18	5	0	1	1	2
D	Aleksandr Smirnov	49	3	13	16	34	12	1	4	5	12
F	German Titov	14	6	6	12	20	0	0	0	0	0
F	Toni Sihvonen	37	2	8	10	6	9	0	1	1	0
F	Jukka Tiilikainen	38	5	4	9	8	11	1	0	1	8
D	Kimmo Timonen	45	3	4	7	10	13	0	1	1	6
D	Kari Harila	18	3	5	8	20	12	2	3	5	16
F	Hannes Hyvönen	9	4	3	7	16	5	0	0	0	0
F	Simo Rouvali	19	4	1	5	10	5	0	0	0	0
D	Erik Kakko	23	3	1	4	8	0	0	0	0	0
D	Mika Lehtinen	9	0	3	3	18	3	0	0	0	4
F	Sami Salo	7	1	2	3	8	1	0	0	0	0
F	Harri Suvanto	11	1	1	2	0	10	2	4	6	4
F	Niko Mikkola	30	0	1	1	24	9	0	1	1	6
F	Arto Vuoti	3	1	0	1	0	0	0	0	0	0
F	Mika Karapuu	1	0	1	1	0	0	0	0	0	0
G	Fredrik Norrena	26	0	0	0	4	13	0	0	0	2
G	Juoni Rokama	43	0	0	0	6	0	0	0	0	0
F	Milka Elomo	1	0	0	0	27	0	0	0	0	0

JYP HT
JYVÄSKYLÄ

		Regular Season					Play-offs				
Pos	Name	GP	G	A	P	PM	GP	G	A	P	PM
F	Jari Lindroos	49	15	24	39	85	4	2	0	2	8
F	Marko Virtanen	50	16	18	34	69	4	0	1	1	4
F	Lasse Nieminen	48	18	15	33	30	4	0	1	1	0
F	Joni Lius	41	9	23	32	12	4	1	1	2	0
F	Pavel Torgajev	50	13	18	31	44	4	0	1	1	25
F	Mikael Nylander	16	11	19	30	63	0	0	0	0	0
D	Markku Heikkinen	50	7	21	28	8	4	0	0	0	2
F	Mika Paananen	50	11	16	27	61	4	0	1	1	6
F	Mika Arvaja	46	15	9	24	38	4	3	0	3	4
F	Kimmo Salminen	50	16	5	21	28	4	0	2	2	0
D	Vesa Ponto	49	3	10	13	28	4	1	1	2	2
D	Jan Latvala	50	3	9	12	40	4	0	2	2	4
F	Markku Ikonen	50	7	5	12	16	4	0	0	0	0
D	Jouni Loponen	42	4	7	11	38	4	0	1	1	4
D	Kalle Koskinen	49	5	5	10	24	4	0	0	0	8
D	Pekka Poikolainen	43	4	4	8	12	4	0	0	0	2
F	Jyrki Jokinen	46	3	3	6	44	4	1	1	2	8
D	Miska Kangasniermi	32	1	5	6	53	4	0	0	0	6
D	Veli-Pekka Hård	29	0	3	3	12	0	0	0	0	0
F	Janne Kurjenniemi	16	1	2	3	8	3	0	0	0	2
F	Tuomo Räty	21	2	0	2	8	0	0	0	0	0
D	Teemu Kohvakka	15	0	2	2	8	1	0	0	0	0
G	Ari-Pekka Siekkinen	49	0	1	1	0	4	0	0	0	0

ÄSSÄT
PORI

		Regular Season					Play-offs				
Pos	Name	GP	G	A	P	PM	GP	G	A	P	PM
F	Jari Korpisalo	50	21	32	53	84	7	2	4	6	6
F	Teppo Kivelä	50	7	32	39	74	7	0	1	1	6
F	Jokke Heinänen	48	21	15	36	40	7	0	2	2	4
F	Rauli Raitanen	50	17	18	35	70	6	0	2	2	2
F	Jaroslav Otevrel	50	13	18	31	26	7	1	4	5	2
D	Karri Kivi	50	10	18	28	20	7	1	1	2	2
F	Ari Saarinen	48	8	19	27	18	7	2	0	2	4
D	Timo Nykopp	47	12	10	22	39	7	0	1	1	4
F	Arto Heiskanen	50	9	10	19	42	7	0	0	0	2
F	Jari Levonen	45	8	9	17	120	7	1	0	1	4
F	Mikael Kotkaniemi	46	6	9	15	12	7	0	0	0	0
F	Janne Virtanen	47	5	9	14	26	7	0	0	0	4
D	Jarno Miikkulainen	36	1	10	11	20	0	0	0	0	0
D	Harri Laurila	50	4	7	11	26	7	0	0	0	2
F	Tomas Kapusta	19	5	4	9	12	7	2	2	4	6
D	Nemo Nookosmaki	31	3	5	8	24	7	0	0	0	0
D	Pasi Peltonen	49	3	5	8	65	7	1	0	1	6
F	Jarno Mäkelä	33	3	2	5	18	1	0	0	0	0
F	Tommi Räjamäki	12	4	1	5	8	7	0	1	1	2
D	Jiri Veber	28	1	3	4	55	0	0	0	0	0
F	Kari Syväsalmi	21	2	1	3	2	4	1	0	1	0
F	Timo Salonen	19	1	2	3	10	0	0	0	0	0
G	Kari Takko	50	0	1	1	4	7	0	1	1	2
F	Jarno Levonen	4	0	1	1	0	0	0	0	0	0
D	Vesa Goman	7	0	0	0	2	0	0	0	0	0
D	Pasi Tuominen	0	0	0	0	0	3	1	0	1	2

		Regular Season					Play-offs			
Pos	Name	GP	G	A	P	PM	GP	G	A	P	PM
F	Juha Ikonen	50	13	22	35	46	4	1	2	3	2
D	Peter Ahola	50	12	21	33	96	4	5	1	6	10
F	Sergei Prjahin	50	13	20	33	49	4	1	4	5	0
D	Sami Nuutinen	50	8	24	32	38	4	0	1	1	0
F	Petro Koivunen	41	11	18	29	36	4	0	0	0	4
F	Jarmo Muukkonen	49	13	12	25	26	4	0	0	0	2
F	Jan Långbacka	48	9	15	24	18	4	2	0	2	4
F	Kimmo Mäki-Kokkila	48	6	12	18	20	4	0	1	1	2
F	Mikko Koivunoro	45	5	12	17	26	4	0	1	1	6
D	Joonas Jääskelainen	50	11	6	17	14	4	1	0	1	0
F	Hannu Järvenpää	45	9	6	15	20	4	0	0	0	2
D	Teemu Sillanpää	50	4	10	14	38	4	0	0	0	4
F	Ilkka Sinisalo	16	7	7	14	6	4	0	3	3	4
F	Mariusz Czerkawski	7	9	3	12	10	0	0	0	0	0
F	Mikko Halonen	39	4	6	10	4	4	1	0	1	2
D	Timo Blomqvist	34	6	4	10	46	4	0	1	1	6
F	Marco Poulsen	27	3	5	8	35	0	0	0	0	0
D	Robert Salo	43	1	6	7	34	4	0	2	2	4
D	Kari Haakana	48	4	3	7	54	4	0	0	0	0
G	Mika Rautio	48	0	5	5	0	4	0	0	0	0
F	Shawn McEachern	8	1	3	4	6	0	0	0	0	0
F	Timo Hirvonen	28	1	3	4	16	4	0	1	1	2
F	Tommi Nyyssönen	20	1	2	3	16	0	0	0	0	0
F	Tero Tiainen	7	1	1	2	2	0	0	0	0	0
F	Vadim Shaidullin	10	1	0	1	2	0	0	0	0	0
F	Teemu Rihijärvi	13	1	0	1	4	0	0	0	0	0
D	Arto Kuki	4	0	1	1	0	0	0	0	0	0
F	Ismo Kuoppala	13	0	0	0	6	0	0	0	0	0
G	Iiro Itamies	45	0	0	0	2	4	0	0	0	0
D	Ismo Kuoppala	13	0	0	0	6	0	0	0	0	0

KIEKKO-ESPOO

		Regular Season					Play-offs			
Pos	Name	GP	G	A	P	PM	GP	G	A	P	PM
F	Petr Korinek	50	14	34	48	68	3	1	2	3	0
F	Arto Sirviö	50	15	21	36	26	3	0	0	0	0
F	Sami Mettovaara	48	22	13	35	24	3	0	0	0	0
F	Pekka Tirkkonen	47	19	12	31	30	3	1	0	1	12
F	Tommi Miettinen	48	13	16	29	26	3	1	1	2	2
D	Kai Rautio	50	5	21	26	42	3	0	0	0	0
F	Janne Kekäläinen	44	8	16	24	12	3	0	0	0	0
D	Petri Matikainen	49	5	13	18	40	3	1	0	1	12
F	Jari Pulliainen	46	7	10	17	18	0	0	0	0	0
D	Jarno Kultanen	47	5	12	17	26	3	0	0	0	8
F	Jussi Tarvainen	45	10	7	17	34	0	0	0	0	0
D	Antti Tuomenoksa	47	3	13	16	56	3	0	0	0	4
F	Kon. Astrahantshev	32	9	6	15	20	0	0	0	0	0
D	Mika Laaksonen	42	6	8	14	44	3	0	1	1	0
D	Miikka Ruokonen	46	2	11	13	36	2	0	0	0	4
F	Veli-Pekka Pekkarinen	50	1	8	9	26	3	0	0	0	0
F	Kimmo Nurro	48	5	4	9	14	3	0	0	0	0
D	Robert Pukalovic	12	3	1	4	0	3	0	1	1	4
F	Sami Simonen	30	1	2	3	22	3	0	0	0	12
G	Pasi Kuivalainen	50	0	1	1	4	3	0	0	0	0
F	Mikko Honkonen	31	1	0	1	6	3	0	1	1	0
D	Jermu Pisto	19	0	0	0	6	1	0	0	0	0
D	Pasi Kemppainen	14	0	0	0	4	0	0	0	0	0

KALPA KUOPIO

HPK HÄMEENLINNA

Pos	Name	GP	G	A	P	PM
F	Kai Nurminen	49	30	25	55	40
F	Risto Jalo	50	12	33	45	30
F	Tony Virta	43	9	24	33	75
F	Igor Boldin	35	8	18	26	12
D	Jarkko Nikander	50	17	9	26	16
F	Juha Järvenpää	41	15	7	22	4
F	Jani Hassinen	41	12	9	21	16
D	Jani Nikko	50	5	13	18	74
F	Aleksandr Andrijevski	17	8	9	17	18
F	Mika Kannisto	23	10	6	16	12
F	Jarkko Varvio	19	7	8	15	4
F	Jari Kauppila	48	4	11	15	40
D	Niko Marttila	48	3	9	12	30
D	Erik Kakko	20	6	6	12	14
F	Geoff Sanderson	12	6	4	10	24
D	Jari Haapamäki	36	2	8	10	73
D	Marko Allen	46	2	7	9	18
D	Mikko Myllykoski	49	3	5	8	28
F	Josef Reznicek	7	1	6	7	6
F	Mika Puhakka	34	1	5	6	10
F	Tommi Varjonen	28	0	6	6	12
F	Tom Koivisto	25	3	3	6	16
F	Ville Tie	15	2	3	5	2
F	Pasi Kivilä	36	2	3	5	32
G	Kari Rosenberg	49	0	3	3	24
F	Toni Mäkiaho	25	1	2	3	8
D	Tommi Hämäläinen	25	1	0	1	22
D	Esa Säteri	15	0	1	1	16
F	Vjatscheslav Fandul	3	0	1	1	2
G	Petri Engman	44	0	0	0	2
D	Kim Vähänen	5	0	0	0	0

TUTO TURKU

Pos	Name	GP	G	A	P	PM
F	Jukka-Pekka Seppo	46	18	33	51	44
F	Jari Hirsimäki	47	19	28	47	66
F	Vesa Karjalainen	47	16	23	39	16
F	Juha Virtanen	50	18	12	30	66
D	Risto Siltanen	44	10	14	24	52
F	Pekka Virta	41	11	9	20	26
F	Jouni Tuominen	46	4	14	18	10
F	Esa Tommila	41	6	9	15	51
D	Brad Turner	43	3	9	12	114
D	Sami Leinonen	42	2	10	12	12
F	Jouko Myrrä	47	9	3	12	10
D	Timo Kulonen	47	4	7	11	26
D	Teppo Numminen	12	3	8	11	4
F	Risto Kurkinen	49	4	7	11	6
F	Ted Donato	14	5	5	10	47
F	Markku Kallio	43	2	8	10	51
F	Tommi Pullola	48	4	6	10	36
D	Petri Kalteva	45	5	3	8	30
D	Jukka Suomalainen	30	4	1	5	42
F	Teemu Numminen	45	0	5	5	14
D	Sebastian Sulku	24	2	0	2	22
F	Tommi Kiiski	9	0	2	2	16
D	Kristian Taubert	18	1	0	1	20
F	Timo Pärssinen	1	1	0	1	0
F	Kimmo Paakki	4	1	0	1	2
	Timo Lehkonen	32	0	0	0	2
D	Craig Woodcroft	12	0	0	0	6

TAPPARA TAMPERE

Pos	Name	GP	G	A	P	PM
F	Janne Ojanen	50	22	33	55	74
D	Timo Jutila	50	11	30	41	66
F	Aleksandr Barkov	50	18	22	40	22
D	Pekka Laksola	50	10	24	34	42
F	Arto Kulmala	48	16	15	31	18
F	Markus Oijennus	47	13	15	28	18
F	Ari Haanpaa	48	12	12	24	67
F	Kari Haikkinen	45	10	11	21	24
F	Pauli Jarvinen	27	8	11	19	12
F	Theoren Fleury	10	8	9	17	22
F	Valeri Krykov	50	7	10	17	24
F	Timo Nurmberg	44	4	9	13	28
D	Jukka Allila	49	1	7	8	34
F	Petr Pavlas	18	1	4	5	6
F	Juha Vuorivirta	39	2	3	5	12
D	Sami Lehtonen	35	2	2	4	34
	Jiri Veber	18	1	3	4	8
	Miikka Kemppi	38	2	1	3	6
	Tommi Haapsaari	30	1	2	3	2
	Pasi Petrilainen	25	3	0	3	14
	Sami-Ville Salomaa	6	0	2	2	2
	Jari Lehtivuori	10	0	2	2	4
	Kai Kuusisto	3	0	1	1	4
	Mikko Konttila	5	1	0	1	0
	Timo Norppa	5	0	1	1	0
G	Ilpo Kauhanen	50	0	1	1	16
F	Marko Toivola	20	0	0	0	4
	Kimmo Hyttinen	15	0	0	0	6
	Jarkko Isotalo	20	0	0	0	12

ILVES TAMPERE

Pos	Name	GP	G	A	P	PM
D	Allan Measures	48	10	23	33	77
F	Hannu Mattila	45	15	16	31	40
F	Sami Ahlberg	50	16	14	30	8
F	Pasi Määttänen	50	11	15	26	26
F	Juha Hautamaa	38	11	11	22	32
F	Timo Peltomaa	49	11	11	22	62
F	Tommy Kiviaho	49	6	15	21	14
F	Reijo Mikkolainen	42	13	6	19	47
F	Sami Pekki	43	8	8	16	12
D	Hannu Henriksson	49	9	7	16	60
F	Jarno Peltonen	32	4	11	15	16
F	Mikko Mäkelä	18	3	11	14	4
F	Marco Poulsen	15	5	8	13	2
D	Petri Kokko	44	6	7	13	46
F	Pasi Huura	32	2	9	11	16
F	Ilkka Sinisalo	30	2	7	9	45
D	Jyrki Lumme	12	4	4	8	28
F	Matti Kaipainen	48	4	4	8	28
D	Martti Järventie	37	1	6	7	18
D	Juha Lampinen	46	3	4	7	48
F	Janne Seva	27	4	3	7	10
F	Jarno Suokko	11	2	3	5	12
G	Jukka Tammi	50	0	4	4	35
D	Brian Tutt	25	1	3	4	42
F	Jari Virtanen	33	1	3	4	18
D	Mikko Niemi	5	0	1	1	4
G	Mika Manninen	50	0	0	0	6
F	Pekka Kangasalusta	2	0	0	0	4

France

Federation:

Federation Francaise des Sports de Glace
President: Bernard Goy
Gen. Secretary: Eugène Peizerat

National Ice Hockey Committee
President: François Deserable
Gen. Secretary: Alain J. Bonnefoy
35, Rue Felicien David
F-75016 Paris
France
Telephone (+33.1) 4527 7575
Fax (+33.1) 4527 3959 or
4527 3961

François Deserable
President
Ice Hockey Committee

Alain J. Bonnefoy
Gen. Secretary
Ice Hockey Committee

Adresses of clubs

Hockey Club Amiens Somme
BP 0704
80007 Amiens

Hockey Club de Reims
8 rue de Taissy
51100 Reims

Rouen Hockey Club
Patinoire de l'Ile Lacroix
76000 Rouen

Chamonix Hockey Club
770 rue Vallot
74400 Chamonix

OHC Viry Essonne
31 Avenue du Général de Gaulle
91170 Viry Chatillon

Angers AGSA
Allee du Haras
49100 Angers

Brest les Albatros
N. Bounoure
12 Park ar Mauer
29850 Gouesnou

Grenoble B. d. L.
Bld. Georges Clemenceau
3800 Grenoble

Regular season 1994/95

Team	GP	Goals	Pts
1. HC Rouen	28	159: 66	46
2. HGA Brest	28	147: 82	36
3. HC Chamonix	28	106:107	33
4. CSG Grenoble	28	89: 90	33
5. HCFB Reims	28	104: 92	29
6. HCS Amiens	28	103:108	25
7. ASG Angers	28	81:141	14
8. OHC Viry	28	81:184	4

Play-off

Quarterfinals

HC Rouen	– OHC Viry	7:0, 15:2, 10:6
HGA Brest	– ASG Angers	9:4, 2:4, 9:5, 3:2
HC Chamonix	– HCS Amiens	4:2, 3:1, 2:4, 5:4
CSG Grenoble	– HCFB Reims	3:4, 3:5, 3:6

Semifinals

HC Rouen – HCFB Reims 10:0, 6:1, 9:2
HGA Brest – HC Chamonix 6:5 (penalty), 6:3, 1:4, 5:2

Final

HC Rouen – HGA Brest 3:3, 4:3 (overtime)

99

Germany

Federation:
Deutscher Eishockey-Bund
Verwaltung:
Betzenweg 34, 81247 München
Germany
Telephone (+49.89) 81820
Fax   (+49.89) 818236
Ligenverwaltung:
Menzinger Straße 68, 80636 München
Telephone (+49.89) 8110044
Fax   (+49.89) 8144447

Rainer Gossmann
President

Clubs
(Deutsche Eishockey-Liga)

Augsburger Panther Eishockey
Senkelbachstraße 2
86153 Augsburg

BSC Preussen Eishockey
Kaiserdamm 89
13053 Berlin

EHC Eisbären Berlin
Steffenstraße
13053 Berlin

DEG Eishockey
Brehmstraße 27a
40239 Düsseldorf

Die Löwen Frankfurt Eishockey
Ostendstraße 83
60314 Frankfurt

Eislauf-Club in Hannover
Am Pferdeturm 7
30625 Hannover

EC Kassel Huskies
Kölnische Straße 42–46
34117 Kassel

Kaufbeurer Eishockey »Die Adler«
Berliner Platz 10
87572 Kaufbeuren

Kölner Haie Eishockey
Heumarkt 52
50667 Köln

Krefelder EV
Krützpoort 16
47804 Krefeld

Federation DEB

President:	Rainer Gossmann
Vicepresident:	Rudolf Schnabel
Treasurer/Schatzmeister:	Wolfgang Sorge
Member/Vorstandsmitgl.:	Dieter Pflügl
Member/Vorstandsmitgl.:	Jochen Daniels
Sport-Director:	Franz Reindl
Secretary/Geschäftsf.:	Franz Hofherr

EV Landshut
Gutenbergweg 32
84034 Landshut

»Die Adler« Mannheim Eishockey
B5, 12
68159 Mannheim

EHC 80 Nürnberg
Äußere Bayreuther Straße 95
90409 Nürnberg

Sportbund DJK Rosenheim
Jahnstraße 28
83022 Rosenheim

SERC Wild Wings Eishockey
Rottweiler Straße 6
78056 Schwenningen

EC Ratingen »Die Löwen«
Am Sandbach 12
40878 Ratingen

ESG Sachsen »Die Füchse«
Weißwasser/Chemnitz
Prof.-Wagenfeld-Ring
02943 Weißwasser

Deutsche Eishockey Liga 1994/95

Regular Season

MAD DOGS München disqualified

Team	GP	W	T	L	Goals	Pts
1. Berliner SC Preussen	44	33	0	11	228:127	69
2. EV Landshut	44	31	3	10	187: 98	67
3. Adler Mannheim	44	29	6	9	164:108	64
4. Krefelder EV	44	29	3	12	203:127	63
5. Düsseldorfer EG	44	29	4	11	196:128	63
6. Kölner Haie	44	28	2	14	185:125	60
7. EC Kassel Huskies	44	22	4	18	145:138	49
8. Star Bulls Rosenheim	44	20	7	17	131:124	48
9. SERC Wild Wings	44	18	7	19	174:148	45
10. Frankfurt Lions	44	16	5	23	110:140	38
11. Kaufbeurer Adler	44	12	7	25	138:181	35
12. EHC 80 Nürnberg	44	11	9	24	151:187	32
13. Augsburger EV	44	12	7	25	137:189	31
14. EC Hannover	44	13	4	27	120:177	31
15. Füchse Sachsen	44	8	5	31	89:182	25
16. Ratingen »Die Löwen«	44	9	5	30	102:214	24
17. EHC Eisbären Berlin	44	10	2	32	136:229	22

Play-off

1. Round (best of 7)		H	H	A	A	H	A	H
Preussen Berlin	– Ratingen	4:0	9:2	4:3	4:1	–	–	–
EV Landshut	– Füchse Sachsen	5:1	5:2	4:1	7:3	–	–	–
Adler Mannheim	– EC Hannover	8:2	6:1	2:4	6:1	8:4	–	–
Krefelder EV	– EV Augsburg	6:2	2:3	10:9**	7:6*	5:2	–	–
Kölner EC	– Kaufbeurer Adler	5:1	4:3	5:1	8:2	–	–	–
Kassel	– Frankfurt	6:5	4:3	2:5	5:3	2:1*	–	–
Rosenheim	– Schwenningen	2:0	3:8	2:6	5:2	4:3*	3:6	5:6*
Düsseldorfer EG	– EC 80 Nürnberg	7:1	5:0	2:4	4:2	9:0	–	–

Quarterfinals						
Preussen Berlin	– SERC Schwenningen	5:1	4:1	3:2*	8:3	–	–
EV Landshut	– EC Kassel Huskies	4:3	8:3	6:3	11:4	–	–
Adler Mannheim	– Kölner EC	3:4	2:3	5:3	2:7	0:6	–
Krefelder EC	– Düsseldorfer EG	1:0	5:4*	3:9	5:3	4:1	–

Semifinals (best of 5)		H	A	H	A	H
Preussen Berlin	– Kölner EC	3:1	2:5	1:5	0:3	–
EV Landshut	– Krefelder EV	3:4*	2:5	6:2	3:2	5:0

Final						
EV Landshut	– Kölner EC	4:3	1:5	4:1	2:8	0:4

Champion: Kölner EC »Die Haie«

* = Overtime   ** = Overtime and Penalty

Regular Season Goalkeeper

NAME	TEAM	GP	MIN	SHOT%	SOG	GS	Ø
1. P. Briza	EVL	39	2215	92.01	1031	83	2.24
2. G. Hegen	ECK	20	1054	90.13	527	52	2.96
3. G. Seliger	SBR	33	1984	89.51	820	86	2.60
4. J. Appel	AM	43	2600	89.41	1052	112	2.58
5. M. Hoppe	SERC	35	2081	88.88	1023	114	3.28
6. J. Kontny	ECK	29	1521	88.41	734	85	3.35
7. K. Friesen	MDM	26	1470	88.38	637	74	3.02
8. H. de Raaf	DEG	35	2039	88.37	869	101	2.97
9. I. Wood	RL	21	1182	88.21	713	84	4.26
10. K. Lang	KEV	30	1792	88.04	761	81	3.04
11. J. Heiss	KEC	42	2474	87.98	999	120	2.91
12. R. Bielke	KEV	14	810	87.87	297	36	2.66
13. K. Merk	BSC	42	2434	87.66	957	118	2.90
14. D. Schrapp	AEV	21	1082	86.13	512	71	3.93
15. B. Englbrecht	EHC 80	24	1334	84.92	617	93	4.18
16. U. Döhler	FL	43	2520	84.37	787	123	2.92
17. J. Schlickenrieder	ECH	40	2340	83.88	1004	162	4.15
18. A. Hanisz	RL	23	1354	83.84	786	127	5.62
19. R. Haider	AEV	28	1528	83.81	729	118	4.63
20. R. Vorderbrüggen	EHC 80	24	1292	82.02	523	94	4.36
21. M. Pethke	KA	32	1816	80.58	654	127	4.19
22. A. Dietzsch	EBB	35	2103	78.56	863	185	5.27
23. P. Franke	ESGS	33	1926	77.25	532	121	3.76

Play-off Goalkeeper

NAME	TEAM	GP	MIN	SHOT%	SOG	GS	Ø
1. J. Heiss	KEC	18	1057	92.64	476	35	1.98
2. H. de Raaf	DEG	9	488	92.59	216	16	1.96
3. K. Merk	BSC	12	726	91.05	302	27	2.23
4. M. Hoppe	SERC	9	517	90.36	301	29	3.36
5. J. Appel	AM	10	560	89.04	292	32	3.42
6. P. Briza	EVL	17	990	88.50	435	50	3.03
7. K. Lang	KEV	15	945	87.97	474	57	3.61
8. R. Haider	AEV	5	270	85.09	161	24	5.33
9. J. Schlickenrieder	ECH	5	300	83.87	186	30	6.00
10. M. Seliger	SBR	7	428	83.68	190	31	4.43
11. P. Franke	ESGS	4	240	83.46	127	21	5.25
12. G. Hegen	ECK	6	321	83.13	166	28	5.23
13. B. Englbrecht	EHC 80	5	300	79.85	134	27	5.40
14. U. Döhler	FL	5	301	77.10	83	19	3.78

Top Scorer
(Regular Season)

Name	Team	GP	G	A	P
1. J. Dopita	EBB	42	28	40	68
2. J. Chabot	BSC	43	20	48	68
3. C. Lindberg	KEV	42	25	41	66
4. M. Bullard	EVL	38	22	43	65
5. P. Draisaitl	KEC	41	26	38	64
6. D. Hegen	DEG/M	40	30	33	63
7. J. Lala	FL	41	18	44	62
8. P. Gross	AM	42	21	41	62
9. J. Dolezal	EHC 80	40	27	34	61
10. O. Sykora	EHC 80	40	20	41	61

Top Scorer
(Play-off)

Name	Team	GP	G	A	P
1. M. Bullard	EVL	18	17	10	27
2. L. Stefan	KEC	18	8	19	27
3. W. Schreiber	EVL	18	11	15	26
4. S. Beresin	KEC	18	17	8	25
5. T. Brandl	KEC	15	8	12	20
6. P. Draisaitl	KEC	18	12	7	19
7. J. Walker	KEV	15	5	13	18
8. C. Valentine	DEG	10	10	7	17
9. J. Chabot	BSC	12	5	12	17
10. F. Sills	KEV	14	11	6	17

FRANKFURT

Name	Pos.	GP	G	A	P	PIM
Waldemar Quapp	G	7	0	0	0	0
Udo Döhler	G	48	0	0	0	4
Alexander Wunsch	D	47	3	17	20	24
Anton Raubal	D	42	0	10	10	44
Florian Stort	D	46	1	6	7	26
Alexander Wedl	D	47	6	4	10	28
Ladislav Strompf	D	39	1	10	11	46
Rudi Gorgenländer	D	48	2	7	9	34
Stefan Königer	D	44	2	1	3	26
Steffen Ziesche	F	45	0	7	7	24
Olaf Scholz	F	22	1	6	7	51
Ilja Vorobjev	F	22	5	15	20	49
Jiri Lala	F	46	22	49	71	43
Andrej Jautmann	F	46	12	9	21	16
Thomas Mühlbauer	F	47	10	4	14	34
Marcus Kempf	F	48	1	2	3	4
Igor Schultz	F	6	1	0	1	8
Martin Schultz	F	48	5	10	15	20
Michael Raubal	F	44	3	5	8	10
Jürgen Schaal	F	47	12	6	18	40
Radek Vit	F	37	1	0	1	10
Patrick Vozar	F	48	13	21	34	26
Rochus Schneider	F	45	19	24	43	41
Robert Reichel	F	21	19	24	43	41
Scott Young	F	1	1	0	1	0

SCHWENNINGEN

Name	Pos.	GP	G	A	P	PIM
Carsten Solbach	G	12	0	0	0	0
Matthias Hoppe	G	44	0	6	6	6
Thomas Gaus	D	52	2	1	3	16
Richard Trojan	D	54	2	20	22	26
Frantisek Frosch	D	44	8	26	34	54
Daniel Nowak	D	52	10	23	33	50
Peter Heinold	D	54	2	11	13	24
Roger Bruns	D	21	0	1	1	2
Andreas Renz	D	43	0	3	3	22
Zdenek Travnicek	D	37	3	20	23	54
Ilmar Toman	F	13	7	8	15	6
Alan Young	F	53	21	14	35	57
Michael Pastika	F	53	3	4	7	6
Andrej Kovalev	F	51	43	29	72	127
Peter Kopta	F	53	19	36	55	74
Robert Brezina	F	52	18	21	39	32
Wayne Hynes	F	48	19	32	51	60
Martin Svedja	F	16	1	1	2	2
George Fritz	F	33	8	14	22	28
Mike Bader	F	31	7	11	18	6
Thomas Deiter	F	38	3	2	5	6
Grant Martin	F	1	0	0	0	0
Karsten Schultz	F	43	1	2	3	24
Alfie Turcotte	F	44	14	45	59	42
Thomas Schädler	F	54	3	7	10	10
Alex Horn	F	22	0	0	0	0
Mike Lay	F	26	15	16	31	41

LANDSHUT

Name	Pos.	GP	G	A	P	PIM
Petr Briza	G	17	0	1	1	4
Christian Künast	G	4	0	0	0	0
Michael Bresagk	D	17	2	7	9	49
Bernd Wagner	D	18	0	3	3	26
Alexander Genze	D	6	0	0	0	0
Eduard Uvira	D	18	0	4	4	14
Peter Gulda	D	18	4	6	10	34
Udo Kießling	D	18	3	7	10	22
Anthony Vogel	F	18	5	7	12	16
Jacek Plachta	F	15	5	4	9	53
Georg Franz	F	18	9	7	16	12
Stephan Retzer	F	17	0	0	0	29
Henri Marcoux	F	18	9	7	16	12
Andreas Loth	F	18	0	1	1	16
Mike Bullard	F	18	17	10	27	28
Markus Berwanger	F	18	2	6	8	44
Wally Schreiber	F	18	11	15	26	26
Ralf Hantschke	F	15	2	8	10	16
Steven McNeil	F	18	4	7	11	28
Jörg Handrick	F	17	3	8	11	18
Helmut Steiger	F	18	2	8	10	12

ROSENHEIM

Name	Pos.	GP	G	A	P	PIM
Oliver Häusler	G	11	0	0	0	0
Marc Seliger	G	40	0	1	1	0
Markus Wieland	D	47	3	6	9	24
Raphael Krüger	D	41	3	3	6	36
Joachim Reil	D	46	0	2	2	26
Ron Fischer	D	36	4	18	22	40
Christian Gegenfurtner	D	45	2	4	6	16
Venci Sebek	D	48	8	19	27	66
Heinrich Schiffl	D	50	0	5	5	44
Sergej Schendelew	D	22	6	14	20	26
Andreas Schneider	F	47	4	7	11	14
Michael Trattner	F	50	2	4	6	40
Tobias Schraven	F	24	1	0	1	6
Rick Boehm	F	50	16	22	38	38
Robert Hock	F	49	13	24	37	10
Radek Toupal	F	20	6	15	21	10
Martin Reichel	F	50	14	29	43	73
Raimond Hilger	F	50	23	21	44	34
Petr Hrbek	F	47	32	26	58	18
Arthur Scheid	F	10	0	0	0	0
Florian Keller	F	27	5	6	11	16
Michael Pohl	F	46	3	6	9	43
Markus Draxler	F	2	0	0	0	2
Duanne Moeser	F	2	1	4	5	4
Doug Weight	F	8	2	3	5	18
Gordon Sherven	F	22	7	21	28	12

NÜRNBERG

Name	Pos.	GP	G	A	P	PIM
Reiner Vorderbrüggen	G	24	0	0	0	6
Bernd Englbrecht	G	29	0	0	0	16
Christian Gerum	D	43	0	8	8	79
Doug Irwin	D	45	4	9	13	42
Miroslav Maly	D	44	2	9	11	132
Stephan Eder	D	18	0	0	0	10
Arno Brux	D	45	2	6	8	14
Michael Weinfurter	D	41	2	9	11	40
Stephan Bauer	D	37	0	1	1	24
Heiko Smazal	D	22	1	5	6	28
Paul Geddes	F	47	26	27	53	2
Ian Young	F	39	5	8	13	60
Stefan Steinbock	F	48	10	12	22	8
Christian Flügge	F	28	0	3	3	10
Klaus Birk	F	44	5	20	25	55
Jürgen Lechl	F	42	9	18	27	8
Thomas Popiesch	F	48	15	12	27	28
Marcus Goerlitz	F	42	0	1	1	10
Jiri Dolezal	F	45	28	35	63	63
Thomas Sterflinger	F	45	2	9	11	34
Sepp Wassermann	F	46	18	19	37	42
Otto Sykora	F	45	22	43	65	79
Peter Cerny	F	11	0	0	0	0
Henrik Hölscher	F	20	3	7	10	14
Ewald Steiger	F	13	3	4	7	2
Roman Horak	F	1	1	2	3	0

AUGSBURG

Name	Pos.	GP	G	A	P	PIM
Reinhard Haider	G	33	0	0	0	2
Dennis Schrapp	G	22	0	0	0	2
Scott Campbell	D	47	5	16	21	26
Dieter Medicus	D	47	2	15	17	36
Thorsten Fendt	D	25	0	0	0	8
Daniel Naud	D	40	11	24	35	28
Fritz Meyer	D	48	3	5	8	22
Christian Curth	D	48	5	8	13	48
Alfred Burkhard	D	10	0	0	0	0
Karl-Heinz Fliegauf	D	17	0	3	3	16
Stefan Mayer	D	35	1	3	4	32
Duanne Moeser	F	22	13	11	24	14
Andreas Römer	F	46	4	5	9	73
Thomas Gröger	F	46	8	20	28	28
Sven Zywitza	F	47	10	6	16	49
Anton Krinner	F	42	11	15	26	26
Patrick Pysz	F	46	5	15	20	67
Heinrich Römer	F	38	4	11	15	8
Ales Polcar	F	44	20	23	43	16
Philip Kukuk	F	42	3	9	12	8
Dietrich Adam	F	18	2	0	2	6
Tim Schnobrich	F	21	1	2	3	6
Tim Ferguson	F	48	15	12	27	64
Robert Heidt	F	47	11	24	35	48
Robert Paclik	F	46	6	11	17	43
Glenn Anderson	F	5	6	2	8	10
Philipp Posch	F	12	0	0	0	0
Christian Brittig	F	18	6	7	13	20
Harald Birk	F	19	6	20	26	28

MÜNCHEN (27. Round †)

Name	Pos.	GP	G	A	P	PIM
Karl Friesen	G	26	0	1	1	0
Christian Frütel	G	3	0	0	0	4
Alexander Genze	D	26	2	4	6	37
Greg Müller	D	27	1	7	8	22
Mike Schmidt	D	27	1	21	22	26
Zdenek Travnicek	D	10	0	0	0	4
Christian Lukes	D	27	1	3	4	38
Sergej Schendelew	D	26	6	16	22	63
Rainer Lutz	D	13	1	2	3	6
Gordon Sherven	F	27	16	21	37	12
Anthony Vogel	F	27	3	16	19	16
Michael Hieus	F	27	7	5	12	14
Dale Derkatch	F	26	14	17	31	49
Christian Brittig	F	27	1	6	7	14
Harald Waibel	F	18	0	0	0	0
Ewald Steiger	F	27	7	7	14	4
Dieter Hegen	F	15	13	12	25	28
Ralf Reisinger	F	27	8	12	20	14
Henrik Hölscher	F	27	1	10	11	24
Tobias Abstreiter	F	27	5	16	21	18
Christoph Sandner	F	26	9	5	14	12
Harald Birk	F	24	6	5	11	18
Chris Straube	F	21	8	2	10	14

KAUFBEUREN

Name	Pos.	GP	G	A	P	PIM
Michael Olbrich	G	1	0	0	0	0
Marc Pethke	G	36	0	1	1	14
Patrick Lange	G	18	0	0	0	2
Kenneth Karpuk	D	46	1	6	7	44
Drahomir Kadlec	D	47	9	26	35	36
Christian Seeberger	D	38	1	1	2	6
Daniel Kunz	D	47	9	13	22	26
Timo Gschwill	D	43	4	5	9	58
Jürgen Simon	D	34	1	1	2	42
Ronny Martin	D	43	0	3	3	18
Jiri Kunce	D	2	0	0	0	0
Elmar Boiger	F	46	12	19	31	30
Oto Hascak	F	45	19	30	49	34
Thorsten Rau	F	47	10	14	24	20
Thomas Martinec	F	32	3	3	6	12
Hans-Jörg Mayer	F	36	10	9	19	33
Manfred Jorde	F	43	10	7	17	22
Roland Timoschuk	F	47	4	10	14	14
Jim Hoffmann	F	47	17	16	33	18
Andreas Volland	F	29	11	10	21	14
Rolf Hammer	F	45	14	19	33	62
Manuel Hess	F	29	1	0	1	0
Axel Kammerer	F	47	9	15	24	12
Norbert Zabel	F	41	0	4	4	22
Moritz Geiselbrechtinger	F	8	0	0	0	2

DÜSSELDORF

Name	Pos.	GP	G	A	P	PIM
Helmut de Raaf	G	44	0	1	1	16
Carsten Gossmann	G	12	0	0	0	0
Kai Fischer	G	1	0	0	0	0
Rafael Jedamzik	D	34	0	2	2	2
Torsten Kienass	D	51	5	11	16	16
Christoph Kreutzer	D	53	4	8	12	38
Andreas Niederberger	D	53	9	24	33	18
Rick Amann	D	52	12	23	35	93
Uli Hiemer	D	50	10	28	38	74
Robert Sterflinger	D	50	5	5	10	22
Markus Kehle	F	51	2	10	12	68
Christian Schmitz	F	28	1	1	2	12
Lorenz Funk	F	53	10	21	31	18
Chris Valentine	F	52	26	41	67	118
Benoit Doucet	F	50	30	38	68	94
Bernd Kühnhauser	F	48	11	14	25	57
Thorsten van Leyen	F	6	0	1	1	2
Bruce Eakin	F	29	7	15	22	22
Pierre Rioux	F	53	18	47	65	14
Andreas Brockmann	F	51	11	19	30	71
Bernd Truntschka	F	53	14	25	39	34
Wolfgang Kummer	F	45	7	11	18	18
Ernst Köpf	F	20	3	12	15	2
Kevin LaVallee	F	49	22	28	50	30
Rainer Zerwesz	F	53	10	12	22	60
Dieter Hegen	F	30	16	24	42	18
Brendan Shanahan	F	3	5	3	8	4

Eisbären BERLIN

Name	Pos.	GP	G	A	P	PIM
Andre Dietzsch	G	35	0	0	0	2
Rupert Meister	G	8	0	0	0	0
Frank Kannewurf	D	40	8	18	26	104
Thomas Graul	D	38	9	13	22	44
Juri Stumpf	D	41	2	7	9	40
Frank Krause	D	36	0	4	4	41
Thorsten Deutscher	D	39	3	5	8	64
Dirk Perschau	D	19	0	4	4	12
Bernd Seyller	D	29	1	3	4	8
Patrick Solf	D	34	1	1	2	28
Nico Pyka	D	13	0	0	0	0
Frank Appel	D	10	0	0	0	4
Jan Gerike	F	15	0	3	3	2
Sven Felski	F	38	15	17	32	102
Moritz Schmidt	F	42	2	3	5	8
Marco Swibenko	F	41	1	3	4	6
Holger Mix	F	42	4	4	8	8
Jiri Dopita	F	42	28	40	68	55
Guido Hiller	F	43	5	4	9	8
Daniel Held	F	39	8	16	24	67
Richard Zemlicka	F	38	23	25	48	32
Thomas Mitew	F	23	4	1	5	16
Jan Schertz	F	43	7	6	13	52
Mike Losch	F	36	6	3	9	10
Mark Jooris	F	12	9	10	19	10

KREFELD

Name	Pos.	GP	G	A	P	PIM
Karel Lang	G	45	0	4	4	14
Rene Bielke	G	14	0	1	1	0
Markus Krawinkel	D	53	1	4	5	12
Earl Spry	D	55	2	15	17	22
Greg Thomson	D	57	10	27	37	52
Brad Bergen	D	58	9	24	33	54
Jayson Meyer	D	58	5	40	45	52
Martin Gebel	D	58	8	18	26	90
Klaus Micheller	D	56	4	13	17	54
Andre Grein	F	55	8	5	13	18
Greg Evtushevski	F	56	28	34	62	132
Herbert Vasiljevs	F	57	5	9	14	34
Ken Petrash	F	57	15	15	30	48
Reemt Pyka	F	57	20	12	32	58
Chris Lindberg	F	57	29	51	80	123
Francois Sills	F	47	25	36	61	50
Peter Ihnacak	F	34	9	10	19	24
Marek Stebnicki	F	41	17	25	42	24
Johnny Walker	F	56	32	39	71	103
Günther Oswald	F	54	29	25	54	129
James Hanlon	F	55	5	19	24	44
Greg Parks	F	11	2	7	9	8

RATINGEN

Name	Pos.	GP	G	A	P	PIM
Andrej Hanisz	G	24	0	0	0	4
Ian Wood	G	26	0	2	2	22
Pavel Mann	D	47	2	8	10	40
Sven Prusa	D	43	0	6	6	50
Otto Keresztes	D	27	2	3	5	14
Michael Kratz	D	1	0	0	0	0
Oliver Schwarz	D	19	1	0	1	6
Christian Althoff	D	28	0	1	1	16
Helmut Elters	D	47	0	2	2	34
Peter Lutter	D	40	1	4	5	63
Thomas Schmidt	D	34	0	1	1	0
Andrej Martemjanov	D	38	3	17	20	68
Christian Kohmann	F	33	2	3	5	4
Jiri Smicek	F	23	0	3	3	4
Richard Brodnicki	F	19	0	1	1	0
Andrej Fuchs	F	46	13	24	37	66
Oliver Kaspar	F	40	10	11	21	20
Klaus Striemitzer	F	21	2	3	5	6
Boris Fuchs	F	46	22	13	35	56
Waldemar Nowosjolow	F	22	5	7	12	36
Thomas Imdahl	F	27	2	4	6	26
Valeri Konstantinow	F	38	2	2	4	12
Udo Schmid	F	46	8	13	21	54
Mark Bassen	F	37	18	11	29	100
Frank Kovacz	F	7	3	3	6	10
Vincent Damphousse	F	11	5	7	12	24
Olaf Scholz	F	19	1	10	11	77
Christian Schmitz	F	19	2	8	10	10
Greg Müller	F	19	4	3	7	16
Christian Flügge	F	16	0	2	2	12

KÖLN

Name	Pos.	GP	G	A	P	PIM
Joseph Heiss	G	18	0	2	2	0
Olaf Grundmann	G	3	0	0	0	0
Mike Schmidt	D	18	2	12	14	28
Jörg Mayr	D	18	3	12	15	32
Mirco Lüdemann	D	17	2	4	6	20
Andreas Pokorny	D	17	3	3	6	6
Karsten Mende	D	18	0	4	4	6
Frank Hohenadl	D	18	0	5	5	28
Marco Heinrichs	D	17	0	0	0	0
Herbert Hohenberger	D	15	5	9	14	24
Thomas Brandl	F	15	8	12	20	16
Stefan Mann	F	18	2	7	9	22
Ronny Reddo	F	18	1	3	4	20
Leo Stefan	F	18	8	19	27	8
Peter Draisaitl	F	18	12	17	19	18
Andreas Lupzig	F	18	7	4	11	36
Michael Rumrich	F	17	3	7	10	39
Martin Ondrejka	F	18	1	3	4	13
Thorsten Sendt	F	18	0	2	2	8
Thorsten Koslowski	F	4	0	0	0	0
Tobias Abstreiter	F	18	2	9	11	22
Franz Demmel	F	18	4	3	7	12
Sergej Beresin	F	18	17	8	25	10

Preussen BERLIN

Name	Pos.	GP	G	A	P	PIM
Klaus Merk	G	54	0	8	8	14
Marc Gronau	G	9	0	0	0	0
Michael Komma	D	40	3	15	18	20
Jochen Molling	D	54	0	6	6	14
Stefan Steinecker	D	56	3	17	20	14
Josef Lehner	D	56	10	16	26	54
Tom O'Regan	D	55	11	52	63	78
Marco Rentzsch	D	54	4	13	17	94
Stephan Sinner	D	55	3	14	17	69
Andreas Schubert	D	54	4	17	21	98
Tony Tanti	F	51	27	35	62	122
Gaetan Malo	F	53	31	21	52	51
Thomas Schinko	F	42	11	15	26	47
Georg Holzmann	F	52	23	25	48	52
Mark Kosturik	F	55	34	30	64	38
Jürgen Rumrich	F	56	30	18	48	18
John Chabot	F	55	25	60	85	62
Harald Windler	F	45	0	3	3	2
Marc Teevens	F	56	27	31	58	16
Bruce Hardy	F	56	15	32	47	28
Fabian Brännström	F	55	5	12	17	4
Andreas Dimbat	F	24	5	1	6	4
Ralf Reisinger	F	26	4	6	10	18

SACHSEN

Name	Pos.	GP	G	A	P	PIM
Thomas Bresagk	G	12	0	0	0	4
Peter Franke	G	37	0	0	0	22
Josef Reznicek	D	32	6	12	18	99
Frank Peschke	D	45	3	18	21	126
Thomas Schubert	D	46	1	2	3	47
Marcel Lichnovsky	D	46	0	8	8	56
Jari Grönstrand	D	41	3	8	11	84
Sebastian Klenner	D	38	0	2	2	24
Antonio Fonso	D	19	1	0	1	12
Andreas Ott	D	45	1	2	3	64
Frantisek Musil	D	1	0	0	0	2
Matthias Kliemann	F	46	8	7	15	32
Branjo Heisig	F	46	18	16	34	123
Jens Schwabe	F	47	5	3	8	10
Torsten Eisebitt	F	47	10	10	20	36
Thomas Knobloch	F	29	3	2	5	8
Falk Herzig	F	42	3	1	4	8
Thomas Wagner	F	42	1	3	4	30
Jan Tabor	F	47	14	14	28	28
Peter Hofmann	F	47	1	4	5	14
Terry Campbell	F	13	4	8	12	29
Michael Flemming	F	44	2	9	11	40
Janusz Janikowski	F	46	7	17	24	45
Ladislav Lubina	F	8	4	1	5	2
Mika Dolazal	F	2	0	0	0	0
Jörg Pohlin	F	10	1	0	1	0

HANNOVER

Name	Pos.	GP	G	A	P	PIM
Marco Herbst	G	5	0	0	0	0
Josef Schlickenrieder	G	45	0	2	2	26
Joachim Lempio	D	47	0	3	3	0
Torsten Hanusch	G	43	3	2	5	87
Thomas Jungwirth	D	41	0	6	6	14
Dave Reierson	D	48	9	14	23	40
Anton Maidl	D	47	1	2	3	80
Rene Ledock	D	47	2	5	7	67
Marc Wittbrock	D	47	2	1	3	24
Craig Topolnisky	D	38	3	6	9	46
Friedhelm Bögelsack	F	45	3	6	9	20
Thomas Werner	F	46	16	16	32	38
Dirk Rohrbach	F	48	3	7	10	16
Harald Kuhnke	F	47	2	6	8	12
Florian Funk	F	46	9	14	23	18
Mark Maroste	F	48	25	29	54	62
Rene Reuter	F	48	7	5	12	30
Milos Vanik	F	48	15	20	35	34
Günther Preuß	F	44	7	24	31	20
Troy Tumbach	F	10	1	2	3	20
Stefan Goldapp	F	29	2	1	3	2
Marcus Bleicher	F	48	15	20	35	75
Harald Waibel	F	26	4	1	5	16

MANNHEIM

Name	Pos.	GP	G	A	P	PIM
Joachim Appel	G	53	0	3	3	14
Markus Flemming	G	2	0	0	0	0
Harold Kreis	D	53	4	13	17	32
Michael Heidt	D	47	10	34	44	42
Steffen Michel	D	51	2	7	9	28
Lars Brüggemann	D	49	1	3	4	84
Toni Plattner	D	49	1	6	7	101
Jörg Hanft	D	53	12	13	25	70
Richard Goldmann	D	41	1	0	1	22
Michael Gabler	D	4	0	0	0	0
Christian Lukes	D	24	2	4	6	22
Mario Gehrig	F	18	1	3	4	12
Pavel Gross	F	48	25	43	68	97
Daniel Körber	F	53	6	7	13	32
Robert Cimetta	F	48	35	37	72	188
Dale Krentz	F	52	17	33	50	67
Jochen Hecht	F	53	16	16	32	80
Dave Latta	F	2	1	1	2	2
Till Feser	F	52	12	11	23	95
Alexander Serikow	F	51	12	19	31	66
Dieter Willmann	F	43	4	4	8	10
Damian Adamus	F	50	11	28	39	16
Frederik Ledlin	F	19	5	10	15	40
David Musial	F	51	4	7	11	77
Sven Valenti	F	51	7	7	14	28
Michael Hreus	F	24	8	12	20	12
Chris Straube	F	24	5	7	12	6

KASSEL

Name	Pos.	GP	G	A	P	PIM
Josef Kontny	G	33	0	0	0	0
Gerhard Hegen	G	26	0	0	0	12
Markus Nachtmann	G	1	0	0	0	0
Milan Mokros	D	47	3	18	21	50
Alexander Engel	D	51	4	9	13	34
Jaroslav Mucha	D	49	3	19	22	70
Murray McIntosh	D	52	0	5	5	20
Georg Güttler	D	51	4	0	7	57
Teja Dambon	D	42	0	0	0	18
Sergej Wikulow	D	51	4	24	28	81
Jamie Bartman	D	11	0	2	2	4
Greg Johnston	F	51	21	33	54	32
Jedrzei Kasperczyk	F	52	20	30	50	38
Dave Morrison	F	38	5	19	24	18
Mike Millar	F	52	45	26	71	100
Ireneusz Pacula	F	48	3	6	9	32
Witalij Grossmann	F	31	8	5	13	45
Manfred Ahne	F	49	4	8	12	59
Peter Kwasigroch	F	48	12	15	27	8
Falk Ozellis	F	51	14	27	41	36
Mario Naster	F	48	9	7	16	14
Brian Hannon	F	44	16	12	28	16
Tino Boos	F	48	2	6	8	10

Great Britain

Federation:
British Ice Hockey Association
Adbolton Lane
Nottingham, NG12 2 LU
Great Britain
Telephone (+44.115) 9821515
Fax   (+44.115) 9821616
President: Frederick Meredith

Gen. Secretary: David Pickles

Frederik Meredith **David Pickles**
President Gen. Secretary

Premier Division 1994/95

Team	GP	W	L	D	Goals	Pts	PIM
1. Sheffield Steelers	44	35	5	4	334:183	74	961
2. Cardiff Devils	44	32	8	4	366:217	68	868
3. Nottingham Panthers	44	32	8	4	372:213	68	1115
4. Edinburgh Racers	44	25	14	5	335:289	55	862
5. Durham Wasps	44	22	19	3	264:242	47	883
6. Fife Flyers	44	20	20	4	271:242	44	583
7. Basingstoke Beavers	44	20	22	2	271:279	42	651
8. Humberside Hawks	44	17	21	6	331:330	40	708
9. Peterborough Pirates	44	12	27	5	248:368	29	886
10. Whitley Warriors	44	10	30	4	242:372	24	1177
11. Milton Keynes Kings	44	9	31	4	248:363	22	636
12. Bracknell Bees	44	6	35	3	189:373	15	786

British Championship Play-off

Group A	GP	W	L	D	Goals	Pts	PIM	Group B	GP	W	L	D	Goals	Pts	PIM
Sheffield	6	4	2	0	35:24	8	137	Edinburgh	6	4	1	1	42:37	9	100
Nottingham	6	3	9	0	35:25	6	139	Cardiff	6	3	1	2	46:30	8	34
Fife	6	3	3	0	29:37	6	88	Basingstoke	6	2	3	1	33:38	5	80
Humberside	6	2	4	0	28:42	4	143	Durham	6	0	4	2	23:39	2	38

Semifinals Sheffield Steelers – Cardiff Devils 7:5
Nottingham Panthers – Edinburgh Racers 11:7

Final Sheffield Steelers – Edinburgh Racers 7:2

**Peterborough Pirates and Milton Kings relegated to „Division one"
Slough Jets promoted to the „Premier Division" 1995/96**

Premier Division 1994/95

Top Scorers

Name	Team	GP	G	A	P
Tony Hand	ED	43	70	137	207
Ivan Matulik	ED	44	87	80	167
Randy Smith	PET	44	53	84	167
Chris Palmer	ED	37	82	85	167
Hilton Ruggles	CAR	44	93	64	157
Rick Brebant	NOT	39	58	94	152
Scott Morrison	HM	44	68	78	146
Paul Adey	NOT	44	72	73	145
Patrick Scott	MK	43	69	71	140
Doug Mc Ewen	CAR	44	62	75	137

Goalkeeper statistic (Minimum 1200 mins)

Name	Team	GP	MIN	SOG	GA	% SV
Martin McKay	SHF	43	1980	1044	128	87.73
Stephen Foster	DUR	44	2513	1565	216	86.19
Bill Morrison	BAS	42	2221	1555	223	85.65
Jason Wood	CR/BS	42	1602	1024	152	85.15
Colin Hamilton	PET	44	1231	1104	169	84.69
Steve Butler	NOT	38	1806	961	152	84.16
John McCrone	FIF	43	1935	1035	169	83.67
Moray Hanson	ED	43	2216	1404	233	83.40
Kevin Dean	WHIT	36	1519	1114	195	82.49
Simon Wren	PET	38	1419	1114	199	82.13

Premier Division Club Secretaries

Basingstoke Beavers
Rick Peters
Woodford Court Hotel
19-23 Studland Rd.
Bouremouth BH4 8H2

Bracknell Bees
Jane Mebougall
John Nike Leisuresport Compl.
John Nike Wat
Bracknell, Berks RG12 4TN

Cardiff Devils
John Lawless
Harlem Court Bute Terrace
Cardiff CF1 2FE

Durham Wasps
Tom Smith
Durham Ice Rink
Durham City DH1 1SQ

Fife Flyers
Betty Mantosh
Kirkcaldy Ice Rink Rosslyn St.
Kirkcaldy, Fife KY1 3HS

Humberside Seahawks
Adrian Florence
Humberside Ice Arena Kingston St.
Hull HU1 2O2

Nottingham Panthers
Rosemary Hardcastle
Nottingham Ice Stadium
Lower Parliment St.
Nottingham NG1 1LA

Peterborough Pirates
David Thorre
170 Parl Rd.
Peterborough PE1 ZUF

Sheffield Steelers
Sharon Lawley
Sheffield Arena Broughton Lane
Sheffield S9 ZDR

Whitley Warriors
Peter Alderson
6 East Farm Terrace
Cramlington, Northumberland
NE23 9DT

Greece

Federation:
Helenic Ice Sports Federation
272 B El. Venizelou (Thisseos Ave.)
Athens
Greece
Telephone (+30.1) 941 4882 or 941 4969
Fax   (+30.1) 941 7939
Telex   215112 gisf gr
President: Christos Hatziathanassiou
Gen. Secretary: Michalis Syrellis

Ch. Hatziathanassiou   **Michalis Syrellis**
President   Gen. Secretary

Season 1994/95 no championship

Last champions
1989	Aris Tessaloniki		1993	Ice Flyers Athens
1990	Aris Tessaloniki		1994	No championship
1991	Aris Tessaloniki		1995	No championship
1992	Aris Tessaloniki			

Hong Kong

Federation:
Hong Kong Ice Hockey Association
B 8–9/F., Causeway Centre, Hong Kong
Telephone (+85.2) 2827 5033 or 2827 5050
Fax   (+85.2) 2827 2698 or 2893 8443
President: Li Guang-Jing
G.P.O. Box 1058, Hong Kong
Telephone (+85.2) 332 7097
Fax   (+85.2) 710 9017
Gen. Secretary: Li Yuan-Sheng
Flat C, 18/F., 520 Nathan Road, Kowloon,
Hong Kong
Telephone (+85.2) 771 1131
Fax   (+85.2) 783 0127

Li Guang-Jing   **Feng Xiang-Chi**
President   Chairman

Season 1994/95
no championship

Hungary

Federation:
Hungarian Ice Hockey Federation
Istvanmezei ut 1–3
Kisstadion
H-1146 Budapest
Hungary
Telephone (+36.1) 157 0007
Fax   (+36.1) 157 0007
President: Dr. Tamas Sarközy
Gen. Secretary: Tamas Harsfalvi

Dr. Tamas Sarközy   Tamas Harsfalvi
President   Gen. Secretary

Championships 1994/95

Team	GP	W	T	L	Goals	Pts
1. FTC Budapest	20	13	3	4	131: 74	29
2. Volan Szekesfehervar	20	13	1	6	117: 74	27
3. Lehel HC	20	12	2	6	102: 71	26
4. Dunaferr	20	10	4	6	114: 62	24
5. Ujpesti T. E. Budapest	20	6	2	12	102: 98	14
6. MAC N. Budapest	20	0	0	20	54:241	0

Play-offs
3th place
Dunaferr   – Lehel HC   4:3, 5:2
Final
FTC Budapest   – Volan Szekesfehervar 2:4, 3:2, 4:2

Awards
Best Scorer
G. Ocskay (Volan)

Best Goalie
K. Ban (Ujpesti)

Best Defense
V. Szelig (Dunaferr)

Best Forward
T. Dobos (FTC)

Clubs National League
Ferencvarosi Torna Club
H-1091 Budapest, Üllöi u. 129
Lehel HC
H-5100 Jaszbereny, Bercsenyi u. 12/a
Ujpesti Torna Egylet
H-1067 Budapest, Eötvös u. 7
Alba-Volan SC
H-8000 Szekesfehervar, Börgöndi u. 14
Miskolci HC
H-3529 Miskolc, Felszabaditok u. 9
Debreceni AHC
H-4024 Debrecen, Piac u. 58
Nepstadion Szabadidö Egyesület
H-1146 Budapest, Istvanmezei u. 1/3
Dunaferr SE
H-2400 Dunaujvaros, Eszperanto u. 4

All Time Champions
Ferencvarosi Torna Club Budapest	20
Ujpesti Dozsa Sport-Club	12
BKE Budapest	7
Vörös Meteor Sport-Club	5
M. T. K. Budapest	3
Bp. Kinizsi Sport-Club	3
B. B. T. E. Budapest	2
Bp. Postas SC	2
Szekesfehervari Volan Sport-Club	1
Lehel SC General	1

Magyar Kupa 1994
FTC Budapest – Dunaferr 5:2
Volan   – Ujpesti   9:1
Final
FTC Budapest – Volan   8:2

India

Federation:
Winter Games Federation of India
Western Naval Command
Att. Vice Admiral S. Jain
Shahid Bhagat Singh Road
Bombay – 400 001
India
Telephone (+9) 286 0932
        (+9) 286 1202
        (+9) 286 4325
President: Vice Admiral S. Jain
Gen. Secretary: Abhay Dogra

Abhay Dogra
Member of the Council and
in charge of ice hockey players

Iceland

Federation:
Icelandic Sport Federation
Laugardal
104 Reykjavik
Iceland
Telephone (+35.41) 813 377
Fax   (+35.41) 678 848
Telex   2314 ISI
President: Ellert B. Schram
Gen. Secretary: Sigurdur Magnusson
Ice Hockey Committee Chairman: Jon Thor Eythorsson

Ellert B. Schram
President

Sigurdur Magnusson
Gen. Secretary

Clubs

Skautafelag Akureyrar
Ishokkideild Ice Rink
Naustavegur 1
600 Akureyri

Björninn
c/o S. Sigurosson
Stararinna 7
112 Reykjavik

Skautafelag Reykjavikur
Asbuortröö 11
220 Hafnarfiröi

Icelandic Championships 1994/95

Team	GP	Goals	Pts
1. Skautafelag Akureyrar A	6	107:19	12
2. Björninn IK	6	55:51	8
3. Skautafelag Reykjavikur	6	29:78	3
4. Skautafelag Akureyrar B	6	22:81	1

Play-off final
Skautafelag Akureyrar A   – Björninn IK   18:7, 11:5

Israel

Federation:
Ice Hockey Federation of Israel
P. O. Box 23510
26 Chissin Street
Tel Aviv, 64284
Israel
Telephone (+972.3) 525 1007
Fax   (+972.3) 525 1349
President: Mark Zeitchik
Gen. Secretary: Lihu Ichilov

Mark Zeitchik
President

Regular season

Team	GP	W	T	L	Goals	Pts
1. HC Bat Yam	8	7	0	1	98: 50	14
2. Jerusalem Capitals	8	6	0	2	66: 48	12
3. HC Haifa	8	4	0	4	68: 35	8
4. HC Metulla	8	3	0	5	38: 64	6
5. HC Tel Aviv	8	0	0	8	32:108	0

Play-off

Semifinal

HC Bat Yam	– HC Metulla	13:5
Jerusalem Capitals	– HC Haifa	7:5

Final

HC Bat Yam	– Jerusalem Capitals	11:3

Last Champion

1990	HC Haifa
1991	HC Haifa
1992	No Championship
1993	No Championship
1994	HC Haifa
1995	HC Bat Yam

Eishockey
Anzeige-
System

Ice hockey
Display
System

- Anzeigesysteme für alle
  Sportarten
- Mikrocomputer-
  Steuerelektronik
- Energiesparende bistabile
  Anzeigenelemente oder
  Leuchtkammersysteme
- Sprechen Sie mit den
  Fachleuten von TELENORMA

- Display systems
  for all kinds of sports
- Microcomputer
  control electronics
- Energy-saving bistable
  indicator-element or
  light-chamber systems
- Talk to the TN specialists

 TELENORMA

BOSCH – TELECOM

Italy

Federation:

Federazione Italiana Sport Ghiaccio
Via G. B. Piranesi 44/B
I-20137 Milano
Italy
Telephone   (+39.2) 7014 1322
Fax   (+39.2) 761 0839 or 715 573

President: Dr. Paul Seeber
Vice-President: Nilo Riva
Gen. Secretary: Nando Buonomini

Dr. Paul Seeber	Nando Buonomini
President	Gen. Secretary

SERIE A CLUBS

Hockey Club Alleghe
c/o Stadio del Ghiaccio
Via Lungolago, 19
32022 Alleghe BL
Telephone (+43.7) 523 300 or 523 343
Fax (+43.7) 723 791
Presidente: Riva Gianfranco

Asiago Hockey
c/o Stadio del Ghiaccio
Via Stazione
36012 Asiago/Vicenza
Telephone (+42.4) 64 580 or 463 082
Fax (+42.4) 64 144
Presidente: Corradin Corrado

HC Bolzano
Casella Postale 258
39100 Bolzano
Telephone (+47.1) 914 983
Fax (+47.1) 200 108
Presidente: Otto Massimo

SG Brunico
Via Castel Lamberto, 1
39031 Brunico/BZ
Telephone (+47.4) 85 599
Fax (+47.4) 84 329
Presidente: Paccagnella Stefano

Devils Milano
Via Piranesi 14
20137 Milano
Telephone (+2) 7000 4220
Fax (+2) 7000 4221
Presidente: Alajmo Gustavo

HC Fassa
c/o Stadio del Ghiaccio
Via Costa 123
38030 Alba di Canazei (TN)
Telephone (+46.2) 62 499
Fax (+46.2) 62 004
Presidente: Vianini Valeriano

HC Gardena
Casello Postale 1
39046 Ortisei (BZ)
Telephone (+47.1) 796 246 or 796 315
Fax (+47.1) 797 551
Presidente: Dell'Antonio Arno

Varese Hockey
Via Albani, 3
21100 Varese
Telephone (+33.2) 241 300
Fax (+33.2) 281 770
Presidente: Blumer Roberto

HC Courmaosta
Piazza Cavalieri di Vittorio Veneto, 7
11100 Aosta
Telephone (+16.5) 238 485
Fax (+16.5) 238 486
Presidente: Rivetti Carlo

SG Milano
Via Egadi, 6
20144 Milano
Telephone (+2)552 201
Fax (+2) 5730 1947
Presidente: Moretti Massimo

All Time Champion Alle Landesmeister	
Cortina d'Ampezzo	15
HC Milano	11
HC Bolzano	12
Inter Milano	5
Diavoli Rosi Neri	4
Gröden	4
Ass. Milanese	3
HC Milan	3
Varese	2
HC Merano	1
Diavoli Milano	1

Serie A
1994/95

Team	GP	W	T	L	Goals	Pts
1 HC Bolzano Wurth S. R. L.	36	26	1	9	215:115	53
2 Shimano Varese Hockey	36	23	3	10	169:111	49
3 HC Stone Island Courmaosta	36	17	7	12	139:120	41
4 SG Milano Saima Avandero	36	16	4	16	141:149	36
5 Hockey Devils Milano SRL	36	14	6	16	156:165	34
6 HC Finstral Gardena	36	15	4	17	158:166	34
7 HC Alleghe Tegola Canadese	36	15	4	17	110:130	34
8 SG Brunico	36	15	2	19	143:176	32
9 HC Fassa Wuber	36	13	2	21	162:183	28
10 Supermercati A&O Asiago Hockey	36	8	3	25	117:195	19

Play-off

Quarterfinals (best of 3)

HC Bolzano	– SG Brunico	8:1	4:2	–
HC Varese	– HC Alleghe	6:1	4:2	–
HC Courmaosta	– HC Gardena	6:3	1:2	12:5
Saima Milano	– Devils Milano	5:6	3:2	5:3

Semifinals (best of 5)

HC Bolzano	– Saima Milano	7:6	5:4	5:6	10:4	–
HC Varese	– HC Courmaosta	4:3	5:1	3:2	–	–

Finals

HC Bolzano	– HC Varese	5:2	3:7	2:5	10:2	5:3

HC BOLZANO

Name	GP	Pt	G	A	PIM
Igor Alberti	4	0	0	0	0
Christian Alderucci	44	9	1	8	56
Alessandro Badiani	37	11	1	10	12
Manuel Bergamo	12	0	0	0	0
Mario Doyon	45	43	13	30	91
Daniele Giacomin	18	5	3	2	34
Ingemar Gruber	5	0	0	0	0
Kim Issel	5	2	0	2	4
Jaromir Jagr	1	0	0	0	0
Enrico Laurati	19	2	0	2	2
Igor Maslennikov	41	78	32	46	39
Robert Oberrauch	45	35	9	26	90
David Pasin	42	108	43	65	80
Martin Pavlu	47	69	18	51	20
Roland Ramoser	46	89	41	48	32
Michael Rosati	47	1	0	1	2
Ruggero de mio Rossi	40	9	4	5	40
Christian Timpone	7	2	1	1	12
Patrick Timpone	20	3	2	1	6
Sergei Vostrikov	43	89	49	40	61
Reinhard Wieser	46	10	5	5	61
Bruno Zarrillo	46	107	42	65	30
Harald Zingerle	44	10	5	5	2

HC VARESE HOCKEY

Name	GP	Pt	G	A	PIM
Chad Biafore	43	41	11	30	84
Paolo Casciaro	40	12	3	9	87
Angelo Catenaro	44	18	4	14	62
Anthony Circelli	43	35	2	33	46
Mark Cupolo	42	34	14	20	101
Stefano Figliuzzi	40	77	40	37	45
Alessandro Gorini	1	0	0	0	0
Piero Greco	27	1	0	1	2
Stefan Mair	37	2	1	1	6
Maurizio Mansi	46	84	40	44	40
John Massara	41	43	19	24	22
Pat Mazzoli	24	1	0	1	10
Giancarlo Merzario	45	6	2	4	52
Mario Nobili	44	60	25	35	65
Luca Orrigoni	37	7	3	4	76
Vezio Sacratini	45	56	21	35	52
Alexander Thaler	45	8	2	6	58
Ivano Zanatta	46	60	23	37	12

HC COURMAOSTA

Name	GP	Pt	G	A	PIM
Giacinto Boni	6	4	1	3	2
Markus Brunner	42	30	19	11	42
Carlo Buemi	2	0	0	0	0
Jim Camazzola	34	42	21	21	49
Pierangelo Cibien	39	35	14	21	77
Jan Czerlinsky	4	7	3	4	4
Luigi da Corte Zandatina	40	9	2	7	8
Giorgio de Bettin	39	23	6	17	24
Paolo de Luca	2	1	0	1	0
Marco Endrizzi	32	15	8	7	22
David Gagner	1	4	0	4	0
David Haas	22	34	14	20	64
Jason Lafreniere	41	72	25	47	24
Bill McDougall	30	64	30	34	107
Corrado Micalef	42	0	0	0	14
Reinhold Oberhofer	29	5	0	5	18
Lorenzo Olivio	32	7	1	6	46
Davide Picco	2	0	0	0	2
Bob Reynolds	16	23	9	14	6
Hermes Sbicego	6	1	0	1	0
Alberto Scapinello	30	3	1	2	6
Marco Scapinello	37	14	5	9	33
Marco Sorbara	5	0	0	0	0
William Stewart	36	17	2	15	70
Adriano Tancon	5	0	0	0	0
Vittorio Zafalon	40	7	2	5	6

SG MILANO SAIMA

Name	GP	Pt	G	A	PIM
Marco Allevato	16	0	0	0	2
Massimo Ansoldi	31	10	7	3	32
Chris Bartolone	42	38	12	26	50
Scott Beattie	43	60	34	26	46
Michele Cereghini	15	1	0	1	8
Georg Comploj	43	32	7	25	100
Kristian Comploi	41	3	0	3	32
Pietro Cotini	1	0	0	0	0
Phil de Gaetano	27	16	3	13	22
Luca de Zordo	21	2	0	2	16
Frank di Muzio	41	53	21	32	77
Joseph Ferraccioli	43	55	16	39	10
Tony Fiore	40	41	14	27	28
Aldo Iaquinta	33	7	2	5	57
Andrea Mosele	40	7	2	5	24
Marco Pietroniro	35	36	15	21	39
Rico Rossi	21	12	3	9	82
Matteo Sala	13	0	0	0	10
Maurizio Scudier	40	32	14	18	12
Carmine Vani	33	38	19	19	70
Giovanni Volante	6	0	0	0	0
Michael Zanier	32	0	0	0	25

HOCKEY DEVILS MILANO

Name	GP	Pt	G	A	PIM
Paul Beraldo	1	0	0	0	0
Roberto Bortot	20	11	7	4	27
Mario Brunetta	33	0	0	0	10
Mirko Ceschini	34	5	3	2	22
Armando Chelodi	33	42	11	31	6
Tom Chorske	7	16	11	5	6
Christian Ciaurro	4	0	0	0	0
Alessandro Cintori	35	15	5	10	16
Mike de Angelis	23	15	4	11	24
Massimiliano Durante	26	7	4	3	8
Dimitri Frolov	29	19	5	14	41
Luca Fusoni	37	11	0	11	38
Robert Anthony Ginnetti	29	55	17	38	24
Anthony Iob	29	52	26	26	71
Emilio Iovio	25	36	17	19	16
Jouri Leonov	3	1	0	1	0
Brian McColgan	8	7	2	5	6
Sergio Momesso	2	5	1	4	2
Santino Pellegrino	7	8	5	3	0
Josef Podlaha	3	1	0	1	0
Frantisek Prochazka	5	2	1	1	6
Alessandro Rossi	10	0	0	0	0
Larry Rucchin	32	19	8	11	12
Fabio Sguazzero	37	16	7	9	6
Ricky Tessari	8	0	0	0	6
Lucio Topatigh	33	56	28	28	127
Marco Vaccani	11	0	0	0	2
Giovanni Volante	3	0	0	0	4
Federico Zancanella	36	9	2	7	32

HC GARDENA

Name	GP	Pt	G	A	PIM
Werner Bernardi	3	0	0	0	0
Patrick Brugnoli	33	30	13	17	8
Frank Caprice	39	0	0	0	0
Aggie Casale	37	80	34	46	51
Ivo Comploj	36	7	6	1	10
Manuel Demetz	15	2	0	2	0
Vincent Guidotti	17	17	8	9	14
Martin Jiranek	8	27	14	13	2
Franz Kasslatter	39	11	3	8	20
Erwin Kostner	36	18	0	18	8
Fabian Kostner	37	2	1	1	16
Thomas Kostner	34	28	12	16	6
Ronni Mesikämmen	23	8	3	5	36
Mirko Moroder	34	32	17	15	34
Jon Morris	38	73	29	44	36
Günther Nocker	37	11	5	6	26
Darryl Olsen	37	26	8	18	49
Leo Pitscheider	16	0	0	0	10
Jlijtsch Prinoth	26	1	0	1	6
Kenneth Strong	28	39	15	24	26

HC FASSA

Name	GP	Pt	G	A	PIM
Antony Amonte	14	38	22	16	10
Mustafa Besic	39	75	18	57	26
Shawn Byram	15	31	15	16	43
Alessandro Carpano	32	4	4	0	49
Ivano Cloch	39	15	6	9	14
Nicola Conforti	34	0	0	0	8
Eric Dandenault	31	31	14	17	87
Renato Daprai	7	0	0	0	0
Alberto Felicetti	28	3	2	1	12
Dino Felicetti	38	62	28	34	95
Dmitri Filippov	3	2	2	0	0
Alexander Gschliesser	39	25	9	16	22
Sergio Liberatore	36	6	3	3	91
Marco Locatin	34	7	4	3	20
Giovanni Marchetti	39	36	7	29	56
Stefano Margoni	32	13	5	8	50
Stefan Nyman	17	10	3	7	12
Elmar Parth	6	0	0	0	2
Francesco Rizzi	2	0	0	0	0
Martino Soracreppa	36	42	13	29	24
Sergej Sorokin	38	46	21	25	12
Igor Viazmikine	12	25	8	17	6

SG BRUNICO

Name	GP	Pt	G	A	PIM
Martin Crepaz	38	33	15	18	14
Franceso de Santis	38	18	10	8	55
Igor Dorofejev	36	71	30	41	45
Vladimir Eremin	38	54	21	33	26
Harald Golser	4	0	0	0	0
Martin Helfer	38	3	0	3	18
Patrick Hellweger	36	3	1	2	16
Angelo Libertucci	37	0	0	0	4
Paul Lochmann	25	0	0	0	18
Ivo Machacka	38	20	8	12	18
Diego Marchiori	15	1	0	1	0
Andrea Paccagnella	34	4	0	4	4
Christian Piccolruaz	38	28	8	20	4
Matthias Prantner	35	18	6	12	43
Alexander Silgener	1	0	0	0	2
Werner Straudi	30	4	2	2	26
Igor Sultanovich	38	56	30	26	6
Thomas Tinkhauser	36	15	9	6	22
Viaczeslav Uvaev	37	26	6	20	28

ASIAGO HOCKEY

Name	GP	Pt	G	A	PIM
Dominic Amodeo	34	51	24	27	4
Gianfranco Basso	2	0	0	0	0
Bruno Campese	39	0	0	0	14
Roberto Cantele	23	1	0	1	18
Enrico Ferretti	2	0	0	0	0
Alexander Ioudine	36	28	11	17	50
Serguei Ivanov	38	32	11	21	16
Gianpiero Longhini	23	1	1	0	12
Oleg Maltsev	22	14	6	8	61
Gaetano Miglioranzi	21	9	2	7	50
Mark Montanari	39	56	22	34	50
Marco Mosele	21	1	0	1	20
Ray Podlosky	8	21	10	11	2
Fabio Rigoni	28	7	4	3	29
Luca Rigoni	30	17	6	11	4
Manuel Rigoni	2	0	0	0	0
Andy Rimsha	8	11	4	7	18
Cristiano Sartori	28	3	1	2	10
Gianluca Schivo	33	11	5	6	53
Stefano Segafredo	32	21	13	8	85
Michele Strazzabosco	33	9	2	7	62
Luca Tessari	24	2	0	2	14
Franco Vellar	29	14	6	8	32
Valentino Vellar	34	4	3	1	109

HC ALLEGHE

Name	GP	Pt	G	A	PIM
Maurizio Bortolussi	36	40	20	20	89
Michael Brewer	35	23	5	18	48
Trevor Burgess	35	16	8	8	93
Giuseppe Busillo	32	29	13	16	73
Boris Bykovski	38	45	16	29	24
Niky Cadorin	9	0	0	0	0
Carlo de Riva	6	0	0	0	0
Lino de Toni	34	38	22	16	32
Marco de Toni	35	7	4	3	18
Matthias de Toni	9	1	0	1	0
Michele de Toni	38	12	5	7	38
Milos de Toni	5	0	0	0	2
David Delfino	38	0	0	0	2
Fabrizio Fontanive	22	2	1	1	14
Carlo Lorenzi	28	7	3	4	14
Christian Moretti	37	0	0	0	36
Diego Riva	3	1	0	1	0
Ilario Riva	36	3	1	2	4
Giulio Soia	37	10	4	6	36
Alen Tormen	22	3	1	2	39
Daniele Veggiato	22	4	1	3	6
Andrei Zhukov	35	32	9	23	98

Japan

Federation:

Japan Ice Hockey Federation
Kishi Memorial Hall
1-1-1, Jin'nan, Shibuya-ku
Tokyo, 150-50
Japan
Telephone (+81.3) 3481 2404
Fax (+81.3) 3481 2407
President: Yoshiaki Tsutsumi
Chief Exec. Director: Shoichi Tomita

Yoshiaki Tsutsumi
President

Shoichi Tomita
Chief Exec. Director

Clubs

Furukawa Denko
Ice Hockey Club
500 Kiyotaki-cho
Nikko-shi
Tochigi 321-14

Nippon Paper Cranes
Ice Hockey Club
2-1-47, Tottori-minami
Kushiro-shi
Hokkaido 084

Kokudo
Ice Hockey Club
6-35-1, Jingumae
Shibuya-ku
Tokyo150

New Oji
Ice Hockey Club
2-1-1, Oji-cho
Tomakomai-shi
Hokkaido 053

Seibu Tetsudo
Ice Hockey Club
3-1-25, Higashifushimi
Hoya-shi
Tokyo 202

Yukijrushi
Ice Hockey Club
6-1-1, Naebo-cho
Higashi-ku, Sapporo-shi
Hokkaido 065

29th Japan Ice Hockey League 1994/95

The First Half (Regular Season)

Team	GP	W	T	L	Goals	Pts
1. Kokudo Tokyo	15	13	1	1	59:25	27
2. New Oji Tomakomai	15	8	2	5	67:47	18
3. Seibu Tetsudo Tokyo	15	8	1	6	56:42	17
4. Nippon Paper Kushiro	15	7	1	7	52:50	15
5. Yukijirushi Sapporo	15	6	1	8	36:48	13
6. Furukawa Denko Nikko	15	0	0	15	23:81	0

The Second Half (Regular Season)

Team	GP	W	T	L	Goals	Pts
1. Seibu Tetsudo Tokyo	15	12	0	3	76:38	24
2. New Oji Tomakomai	15	12	0	3	72:42	24
3. Kokudo Tokyo	15	9	0	6	68:48	18
4. Nippon Paper Kushiro	15	7	0	8	51:59	14
5. Yukijirushi Sapporo	15	4	1	10	35:70	19
6. Furukawa Denko Nikko	15	0	1	14	27:72	1

Play-off Final

Kokudo – Seibu Tetsudo 3:2 in 5 games
4:3, 2:2 (PS 1:0), 2:1, 1:1 (PS 1:0), 4:1

Top Scorers (Regular Season)

	Name	Team	GP	P	G	A
1.	Ryan Fujita	Seibu Tetsudo	30	46	25	21
	Norio Suzuki	New Oji	30	46	16	30
3.	Akihito Sugisawa	New Oji	30	38	17	21
4.	Taku Takahashi	Seibu Tetsudo	27	35	16	19
	Hiroshi Matsuura	New Oji	30	35	24	11
6.	Steven Tsujiura	Kokudo	29	32	12	20
	Toshiyuki Sakai	Kokudo	26	32	10	22
8.	Chris Yule	Kokudo	28	30	23	7
	Taro Nihei	Kokudo	28	30	15	15
10.	Hideyuki Ueno	Seibu Tetsudo	30	29	15	14

Korea

Federation:
Korean Ice Hockey Association
106 Olympic Gym. No 2
Oyun-Dong, Songpa-Ku
Seoul
Korea
Telephone (+82.2) 420 4291 + 423 2407
Fax   (+82.2) 420 4160
President: Kap-Chul Park
Secretary: Jae-Jung Koh

Kap-Chul Park
President

Jae-Jung Koh
Secretary

Korean league 1994/95

Teams	GP	W	T	L	Goals	Pts
1. Seoktop	15	10	3	2	56:40	23
2. Yonsei	15	11	0	4	74:35	22
3. Korea	15	7	1	7	62:65	15
4. Hanyang	15	6	2	7	52:60	14
5. Kwangwoon	15	4	1	10	41:58	9
6. Kyunghee	15	3	1	11	39:66	7

Championship final
Seoktop – Yonsei   1:0, 2:3, 3:1

Top scorers

Name	Team	GP	G	A	P
1. Cho Chul-Woo	Kwangwoon	15	14	4	18
2. Kim Hee-Woo	Seoktop	15	9	8	17
3. Youn Kook-Il	Yonsei	15	12	4	16
4. Kim Sung-Bok	Yonsei	15	10	5	15
Kim Young-Nam	Korea	15	9	6	15
Song Hyun-Suk	Yonsei	15	8	7	15
7. Oh Keun-Young	Kwangwoon	15	9	5	14
Bae Young-Ho	Hanyang	15	7	7	14
9. Park Sung-Min	Korea	15	8	5	13
Chang Eun-Suk	Yonsei	15	6	7	13

DPR Korea

Federation:
Ice Hockey Association of the
Democratic People's Republic of
Korea
Kumsongdong 2
Mangyongdae District
Pyongyang D.P.R. Korea

President: Kang Duk Chun
Secretary: Mun Yong-Song
Telephone (+85.02) 814 164
Fax   (+85.02) 814 403
Telex   5472 Kp

Kazakhstan

KIHF

Federation:

Kazakhstan Ice Hockey Federation
Kosmitcheskaya Street 12/1
492022 Ust-Kamenogorsk
Kazakhstan
Telephone   (+7.323) 247 5934
                    (+7.323) 247 5428
Fax   (+7.323) 247 5934
Fax Moscow (+7.095) 432 9400
President: Anatoly P. Zlotnikov
Gen. Secretary: Mark E. Dolgov

Anatoly P. Zlotnikov   Mark E. Dolgov
President   Gen. Secretary

Kazakhstan Championships 1994/95

Team	GP	W	T	L	Goals	Pts
1. Torpedo Ust-Kamenogorsk	12	10	1	1	88:38	21
2. Bulat Temirtau	12	7	1	4	48:41	15
3. Stroitel Karaganda	12	6	0	6	39:57	12
4. Torpedo II Ust-Kamenogorsk	12	0	0	12	28:67	0

Top Scorers

Name	Team	P	G+A
1. Konstantin Spodarenko	Torpedo	14	11+3
2. Sergei Antipov	Torpedo	12	6+6
3. Andrei Samokhvalov	Torpedo	12	5+7
4. Yury Karatayev	Torpedo	12	4+8
5. Alexander Filippov	Stroitel	11	9+2
6. Andrei Savenkov	Torpedo	11	8+3
7. Sergei Mogilnikov	Torpedo	10	4+6
8. Vladimir Tushentsov	Bulat	10	3+7

Best Players of the Championship

Goalkeeper: Vladimir Ryaguzov   Bulat Temirtau
Defence: Andrei Savenkov   Torpedo Ust-Kamenogorsk
Forward: Alexander Filippov   Stroitel Karaganda

Latvia

Federation:

Latvian Ice Hockey Federation
Krisjana Barona Street 88
LV-1450 Riga
Latvia
Telephone (+371.2) 273 661
                (+371.2) 278 380
Fax   (+371.2) 278 380
President: Kirovs Lipmans
Gen. Secretary: Harijs Vitolins

Kirovs Lipmans
President

Harijs Vitolins
Gen. Secretary

Latvian Championships 1994/95

Team	GP	W	T	L	Goals	Pts
1. NIK'S Brih Riga	24	22	0	2	203: 93	44
2. Essamika Ogre	24	19	0	5	211: 89	38
3. Pardaugava Riga II	24	11	1	12	121:135	23
4. NIK'S Riga Juniors	24	4	1	19	84:163	9
5. Latvijas Zelts Riga	24	3	0	21	92:231	6

Team for European Cup:
Pardagauva Riga I (ISIHL)

Best players awards

Goalkeeper:	Viktors Durnovs	NIK'S Brih
Defender:	Martins Grundmanis	Ogre
Forward:	Sergejs Nikitins	NIK'S Brih

Top Scorers

Name	Team	GP	G	A	P
1. Aigars Razgals	Essamika	23	36	33	69
2. Ingus Eglitis	Essamika	24	17	38	55
3. Sergejs Nikitins	NIK'S Brih	24	27	26	53
4. Martins Grundmanis	Essamika	24	24	27	51
5. Normunds Karpinskis	NIK'S Brih	23	28	22	50
6. Nikolajs Sirotkins	NIK'S Brih	23	21	25	46
7. Maris Drelings	NIK'S Brih	23	20	24	44
8. Andris Vitolins	Essamika	24	20	23	43
9. Girts Ankipans	Essamika	24	17	22	39
10. Aleksandrs Golubovics	NIK'S Brih	23	20	16	36

Latvian First Division

Team	Goals	Pts
1. Riga Alianse	146: 41	26: 2
2. Lido	106: 65	22: 6
3. RTU Hanza	87: 82	19: 9
4. Essamika Ogre II	101: 71	18:10
5. Baldera Hokeja Skola	51: 63	11:17
6. HK Riga	70: 69	10:18
7. Saga	58:106	5:23
8. Dispeceri	54:176	1:27
9. THK Talsi	139: 20	20: 0
10. Valmiera	92: 45	14: 6
11. Smiltenes Vanagi	55: 62	8:12
12. Seda	41: 92	6:14
13. Rig. Sin	35:118	6:14
14. Vecemeistars	35: 50	6:14

Lithuania

Federation:
Lithuanian Ice Hockey Federation
Zemaitis 6
2675 Vilnius
Lithuania
Telephone (+37.0) 263 4587
Fax   (+37.0) 266 1223
Telex   261-118 LSK
President: Vytautas Gudiskis
Gen. Secretary: Rimantas Dziautas

Vytautas Gudiskis
President

Rimantas Dziautas
Gen. Secretary

Lithuanian Championships 1994/95

Team	GP	W	T	L	Goals	Pts
1. Energija Elektrenai	19	18	1	0	207: 45	37
2. Germantas Telsiai	20	13	1	6	107: 81	27
3. Solvita Kaunas	20	11	1	8	143:116	23
4. Junior Nationalteam	20	10	1	9	133: 98	21
5. Poseidonas Elektrenai	20	3	0	17	74:211	6
6. Nemunas Rokiskis	19	2	0	17	70:183	4

Top Scorers

Name	Team	GP	G
1. V. Skadauskas	Energija Elektrenai	18	30
2. S. Kuliesius	Junior Nationalteam	20	28
J. Merkutov	Germantas Telsiai	20	28
4. E. Bauba	Junior Nationalteam	15	27
5. G. Sagaika	Solvita Kaunas	19	26

Luxembourg

Federation:
Fédération Luxembourgeoise
de Hockey sur Glace
Mme. Monique Scheier-Schneider
Boite postale 1632
L-1016 Luxembourg

Telephone (+352) 492 198
Fax   (+352) 402 228
President:
Christian Thiry
Gen. Secretary:
Monique Scheier-Schneider

Season 1994/95 no championship

Championship was not played because of differences among Tornado Luxembourg and other teams (EHC Beaufort, Rapid Remich and Lokomotive Luxembourg). Too in this season Tornado Luxembourg played in one of Germany's lower league. Only the cup competition was played.

Luxembourg Cup 1995

Team	Country	GP	Goals	Pts
1. Tornado Luxembourg	LUX	10	143: 58	18
2. Leuven Chiefs	BEL	10	163: 34	18
3. ESU Kaiserslautern	GER	10	65: 94	8
4. Epinal Image Club	FRA	10	37: 94	8
5. Trier/Dillingen	GER	10	45: 70	6
6. Lokomotive Luxembourg	LUX	10	28:134	2

Tornado Luxembourg
as the winner of the cup will represent Luxembourg in European cup 1995/96.

Mexico

Federation:
Federación Mexicana de Deportes Invernales A. C.
Via Lactea 351
Jardines de Satelite
Naucalpan de Juarez
Estado de Mexico
531129 Mexico
Telephone (+52.5) 343 0855, 645 4570
          (+52.5) 652 9223, 557 4544 (Ext. 164)
Fax   (+52.2) 343 0855, 645 6308, 652 7232
President: José Luis Aguilar-Urzaiz
Gen. Secretary: Ignacio Goyarzu-Gonzales

J. L. Aguilar-Urzaiz
President

New Zealand

Federation:
New Zealand Ice Hockey Federation
P. O. Box 488
Christchurch
New Zealand
Telephone (+64.3) 364 2122
Fax   (+64.3) 364 2124
President: Ron O'Reilly
Gen. Secretary: Stanley Green

Ron O'Reilly
President

Stanley Green
Gen. Secretary

Season 1994

Champion 1994:	Auckland
Juniors:	Canterbury
Midget:	Canterbury

Last Champions

1990	Auckland
1991	Auckland
1992	No Champion
1993	No Champion
1994	Auckland

Netherlands

Federation:

Nederlandse Ijshockey Bond
P. O. Box 292
NL-2700 AG Zoetermeer
Netherlands
Telephone (+31.79) 417574
Fax (+31.79) 41302
President: John Th. M. C. Ponsioen
Secretary: Jack Ham
Exec. Director: Rob van Rijswijk

Rob van Rijswijk
Exec. Director

Elite Division Clubs

Geleen
P. O. Box 161
NL-6160 AD Geleen

Heerenveen
P. O. Box 715
HL-8440 AG Heerenveen

Nijmegen
Saltshof 17-08
NL-6604 EM Wychen

Panda's Rotterdam
P. O. Box 248
NL-3000 AE Rotterdam

Tilburg Trappers
P. O. Box 438
NL-5000 Ak Tilburg

Ehrendivision 1994/95

Team	GP	W	T	L	Pt	Goals
1. Couwenberg Trappers Tilburg	24	22	1	1	45	220: 52
2. Hatulek Heaters Geleen	24	17	2	5	36	189: 74
3. Fulda Tigers Nijmegen	24	17	1	6	35	118: 92
4. CP & A Eindhoven	24	13	1	10	27	124:136
5. Gunco Panda's Rotterdam	24	7	0	17	14	98:151
6. Heerenveen Flyers	24	2	2	20	6	70:159
7. Dordrecht Lions	24	2	1	21	5	68:223

Play-off

Semi finals

Trappers Tilburg	–	Eindhofen	7:0, 5:2, 5:4
Heaters Geleen	–	Tigers Nijmegen	0:3, 6:4, 6:3, 7:5

Final

Trappers Tilburg	–	Heaters Geleen	5:4, 5:2, 14:2

Top Scorers 1994/95

Name	Team	GP	G	A	P
1. David Livingston	Tilburg	29	46	46	92
2. Antoine Geesink	Tilburg	30	13	63	76
3. Tomy Speel	Geleen	31	27	39	66
4. Kip Noble	Tilburg	30	25	41	66
5. Frank Versteeg	Geleen	31	24	41	65
6. Al Raymond	Geleen	30	28	36	64
7. Theo van Gerwen	Tilburg	30	28	35	63
8. Mark Bultje	Geleen	23	30	29	59
9. Igor Akulinin	Eindhoven	27	32	25	57
10. Theo Kruger	Eindhoven	23	24	32	56

Norway

Federation:
Norges Ishockeyforbund
Normannsgt. 47
N-0655 Oslo 6
Norway
Telephone (+47.22) 682 880
Fax   (+47.22) 681 583
President: Bjørn Ruud
Managing Director: Rune Hauger

Bjørn Ruud	Rune Hauger
President	Managing Director

Clubs

Lillehammer IK
Box 1105 – Skurva
2601 Lillehammer
Phone (+47.61) 260 015
Telefax (+47.61) 260 615

Storhamar IL
Box 1002
2301 Hamar
Phone (+47.62) 527 145
Telefax (+47.62) 529 138

Trondheim IK
Box 60
7001 Trondheim
Phone (+47.73) 916 246
Telefax (+47.73) 916 246

IL Sparta
Box 1088 – Valaskjold
1701 Sarpsborg
Phone (+47.69) 155 077
Telefax (+47.69) 155 057

Viking IHK
Box 121
4001 Stavanger
Phone (+47.51) 533 615
Telefax (+47.51) 536 840

IL Stjernen
Box 185
1601 Fredrikstad
Phone (+47.69) 319 980
Telefax (+47.69) 318 709

VIF Hockey
Box 9401 – Valerenga
0610 Oslo
Phone (+47.22) 687 206
Telefax (+47.22) 571 669

Championships 1994/95

Team	GP	W	T	L	Goals	Pts
1. Storhamar IL Hamar	28	21	5	2	195: 52	47
2. VIF Hockey Oslo	28	18	4	6	134: 91	40
3. Lillehammer IK	28	17	4	7	117: 97	38
4. Spektrum Flyers Oslo	28	15	3	10	118: 87	33
5. Stjernen Fredrikstad	28	13	3	12	134:125	29
6. Viking Stavanger	28	7	2	19	88:128	16
7. Trondheim IK	28	7	1	20	79:138	15
8. Sparta Sarpsborg	28	2	2	24	70:217	6

Quarter Finals A
1. Stjernen	19:16	6:2
2. Storhamar	12:11	6:2
3. Spektrum Oslo	14:18	0:8

Quarter Finals B
1. VIF Oslo	18:12	6:2
2. Lillihammer	14:13	4:4
3. Viking	15:22	2:6

Semi Finals
VIF Oslo	– Storhamar Hamar	2:4, 4:5
Stjernen Fredrikstad	– Lillehammer	6:3, 4:3

Final
Storhamar Hamar	– Stjernen Fredrikstad	4:1, 7:2, 6:1

Season Top Scorers

Name	Team	GP	G	A	P
Martin Åhlberg	Storhamar	37	49	22	71
Kyle McDonough	Stjernen	37	38	24	62
Dan O'Connell	Viking	32	37	21	58
Morten Finstad	Stjernen	37	26	32	58
Ørjan Løvdal	Stjernen	34	18	39	57
Eirik Paulsen	Viking	29	22	27	49
Tom Erik Olsen	Storhamar	36	26	21	47
Ole E. Dahlstrøm	Storhamar	33	25	22	47
Trond Magnussen	Lillehammer	34	27	19	46
Erik Kristiansen	Storhamar	37	17	28	45
Petter Salsten	Storhamar	37	18	23	41

All Star Team: Marthinsen (Storh.); Salsten (Storh.); Jakobsen (Spektrum); Magnussen (Lilleh.); Løvdal (Stjernen); Åhlberg (Storh.).
Coach of the year: S. Tholsson (Stjernen)
Gold puck award: Trond Magnussen (Lillehammer)

Poland

Federation:
Polish Ice Hockey Federation
Zieleniecka 1
Stadion X-Lecia
03-901 Warszawa
Poland
Telephone (+48.2) 617 6064
         (+48.2) 617 4564
Fax   (+48.2) 617 6064
President: Bogdan Tyszkiewicz
Gen. Secretary: Zenon Hajduga

Bogdan Tyszkiewicz
President

Zenon Hajduga
Gen. Secretary

Clubs

Autosan Sanok
Mickiewicza 12
38-500 Sanok

MHKS Polonia Bytom
Pulaskiego 71
41-902 Bytom

NKS Podhale Nowy Targ
Parkowa 14
34-400 Nowy Targ

GKS Naprzod Janow
Nalkowskiej 10
40-425 Katowice-Janow

RKS Stoczniowiec
Bazynskiego 1
80-868 Gdansk

KS Unia Oswiecim
Ul. Chemikow 4
32-601 Oswiecim

TTH Torun
Ul. Bema 23
87-100 Torun

SMS PZHL Sosnowiec
Ul. Maja 41
41-200 Sosnowiec

KKH Katowice
Ul. Dworcowa 15
40-012 Katowice

MKH Tysovia
Findera 2
43-100 Tychy

Championships 1994/95

Team	GP	W	T	L	Goals	Pts
1. NKS Podhale Nowy Targ	32	25	5	2	196: 77	55
2. KS Unia Oswiecim	32	23	3	6	202: 78	49
3. KKH Katowice	32	21	3	8	182: 86	45
4. GKS Naprzod Janow	32	16	7	9	152: 95	39
5. TTH Metron Torun	32	15	6	11	131:121	36
6. MHKS Polonia Bytom	32	11	3	18	97:167	25
7. RKS Stoczniowiec Gdansk	32	16	5	11	138:131	37
8. MKH Tysovia	32	16	2	14	122:101	34
9. STS Autosan Sanok	32	16	2	14	140:122	34
10. SMS PZHL Sosnowiec	32	8	1	23	77:159	17
11. BTH Bydgoszcz	32	4	1	27	65:165	9
12. KS Cracovia	32	1	2	29	85:285	4

Games for place 9–11

9. STS Autosan Sanok	4	4	0	0	27: 6	8
10. BTH Bydgoszcz	4	2	0	2	16: 19	4
11. KS Cracovia	4	0	0	4	11: 29	0

SMS PZHL Sosnowiec didn't play for 9th place

Play-off
Quarter finals

NKS Podhale	– MKH Tysovia	11:1, 6:2
KC Unia	– RKS Stozniowiec	5:1, 6:4
KKH Katowice	– MHKS Polonia	6:2, 9:2
GKS Naprzod	– TTH Metron	2:4, 2:3, 3:3, 2:1 P, 4:0

Semi finals

KS Unia	– KKH Katowice	3:7, 2:5, 5:3, 4:2, 5:3
NKS Podhale	– GKS Naprzod	10:0, 6:5, 5:1

Final

NKS Podhale	– KS Unia	9:5, 2:5, 7:0, 7:0

Rumania

Federation:

Federation Romana de Hochei pe Gheata
Blvd. Basarabia 35–37
73403 Bucuresti
Rumania
Telephone (+40.1) 6476 535
Fax   (+40.1) 3210 114
President: Dr. Dan Voiculescu
Secretary: Eduard Pana

Dr. Dan Voicuzescu   **Eduard Pana**
President   Secretary

Rumanian National League 1994/95

Team	GP	W	T	L	Goals	Pts
1. Steaua Bucuresti	20	17	2	1	146: 54	36
2. Sport Club M. Ciuc	20	13	2	5	114: 64	28
3. Sportul Studentesc	20	8	3	9	68:109	19
4. Dunarea Galati	20	7	2	11	67: 81	16
5. I.S.A.M.A. & Plastico	20	0	1	19	31:118	1

Top Scorer

Name	Team	G	A	P
1. Marius Gilga	Steaua Bucuresti	18	17	35
2. Ion Zaharia	Steaua Bucuresti	11	22	33
3. Levente Elekes	Sport Club M. Ciuc	24	8	32
4. Catalin Geru	Steaua Bucuresti	17	13	30
5. Peter Szabolcs	Sport Club M. Ciuc	15	14	29
6. Attila Balla.	Sport Club M. Ciuc	12	16	28
7. Zoltan Kertesz	Sport Club M. Ciuc	15	10	25
8. Gheorghe Daniel	Sportul Studentsc	16	7	23
9. Vasile Jumatate	Steaua Bucuresti	9	14	23
10. Eugen Radu	Steaua Bucuresti	13	8	21

All Time Champions

Team	Title	Team	Title
Steaua Bucuresti	31	Vointa Miercnrea Ciuc	2
CS Dinamo Bucuresti	7	Brasovia Brasov	1
Tenis Club Bucuresti	5	H. C. Bragadiri Bucuresti	1
H. C. Juventus Bucuresti	4	Dragos Voda Cernauti	1
Hockei Club Bucuresti	3	Venus Bucuresti	1
Telefon Club Bucuresti	2	H. C. Ciocanul Bucuresti	1
H. C. Rapid Bucuresti	2	Stiinta Cluj	1
Locomotiva Tirgun Mures	2	Recolta Miercurea Ciuc	1
Avintul IPEIL Miercurea Ciuc	2		

IIHF REFEREE SEMINAR
Hotel ASTORIA-Bled – July 16–23. 1995

IIHF-PARTNERS
NIKE · CANSTAR · BAUER · COOPER

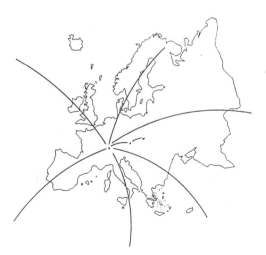

TATRA AIR

for further information
please contact our office:

Telephone: +42-7-236054
Fax: +42-7-294259

We fly the world to Slovakia and Slavakia to the world
TATRA AIR, the only Slovakian carrier, offers you convenient link to and from
Bratislava, capital of Slovakia
All destinations are easily connected with all major airports in the world
TRY EASY WAY: The direct link

Russia

Federation:
Ice Hockey Federation of Russia
Luzhnetskaja Naberezhnaja 8
119871 Moscow/Russia
Telephone (+70.95) 201 0820
(V. Sych)   (+70.95) 201 0277
            (+70.95) 201 1314
(Samoilov) (+70.95) 201 1132
Fax   (+70.95) 248 0322
President: Valentyn Sych
Vice President: Yuri Korolev
Gen. Secretary: Sergej Samoilov

Valentyn Sych
President

Sergej Samoilov
Gen. Secretary

All time champions 1947–1995

1947	Dynamo Moscow
1948 – 1950	CSKA Moscow
1951 – 1953	VVS Moscow
1954	Dynamo Moscow
1955/56	CSKA Moscow
1957	Krylja Moscow
1958 – 1961	CSKA Moscow
1962	Spartak Moscow
1963 – 1966	CSKA Moscow
1967	Spartak Moscow
1968	CSKA Moscow
1969	Spartak Moscow
1970 – 1973	CSKA Moscow
1974	Krylja Moscow
1975	CSKA Moscow
1976	Spartak Moscow
1977 – 1989	CSKA Moscow
1990	Dynamo Moscow
1991	Dynamo Moscow
1992 + 1993	Dynamo Moscow
1994	Lada Togliatti

Titels

CSKA Moscow	32
Dynamo Moscow	7
Spartak Moscow	4
VVS Moscow	3
Krylja Moscow	2
Lada Togliatti	1

Season 1994/95

Western Division

Team	GP	W	L	T	Goals	Pts
1. Torpedo Yaroslavl	52	33	15	4	152: 96	70
2. Krylja Sovetov Moscow	52	30	14	8	173:120	68
3. Dynamo Moscow	52	30	16	6	172:107	66
4. Torpedo Nizhny Novgorod	52	26	16	10	137:111	62
5. Itil Kazan	52	27	18	7	150:123	61
6. CSKA Moscow	52	25	20	7	158:114	57
7. SKA St. Petersburg	52	26	21	5	127:122	57
8. Khimik Voskresensk	52	23	21	8	122:125	54
9. Spartak Moscow	52	23	24	5	132:154	51
10. Severstal Cherepovets	52	20	28	4	111:151	44
11. Kristall Elektrostal	52	17	31	4	112:157	38
12. Tivali Minsk	52	13	31	8	102:151	34
13. Sokol Kiev	52	12	30	10	104:142	34
14. Pardaugava Riga	52	14	34	4	99:168	32

Eastern Division

Team	GP	W	L	T	Goals	Pts
1. Lada Togliatti	52	41	7	4	229: 83	86
2. Avangard Omsk	52	36	8	8	220:100	80
3. Metallurg Magnitogorsk	52	37	12	3	260:134	77
4. Salavat Yulayev Ufa	52	31	10	11	219:126	73
5. Traktor Chelyabinsk	52	26	21	5	177:146	57
6. Molot Perm	52	27	22	3	144:140	57
7. Torpedo Ust-Kamenogorsk	52	24	24	4	173:171	52
8. Avtomobilist Yekatarinenburg	52	18	22	12	126:137	48
9. CSK VVS Samara	52	19	26	7	161:169	45
10. Kristall Saratov	52	19	28	5	134:173	43
11. Rubin Tyumen	52	18	30	4	155:205	40
12. Sibir Novosibirsk	52	14	35	3	158:273	31
13. Metallurg Novokuznetsk	52	11	33	8	125:185	30
14. Stroitel Karaganda	52	3	46	3	99:338	9

Western Division

Top scorer

Name	Team	GP	G	A	Pts
1. Andrei Tarasenko	Torpedo	50	17	37	54
2. Sergei Zolotov	Krylja	45	14	31	45
3. Alexei Traseukh	Torpedo	51	21	22	43
4. Oleg Belov	CSKA	45	21	18	39
5. Alexei Chupin	Itil	49	23	14	37
6. Alexander Zybin	Torpedo	46	9	28	37
7. Vladimir Samylin	Torpedo	50	19	17	36
8. Albert Leschev	CSKA	51	12	24	36
9. Alexander Chibiryaev	Khimik	52	12	24	36
10. Dmitri Gogolev	Krylja	49	21	14	35

Top defensemen

Name	Team	GP	G	A	Pts
1. Vadim Brezgunov	Krylja	49	10	11	21
2. Dmitri Yerofeyev	Krylja	51	10	11	21
3. Andrei Skopintsev	Krylja	52	8	12	20
4. Alexei Putilin	Spartak	36	6	12	18
5. Karlis Skrastynsh	Riga	52	4	14	18

Eastern Division

Top scorer

Name	Team	GP	G	A	Pts
1. Dmitri Denisov	Salavat	52	43	17	60
2. Yevgeny Koreshkov	Metallurg	51	33	20	53
3. Konstantin Shafranov	Metallurg	47	21	30	51
4. Pavel Lazarev	Traktor	52	27	23	50
5. Igor Varitsky	Traktor	51	26	21	47
6. Boris Timofeyev	Salavat	52	22	24	46
7. Alexander Koreshkov	Metallurg	44	22	23	45
8. Sergei Osipov	Metallurg	52	26	18	44
9. Igor Dyakiv	Avangard	52	12	30	42
10. Oleg Kryazhev	Avangard	52	21	20	41

Top defensemen

Name	Team	GP	G	A	Pts
1. Valeri Nikulin	Traktor	52	14	14	28
2. Mikhail Shubinov	Kristall	46	10	17	27
3. Vladimir Antipin	Torpedo	52	8	15	23
4. Vadim Glovatsky	Traktor	52	2	17	19
5. Konstantin Maslyukov	Avangard	43	10	7	17

Play-offs

1th round (best of 3)

Teams		H	A	A
Avtomobilist Yekatarinenburg	– Torpedo Jaroslavl	1:2	1:4	–
Itil Kazan	– Salavat Yulayev Ufa	2:5	0:6	–
Molot Perm	– Dynamo Moscow	1:5	4:2	0:2
SKA St. Petersburg	– Avangard Omsk	2:1	1:2	1:3
Torpedo Ust-Kamenogorsk	– Krylja Moscow	0:7	2:7	–
CSKA Moscow	– Metallurg Magnitogorsk	2:3	2:5	–
Traktor Chelyabinsk	– Torpedo Nishny Novgorod	2:1	2:5	2:4
Chimik Woskresensk	– Lada Togliatti	0:1	1:8	–

Quarterfinals (best of 3)

Teams		H	A	A
Salavat Yulayev Ufa	– Torpedo Yaroslavl	2:1	3:2	–
Dynamo Moscow	– Avangard Omsk	7:3	2:5	7:2
Metallurg Magnitogorsk	– Krylja Moscow	4:3	4:2	–
Torpedo Nishny Novgorod	– Lada Togliatti	1:2	0:3	–

Semifinals (best of 3)

Teams		A	H	H
Dynamo Moscow	– Salavat Yulayev Ufa	4:3	1:2	2:1
Lada Togliatti	– Metallurg Magnitogorsk	1:4	8:1	3:2

Final (best of 5)

Teams		A	A	H	H	H
Lada Togliatti	– Dynamo Moscow	1:3	4:5	3:2	4:3	0:6

SEASON-AWARDS

Most productive line „TRUD TROPHY":
Shafranov – Y. Koreshov – A. Koreshov (Magnitogorsk)

Scoring leader „ISVISTIJA TROPHY":   Dmitri Denisov (Ufa) 64 Pts

Most HAT-TRICKS TROPHY: Nikolaj Marinenko (Omsk) 2 hat-tricks

Fair play cup „OGONEK TROPHY":   Torpedo Yaroslavl

Player of the year: Dmitri Denisov (Ufa)

Rookie of the year: Sergej Gusev (Samara)

WESTERN DIVISION	EASTERN DIVISION
Most valuable player	**Most valuable player**
Oleg Belov (CSKA)	Dmitri Denisov (Samara)
Rookie of the year	**Rookie of the year**
Alexej Morozov (Krylja)	Sergej Gusev (Samara)

ALL STAR TEAM

Sergej Abramov (Itil)	**GOALIE**	Alexej Marjin (Lada)
Dmitri Krasotkin (Yaroslavl) Andrej Skopintsev (Krylja)	**DEFENSEMEN**	Rafik Yakubov (Lada) Konstantin Maslyukov (Omsk)
Andrej Tarasenko (Yaroslavl) Oleg Belov (CSKA) Roman Iljin (Dynamo Moscow)	**FORWARDS**	Konstantin Shafranov (Magnitogorsk) Yevgeny Koreshkov (Magnitogorsk) Dmitri Denisov (Ufa)

Play-off   Scoring leaders

	Name	Team	GP	G	A	Pts
1.	Roman Iljin	Dynamo Moscow	14	7	9	16
2.	Vladimir Grachev	Dynamo Moscow	14	7	2	9
3.	Anatoli Yemelin	Lada	12	6	3	9
4.	Konstantin Shafranov	Metallurg Magnitogorsk	7	5	4	9
5.	Denis Metlyuk	Lada Togliatti	12	4	5	9
6.	Yuri Zlov	Lada Togliatti	12	5	3	8
7.	Yevgeny Koreshkov	Metallurg Magnitogorsk	7	3	5	8
8.	Vladimir Vorobjev	Dynamo Moscow	14	1	7	8
9.	Alexander Prokopjev	Dynamo Moscow	14	4	3	7
10.	Ravil Yakubov	Dynamo Moscow	14	4	3	7
11.	Ivan Svintsitsky	Lada Togliatti	10	3	4	7

Coaches Inter State Hockey League

Team	Head Coach	Assistant Coaches
Dynamo Moscow	Ravil Yakubov	Vladimir Semenov
CSKA Moscow	Viktor Tichonov	Viktor Kuskin, VI. Popov
Spartak Moscow	Valentin Gureyev (fired) Viktor Shalimov	Viktor Shalimov Nikolay Uryupin
Krylja Moscow	Igor Dmitriev	Sergej Kotov, Al. Zarubin
Chimik Woskresensk	Gennady Vlasyuk	Alexander Yerokhov
SKA St. Petersburg	Boris Michailov	A. Michailov, A. Zhukov
Pardaugava Riga	Mikhail Beskasov (fired) Leonid Beresnev	Leonid Beresnev Maris Baldonieks
Sokol Kiev	Alexander Seukand	Viktor Chibirev
Tivali Minsk	Andrej Sidorenko	A. Vladykin, V. Semenov
Nizhny Novgorod	Mikhail Varankov	V. Fedorov, S. Tyulapkin
Torpedo Yaroslavl	Sergeij Nikolayev	V. Shaposhnikov, V. Kiselev
Itil Kazan	Viktor Kuznetsov (fired) Vsevolod Yelfimov	V. Yelfinov, A. Cernetsov Alexander Cernetsov
Salavat Yulayev Ufa	Rafael Ishmatov	A. Antipin, L. Makarov
Severstal Cherepovets	Vladimir Golev	O. Galyamin, S. Ivanov
Kristall Saratov	Vladimir Kuplinov	Y. Korchin, S. Myasnikov
Lada Togliatti	Gennady Tsygurov	S. Mikhalev, A. Tychkin
Avangard Omsk	Leonid Kiselev	Y. Sinyugin, V. Shevchenko
Traktor Cheljabinsk	Valeri Belousov	S. Grigorkin, A. Timofeyev
Yekatarinenburg	Viktor Kutergin	V. Prokovjev, S. Selivanov
Magnitogorsk	Valeri Postnikov	A. Makhinov, V. Sukhov
Novokuznetsk	Viktor Laukin	M. Gomberg, S. Lantratov
Molot Perm	Vasili Spiridonov	G. Kosolapov, V. Sapichev
Ust Kamenogorsk	Vladimir Koptsov	V. Golts, V. Kirichenko
Stroitel Karaganda	Reikhan Ukanov	P. Pavlyuckenko, N. Krasev
Kristall Elektrostal	Vladimir Marinichev	M. Shikin, A. Zachesov
Sibir Novosibirsk	Sergej Akimov	Arkady Bagayev
VVS Samara	Yuri Moiseyev	V. Ivanov, A. Dolganov
Rubin Tyumen	Alexander Kuzmin	Y. Konovalov, G. Balashov

Dynamo Moscow

Pos	Name	GP	G	A	P	PM	GP	G	A	P	PM
							Play-off				
F	Vladimir Vorobjev	48	9	20	29	28	14	1	7	8	2
C	Alexander Prokopjev	46	17	9	26	74	14	4	3	7	14
F	Igor Bakhmutov	33	10	15	25	8	13	4	1	5	2
C	Ravil Yakubov	49	15	8	23	38	14	4	3	7	20
F	Roman Iljin	44	12	10	22	53	14	7	9	16	31
F	Vladimir Grachev	48	13	8	21	20	14	7	2	9	10
D	Yevgeny Gribko	44	10	7	17	38	14	0	2	2	8
F	Alexander Kuvaldin	47	7	8	15	10	14	1	2	3	10
F	Dmitri Chumachneko	36	7	8	15	14	14	3	2	5	20
D	Sergej Vyshedkevich	49	6	7	13	67	14	2	0	2	12
F	Dmitri Nazarov	47	10	3	13	16	14	3	1	4	4
F	Yuri Leonov	20	7	5	12	6	12	3	4	7	2
C	Dmitri Sergeyev	41	7	4	11	4	14	1	1	2	4
F	Igor Korolev	13	4	6	10	18	0	0	0	0	0
F	Andrei Kuzmin	38	6	4	10	26	13	1	3	4	16
F	Valerj Belov	36	5	5	10	38	0	0	0	0	0
F	Andrej Nikolishin	12	7	2	9	6	0	0	0	0	0
F	Valerj Cherny	26	4	3	8	6	3	0	0	0	0
D	Sergej Voronov	44	3	4	7	80	12	4	1	26	26
D	Alexej Troschnisky	41	1	5	6	28	6	0	1	1	4
D	Dmitri Sukhanov	31	1	3	4	10	12	0	0	0	4
D	Ruslan Batyrshin	36	2	2	4	65	12	1	1	2	6
D	Roman Zolotov	25	0	2	2	24	8	1	2	3	6
F	Viktor Kozlov	3	1	1	2	2	0	0	0	0	0
F	Eduard Pershin	4	1	1	2	2	3	0	0	0	2
D	Alexander Karpovtsev	13	0	2	2	10	0	0	0	0	0
D	Oleg Orekhovsky	30	0	1	1	18	0	0	0	0	0
D	Viktor Glushenko	3	0	1	1	4	13	1	1	2	4
F	Sergej Lantratov	7	1	0	1	2	0	0	0	0	0
F	Eduard Dmitriyev	11	0	1	1	10	2	1	0	1	0
C	Petr Devyatkin	3	1	0	1	0	0	0	0	0	0
C	Sergej Klimovich	4	1	0	1	2	0	0	0	0	0
F	Sergej Luchinkin	6	1	0	1	4	0	0	0	0	0
F	Denis Kartsev	7	1	0	1	0	2	0	0	0	0
F	Sergei Gorbachev	4	0	1	1	2	0	0	0	0	0
F	Igor Dorofeyev	3	1	0	1	2	6	0	0	0	4
F	Eduard Pershin	4	1	1	2	2	0	0	0	0	0
D	Sergej Sorokin	0	0	0	0	0	5	1	3	4	6
D	Vadim Gusev	35	0	0	0	18	0	0	0	0	0
D	Dmitri Ryabkin	48	0	0	0	12	11	0	2	2	0
D	Vladimir Kramskoi	0	0	0	0	0	8	1	0	1	12
D	Sergej Sorokin	0	0	0	0	0	5	1	3	4	6

Goaltenders	GP	MIN	GA	GAA	GP	MIN	GA	GAA
Yevegeny Nabokov	24	1265	40	1.89	13	810	30	2.22
Sergej Podpuzko	2	90	5	3.33	0	0	0	0
Ildar Mukhometov	31	1785	60	2.01	1	60	2	2.00

CSKA Moscow

Pos	Name	GP	G	A	P	PM	GP	G	A	P	PM
							Play-off				
C	Oleg Belov	46	21	18	39	51	0	0	0	0	0
F	Albert Leschev	51	12	24	36	51	2	0	2	2	0
F	Vladimir Zhashkov	52	17	18	35	10	2	1	0	1	0
C	Andrei Raisky	51	13	14	27	62	2	0	1	1	4
F	Stanislav Romanov	42	13	14	27	4	2	0	1	1	4
F	Denis Vinokurov	49	13	12	25	22	2	0	1	1	0
F	Valentin Morozov	47	9	4	13	102	2	2	0	2	0
C	Alexander Kharlamov	45	8	4	12	12	0	0	0	0	0
D	Alexander Osadchy	52	8	4	12	100	2	0	0	0	0
F	Vadim Sharifjanov	34	7	3	10	26	2	0	0	0	0
C	Nikolai Zavarukhin	35	5	5	10	26	2	0	0	0	2
C	Vyacheslav Kozlov	10	3	4	7	14	0	0	0	0	0
C	Dmitri Gorenko	33	5	2	7	35	0	0	0	0	0
F	Boris Zelenko	35	5	1	6	12	1	0	0	0	0
D	Stanislav Shalnov	52	1	5	6	24	2	0	0	0	0
D	Alexei Krivchenkov	46	1	4	5	43	0	0	0	0	0
D	Alexei Kasatonov	9	2	3	5	6	0	0	0	0	0
D	Artur Oktyabrev	46	1	3	4	36	0	0	0	0	0
D	Andrei Yakovenkov	16	2	2	4	10	0	0	0	0	0
F	Sergei Samsonov	13	2	2	4	14	2	0	0	0	0
D	Vasili Turkovsky	46	1	2	3	22	2	0	0	0	2
F	Andrei Dolgov	20	3	0	3	14	1	0	0	0	0
D	Roman Mozgunov	48	2	1	3	20	2	0	0	0	2
D	Yuri Yeresko	38	0	1	1	8	2	0	0	0	0
D	Sergei Reshetnikov	27	1	0	1	6	0	0	0	0	0
F	Dmitri Shulga	10	1	0	1	2	0	0	0	0	0
F	Denis Pigolitsyn	25	1	0	1	8	2	0	0	0	0
F	Andrei Petrunin	7	0	1	1	0	2	0	0	0	0
C	Alexander Titov	32	1	0	1	6	0	0	0	0	0
D	Nikolai Tsulygin	16	0	0	0	12	0	0	0	0	0
D	Levon Mikaelyan	12	0	0	0	4	2	0	0	0	4
D	Alexei Isaikin	4	0	0	0	2	0	0	0	0	0
D	Maxim Tsvetkov	17	0	0	0	2	1	1	0	1	0
F	Alexei Lazarenko	5	0	0	0	0	0	0	0	0	0
F	Vladislav Yakovenko	2	0	0	0	0	0	0	0	0	0
C	Alexander Zhinkov	22	0	0	0	6	2	0	0	0	0
F	Ivan Prokich	7	0	0	0	2	0	0	0	0	0

Goaltenders	GP	MIN	GA	GAA	GP	MIN	GA	GAA
Vitali Yeremeyev	49	2733	97	2.13	2	120	8	4.00
Andrei Tsarev	9	335	17	3.04	0	0	0	0

134

Pos	Name	GP	G	A	P	PM	GP	G	A	P	PM
							Play-off				
F	Sergei Zolotov	45	14	31	45	16	4	0	3	3	0
F	Dmitri Gogolev	49	21	14	35	10	4	2	3	5	0
C	Alexander Korolyuk	52	16	13	29	62	4	1	2	3	4
F	Dmitri Nabokov	49	15	12	27	32	4	5	0	5	6
F	Alexei Morozov	48	15	12	27	53	4	0	3	3	0
C	Alexei Pogonin	52	7	15	22	44	4	1	2	3	2
F	Alexander Savchenkov	50	11	10	21	26	4	4	0	4	4
D	Dmitri Yerofeyev	51	10	11	21	44	4	1	2	3	2
D	Vadim Brezgunov	49	10	11	21	30	4	1	0	1	2
D	Andrei Skopintsev	52	8	12	20	55	4	1	1	2	0
F	Toivo Suursoo	47	10	5	15	36	4	0	0	0	4
D	Igor Ivanov	52	3	11	14	40	4	0	0	0	0
C	Vitali Tomilin	47	4	5	9	43	2	0	0	0	2
F	Igor Boriskov	12	4	4	8	18	1	0	0	0	2
F	Alexander Boikov	30	3	4	7	8	0	0	0	0	0
F	Pavel Boichenko	31	6	1	7	10	4	1	1	2	0
C	Ruslan Revyakin	33	4	2	6	12	3	0	0	0	0
D	Ilja Stashenkov	51	3	3	6	40	4	1	0	1	0
C	Vladimir Terekhov	29	3	2	5	12	0	0	0	0	0
F	Vadim Popov	45	3	1	4	8	2	0	1	1	0
C	Alexei Isakov	32	1	2	3	6	2	0	0	0	2
F	Konstantin Rachkov	5	0	2	2	2	0	0	0	0	0
D	Maxim Chukanov	41	1	1	2	16	4	0	0	0	0
D	Ilja Makarov	18	1	0	1	6	0	0	0	0	0
D	Aycholos Escher	3	0	0	0	0	0	0	0	0	0
D	Nikolai Schedrov	33	0	0	0	12	4	0	0	0	4
C	Alexei Kolkunov	7	0	0	0	0	4	1	0	1	0
F	Pavel Baulin	17	0	0	0	8	0	0	0	0	0
F	Igor Zelenchev	1	0	0	0	0	3	0	1	1	0
C	Yuri Litvinov	6	0	0	0	8	0	0	0	0	0

Goaltenders	GP	MIN	GA	GAA	GP	MIN	GA	GAA
Viktor Christov	21	1077	41	2.28	2	73	5	4.11
Andrei Karpin	37	2093	78	2.23	4	168	5	1.79

Krylja Sovetov Moscow

Pos	Name	GP	G	A	P	PM	GP	G	A	P	PM
							Play-off				
C	Alexander Chibiryaev	42	12	24	36	104	2	0	0	0	2
F	Yevgeny Garanin	50	19	8	27	6	2	0	0	0	0
F	Alexander Syrtsov	45	9	12	21	26	2	0	0	0	0
C	Vladimir Iljin	52	12	5	17	94	2	0	0	0	6
F	Sergei Kutasov	35	9	4	13	18	2	0	0	0	0
D	Nikolai Syrtsov	50	5	7	12	55	2	0	0	0	0
D	Vladimir Tolokonnikov	52	4	7	11	46	2	0	0	0	0
F	Alexander Kazakov	52	4	7	11	28	2	0	0	0	2
F	Andrei Dolgov	26	9	2	11	10	0	0	0	0	0
C	Mikhail Belobragin	51	5	3	8	24	2	0	0	0	0
F	Igor Alexandrov	24	4	4	8	6	2	0	0	0	2
D	Oleg Kobzev	40	3	4	7	26	2	0	0	0	0
D	Andrei Doronin	46	3	4	7	32	2	0	0	0	4
F	Sergei Korolev	45	3	4	7	22	2	0	0	0	0
F	Sergei Artyushenko	50	4	3	7	32	2	0	1	1	0
D	Alexei Miroshnikov	39	3	2	5	8	2	0	0	0	2
D	Andrei Loginov	51	2	2	4	14	1	0	0	0	4
F	Alexander Galkin	24	3	1	4	20	2	0	1	1	0
F	Vadim Gusev	45	3	1	4	14	1	0	0	0	0
D	Vitali Dryndin	50	2	1	3	36	2	0	0	0	0
C	Alexander Levenok	51	1	2	3	28	2	1	0	1	0
D	Boris Verigin	52	0	2	2	34	2	0	0	0	0
F	Alexander Maksimov	332	0	2	2	8	2	0	0	0	0
F	Alexei Krutov	26	2	0	2	4	0	0	0	0	0
D	Dmitri Chelnokov	24	1	0	1	26	0	0	0	0	0
F	Alexander Shlykov	9	0	1	1	2	0	0	0	0	0
D	Andrei Yershov	16	0	0	0	6	0	0	0	0	0
D	Igor Grachev	13	0	0	0	18	2	0	0	0	4

Goaltenders	GP	MIN	GA	GAA	GP	MIN	GA	GAA
Andrei Kozlov	1	8	21	5.00	0	0	0	0
Sergei Nikolayev	18	1016	34	2.00	1	9	0	0
Oleg Lavrestky	37	2455	87	2.12	1	111	9	4.86

Khimik Voskre-senk

SKA St. Petersburg

							Play-off				
Pos	**Name**	**GP**	**G**	**A**	**P**	**PM**	**GP**	**G**	**A**	**P**	**PM**
F	Vladimir Andreyev	43	14	15	29	18	3	0	0	0	0
C	Yuri Tsyplakov	52	13	10	23	37	3	0	0	0	2
F	Alexander Vinogradov	46	11	11	22	65	2	0	0	0	28
F	Maxim Sushinsky	52	11	11	22	57	3	1	0	1	6
C	Viktor Belyakov	51	10	11	21	34	3	1	1	2	10
F	Alexei Yefimov	48	9	10	19	54	3	0	0	0	0
F	Pavel Yevstigneyev	49	11	7	18	22	3	0	0	0	0
F	Vasili Kamenev	48	7	9	16	24	3	0	1	1	4
D	Vladimir Alexushin	51	4	8	12	40	3	0	0	0	26
F	Yevgeny Pavlov	36	6	5	11	12	0	0	0	0	0
D	Alexander Khavanov	49	7	0	7	32	3	0	0	0	0
F	Gennady Levedev	17	3	4	7	18	3	0	1	1	4
C	Alexei Popov	46	5	2	7	4	3	0	0	0	0
D	Dmitri Tsvetkov	48	2	4	6	10	3	0	0	0	2
D	Marat Davydov	30	4	1	5	20	2	0	0	0	2
D	Dmitri Kukushkin	43	2	2	4	28	3	0	0	0	0
D	Yevgeny Filinov	51	0	4	4	46	3	0	0	0	0
F	Ilja Gorbushin	10	1	2	3	4	0	0	0	0	0
C	Alexei Yegorov	10	2	1	3	10	0	0	0	0	0
F	Vladimir Samsonik	14	1	1	2	2	2	1	0	1	0
F	Yegor Mikhailov	32	1	1	2	8	0	0	0	0	0
F	Pavel Klemantovich	32	0	2	2	6	2	0	0	0	0
D	Alexander Sivov	30	0	1	1	6	3	0	0	0	12
D	Roman Kukhtinov	5	1	0	1	2	0	0	0	0	0
D	Yuri Gailik	51	0	1	1	14	3	0	1	1	2
F	Sergei Iliyuschenko	37	1	0	1	12	3	0	0	0	2
C	Konstantin Gorovikov	13	1	0	1	4	2	0	0	0	0
D	Alexei Rubov	38	0	0	0	43	0	0	0	0	0
D	Dmitri Alekhin	11	0	0	0	4	0	0	0	0	0
C	Andrei Maslov	6	0	0	0	0	0	0	0	0	0
D	Oleg Timofeyev	30	0	0	0	22	0	0	0	0	0

Goaltenders	**GP**	**MIN**	**GA**	**GAA**	**GP**	**MIN**	**GA**	**GAA**
Kirill Korenkov	20	1022	43	2.52	0	0	0	0
Maxim Soklov	38	2098	79	2.26	3	190	6	1.89

Torpedo Nizhny Novgorod

							Play-off				
Pos	**Name**	**GP**	**G**	**A**	**P**	**PM**	**GP**	**G**	**A**	**P**	**PM**
F	Alexei Rotanov	47	24	10	34	10	4	1	0	1	2
F	Anatoli Vodopjanov	44	7	14	21	28	5	1	1	2	6
C	Vyacheslav Rjanov	46	7	11	18	42	5	1	0	1	6
F	Vladimir Krutov	51	12	4	16	44	0	0	0	0	0
F	Andrei Smirnov	48	12	4	16	26	5	1	1	2	10
F	Vladimir Konkov	51	12	4	16	44	5	1	0	1	6
F	Vladimir Kireyev	39	11	4	15	26	1	0	0	0	0
F	Vladimir Orlov	52	9	6	15	40	5	1	0	1	6
C	Yevgeny Bobariko	41	10	4	14	12	5	0	2	2	0
D	Andrei Mazhugin	51	3	9	12	32	5	0	1	1	6
D	Oleg Namestnikov	51	4	6	10	28	5	1	0	1	0
D	Vadim Galikhmanov	52	4	5	9	90	5	1	1	2	29
D	Nikolai Voevodin	52	2	7	9	36	5	0	0	0	4
C	Igor Sirotinin	34	5	4	9	18	5	1	0	1	27
C	Sergei Shesterikov	45	8	1	9	12	5	1	0	1	0
C	Vasili Smirnov	45	6	3	9	8	2	0	1	1	0
F	Sergei Makarov	8	1	5	6	6	5	0	1	1	8
D	Sergei Zalipyatskikh	45	2	3	5	38	2	0	0	0	0
D	Alexander Kupriyanov	43	0	5	5	38	5	0	0	0	6
F	Yuri Bogusevich	27	3	0	3	4	0	0	0	0	0
F	Andrei Zhelnov	31	2	1	3	8	5	1	0	1	2
D	Alexander Danchishin	27	1	1	2	4	0	0	0	0	0
F	Alexei Ushakov	31	1	1	2	22	1	0	0	0	2
C	Vadim Averkin	3	1	1	2	0	0	0	0	0	0
D	Lev Latin	49	0	1	1	36	5	0	1	1	6
D	Sergei Klishin	14	1	0	1	2	0	0	0	0	0
D	Pavel Komarov	26	0	1	1	38	3	0	0	0	0
C	Alexei Vorobjev	6	0	1	1	2	0	0	0	0	0
F	Sergei Braitsev	7	1	0	1	0	0	0	0	0	0
F	Sergei Kiselev	6	0	1	1	0	0	0	0	0	0
F	Alexei Pugin	17	0	1	1	12	0	0	0	0	0
C	Mikhail Petrov	30	0	1	1	8	4	0	1	1	0

Goaltenders	**GP**	**MIN**	**GA**	**GAA**	**GP**	**MIN**	**GA**	**GAA**
Alexei Ignatenko	9	313	16	3.06	2	80	2	1.50
Sergei Fadeyev	49	2860	94	1.97	4	220	0	2.45

Pos	Name	GP	G	A	P	PM	GP	G	A	P	PM
							Play-off				
F	Andrei Tarasenko	50	17	37	54	50	4	4	0	4	0
C	Alexei Traseukh	51	21	22	43	16	4	0	2	2	2
F	Alexander Zybin	46	9	28	37	14	4	0	3	3	0
C	Vladimir Samylin	50	19	17	36	30	4	0	3	3	4
F	Alexander Ardashev	51	14	20	34	16	4	2	2	4	2
C	Alexei Gorshkov	51	14	7	21	20	4	0	0	0	2
D	Dmitri Krasotkin	48	4	10	14	40	4	0	0	0	4
F	Igor Melyakov	50	6	8	14	34	4	0	1	1	0
C	Dmitri Zatevakhin	52	5	9	14	16	4	0	0	0	4
D	Igor Martynov	51	5	8	13	18	4	0	0	0	2
F	Dmitri Zinin	36	7	6	13	16	4	2	2	4	2
D	Alexei Amelin	50	3	9	12	20	4	0	0	0	2
F	Vyacheslav Kurochkin	43	6	4	10	16	4	0	0	0	0
D	Oleg Komissarov	36	2	7	9	34	4	0	0	0	0
F	Alexander Skoptsov	50	4	5	9	2	4	0	0	0	0
D	Andrei Sobolev	51	0	8	8	24	4	0	1	1	4
D	Dmitri Yushkevich	10	3	4	7	8	0	0	0	0	0
D	Yevgeny Shaldybin	42	4	5	7	10	4	0	1	1	0
F	Roman Kostromin	19	4	2	6	2	4	0	0	0	0
F	Anatoli Lvov	16	1	4	5	12	0	0	0	0	0
F	Alexander Ageyev	17	0	5	5	0	0	0	0	0	0
F	Mikhail Vasiljev	7	0	4	4	8	0	0	0	0	0
F	Mikhail Kazakevich	11	1	3	4	2	0	0	0	0	0
D	Vladislav Shvedov	50	1	2	3	10	4	0	0	0	0
C	Dmitri Dyakiv	6	1	2	3	2	0	0	0	0	0
D	Ildar Yubin	44	0	2	2	18	1	0	0	0	0
F	Leonid Toropchenko	16	1	1	2	10	1	1	0	1	0
D	Sergei Zhukov	27	1	0	1	4	4	0	0	0	0
D	Sergei Suyarkov	10	0	0	0	4	0	0	0	0	0
C	Anatoli Tarabanov	7	0	0	0	0	0	0	0	0	0
F	Anatoli Ustyugov	5	0	0	0	0	0	0	0	0	0
F	Konstantin Kasatkin	4	0	0	0	2	0	0	0	0	0

Goaltenders	GP	MIN	GA	GAA	GP	MIN	GA	GAA
Alexei Chervyakov	46	2653	79	1.78	4	250	7	1.68
Sergei Nikolayev	1	65	1	0.92	0	0	0	0
Yevgeny Tarasov	11	387	15	2.32	0	0	0	0

Torpedo Yaroslavl

Pos	Name	GP	G	A	P	PM	GP	G	A	P	PM
							Play-off				
C	Alexei Chupin	49	23	14	37	87	2	0	0	0	2
F	Roman Baranov	44	17	15	32	30	2	1	1	2	2
F	Kirill Golubev	49	12	19	31	73	2	0	1	1	0
C	Oleg Tolokontsev	51	18	9	27	14	2	1	0	1	0
F	Airat Kadeikin	51	13	10	23	38	2	0	0	0	27
F	Ilnur Gizatullin	50	12	11	23	26	2	0	0	0	0
C	Rinat Kasjanov	51	7	12	19	20	2	0	0	0	0
F	Mikhail Sarmatin	50	7	8	15	38	2	0	0	0	0
D	Dmitri Balmin	42	2	12	14	80	2	0	0	0	2
D	Andrei Zubkov	49	4	7	11	22	2	0	0	0	0
F	Gleb Veselov	51	9	2	11	35	2	0	0	0	2
D	Vladislav Makarov	52	3	7	10	32	2	0	0	0	2
D	Sergei Selyanin	31	2	7	9	36	0	0	0	0	0
F	Eduard Kudermetov	26	6	2	8	10	0	0	0	0	0
C	Almaz Garifullin	51	6	2	8	10	2	0	0	0	0
D	Alexander Zavjalov	52	3	4	7	38	2	0	0	0	2
C	Sergei Kanyukov	39	1	5	6	10	2	0	0	0	0
D	Artem Anisimov	46	3	2	5	55	1	0	0	0	0
D	Leonid Labzov	48	2	1	3	30	2	0	0	0	2
D	Eduard Valiullin	49	0	1	1	22	2	0	0	0	2
F	Andrei Tsarev	10	0	1	1	2	2	0	0	0	0
D	Alexei Puchkov	9	0	0	0	8	0	0	0	0	0
D	Yevgeny Petrov	14	0	0	0	2	0	0	0	0	0
D	Dmitri Petrov	36	0	0	0	18	2	0	0	0	0
F	Alexander Sukhenko	26	0	0	0	6	2	0	0	0	0
F	Denis Yelakov	32	0	0	0	8	0	2	2	0	0
F	Igor Ageyev	4	0	0	0	2	0	0	0	0	0
F	Rustem Amirov	18	0	0	0	2	0	0	0	0	0

Goaltenders	GP	MIN	GA	GAA	GP	MIN	GA	GAA
Sergei Abramov	51	3049	120	2.36	2	104	11	6.34
Dmitri Yachanov	4	111	3	1.62	1	16	0	0

Itil Kazan

Salavat Yulayev Ufa

Pos	Name	GP	G	A	P	PM	GP	G	A	P	PM
							| Play-off				
F	Dmitri Denisov	52	43	17	60	22	7	3	1	4	0
F	Boris Timofeyev	52	22	24	46	22	7	4	2	6	0
C	Rail Muftiyev	49	10	29	39	22	7	0	3	3	4
F	Konstantin Polozov	50	17	15	32	16	7	4	2	6	2
F	Aidar Khairullin	50	15	16	31	12	7	2	3	5	25
C	Ruslan Suleimanov	51	14	15	29	52	7	1	2	3	4
F	Denis Afinogenov	51	11	10	21	12	3	0	2	2	0
C	Andrei Davletov	51	11	7	18	28	7	1	1	2	4
F	Alik Gareyev	49	11	5	16	53	7	2	1	3	12
C	Alexander Semak	9	9	6	15	4	0	0	0	0	0
F	Rustem Gabdullin	45	6	5	11	18	7	0	2	2	2
D	Valeri Davletshin	51	4	7	11	38	5	0	0	0	4
D	Andrei Volkov	51	6	4	10	22	7	1	0	1	6
D	Andrei Yakhanov	52	3	7	10	50	7	1	0	1	10
D	Oleg Vasiljev	44	6	3	9	14	7	0	0	0	4
F	Vadim Plotnikov	50	5	2	7	37	4	0	1	1	0
D	Mikhail Potapov	32	4	3	7	6	7	0	3	3	2
D	Rustem Kamaletdinov	51	5	2	7	24	7	1	0	1	8
F	Alexander Sverzhov	40	3	2	5	14	7	0	0	0	6
D	Vladimir Alexeyev	48	2	2	4	14	5	0	0	0	4
D	Nikolai Tsulygin	13	2	2	4	10	7	0	0	0	4
D	Andrei Zyuzin	30	3	0	3	16	0	0	0	0	0
D	Alexei Plotnikov	41	3	0	3	4	7	0	0	0	0
F	Alfred Yunusov	4	0	3	3	0	0	0	0	0	0
D	Sergei Lopatin	10	0	2	2	8	0	0	0	0	0
C	Ruslan Shafikov	30	2	0	2	10	0	1	1	2	4
D	Vener Safin	4	1	0	1	0	6	0	2	2	0
F	Oleg Artamonov	11	1	0	1	4	0	0	0	0	0
F	Andrei Sidyakin	7	0	1	1	0	0	0	0	0	0
F	Vyacheslav Sidorov	7	0	0	0	0	0	0	0	0	0
C	Enrest Salishev	5	0	0	0	2	0	0	0	0	0

Goaltenders	GP	MIN	GA	GAA	GP	MIN	GA	GAA
Vladimir Tikhomirov	32	1880	75	2.39	7	429	12	1.67
Alexander Nikiforov	17	958	32	2.00	7	1	0	0
Igor Vasiljev	7	335	19	3.40	0	0	0	0

Lada Togliatti

Pos	Name	GP	G	A	P	PM	GP	G	A	P	PM
							| Play-off				
F	Anatoli Yemelin	51	19	16	35	22	12	5	3	8	4
F	Alexander Ivanov	46	22	13	35	28	12	1	4	5	8
C	Ivan Svintsitsky	49	17	17	34	36	10	2	3	5	4
C	Vyacheslav Bezukladnikov	52	14	19	33	26	12	5	0	5	4
F	Eduard Gorbachev	43	14	19	33	44	12	4	1	5	12
F	Konstantin Peregudov	43	16	5	21	10	12	0	3	3	0
C	Alexander Nesterov	51	14	7	21	16	12	1	2	3	10
F	Igor Trukhachev	43	10	8	18	14	11	2	2	4	8
F	Yuri Zlov	29	8	9	17	18	12	5	4	9	0
F	Alexei Kovalev	12	8	8	16	49	0	0	0	0	0
D	Rafik Yakubov	51	7	8	15	36	12	0	0	0	16
C	Denis Metlyuk	25	8	6	14	10	12	6	4	10	10
F	Eduard Valiullin	24	8	5	13	6	0	0	0	0	0
D	Maxim Galanov	45	5	6	11	54	9	0	1	1	12
C	Sergei Martynyuk	42	6	5	11	28	11	0	1	1	4
F	Andrei Kovalenko	11	9	2	11	14	0	0	0	0	0
F	Denis Tsygurov	10	3	7	10	4	0	0	0	0	0
C	Konstantin Tatrintsev	22	7	3	10	4	9	0	0	0	0
D	Oleg Volkov	46	4	5	9	65	12	0	0	0	35
D	Oleg Koftun	40	3	6	9	20	12	0	0	0	0
C	Oleg Belkin	20	6	3	9	22	11	1	0	1	14
D	Yuri Panov	49	5	3	8	18	12	1	0	1	8
C	Vyacheslav Butsayev	9	2	6	8	6	0	0	0	0	0
D	Oleg Burlutsky	44	1	6	7	14	12	0	2	2	6
D	Vladimir Tarasov	51	3	4	7	49	12	0	1	1	14
F	Sergei Zherebtsov	38	4	3	7	10	9	1	0	1	8
D	Igor B. Nikitin	50	1	5	6	28	11	0	1	1	4
F	Vladimir Zorkin	11	3	3	6	0	11	1	2	3	27
D	Igor V. Nikitin	36	0	5	5	8	12	2	1	3	2
F	Konstantin Kuzmichev	13	0	4	4	8	0	0	0	0	0
C	Pavel Desyatkov	13	2	0	2	6	0	0	0	0	0

Goaltenders	GP	MIN	GA	GAA	GP	MIN	GA	GAA
Alexei Marjin	30	1670	45	1.61	12	619	21	2.03
Andrei Bolsunovsky	26	1474	38	1.54	4	127	7	3.30

Pos	Name	GP	G	A	P	PM	GP	G	A	P	PM
							Play-off				
F	Igor Dyakiv	52	12	30	42	18	5	1	3	4	6
F	Oleg Kryazhev	52	21	10	41	26	6	1	0	1	0
C	Sergei Yelakov	52	17	23	40	14	6	0	4	4	2
F	Igor Zhilinsky	50	17	12	29	14	6	3	1	4	6
C	Andrei Rasolko	48	14	15	29	20	3	1	0	1	0
F	Nikolai Marinenko	22	20	8	28	10	6	3	3	6	4
F	Yevgeny Shastin	52	12	15	27	77	6	1	1	2	6
F	Yerlan Sagymbayev	37	17	6	23	4	5	0	0	0	2
C	Igor Latyshev	47	12	8	20	14	6	0	1	1	6
D	Konstantin Maslyukov	43	10	7	17	58	5	1	1	2	12
D	Dmitri Parkhomenko	48	9	8	17	26	6	0	2	2	27
C	Konstantin Butsenko	44	10	6	16	12	6	2	1	3	6
D	Sergei Korobkin	52	8	6	14	46	5	0	1	1	10
F	Eduard Zankovets	49	5	9	14	41	3	0	0	0	0
F	Vitali Chinakhov	18	5	7	12	6	6	1	0	1	6
F	Alexei Zhdakhin	38	5	6	11	62	2	0	0	0	0
D	Igor Khatsei	51	6	3	9	32	6	0	1	1	8
D	Albert Loginov	51	2	7	9	55	6	0	0	0	6
D	Oleg Uglnikov	52	4	4	8	16	6	0	0	0	2
C	Ramil Saifullin	23	4	4	8	4	1	0	0	0	0
F	Eduard Polyakov	26	5	3	8	0	6	1	3	4	4
F	Bogdan Rudenko	14	3	1	4	0	5	1	0	1	4
F	Andrei Kolesnikov	35	1	2	3	14	3	0	1	1	2
D	Alexander Myagkikh	36	0	2	2	20	6	0	0	0	0
D	Ilnaz Zakitov	4	0	2	2	4	0	0	0	0	0
D	Dmitri Mekeshkin	16	0	2	2	4	6	0	0	0	0
F	Vadim Tupitsyn	9	0	2	2	4	0	0	0	0	0
C	Eduard Dmitriyev	18	1	1	2	20	0	0	0	0	0
D	Vladimir Kapulovsky	23	0	1	1	18	0	0	0	0	0
D	Oleg Gorbenko	6	0	0	0	2	0	0	0	0	0
D	Oleg Kachesov	4	0	0	0	10	0	0	0	0	0
F	Alexei Sergiyevsky	4	0	0	0	2	0	0	0	0	0

Goaltenders	GP	MIN	GA	GAA	GP	MIN	GA	GAA
Alexander Vjyukhin	30	1687	58	2.06	3	173	12	4.16
Toomas Kuli	1	9	0	0	0	0	0	0
Sergei Khramtsov	27	1467	42	1.71	4	197	7	2.13

Avangard Omsk

Pos	Name	GP	G	A	P	PM	GP	G	A	P	PM
							Play-off				
F	Pavel Lazarev	52	27	23	50	48	3	0	3	3	14
F	Igor Varitsky	51	26	21	47	26	3	3	0	3	6
C	Sergei Gomolyako	23	10	24	34	54	3	1	3	4	28
D	Valeri Nikulin	52	14	14	28	48	3	0	0	0	10
C	Vyacheslav Dolishnya	52	17	11	28	22	3	1	0	1	6
C	Oleg Cherkasov	52	12	11	23	26	3	0	0	0	2
D	Vadim Glovatsky	52	2	17	19	56	3	0	0	0	28
C	Yevgeny Zinovjev	31	9	9	18	6	3	0	0	0	0
F	Yevgeny Bobykin	33	8	9	17	14	1	0	0	0	0
C	Dmitri Demidov	51	11	6	17	26	3	0	0	0	4
F	Valeri Karpov	10	6	8	14	8	0	0	0	0	0
F	Maxim Smelnitsky	49	9	5	14	22	3	0	0	0	4
F	Andrei Didenko	45	6	3	9	22	3	0	0	0	0
D	Oleg Davydov	52	3	5	8	36	3	0	1	1	0
D	Alexei Chikalin	51	2	6	8	52	3	0	0	0	4
D	Alexander Shvarev	52	4	3	7	34	3	0	1	1	4
F	Oleg Maltsev	5	3	2	5	4	3	0	1	1	37
F	Yevgeny Momot	44	2	1	3	20	3	0	0	0	2
F	Matvei Belousov	41	2	1	3	6	1	0	0	0	0
D	Dmitri Tertyshny	38	0	3	3	14	1	0	0	0	0
F	Viktor Marusov	18	2	0	2	14	3	0	0	0	0
F	Vasili Kulikov	4	0	1	1	0	0	0	0	0	0
D	Anvar Gatiyatulin	34	0	1	1	16	3	0	0	0	0
F	Sergei Purtov	13	1	0	1	8	0	0	0	0	0
F	Alexei Kokovin	7	1	0	1	0	0	0	0	0	0
D	Sergei Kolesnik	18	0	0	0	4	0	0	0	0	0
D	Mikhail Okhotnikov	32	0	0	0	10	3	0	0	0	0
D	Yuri Usenko	10	0	0	0	14	0	0	0	0	0
D	Andrei Sapozhnikov	18	0	0	0	14	3	1	0	1	6
C	Stanislav Tugolukov	22	0	0	0	14	2	0	0	0	0
C	Maxim Orlov	8	0	0	0	2	0	0	0	0	0
C	Anton Gallyamov	4	0	0	0	0	0	0	0	0	0

Goaltenders	GP	MIN	GA	GAA	GP	MIN	GA	GAA
Andrei Batalov	8	364	18	2.96	0	0	0	0
Mikhail Yemeljanov	6	201	13	3.88	1	44	1	1.36
Andrei Zuyev	45	2580	115	2.67	3	136	9	3.97

Traktor Chelyabinsk

Avto-mobilist Yekata-rinenburg

							Play-off				
Pos	Name	GP	G	A	P	PM	GP	G	A	P	PM
C	Denis Mitin	45	8	12	20	22	2	0	0	0	2
F	Andrei Khazov	47	12	8	20	36	2	0	0	0	0
F	Dmitri Popov	49	11	9	20	18	2	0	0	0	0
F	Igor Koreshkov	32	12	7	19	6	2	0	0	0	0
F	Andrei Subbotin	49	9	9	18	34	2	1	0	1	2
F	Dmitri Subbotin	52	9	6	15	75	2	0	0	0	2
F	Dmitri Pirozhkov	39	11	4	15	20	2	0	0	0	0
F	Vladimir Maslov	39	9	6	15	18	2	0	0	0	25
C	Vladimir Yelovikov	51	5	9	14	26	2	0	0	0	0
F	Vitali Zybin	51	7	6	13	12	1	0	0	0	0
D	Vyacheslav Mishenin	47	1	8	9	22	2	0	0	0	0
D	Pavel Velizhanin	40	5	4	9	34	2	0	0	0	0
D	Alexander Bezrodnov	52	1	6	7	28	1	0	0	0	0
F	Alexei Permyakov	49	5	2	7	10	2	0	0	0	0
D	Andrei Skomorokha	52	3	3	6	8	2	0	0	0	2
D	Oleg Porotnikov	43	2	4	6	22	2	1	0	1	0
C	Stanislav Chemodanov	47	5	1	6	34	2	0	0	0	0
F	Ilja Byakin	4	3	2	5	14	0	0	0	0	0
D	Vasili Zagvozdkin	51	1	2	3	34	2	0	0	0	0
D	Sergei Narushko	33	2	1	3	42	2	0	0	0	0
F	Igor Lukiyanov	14	0	3	3	2	2	0	1	1	0
C	Alexander Chelushkin	11	2	1	3	4	0	0	0	0	0
D	Yevgeny Mukhin	42	1	1	2	32	2	0	0	0	0
D	Vladislav Otmakhov	38	0	2	2	12	2	0	0	0	0
F	Andrei Petrakov	11	1	1	2	6	1	0	0	0	0
F	Alexei Makarov	29	1	1	2	8	2	0	0	0	0
F	Alexander Yargin	8	0	0	0	0	0	0	0	0	0
F	Dmitri Shpakovsky	4	0	0	0	0	0	0	0	0	0
C	Alexander Krapivin	18	0	0	0	6	0	0	0	0	0

Goaltenders	GP	MIN	GA	GAA	GP	MIN	GA	GAA
Albert Shirgaziyev	28	1622	65	2.40	1	60	4	4.00
Yevgeny Loiferman	27	1558	71	2.73	1	60	2	2.00

Metallurg Magnit-ogorsk

							Play-off				
Pos	Name	GP	G	A	P	PM	GP	G	A	P	PM
C	Yevgeny Koreshkov	51	33	20	53	32	3	3	5	8	4
F	Konstantin Shafranov	47	21	30	51	24	7	5	4	9	12
F	Alexander Koreshkov	44	22	23	45	12	7	2	1	3	2
F	Sergei Osipov	52	26	18	44	8	7	0	1	1	6
C	Mikhail Borodulin	43	16	17	33	60	6	0	1	1	6
C	Sergei Solomatov	50	13	19	32	16	7	1	2	3	0
F	Igor Starkovsky	48	20	10	30	30	6	0	0	0	0
F	Sergei Devyatkov	48	17	9	26	44	6	2	2	4	29
C	Andrei Razin	49	11	14	25	12	7	3	2	5	6
F	Alexander Golts	48	12	11	23	12	4	0	0	0	0
F	Alexei Stepanov	52	11	12	23	18	7	4	1	5	6
D	Andrei Sokolov	48	4	13	17	46	6	0	1	1	12
F	Dmitri Voronezhey	46	9	7	16	14	2	0	0	0	0
D	Vadim Podrezov	48	4	11	15	28	7	0	0	0	6
C	Igor Knyazev	37	5	9	14	8	5	0	0	0	2
F	Alexei Pogodin	26	7	6	13	4	7	1	1	2	2
D	Yuri Isayev	41	6	6	12	32	5	0	2	2	8
D	Sergei Simonov	44	6	3	9	8	4	0	0	0	2
D	Konstantin Isakov	48	2	4	6	10	7	0	1	1	4
C	Dmitri Ivanov	30	3	3	6	12	5	1	0	1	2
D	Yevgeny Shalygin	48	2	3	5	34	7	0	0	0	8
F	Sergei Ivlev	15	4	1	5	4	5	0	1	1	27
D	Oleg Achapkin	39	1	3	4	22	6	0	0	0	2
D	Georgy Mustayev	41	1	3	4	14	7	1	0	1	4
D	Sergei Usanov	20	1	3	4	24	2	0	0	0	6
D	Yevgeny Gubarev	36	2	0	2	22	0	0	0	0	0
D	Marat Askarov	4	1	1	2	0	6	0	0	0	0
D	Vladimir Leshko	14	0	1	1	2	0	0	0	0	0
F	Dmitri Maximov	3	0	1	1	0	0	0	0	0	0

Goaltenders	GP	MIN	GA	GAA	GP	MIN	GA	GAA
Yevgeny Ryabchikov	1	60	1	1.00	0	0	0	0
Boris Tortunov	18	785	33	2.52	5	274	11	2.40
Valeri Ivannikov	42	2288	100	2.62	3	146	10	4.11

Pos	Name	GP	G	A	P	PM	GP	G	A	P	PM
F	Boris Alexandrov	30	14	19	33	18	2	0	0	0	0
F	Sergei Antipov	52	19	11	30	40	2	0	0	0	0
C	Andrei Pechelyakov	48	17	11	28	24	2	0	0	0	0
C	Pavel Kamentsev	49	14	11	25	40	2	1	0	1	2
D	Vladimir Antipin	52	8	15	23	64	2	0	0	0	6
F	Andrei Samokhvalov	44	13	9	22	6	2	0	0	0	2
F	Vladimir Yefremov	43	12	6	18	32	2	0	0	0	0
F	Yuri Karatayev	48	9	7	16	16	1	1	0	1	0
D	Andrei Savenkov	51	9	6	15	30	2	0	1	1	0
F	Maxim Komissarov	44	9	5	14	39	2	0	0	0	0
F	Anatoli Filatov	33	6	6	12	30	1	0	0	0	0
D	Igor Zemlyanoi	51	7	5	12	48	2	0	0	0	0
C	Roman Shipulin	48	6	5	11	10	2	0	0	0	0
D	Viktor Bystryantsev	45	2	8	10	30	2	0	0	0	2
C	Andrei Tsyba	36	3	5	8	14	2	0	1	1	0
C	Sergei Mogilnikov	19	1	7	8	2	1	0	0	0	0
D	Oleg Kovalenko	51	3	4	7	53	2	0	1	1	4
D	Igor Medvedev	46	3	4	7	32	2	0	0	0	4
C	Igor Kravets	51	5	2	7	22	2	0	0	0	0
F	Roman Zavodov	5	3	2	5	0	2	0	1	1	0
D	Viktor Fedorchenko	39	0	4	4	12	2	0	0	0	2
F	Dmitri Dudarev	30	2	2	4	22	2	0	0	0	0
D	Igor Polischuk	12	1	2	3	0	0	0	0	0	0
D	Vitali Tregubov	44	2	1	3	8	2	0	0	0	2
F	Vladimir Zavjalov	29	2	1	3	4	2	0	0	0	0
D	Alexander Artemenko	21	0	1	1	6	2	0	0	0	0
F	Konstantin Spodarenko	18	1	0	1	0	1	0	0	0	0
D	Sergei Kislitsyn	18	1	0	1	6	0	0	0	0	0
F	Andrei Singeleyev	16	1	0	1	0	1	0	0	0	0
D	Andrei Pruchkovsky	4	0	0	0	0	0	0	0	0	0

Goaltenders	GP	MIN	GA	GAA	GP	MIN	GA	GAA
Alexander Shimin	16	751	45	3.59	1	54	5	5.55
Vladimir Borodulin	26	1487	77	3.10	2	66	9	8.18
Konstantin Kapkaikin	16	909	48	3.16	0	0	0	0

Pos	Name	GP	G	A	P	PM	GP	G	A	P	PM
F	Dmitri Romanov	52	26	8	34	20	3	0	1	1	0
F	Alexander Gulyavtsev	51	15	9	24	64	3	0	0	0	6
C	Mikhail Ipatov	45	9	14	23	38	3	0	0	0	0
F	Sergei Nechayev	46	8	12	20	12	3	0	0	0	4
C	Rinat Khasanov	51	9	9	18	107	3	1	1	2	2
F	Anatoli Lvov	34	12	5	17	24	3	1	0	1	2
C	Vadim Schelkunov	46	10	6	16	36	3	0	0	0	0
F	Yevgeny Akmetov	50	11	5	16	24	3	0	0	0	2
C	Sergei Gubanov	42	7	4	11	32	2	0	0	0	0
D	Valeri Oleinik	52	6	4	10	24	3	0	0	0	0
F	Alexei Panin	45	5	5	10	10	3	2	0	2	2
F	Nikolai Bardin	35	4	6	10	2	3	1	1	2	2
F	Alexander Ageyev	14	6	3	9	2	3	0	0	0	0
F	Andrei Koshkin	21	3	4	7	6	3	0	0	0	0
D	Sergei Marchenko	52	2	3	5	61	3	0	0	0	2
F	Gennady Lebedev	20	0	4	4	12	0	0	0	0	0
F	Pavel Smirnov	48	2	2	4	34	3	0	0	0	0
D	Murat Sterzhanov	51	1	3	4	38	3	0	0	0	4
D	Vladimir Kapulovsky	18	1	2	3	10	3	0	0	0	4
D	Andrei Yemelin	44	0	3	3	14	3	0	0	0	0
D	Andrei Basalgin	33	0	3	3	16	3	0	0	0	0
C	Vitali Chinakhov	14	2	1	3	4	0	0	0	0	0
C	Vadim Tupitsyn	16	0	3	3	2	0	0	0	0	0
D	Mikhail Kovalkov	52	2	0	2	30	3	0	0	0	0
D	Sergei Suyarkov	27	2	0	2	14	3	0	0	0	0
D	Dmitri Bernatavichus	18	1	1	2	31	3	0	1	1	4
D	Sergei Makarov	13	0	1	1	10	3	0	0	0	0
D	Sergei Usanov	8	0	0	0	6	0	0	0	0	0
D	Vadim Galkin	10	0	0	0	4	0	0	0	0	0

Goaltenders	GP	MIN	GA	GAA	GP	MIN	GA	GAA
Rushan Yavayev	27	1635	74	2.71	0	0	0	0
Valeri Yerokhin	25	1500	64	2.56	3	180	9	3.00

Spartak Moscow

Pos	Name	GP	G	A	P	PM
F	Mikhail Ivanov	36	18	14	32	64
F	Dmitri Shamolin	51	9	18	27	20
C	Konstantin Korotkov	49	6	19	25	24
F	Dmitri Klevakin	52	12	10	22	4
C	Georgy Yevtyukhin	45	8	13	21	56
F	Alexei Tkachuk	31	13	6	19	18
D	Alexei Putilin	36	6	12	18	50
F	Igor Mishukov	38	16	1	17	24
F	Sergei Shalamai	44	10	5	15	30
C	Vadim Yepanchintsev	43	4	8	12	24
F	Dmitri Rozhkov	27	3	8	11	20
D	Dmitri Podlegayev	45	4	2	6	32
F	Nikolai Borschevsky	9	5	1	6	14
F	Maxim Stepanov	41	4	1	5	2
F	Vitali Prokhorov	8	1	4	5	8
F	Vladislav Yakovenko	12	4	1	5	29
D	Sergei Butko	52	1	3	4	22
D	Yuri Yaschin	28	2	1	3	10
F	Konstantin Mitroshkin	29	3	0	3	6
D	Yevgeny Petrochinin	45	0	2	2	14
F	Pavel Bure	1	2	0	2	2
C	Yuri Smirnov	22	1	0	1	0
C	Vladimir Sirotkin	19	0	1	1	12
D	Vyacheslav Fetisov	1	0	1	1	4
F	Vladimir Uvarov	29	0	1	1	8
F	Alexander Mogilny	1	0	1	1	0
D	Nikolai Semin	34	0	1	1	18
D	Daniil Markov	39	0	1	1	36
D	Alexander Yudin	26	0	0	0	41

Goaltenders	GP	MIN	GA	GAA
Oleg Shevtsov	33	1915	87	2.72
Andrei Fedotov	4	311	9	1.73
Alexei Ivashkin	22	1248	57	2.74

Pardaugava Riga

Pos	Name	GP	G	A	P	PM
F	Leonis Tambiyev	47	21	7	28	56
F	Andrei Ignatovich	46	9	11	20	69
D	Karlis Skrastynsh	52	4	14	18	69
C	Alexander Semenov	47	12	2	14	52
C	Sergei Senin	41	5	7	12	30
F	Alexander Nizhivy	47	2	9	11	16
F	Yanis Tomans	51	10	1	11	38
C	Alexei Khromchenkov	49	5	4	9	45
C	Alexei Frolikov	38	4	3	7	28
F	Pavel Parkhomenko	35	6	1	7	20
F	Alexander Matsiyevsky	32	2	4	6	12
F	Viktor Filatov	41	4	2	6	32
C	Mikhail Kozlov	44	4	2	6	32
D	Oleg Sorokin	37	1	4	5	8
F	Alexander Kerch	11	4	0	4	4
D	Agris Roshtoks	43	0	3	3	26
D	Marek Yasas	14	1	1	2	4
F	Oleg Yurenko	21	1	1	2	4
C	Valeri Kulibaba	13	1	1	2	2
F	Mikhail Saliyenko	17	1	1	2	4
F	Edgars Rozentals	4	1	0	1	0
D	Alexander Shishkovich	46	1	0	1	40
F	Alexander Kolchanov	10	0	1	1	4
D	Dmitri Rodin	21	0	0	0	0
D	Atvars Tribuntsov	12	0	0	0	8
D	Andris Keisters	24	0	0	0	6
D	Aigars Mironovich	39	0	0	0	24
D	Gatis Tseplis	36	0	0	0	28
D	Ronalds Ozolinsh	43	0	0	0	26
D	Kaspars Astashenko	25	0	0	0	24
F	Artis Abols	13	0	0	0	10

Goaltenders	GP	MIN	GA	GAA
Andrei Zinkov	38	2029	101	2.98
Yuris Klodans	22	1111	66	3.56

Sokol Kiev

Pos	Name	GP	G	A	P	PM
F	Vitali Litvinenko	45	13	14	27	8
F	Viktor Goncharenko	49	12	10	22	36
C	Valentin Oletsky	51	10	8	18	46
C	Vadim Shakhraichuk	45	10	4	14	83
F	Andrei Nikolayev	42	7	7	14	16
F	Vasili Bobrovnikov	43	7	7	14	14
F	Anatoli Stepanishchev	30	7	7	14	50
D	Anatoli Khomenko	31	4	4	8	58
F	Anatoli Koveshnikov	51	8	0	8	10
D	Oleg Polkovnikov	38	0	7	7	70
F	Vitali Semenchenko	41	4	3	7	16
C	Dmitri Pidgursky	49	2	4	6	61
F	Artem Ostroushko	37	3	2	5	34
D	Alexander Savitsky	14	2	2	4	20
D	Yuri Gunko	25	4	0	4	18
D	Vyacheslav Timchenko	20	2	1	3	22
D	Sergei Garkusha	48	1	2	3	28
D	Igor Yankovich	20	1	1	2	12
F	Yevgeny Mlinchenko	18	2	0	2	8
F	Oleg Turyshev	30	1	1	2	2
D	Andrei Olexiyenko	19	1	0	1	20
D	Vyacheslav Zavalnyuk	41	1	0	1	26
F	Vladislav Zozovsky	7	1	0	1	6
C	Nikolai Maiko	39	0	1	1	4
C	Konstantin Butsenko	5	0	1	1	4
F	Sergei Karnaukh	29	1	0	1	12
C	Sergei Chubenko	6	0	1	1	2
D	Igor Drifan	6	0	0	0	6
D	Yuri Rivny	20	0	0	0	10
D	Alexei Bernatsky	11	0	0	0	2
D	Alexander Mukhanov	21	0	0	0	20
C	Dmitri Mozheiko	8	0	0	0	4

Goaltenders	GP	MIN	GA	GAA
Yevgeny Brul	6	332	16	2.89
Yuri Shundrov	26	1549	65	2.51
Igor Karpenko	23	1292	67	3.11

Tivali Minsk

Pos	Name	GP	G	A	P	PM
F	Andrei Skabelka	49	12	11	23	18
C	Vasili Pankov	50	10	10	20	49
F	Oleg Antonenko	46	12	7	19	30
D	Oleg Khmyl	48	4	12	16	20
F	Sergei Shitkovsky	41	9	3	12	54
F	Konstantin Frolov	52	8	4	12	44
F	Dmitri Ovsyannikov	42	8	4	12	4
F	Vladimir Deyev	50	6	5	11	20
D	Alexander Makritsky	43	1	5	6	50
D	Ruslan Salei	51	4	2	6	44
C	Igor Leonovich	46	3	3	6	42
D	Oleg Romanov	47	3	3	5	42
F	Vladimir Khailak	31	3	2	5	14
F	Sergei Chernyavsky	34	1	4	5	18
D	Sergei Yerkovich	45	3	1	4	52
F	Pavel Derkach	44	3	1	4	16
C	Anton Yurkin	15	1	3	4	12
C	Anatoli Varivonchik	28	1	3	4	12
D	Mark Velichkov	33	2	1	3	12
D	Andrei Protopopov	44	1	2	2	14
F	Valeri Yermolov	15	1	1	2	35
C	Yuri Karpenko	44	2	0	2	20
F	Alexander Andriyevsky	4	1	1	2	4
F	Igor Tarnovsky	16	1	0	1	2
F	Alexei Monakhov	12	0	1	1	0
D	Pavel Mikulchik	14	0	0	0	6
D	Oleg Teterev	33	0	0	0	6
D	S. Galkin	9	0	0	0	18
C	Alexander Zapolsky	5	0	0	0	2
F	Alexander Rymsha	23	0	0	0	6

Goaltenders	GP	MIN	GA	GAA
Alexander Gavrilenok	40	2380	111	2.79
Yuri Ivashin	15	845	40	2.84

CIC PLAY-OFF NON-QUALIFIERS

Severstal Cherepovets

Pos	Name	GP	G	A	P	PM
F	Igor Petrov	50	13	15	28	46
F	Igor Nikulin	52	14	12	26	28
F	Vladimir Kochin	50	16	8	24	32
C	Andrei Konarev	50	9	8	17	49
C	Oleg Savchuk	51	8	7	15	26
D	Alexander Terekhov	52	5	8	13	48
F	Sergei Ichensky	20	6	4	10	6
D	Andrei Dylevsky	51	2	7	9	58
F	Sergei Kondrashkin	51	7	2	9	22
F	Sergei Kozlov	48	3	5	8	22
D	Alexander Zhdan	22	6	0	6	12
F	Vladimir Uimanov	44	4	2	6	12
F	Oleg Boltunov	37	4	2	6	24
C	Alexei Koznev	41	2	3	5	10
F	Alexei Sokolov	43	3	2	5	12
D	Sergei Karpov	6	0	4	4	4
D	Yuri Lynov	32	1	2	3	14
D	Vladimir Tyagin	52	1	2	3	44
D	Vitali Solin	17	1	1	2	2
F	Andrei Shutov	14	2	0	2	6
F	Alexei Ivanov	14	1	0	1	0
F	Sergei Shumilov	12	1	0	1	2
C	Alexei Skvortsov	35	0	1	1	22
F	Alexander Agnevschikov	13	1	0	1	2
F	Alexei Barsukov	5	0	1	1	0
F	Dmitri Konovalov	19	1	0	1	4
D	Viktor Zavarzin	4	0	0	0	6
D	Alexei Danilov	17	0	0	0	6
D	Andrei Kozyrev	40	0	0	0	36
D	Alexei Vasiljev	4	0	0	0	0
D	Sergei Semenov	26	0	0	0	18
D	Andrei Khaidin	37	0	0	0	26
F	Andrei Smirnov	5	0	0	0	0

Goaltenders	GP	MIN	GA	GAA
Alexei Gribakin	17	881	63	4.29
Alexander Chizhevsky	13	681	30	2.64
Sergei Polyakov	28	1524	57	2.24

Kristall Elektrostal

Pos	Name	GP	G	A	P	PM
F	Andrei Sidlyarov	51	19	8	27	46
F	Sergei Nikonorov	51	15	11	26	4
C	Dmitri Vershinin	49	8	11	19	18
F	Vadim Pokatilo	52	10	8	18	16
D	Dmitri Kamyshnikov	28	5	9	14	44
C	Vladimir Khamrakulov	38	9	4	13	20
F	Vitali Kabanov	52	9	3	12	16
C	Vladimir Potapov	51	4	7	11	24
F	Sergei Novikov	20	4	4	8	6
F	Sergei Makarov	33	5	3	8	30
D	Vladimir Cherbaturkin	52	2	6	8	90
D	Sergei Karpov	18	1	5	6	10
F	Yakov Deyev	32	3	3	6	10
D	Alexander Grishin	50	1	3	4	75
D	Eduard Matyukhov	39	1	3	4	52
D	Andrei Simashov	43	1	3	4	12
C	Sergei Selyutin	28	2	2	4	16
C	Igor Shevtsov	37	3	1	4	14
C	Alexei Budayev	25	2	1	3	12
D	Alexander Golovkin	41	2	1	3	61
F	Igor Petrushkin	12	3	0	3	0
D	Gennady Yefimov	45	0	3	3	14
F	Vladislav Bryzgalov	34	2	0	2	22
D	Vitali Proshkin	29	0	1	1	20
F	Yevgeny Sultanovich	6	1	0	1	0
F	Vasili Christokletov	25	0	1	1	8
D	Vadim Musatov	49	0	0	0	53
D	Roman Kablin	3	0	0	0	0
D	Yuri Medvedev	7	0	0	0	0
D	Alexander Sapogov	6	0	0	0	2
F	Andrei Smirnov	6	0	0	0	4
C	Alex. Korolev	8	0	0	0	6
F	Alexander Golovin	11	0	0	0	2
F	Vyacheslav Vorobjev	27	0	0	0	36

Goaltenders	GP	MIN	GA	GAA
Igor Galkin	25	1344	66	2.94
Denis Kuzmenko	32	1796	90	3.00

Kristall Saratov

Pos	Name	GP	G	A	P	PM
C	Igor Stepanov	52	21	20	41	74
F	Andrei Korolev	42	20	19	39	75
F	Ali Burkhanov	48	21	16	37	54
D	Mikhail Shubinov	46	10	17	27	56
C	Sergei Tostykh	52	11	6	17	30
D	Sergei Fedotov	52	5	8	13	42
D	Oleg Leontjev	52	6	4	10	47
F	Kirill Dvurechensky	45	8	2	10	12
F	Vadim Molotilov	52	7	2	9	18
D	Dmitri Stulov	52	1	8	9	61
F	Vadim Umnov	51	5	2	7	10
C	Sergei Samoshkin	52	3	3	6	36
C	Alim Aleyev	49	4	2	6	28
F	Alexander Ivanov	50	4	1	5	73
F	Vitali Sedov	14	3	1	4	10
D	Alexei Krivonozhkin	52	1	2	3	22
F	Dmitri Yermoshin	50	1	2	3	10
F	Mikhail Schetinin	36	2	1	3	2
D	Alexander Mikhailov	52	0	1	1	20
D	Vladimir Dumnov	49	0	1	1	12
F	Roman Pustovoi	20	1	0	1	2
F	S. Zemskov	13	0	1	1	0
D	Dmitri Chikin	1	0	0	0	0
D	Ivan Polischuk	50	0	0	0	53
D	Nikolai Cherepukha	2	0	0	0	0
C	Yevgeny Tarasov	2	0	0	0	0
F	Yevgeny Shishkin	13	0	0	0	8
F	Yevgeny Chulkov	10	0	0	0	0

Goaltenders	GP	MIN	GA	GAA
Dmitri Melnikov	29	1399	68	2.91
Dmitri Sychkov	33	1752	104	3.56

Metallurg Novokuznetsk

Pos	Name	GP	G	A	P	PM
C	Alexander Kitov	47	18	5	23	22
F	Alexander Voronov	51	14	9	23	8
F	Mikhail Sigarev	41	13	5	18	117
F	Oleg Gross	32	10	7	17	8
C	Arkadi Pavlyuchenko	51	7	8	15	47
C	Alexander Malakhov	42	5	7	12	8
D	Andrei Troschenkov	49	7	5	12	44
F	Andrei Smirnov	48	5	7	12	12
F	Vladislav Morozov	24	10	1	11	32
D	Yuri Zuyev	34	4	6	10	46
D	Andrei Yevstafjev	46	4	5	9	36
F	Sergei Kalinin	46	5	3	8	6
D	Alexei Giro	52	0	5	5	36
F	Yevgeny Baklanov	48	4	1	5	18
F	Vladimir Kormachev	37	2	3	5	10
D	Dmitri Voinsky	40	0	4	4	22
D	Dmitri Butsenko	18	0	3	3	0
D	Alexei Kitsyn	52	3	0	3	50
C	Alexander Skvortsov	30	3	0	3	6
F	Sergei Kharchenko	44	3	0	3	8
F	Sergei Moskalev	30	1	1	2	16
D	Sergei Trofilov	42	1	1	2	10
D	Sergei Yapparov	30	1	1	2	6
F	Andrei Vara	25	2	0	2	8
C	Valeri Gudozhnikov	14	2	0	2	2
F	Mikhail Pashin	13	1	0	1	0
D	Roman Romanov	18	0	0	0	10
D	Vyacheslav Potapov	8	0	0	0	2
C	Stanislav Komarov	32	0	0	0	14
F	Pavel Borzunov	15	0	0	0	2

Goaltenders	GP	MIN	GA	GAA
Vyacheslav Lisovets	12	558	43	4.62
Dmitri Kuroshin	45	2608	142	3.26

CIC PLAY-OFF NON-QUALIFIERS

Stroitel Karaganda

Pos	Name	GP	G	A	P	PM
F	Alexei Murzin	46	11	13	24	26
F	Alexander Filippov	49	15	3	18	2
F	Valeri Minayev	32	4	4	8	2
F	Andrei Zalipyatskikh	38	4	3	7	12
C	Alexander Kharitonov	48	5	2	7	34
D	Oleg Bolyakin	36	8	6	14	32
D	Dmitri Dubrovsky	43	6	0	6	54
F	Vladimir Sapozhnikov	33	5	1	6	19
F	Bulat Gabdrakhmanov	33	4	1	5	14
C	Oleg Martjanov	21	3	2	5	4
C	Valeri Tushentsov	11	2	3	5	4
D	Viktor Alexandrov	16	2	2	4	12
F	Pavel Tsukanov	7	3	1	4	2
C	Vladimir Zhabunin	8	2	2	4	2
F	A. Moskalev	10	2	2	4	0
C	Alexander Mokshantsev	32	2	2	4	26
F	Yevgeny Avdeyev	46	3	1	4	6
D	Alexander Bolchugov	28	1	2	3	4
F	Sergei Kuksov	19	1	2	3	8
F	Roman Malov	15	2	1	3	0
F	Denis Orlov	48	2	1	3	14
F	Denis Leonov	12	1	2	3	4
C	Alexei Anisimov	10	0	3	3	0
D	Alexander Gasnikov	49	0	2	2	36
C	Galim Mambetaliyev	10	0	2	2	6
C	Viktor Buyalsky	8	1	1	2	0
F	Leonid Zavitsyev	5	2	0	2	2
D	V. Kharchenko	2	1	0	1	2
D	Ivan Peltek	3	0	1	1	8
D	Alexander Fomichev	6	1	0	1	2
D	Alexei Mikhailov	32	1	0	1	12
D	Sergei Yakovenko	31	1	0	1	12
D	Denis Pavlov	31	0	1	1	10
D	Vladislav Kern	49	1	0	1	32
F	P. Glotov	2	1	0	1	0
F	Vadim Avdeyev	23	1	0	1	0
F	A. Obukhov	2	1	0	1	0
D	Vitali Kats	42	0	0	0	38
D	Pavel Starodubov	27	0	0	0	16
D	Oleg Stryukov	18	0	0	0	10
D	Yuri Petrushin	16	0	0	0	12
F	Dauren Zhunusov	19	0	0	0	6

Goaltenders	GP	MIN	GA	GAA
A. Dryamin	5	122	19	9.34
Sergei Fedorovich	2	23	6	15.65
Yevgeny Shmetis	2	51	9	10.58
Nikolai Kolioglov	27	1448	176	7.29
Vladimir Balandin	26	1500	128	5.12

CSK VVS Samara

Pos	Name	GP	G	A	P	PM
C	Vladimir Boyarintsev	50	15	15	30	26
F	Alexei Klimantov	52	14	15	29	18
F	Sergei Shumikhin	52	18	10	28	24
C	Dmitri Vanyasov	52	14	14	28	40
F	Yuri Mordvintsev	50	17	7	24	20
F	Igor Krasheninnikov	52	16	7	23	22
F	Alexei Zuyev	48	12	9	21	38
C	Aidar Musakayev	52	6	12	18	10
F	Andrei Nizamayev	51	8	10	18	34
D	Sergei Mordvintsev	47	7	8	15	12
D	Oleg Yushin	52	7	7	14	16
D	Sergei Vologzhanin	50	3	11	14	18
D	Sergei Gusev	50	5	8	13	58
C	Andrei Kuznetsov	47	5	3	8	12
F	Oleg Larionov	49	6	1	7	14
D	Alexei Buldakov	47	1	3	4	36
F	Alexei Igonchenko	16	2	2	4	4
F	Sergei Nikolayev	27	2	1	3	4
D	Andrei Kulikov	34	1	1	2	14
D	Oleg Kuznetsov	40	0	2	2	26
F	Oleg Naumenko	26	1	1	2	16
F	Konstantin Isupov	16	1	1	2	31
D	Pavel Zubov	22	0	1	1	6
F	Andrei Morozov	11	1	0	1	0
F	Alexei Alexeyev	15	1	0	1	6
D	Vladimir Shuklin	8	0	0	0	0

Goaltenders	GP	MIN	GA	GAA
Rashid Davydov	27	1486	78	3.15
Alexei Shamin	32	1670	91	3,27

Sibir Novosibirsk

Pos	Name	GP	G	A	P	PM
F	Dmitri Zatonsky	52	23	12	35	32
F	Vladimir Gromilin	45	14	16	30	22
C	Sergei Gubarev	48	16	13	29	34
F	Sergei Korchagin	49	15	12	27	40
F	Yevgeny Babayev	52	11	15	26	38
F	Vladimir Yablonsky	44	12	13	25	12
C	Viktor Fominykh	51	11	12	23	54
F	Igor Khramtsov	50	7	13	20	58
C	Igor Bukhtoyarov	48	10	5	15	14
D	Amir Alyamov	48	10	4	14	32
D	Igor Ryzhikh	52	7	3	10	36
D	Oleg Prokopenko	47	3	5	8	18
D	Valeri Shestitko	52	3	4	7	42
C	Igor Ulshin	22	4	3	7	6
F	Igor Korovashkin	37	5	1	6	44
F	Sergei Zhukov	36	1	4	5	22
F	Igor Gorbenko	8	2	2	4	4
D	Alexei Prokopev	34	1	2	3	18
D	Yevgeny Tyutikov	18	0	3	3	22
F	V. Klochkov	17	2	0	2	6
D	Andrei Barsukov	45	1	0	1	38
F	Alexander Vlasov	19	0	1	1	4
D	Yevgeny Ushkov	35	0	0	0	6
D	Vyacheslav Gerold	4	0	0	0	8
D	Alexei Godny	27	0	0	0	16
F	Vyacheslav Karpov	12	0	0	0	0
C	Mikhail Rogoza	9	0	0	0	0
F	Alexei Logutenko	19	0	0	0	18

Goaltenders	GP	MIN	GA	GAA
Konstantin Kapkaikin	12	664	48	4.33
Sergei Moshalev	7	316	24	4.55
Anton Scherbakov	3	104	11	6.34
Yuri Shevchenko	24	1359	127	5.60
Nikolai Krivtsov	15	696	63	5.43

Rubin Tyumen

Pos	Name	GP	G	A	P	PM
F	Nikolai Babenko	49	20	21	41	16
F	Alexei Galynsky	44	14	4	18	12
C	Sergei Zaitsev	50	11	7	18	16
F	Vladimir Zorkin	22	9	8	17	12
D	Pavel Plotnikov	52	8	7	15	95
F	Vladimir Sinitsyn	52	7	8	15	12
C	Sergei Mogilnikov	51	5	9	14	10
C	Nikolai Ustinov	26	5	9	14	18
C	Vyacheslav Khayev	48	8	6	14	24
F	Eduard Valiullin	16	10	3	13	2
F	Alexander Samopalnikov	45	10	3	13	10
C	Vladislav Khromykh	51	6	6	12	20
C	Vladislav Gromov	50	6	5	11	6
D	Rashit Galimzhanov	45	4	7	11	14
C	Alexei Zhukov	50	7	3	10	14
F	Konstantin Makarov	44	5	1	6	10
C	Konstantin Kurochkin	43	3	3	6	14
F	Alexei Kokovin	22	4	2	6	0
D	Denis Denisov	32	1	4	5	10
F	Viktor Belyakov	10	3	2	5	6
D	Khalim Nigmatullin	52	3	0	3	44
D	Oleg Kachesov	32	3	0	3	42
D	Dmitri Sayenko	40	1	2	3	26
D	Yuri Mikhailis	39	0	3	3	28
D	Valeri Ganzha	14	0	1	1	4
D	Sergei Milto	12	0	1	1	2
D	Alexander Vetrov	20	0	1	1	14
F	Igor Gorbenko	5	1	0	1	2
F	Andrei Kuznetsov	10	1	0	1	4
D	Vladimir Koilov	24	0	0	0	8
D	Dmitri Burlutsky	47	0	0	0	57
D	Pavel Yeremeyv	18	0	0	0	6

Goaltenders	GP	MIN	GA	GAA
Pavel Bessonov	23	1131	89	4.72
Andrei Vasilevsky	38	2013	116	3.45

CIC PLAY-OFF NON-QUALIFIERS

SCANDIC
CROWN HOTEL
VIENNA

Handelskai 269
A-1020 Wien
Telephone +43/1/727 77
Fax +43/1/727 77-199

The official hotel of
the IIHF, UEFA,
Davis Cup

Unique on the Danube with the largest standard rooms in Vienna

Cost saving conference packages for sports clubs

Neueste original US-Profi-Banden-
systeme ab Werk Deutschland

uniVersal *sport products*

EISBAHN-ANLAGEN

Beratung · Planung · Lieferung
Ihr Fachmann Erhard Waldapfel

Drosselweg 5 · D-73249 Wernau/Neckar
Telefon 0 71 53/33 71 · Fax 0 71 53/3 82 70

Eisbahn-Banden-Technik · Eishockey-Schutzeinrichtungen

Makralon oder Netze, Eishockey-Markierungen, umweltfreundlich – keine Farbe,
Mannschafts-, Strafbank- und Jury-Einrichtungen, neueste orig.
Canada-Eishockey-Tore, 4-Punkt-Eisverankerung, Schutzverglasungen,
spezielle Kunststoff-Banden-Stoßleisten, Verleihschuhständer, Gummiboden.
Alles nach internationalen Vorschriften.

Teil- und Komplettsanierungen

145

Sweden

Federation:
Svenska Ishockeyförbundet
Box 5204
S-12116 Johanneshov/Stockholm
Sweden
Telephone (+46.8) 602 6600
Fax   (+46.8) 910 035
President: Rickard Fagerlund
Executive Director: Bo Berglund

Rickard Fagerlund	Bo Berglund
President	Executive Director

Clubs

AIK Solna Stockholm
Box 1408
17127 Solna

Malmö IF
Isstadion E. Perssons Väg
21762 Malmö

Brynäs IF
Idrottsvägen 7
80633 Gävle

Djurgarden IF
Box 5134
12117 Johanneshov

Färjestad BK
Box 318
65108 Karlstad

Leksand IF
Box 118
79323 Leksand

Luleå HF
Ishallen Delfinen
97334 Luleå

MoDo Domsjö
Box 76
89222 Domsjö

Rögle BK
Box 1185
26223 Ängelholm

HV 71 Jonköping
Rosenlundshallen
55454 Jönköping

Västeras IK
Box 7062
72217 Västeras

Västra Frölunda HC
Box 5014
40221 Göteborg

Elite Division 1994/95
Regular Season Standings

Team	GP	W	L	T	Goals	Pts
1. Djurgarden Stockholm	40	24	9	7	139: 96	55
2. Malmö IF	40	20	7	13	130:105	53
3. Luleå HF	40	21	9	10	164:116	52
4. Leksand IF	40	21	13	6	155:132	48
5. Brynäs Gävle	40	17	15	8	119:127	42
6. Färjestad Karlstad	40	17	17	6	128:135	40
7. Västeras IK	40	15	18	7	145:137	37
8. HV 71 Jonköping	40	12	19	9	117:143	33
9. AIK Solna Stockholm	40	11	21	8	111:146	30
10. MoDo Hockey Domsjö	40	8	22	10	121:140	26
11. Västra Frölunda	22	6	11	5	63: 70	17
12. Rögle Angelholm	22	5	16	1	49: 93	11

Top eight teams qualified for the playoffs.
All return to Eliteserien next season.

Play-off
Quarterfinals (best of 5)

HV 71 Jönköping	– Djurgarden IF	5:2, 3:2, 5:2
Brynäs Gävle	– Leksand IF	2:3, 1:0, 4:3, 8:3
Luleå HF	– Färjestad BK	5:7, 8:4, 4:1, 3:2
Malmö IF	– Västeras IK	4:3, 1:2, 5:3, 4:2

Semifinals

HV 71 Jönköping	– Malmö IF	2:3, 0:4, 3:2, 5:3, 6:2
Brynäs Gävle	– Luleå HF	1:4, 3:6, 2:1, 4:3, 4:3

Finals

HV 71 Jönköping	– Brynäs Gävle	2:4, 4:0, 2:3, 4:2, 5:4

Regular Season

Leading Elitserien Scorers

Name	Team	GP	G	A	P	PM
1. Mika Nieminen	Luleå	38	18	31	49	26
2. Per Erik Eklund	Leksand	32	13	36	49	12
3. Niklas Eriksson	Leksand	39	17	26	43	32
4. Esa Keskinen	HV 71	39	15	28	43	48
5. Marcus Akerblom	Leksand	40	14	29	43	18
6. Anders Carlsson	Västeras	39	16	22	38	40
7. Hakan Loob	Färjestad	39	13	25	38	58
8. Morgan Samuelsson	AIK	40	16	21	37	14
9. Alexei Salomatin	Västeras	37	17	18	35	10
10. Tomas Forslund	Leksand	34	24	10	34	46
11. Stefan Nilsson	Luleå	39	9	25	34	55
12. Mishat Fahrutdinov	Västeras	39	8	25	33	15
13. Johan Rosen	Luleå	40	18	14	32	52
14. Stefan Hellkvist	Västeras	39	14	18	32	14
15. Mats Lindgren	Västeras	37	17	15	32	20

Goaltending

Name	Team	GP	Mins	GA	SO	GAA
Sam Lindstahl	AIK Solna	10	600	43	0	4.30
Joakim Persson	AIK Solna	30	1800	103	1	3.43
Michael Sundlof	Brynäs	34	2040	105	2	3.08
Lars Karlsson	Brynäs	4	240	17	0	4.25
Tomas Ostlund	Djurgarden	39	2340	95	4	2.43
Jonas Forsberg	Djurgarden	1	60	1	0	1.00
Jonas Eriksson	Färjestad	23	1324	84	1	3.81
Patrik Haltia	Färjestad	17	956	44	0	2.76
Peter Aslin	HV 71	19	1095	70	0	3.83
Boo Ahl	HV 71	23	1305	73	0	3.36
Ake Lilljebjorn	Leksand	23	1380	68	0	3.16
Johan Hedberg	Leksand	17	986	58	1	3.53
Fredrik Andersson	MoDo	13	740	46	0	3.73
Petter Ronnqvist	MoDo	28	1600	94	1	3.52
Hakan Algotsson	Frölunda	14	829	47	0	3.40
Mikael Sandberg	Frölunda	9	491	23	1	2.81
Jarmo Myllys	Luleå	37	2220	106	4	2.85
Erik Granqvist	Luleå	3	180	10	0	3.33
Peter Lindmark	Malmö	14	840	34	3	2.43
Roger Nordstrom	Malmö	26	1560	72	1	2.77
Kenneth Johansson	Rögle	14	760	56	0	4.42
Magnus Svard	Rögle	9	500	32	0	3.84
Mats Ytter	Västeras	36	2053	111	1	3.24
Erik Bergstrom	Västeras	6	277	19	0	4.11
Henrik Nordfeldt	Västeras	1	10	2	0	12.00

Final Allsvenskan Standings

Name	GP	W	L	T	Goals	Pts
1. Rögle BK*	18	13	2	3	84:46	29
2. Västra Frölunda*	18	12	4	2	106:50	26
3. Troja/Ljungby	18	11	5	2	70:51	24
4. Kiruna	18	7	5	6	54:54	20
5. Boden	18	8	9	1	71:65	17
6. Huddinge	18	5	8	5	57:73	15
7. Vita Hasten	18	6	10	2	54:61	14
8. Mora	18	5	9	4	55:81	14
9. Orebro	18	5	11	2	51:80	12
10. Hammarby	18	3	12	3	46:87	9

* Return to Elitserien for 1995/96 season

Play-off

Leading Scorers

Name	Team	GP	G	A	P	PM
1. Mika Nieminen	Luleå	9	5	8	13	16
2. Per Gustafsson	HV 71	13	7	5	12	6
3. Marko Palo	HV 71	13	5	7	12	20
4. Stefan Ornskog	HV 71	13	4	8	12	4
5. Johan Rosen	Luleå	9	7	4	11	10
6. Jonas Johnsson	Brynäs	14	4	6	10	14
7. Ove Molin	Brynäs	14	4	6	10	4
8. Stefan Falk	HV71	13	6	3	9	14
9. Bedrich Scerban	Brynäs	14	4	5	9	12
10. Hakan Ahlund	Malmö	9	4	5	9	10
11. Jiri Kucera	Luleå	9	2	7	9	6
12. Stefan Ketola	Brynäs	13	2	7	9	26
13. Peter Larsson		14	4	4	8	6
14. Mikael Wahlberg	Brynäs	14	4	4	8	39
15. Fredrik Modin	Brynäs	14	4	4	8	6

Goaltending

Name	Team	GP	Mins	GA	SO	GAA
Michael Sundlof	Brynäs	12	696	28	1	2.41
Lars Karlsson	Brynäs	3	144	15	0	6.25
Tomas Oslund	Djurgarden	3	180	13	0	4.33
Jonas Eriksson	Färjestad	2	120	13	0	6.50
Patrik Haltia	Färjestad	2	120	7	0	3.50
Boo Ahl	HV 71	13	780	33	1	2.54
Ake Lilljebjorn	Leksand	4	221	7	0	1.90
Johan Hedberg	Leksand	4	221	8	0	2.17
Jarmo Myllys	Luleå	9	540	28	0	3.11
Peter Lindmark	Malmö	2	120	5	0	2.50
Roger Nordstrom	Malmö	7	420	21	0	3.00
Mats Ytter	Västeras	4	240	14	0	3.50

All Time Champions 1922–1995

Team	Title
Djurgarden Stockholm	14
Brynäs Gävle	11
IK Göta	9
Hammarby IF	8
AIK Stockholm	7
Södertälje SK	7
IF Leksand	4
Färjestad Karlstad	3
Malmö IF	2
Västra Frölunda	1
Skelleftea AIK	1
MoDo Domsjö	1
IF Björklöven	1
HV 71 Jonköping	1

Djurgarden Stockholm

Pos	Name	Reguar Season					Play-offs				
		GP	G	A	P	PM	GP	G	A	P	PM
F	Charles Berglund	19	11	20	31	20	3	1	3	4	4
F	Per Eklund	40	19	10	29	20	3	1	1	2	4
F	Fredrik Lindqvist	40	11	16	27	14	3	0	0	0	2
F	Patrik Erickson	40	10	14	24	18	3	0	1	1	8
F	Peter Nilsson	39	6	16	22	20	3	0	0	0	2
F	Espen Knutsen	30	6	14	20	18	3	0	1	1	0
F	Anders Huusko	36	12	7	19	28	1	0	0	0	0
D	Robert Nordmark	34	7	11	18	50	3	1	0	1	2
D	M. Ragnarsson	38	7	9	16	20	3	0	0	0	4
D	Erik Huusko	40	7	9	16	28	3	0	1	1	2
D	Bjorn Nord	39	7	7	14	42	3	0	0	0	2
F	Jens Ohling	28	6	7	13	4	3	0	2	2	0
D	Thomas Johansson	38	5	6	11	14	3	1	0	1	0
F	Mats Sundin	12	7	2	9	14	0	0	0	0	0
D	Mikael Magnusson	38	2	7	9	61	3	0	2	2	2
F	Ola Josefsson	27	5	2	7	20	2	0	0	0	0
D	Christian Due-Boje	38	1	6	7	55	3	0	0	0	0
F	Magnus Jansson	12	4	2	6	10	1	0	0	0	0
D	Joakim Lundberg	38	1	3	4	10	3	0	0	0	6
D	Joakim Musakka	39	2	1	3	28	3	1	0	1	4
G	Tomas Ostlund	40	0	0	0	8	3	0	0	0	4
F	Mattias Hallback	25	0	0	0	2	3	0	0	0	0
F	Kristoffer Ottosson	30	0	0	0	2	3	0	0	0	0
F	Jonas Borgar	4	0	0	0	0	0	0	0	0	0
G	Jonas Forsberg	26	0	0	0	0	3	0	0	0	0
G	Micheal Turnqvist	14	0	0	0	0	0	0	0	0	0
	Jonas Borger	4	0	0	0	0	0	0	0	0	0

Brynäs Gävle

Pos	Name	Reguar Season					Play-offs				
		GP	G	A	P	PM	GP	G	A	P	PM
F	Andreas Dackell	39	16	14	30	34	14	3	3	6	14
F	Peter Larsson	40	6	23	29	28	14	4	4	8	6
F	Jonas Johnsson	39	9	15	24	22	14	4	6	10	14
F	Ove Mohlin	36	10	10	20	26	14	4	6	10	4
F	Fredrik Modin	30	9	9	18	31	14	4	4	8	6
F	Anders Huss	31	8	8	16	14	14	5	1	6	22
F	Sergei Pushkov	35	5	9	14	10	0	0	0	0	0
F	Mikael Wahlberg	39	5	9	14	50	13	4	4	8	39
D	Bedrich Scerban	40	4	9	13	26	14	4	5	9	12
D	Christer Olsson	39	6	5	11	18	14	1	3	4	6
F	Stefan Ketola	32	2	7	9	12	14	2	7	9	20
F	Per-Johan Johansson	39	5	4	9	24	14	3	0	3	12
D	Stefan Klockare	40	5	4	9	14	14	0	3	3	8
F	Stefan Polla	37	5	3	8	10	13	1	3	4	31
F	Thomas Tallberg	15	5	3	8	8	0	0	0	0	0
	Per Lofstrom	30	2	3	5	12	14	1	4	5	10
	Mikael Lindh	22	3	1	4	4	13	1	0	1	2
	Jonas Lofstrom	23	1	2	3	12	14	1	4	5	8
D	Tommy Melkersson	39	1	2	3	44	14	0	1	1	22
D	Mikael Enander	34	2	1	3	24	13	0	0	0	2
D	Daniel Casselstahl	29	2	1	3	10	3	0	0	0	0
D	Johan Tornberg	37	1	1	2	20	4	0	0	0	0
G	Michael Sundlof	39	0	0	0	8	12	0	0	0	6
	Lars Karlsson	40	0	0	0	0	14	0	0	0	2
	Mattias Pettersson	1	0	0	0	0	2	0	0	0	0
F	Max Wikman	4	0	0	0	4	0	0	0	0	0
	Mikael Lindman	0	0	0	0	0	14	0	1	1	6
	Sergei Pushov	0	0	0	0	0	13	0	0	0	2

Färjestad Karlstad

Pos	Name	Reguar Season					Play-offs				
		GP	G	A	P	PM	GP	G	A	P	PM
F	Hakan Loob	39	13	25	38	58	4	2	0	2	2
F	Mats Lindgren	37	17	15	32	20	3	0	0	0	4
F	Jonas Hoglund	40	14	12	26	16	4	3	2	5	0
F	Claes Eriksson	40	11	10	21	32	4	2	3	5	8
F	Niklas Brannstrom	40	10	9	19	22	4	1	0	1	2
F	Andreas Johansson	36	9	10	19	42	4	0	0	0	10
D	Per Lundell	40	4	13	17	18	4	0	4	4	0
F	Stefan Nilsson	39	9	8	17	32	4	1	0	1	2
F	Mattias Johansson	40	7	8	15	30	4	4	3	7	2
D	Sergei Fokin	39	8	5	13	30	4	0	2	2	0
F	Peter Ottosson	35	7	4	11	16	4	0	1	1	2
D	Tommy Samuelsson	38	2	7	9	20	4	0	0	0	2
D	Thomas Rhodin	40	3	4	7	80	4	0	0	0	2
F	Magnus Arvedsson	36	1	6	7	45	4	0	0	0	6
D	Jesper Duus	39	2	4	6	20	4	0	0	0	6
D	Mattias Olsson	40	2	4	6	16	4	0	1	1	0
D	Olli Kaski	36	2	3	5	18	4	1	0	1	6
F	Bjorn Eriksson	31	0	2	2	4	4	0	0	0	0
	Jan Labraaten	2	0	1	1	2	1	0	0	0	0
G	Jonas Eriksson	40	0	0	0	22	4	0	0	0	0
G	Patrik Haltia	40	0	0	0	2	4	0	0	0	0
	Patrik Wallenberg	2	0	0	0	2	0	0	0	0	0
	Per Sveder	7	0	0	0	0	0	0	0	0	0

HV 71 Jonköping

Pos	Name	Reguar Season					Play-offs				
		GP	G	A	P	PM	GP	G	A	P	PM
F	Esa Keskinen	39	15	28	43	48	13	3	5	8	10
F	Marko Palo	37	16	13	29	24	13	5	7	12	20
D	Fredrik Stillman	39	9	16	25	47	13	2	5	7	22
D	Ken Kennholt	37	9	14	23	64	13	2	5	7	6
F	Patric Kjellberg	29	5	15	20	12	0	0	0	0	0
F	Peter Hammarstrom	40	12	7	19	26	13	3	3	6	12
F	Stefan Ornskog	32	5	11	16	6	13	4	8	12	4
F	Johan Lindbom	39	9	7	16	30	13	2	5	7	12
D	Per Gustafsson	38	10	6	16	14	13	7	5	12	8
F	Johan Davidsson	37	4	7	11	28	13	3	2	5	0
F	Ove Tornberg	38	6	5	11	54	13	0	0	0	4
F	Stefan Falk	40	3	7	10	26	13	6	3	9	14
D	Mattias Svedberg	40	3	3	6	24	13	1	0	1	8
F	Thomas Ljungberg	40	2	4	6	24	13	1	3	4	6
F	Peter Ekelund	40	2	4	6	12	13	3	1	4	11
D	Niklas Rahm	32	0	5	5	10	13	2	1	3	14
D	Hans Abrahamsson	34	1	4	5	36	13	2	2	4	12
D	Andreas Schultz	23	1	2	3	6	2	0	0	0	0
F	Magnus Salmi	28	1	0	1	6	13	0	0	0	0
D	David Halvarsson	20	1	0	1	0	12	0	0	0	0
D	David Petrasek	30	0	1	1	6	11	0	0	0	0
F	Thomas Gustavsson	10	0	0	0	2	12	0	0	0	2
G	Peter Aslin	32	0	0	0	0	13	0	0	0	0
G	Boo Ahl	40	0	0	0	2	13	0	0	0	4
	Howard Lindersson	7	0	0	0	0	0	0	0	0	0

Leksand IF

		Reguar Season					Play-offs			
Pos	Name	GP	G	A	P	PM	GP	G	A	P	PM
F	Niklas Eriksson	39	17	26	43	32	4	1	2	3	4
F	Marcus Akerblom	40	14	29	43	18	4	0	2	2	2
F	Per-Erik Eklund	32	13	36	49	12	2	0	1	1	4
F	Tomas Forslund	34	24	10	34	46	3	1	0	1	25
F	Jonas Bergqvist	33	17	12	29	16	4	0	0	0	4
D	Tomas Jonsson	37	8	17	25	38	4	1	3	4	27
F	Mikael Holmberg	40	16	8	24	20	4	2	0	2	0
D	Jan Huokko	40	10	8	18	14	4	0	1	1	6
F	Jarmo Makitalo	35	5	10	15	14	4	0	0	0	0
F	Andr. Karlsson	24	7	8	15		4	0	1	1	0
F	Andy Schneider	39	6	8	14	71	4	1	1	2	31
F	M. Thuresson	39	3	10	13	42	4	1	0	1	0
D	Orjan Lindmark	30	2	7	9	16	4	0	0	0	4
D	Mats Lusth	40	1	8	9	60	4	0	0	0	6
D	Jergus Baca	38	2	5	7	50	4	1	1	2	6
F	Markus Eriksson	40	5	1	6	8	4	1	1	2	0
D	Hans Lodin	40	3	1	4	50	4	0	0	0	4
D	Nicklas Nordqvist	31	0	2	2	4	4	0	1	1	0
G	Johan Hedberg	39	0	1	1	2	4	0	0	0	0
D	Peter Casparsson	15	1	0	1	2	2	0	0	0	0
F	Peter Nordstrom	13	1	0	1	0	0	0	0	0	0
G	Ake Lilljebjorn	40	0	1	1	2	4	0	0	0	2
D	Roger Johansson	7	0	0	0	14	0	0	0	0	0
	Niklas Nordqvist	23	0	0	0	2	0	0	0	0	0
D	Ulf Samuelsson	2	0	0	0	8	0	0	0	0	0
	Andreas Ost	3	0	0	0	0	0	0	0	0	0
	Jonas Nilsson	4	0	0	0	0	0	0	0	0	0
	Kenrik Persson	4	0	0	0	0	0	0	0	0	0

Luleå HF

		Reguar Season					Play-offs			
Pos	Name	GP	G	A	P	PM	GP	G	A	P	PM
F	Mika Nieminen	38	18	31	49	26	9	5	3	8	16
F	Stefan Nilsson	39	9	25	34	55	9	0	5	5	2
F	Johan Rosen	40	18	14	32	52	9	7	4	11	10
F	Robert Nordberg	39	15	15	30	18	9	6	0	6	22
F	Lars Hurtig	40	13	16	29	59	9	5	0	5	30
F	T. Holmstrom	40	14	14	28	56	8	1	2	3	20
F	Jiri Kucera	40	15	12	27	24	9	2	7	9	8
D	Roger Akerstrom	39	5	16	21	38	8	1	1	2	12
F	Johan Stromvall	37	16	5	21	16	9	3	3	6	6
F	Tomas Berglund	37	4	14	18	69	9	0	6	6	10
D	Mattias Ohlund	34	6	10	16	34	9	4	0	4	16
D	Lars Modig	37	5	9	14	14	9	0	3	3	6
F	Mikael Renberg	10	9	4	13	16	0	0	0	0	0
D	Petter Nilsson	35	6	5	11	18	9	2	4	6	4
D	Tomas Lilja	28	2	7	9	22	6	0	0	0	12
D	Stefan Jonsson	39	4	4	8	38	8	0	1	1	4
F	Anders Burstrom	35	1	5	6	14	0	0	0	0	0
F	Anders Burstrom	35	1	5	6	14	0	0	0	0	0
F	Mikael Lovgren	34	1	0	1	4	9	0	1	1	0
F	Mikael Engstrom	32	1	4	5	4	9	0	0	0	0
D	Torbjorn Lindberg	29	1	4	5	4	0	0	0	0	0
D	Patrik Hoglund	23	0	4	4	2	9	0	0	0	0
G	Jarmo Myllys	37	0	4	4	22	9	0	0	0	14
F	Anders Burstrom	35	1	5	6	14	9	0	0	0	0
F	Mikael Lovgren	34	1	0	1	4	0	0	0	0	0
	Jakob Gunler	13	1	0	1	4	2	0	0	0	0
G	Erik Granqvist	40	0	0	0	0	9	0	0	0	0

Malmö IF

Pos	Name	Reguar Season					Play-offs				
		GP	G	A	P	PM	GP	G	A	P	PM
F	Raimo Helminen	35	10	19	29	55	7	3	2	5	4
D	Robert Svehla	32	11	13	24	83	9	2	3	5	6
F	Tero Lethera	37	12	11	23	30	9	0	1	1	0
F	Roger Hansson	39	8	14	22	18	9	4	2	6	2
F	Peter Sundstrom	40	9	13	22	30	9	1	4	5	2
D	Roger Ohman	40	8	10	18	18	9	1	4	5	0
D	Ricard Persson	31	3	13	16	38	9	0	2	2	6
F	Tomas Sandstrom	12	10	5	15	14	0	0	0	0	0
F	Bo Svanberg	35	5	10	15	26	9	2	4	6	8
F	Daniel Rydmark	23	8	7	15	24	9	1	2	3	31
F	Jesper Mattsson	37	9	6	15	18	9	2	0	2	18
F	Patrik Sylvegard	31	9	6	15	14	0	0	0	0	0
F	Hakan Ahlund	37	4	10	14	26	9	4	5	9	10
D	Petri Liimatainen	34	9	3	12	8	9	2	5	7	6
F	Marcus Magnertoft	30	5	5	10	16	0	0	0	0	0
D	Peter Andersson	27	1	9	10	18	9	5	0	5	16
F	Mattias Bosson	40	2	7	9	18	9	0	2	2	6
D	Peter Hasselblad	40	3	5	8	38	9	1	2	3	8
D	Johan Salle	38	2	3	5	12	9	0	0	0	8
F	Jens Hemstrom	20	0	2	2	0	0	0	0	0	0
F	Mikael Burakovsky	7	1	0	1	0	2	0	0	0	0
	Patrik Boli	9	1	0	1	2	7	0	0	0	0
	Andreas Larsson	2	0	1	1	0	0	0	0	0	0
D	Kim Johnsson	13	0	0	0	4	1	0	0	0	0
D	Jesper Damgaard	16	0	0	0	2	0	0	0	0	0
G	Roger Nordstrom	39	0	0	0	4	9	0	0	0	0
D	Johan Norgren	14	0	0	0	2	0	0	0	0	0
	Peter Lindmark	38	0	0	0	0	9	0	0	0	0
	Jesper Damgaard	12	0	0	0	2	0	0	0	0	0

Västeras IK

Pos	Name	Reguar Season					Play-offs				
		GP	G	A	P	PM	GP	G	A	P	PM
F	Anders Carlsson	39	16	22	38	40	4	1	3	4	4
F	Alexei Salomatin	37	17	18	35	10	4	0	0	0	6
F	Mishat Fahrutdinov	39	8	25	33	15	4	0	0	0	4
F	Stefan Hellqvist	39	14	18	32	14	4	1	1	2	6
F	Claes Lindblom	40	13	11	24	34	4	2	0	2	6
D	Leif Rohlin	39	15	15	30	46	4	2	0	2	2
F	Paul Andersson	33	11	10	21	12	4	1	0	1	2
F	Johan Brummer	38	11	9	20	36	4	1	0	1	2
D	Thomas Eriksson	40	8	7	15	46	4	0	1	1	0
F	Patrik Juhlin	11	5	9	14	8	0	0	0	0	0
D	Nicklas Lidstrom	13	2	10	12	4	0	0	0	0	0
F	Mikael Pettersson	31	4	8	12	6	4	1	2	3	0
D	Mikael Wiklander	40	6	6	12	36	4	1	0	1	0
F	Henrik Nilsson	40	4	7	11	10	4	0	1	1	0
D	Lars Ivarsson	32	3	7	10	26	3	0	0	0	2
F	Patrik Zetterberg	29	2	6	8	12	4	0	1	1	2
F	Jarmo Kekalainen	23	1	5	6	24	1	0	0	0	0
D	Ville Siren	37	1	4	5	44	4	0	1	1	4
D	Thomas Carlsson	33	1	3	4	16	3	0	0	0	2
F	Peter Popovic	11	0	3	3	10	0	0	0	0	0
D	Edvin Frylen	25	2	1	3	14	4	0	0	0	4
F	Henrik Nordfelt	35	0	3	3	10	4	0	0	0	2
D	Peter Jacobsson	22	1	1	2	14	0	0	0	0	0
G	Mats Ytter	40	0	0	0	4	4	0	0	0	0
D	Kristian Andersson	2	0	0	0	0	0	0	0	0	0
	Erik Bergstrom	40	0	0	0	0	4	0	0	0	0

Play-off Non-qualifiers

AIK Stockholm

Pos	Name	GP	G	A	P	PM
F	Morgan Samuelsson	40	16	21	37	14
F	Tomas Strandberg	40	7	20	27	26
D	Rickard Franzen	39	12	13	25	42
F	Mats Lindberg	40	14	10	24	8
F	Patric Englund	39	11	12	23	18
F	Anders Gozzi	35	6	10	16	18
F	Kristian Gahn	38	9	6	15	22
F	Tommy Lehmann	35	4	11	15	16
F	Anders Johnson	35	6	9	15	24
D	Dick Tarnstrom	37	8	4	12	26
D	Nicklas Havelid	40	3	7	10	38
F	Peter Gerhardsson	38	4	4	8	12
F	Stefan Gustavsson	39	6	1	7	18
F	Bjorn Ahlstrom	35	2	5	7	20
D	Brett Hauer	37	1	3	4	38
D	Johan Akerman	38	1	3	4	8
D	Patrik Aberg	39	1	2	3	36
F	Sacha Molin	29	0	2	2	6
D	Tony Barthelson	39	1	1	2	30
F	Tony Skopac	22	0	1	1	24
D	Sam Lindstahl	36	0	0	0	4
G	Joakim Persson	30	0	0	0	2
D	Johan Olsson	10	0	0	0	2
D	Peter Wallin	10	0	0	0	0
	Jimmy Marlboro	1	0	0	0	0
	Dan Vangring	5	0	0	0	0
	Hans Lahteenmaki	1	0	0	0	0

MoDo Hockey

Pos	Name	GP	G	A	P	PM
F	Martin Hostak	40	14	17	31	30
F	Magnus Wernblom	38	12	10	22	50
F	Anders Soderberg	38	9	13	22	2
F	Niklas Sundstrom	33	8	13	21	30
D	Mattias Timander	39	8	9	17	24
F	Lars Bystrom	39	5	11	16	2
F	Kyosti Karjalainen	35	7	9	16	20
F	Per Svartvadet	40	6	9	15	31
F	Peter Forsberg	11	5	9	14	20
F	Andreas Salomonsson	40	5	9	14	34
D	Jiri Vykoukal	40	7	6	13	36
F	Lennart Hermansson	30	2	9	11	22
D	Hans Jonsson	39	4	6	10	30
F	Mikael Hakansson	37	3	7	10	16
D	Anders Eriksson	39	3	6	9	54
F	Andreas Olsson	31	4	5	9	16
D	Lars Jansson	39	8	0	8	14
D	Fredrik Bergqvist	29	4	2	6	18
F	Petter Ronnqvist	36	0	2	2	0
D	Anders Berglund	16	1	0	1	10
D	Tomas Nanzen	25	1	0	1	12
	Per Hallberg	2	0	1	1	0
F	Marcus Ramen	10	0	0	0	0
G	Fredrik Andersson	38	0	0	0	4
	Stefan Olsson	4	0	0	0	0
	Daniel Olsson	3	0	0	0	0

Teams relegated MID-Season

Rögle Angelholm

Pos	Name	GP	G	A	P	PM
F	Stefan Elvenes	22	11	8	19	14
F	Jorgen Jonsson	22	4	6	10	18
F	Mikael Hjalm	22	4	6	10	6
F	Mats Loov	22	5	4	9	6
F	Pelle Svensson	22	6	2	8	16
F	Per Wallin	16	1	6	7	12
F	Mattias Loof	22	1	6	7	24
D	D. Johansson	22	4	2	6	16
F	Arto Ruotanen	19	1	4	5	8
D	Kari Suoraniemi	19	0	5	5	6
F	Tomas Srsen	16	3	1	4	30
F	Roger Elvenes	22	3	1	4	10
D	Kari Eloranta	17	1	3	4	8
D	Kenny Jonsson	8	3	1	4	20
F	Jens Nielsen	22	1	2	3	6
F	Daniel Tjarnqvist	18	0	1	1	2
F	Peter Lundmark	22	1	0	1	6
D	Mikael Johansson	20	0	1	1	2
D	Stanislav Meciar	16	0	1	1	4
D	Johan Finnstrom	19	0	0	0	10
F	Magnus Hermansson	6	0	0	0	0
F	Fredrik Moller	4	0	0	0	0
G	Kenneth Johansson	22	0	0	0	2
G	Magnus Svard	22	0	0	0	0
D	Pierre Johansson	22	0	0	0	6

Västra Frölunda Göteborg

Pos	Name	GP	G	A	P	PM
F	Marko Jantunen	22	15	8	23	22
F	Daniel Alfredsson	22	7	11	18	22
F	Thomas Sjogren	22	2	10	12	6
F	Terho Koskela	18	6	5	11	26
D	Per Djoos	22	5	4	9	12
F	Patrik Carnback	14	2	6	8	20
D	Stefan Larsson	20	4	3	7	30
F	Peter Berndtsson	21	4	3	7	10
D	Ronnie Sundin	11	3	4	7	6
F	Alexander Beliavski	19	2	4	6	8
D	Joacim Esbjors	22	1	4	5	22
F	Lars Edstrom	16	4	1	5	4
F	Jonas Esbjors	16	1	3	4	4
D	Oskar Ackestrom	22	1	2	3	6
F	Lars Dahlstrom	21	0	3	3	4
F	Per Edlund	22	1	2	3	18
F	Peter Strom	16	0	3	3	10
F	Per-Johan Axelsson	8	2	1	3	6
D	J.-Ander.-Junkka	16	0	2	2	2
F	Stefan Axelsson	22	1	1	2	6
F	Jerry Persson	20	1	0	1	0
D	Ulf Jansson	11	0	1	1	0
D	Mikael Andersson	7	1	0	1	31
D	Joacim Esbjors	4	0	1	1	8
F	Peter Hogardh	4	0	0	0	0

Switzerland

Federation:
Schweizerischer Eishockeyverband
Postfach 125
CH-8062 Zürich
Telephone   (+41.1) 317 7080
Fax   (+41.1) 312 6314

President: Josef Brunner

Gen. Secretary: Peter Lüthi

Manager National Teams: Peter Zahner

Josef Brunner
President

Peter Zahner
Manager National Teams

Clubs

EHC Biel
Postfach 1172
2500 Biel/Bienne

**Zürcher
Schlittschuhclub**
Postfach 486
8021 Zürich

HC Fribourg
Postfach 402
1701 Fribourg

EHC Kloten
Verenagasse 9
8302 Kloten

HC Lugano
Casella Postale 2694
6901 Lugano

HC Ambri-Piotta
6775 Ambri

HC Davos
Postfach
7270 Davos-Platz

EV Zug
Postfach 3115
6300 Zug 3

SC Bern
Zikadenweg 7
3006 Bern

SC Rapperswil-Jona
Postfach 1106
8640 Rapperswil

Nationalliga A 1994/95
Regular Season

Team	GP	Goals	Pts
1. EV Zug	36	152:125	48:24
2. HC Lugano	36	147:102	47:25
3. HC Ambri-Piotta	36	141:136	43:29
4. HC Davos	36	139:125	42:30
5. HC Fribourg	36	177:140	41:31
6. SC Bern	36	146:123	39:33
7. EHC Kloten	36	116:119	38:34
8. Zürcher SC	36	129:152	27:45
9. SC Rapperswil	36	102:165	19:53
10. EHC Biel	36	108:170	16:56

Play-offs
Quarterfinals (best of 5)

EV Zug	– Zürcher SC	6:2, 4:8, 3:0, 4:6, 8:3
HC Lugano	– EHC Kloten	5:0, 4:6, 1:2, 1:0, 3:5
HC Ambri-Piotta	– SC Bern	3:6, 4:5, 1:5
HC Davos	– HC Fribourg	3:4, 5:3, 2:4, 3:2, 3:4

Semifinals

EV Zug	– HC Fribourg	5:4, 4:3, 5:1
SC Bern	– EHC Kloten	2:3, 0:3, 1:4

Final

EV Zug	– EHC Kloten	3:8, 1:4, 5:2, 3:4

All Time Champions / Alle Landesmeister

HC Davos	25	Zürcher SC	3
EHC Arosa	9	EHC Biel	3
SC Bern	9	HC Bellerive Vevey	2
EHC St. Moritz	7	HC Villars	2
La Chaux de Fonds	6	Grasshoppers Zürich	2
HC Rosey Gstaad	4	SC Langnau	1
HC Lugano	4	EHC Visp	1
EHC Kloten	4		

EV ZUG

Name	GP	G	A1	A2	Pt	PIM
Ken Yarenchuck	36	26	27	10	63	55
Misko Antisin	32	14	21	7	42	32
Steve Aebersold	36	19	7	6	32	28
Dino Kessler	34	8	13	9	30	30
Patrick Fischer	36	10	13	5	28	30
Tom Fergus	22	12	11	1	24	56
Colin Müller	38	9	7	8	24	12
Ph. Neuenschwander	36	11	8	4	23	36
Daniel Meier	36	6	6	3	15	33
André Künzi	36	4	4	6	14	53
Dan Quinn	7	7	3	3	13	26
Thomas Künzi	36	6	4	3	13	48
Bill Schafhauser	36	4	3	5	12	43
Franz Steffen	21	6	4	1	11	26
Andreas Fischer	25	4	3	3	18	24
Fausto Mazzoleni	36	5	4	–	9	16
Daniel Giger	36	–	3	4	7	8
Jakub Horak	35	–	1	2	3	6
Thomas Seitz	35	1	–	–	1	–
Marco Köppel	7	–	1	–	1	–
Marc Habscheid	5	–	1	–	1	–
Livio Fazio	35	–	1	–	1	2

EHC KLOTEN

Name	GP	G	A1	A2	Pt	PIM
Mikael Johansson	35	14	22	14	50	8
Roman Wäger	34	25	15	7	47	44
Felix Hollenstein	36	16	23	5	44	71
Anders Eldebrink	25	8	8	8	24	16
Martin Bruderer	36	8	3	3	14	58
Bruno Erni	27	9	1	1	11	24
Roger Meier	36	3	8	–	11	28
Marco Bayer	35	2	6	3	11	34
Oliver Hoffmann	30	5	3	1	9	10
Sacha Ochsner	35	5	3	1	9	12
Daniel Sigg	35	6	1	1	8	30
Martin Kout	36	5	–	1	6	12
Michael Diener	35	3	2	–	5	10
Manuele Celio	25	2	3	–	5	10
Mathias Holzer	36	2	2	1	5	12
Calle Johansson	5	1	–	2	3	8
Patrik della Rossa	38	2	–	–	2	6
Marco Klöti	36	–	2	–	2	6

HC FRIBOURG

Name	GP	G	A1	A2	Pt	PIM
Andrej Khomutov	35	41	32	13	86	32
Slava Buykov	30	24	36	15	75	35
Pascal Schaller	36	17	13	12	42	4
Patrice Brasey	33	18	16	3	37	44
Chad Silver	36	6	13	9	28	12
Mario Rottaris	35	11	9	4	24	22
Marc Leuenberger	36	13	5	5	23	12
Fredy Bobillier	35	6	5	8	19	54
Alain Reymond	36	6	7	1	14	18
Doug Honegger	33	4	6	4	14	54
Christophe Brown	36	11	1	–	12	6
Bruno Maurer	35	6	2	3	11	28
Antoine Descloux	36	4	2	2	8	28
Olivier Keller	35	5	1	–	6	56
Joel Aeschlimann	36	3	1	1	5	6
Mathias Bächler	34	–	4	–	4	6
David Leibzig	36	–	–	3	3	10
Chr. Hofstetter	26	–	2	1	3	10
Nicolas Gauch	18	1	1	–	2	–
Marty Dallman	4	1	1	–	2	4

HC DAVOS

Name	GP	G	A1	A2	Pt	PIM
Dan Hodgson	35	23	15	12	50	32
Gilles Thibaudeau	36	17	11	9	37	24
Magnus Svensson	35	8	18	7	33	46
Christian Weber	25	12	10	7	29	2
René Müller	36	14	7	3	24	10
Gian-Marco Crameri	36	11	11	2	24	32
Olivier Roth	37	7	11	2	20	22
Peter Bärtschi	30	11	5	3	19	8
Andy Näser	36	7	11	1	19	4
Sämi Balmer	21	4	5	4	13	4
Riccardo Signorell	35	6	3	3	12	26
Reto Stirnimann	36	4	6	2	12	8
Beat Equilino	35	2	3	3	8	58
Roger Sigg	32	5	2	–	7	44
Ivo Rüthemann	25	4	1	2	7	2
Martin Brich	34	2	3	1	6	22
Marc Gianola	30	–	1	4	5	18
Andy Rufener	18	1	1	2	4	8
Andy Egli	28	1	1	–	2	18
Mario Schocher	24	–	2	–	2	4
Andrea Haeller	36	–	2	–	2	12
Nando Wieser	36	–	1	1	2	4

HC AMBRI-PIOTTA

Name	GP	G	A1	A2	Pt	PIM
Dimitri Kwartalnov	27	24	14	4	42	30
Igor Fedulov	33	17	17	8	42	28
Peter Jaks	32	21	13	5	39	26
Theo Wittmann	34	16	9	9	34	4
Keith Fair	36	10	14	4	28	34
Thomas Heldner	36	6	10	4	20	16
Valeri Kamenski	12	13	5	1	19	2
John Fritsche	20	5	6	8	19	18
Nicola Celio	36	6	9	2	17	2
Luca Vigano	36	5	8	3	16	24
Rick Tschumi	35	2	2	4	8	18
Markus Studer	36	7	–	–	7	8
Brenno Celio	36	3	3	1	7	16
Blair Müller	36	2	3	1	6	8
Tiziano Gianini	26	1	3	2	6	8
Ivan Gazzaroli	35	2	3	–	5	16
Luigi Riva	34	1	3	1	5	24
Stefano Togni	28	–	2	1	3	–

ZÜRCHER SC

Name	GP	G	A1	A2	Pt	PIM
Patrick Lebeau	36	27	17	8	52	22
Marc Fortier	35	11	30	10	51	104
Adrian Bachofner	36	18	8	7	33	44
Andreas Zehnder	36	9	11	8	28	88
Claudio Micheli	36	11	6	5	22	22
Bruno Vollmer	36	13	4	2	19	66
Vjeran Ivankovic	36	10	7	2	19	12
Didier Princi	36	10	6	3	19	24
Roger Thöny	36	5	6	4	15	32
Edgar Salis	33	3	5	5	13	36
Michael Zeiter	36	2	6	3	11	24
Patrizio Morger	35	3	4	1	8	8
Mario Brodmann	29	2	1	4	7	16
Jiri Faic	35	–	3	3	6	4
Bruno Steck	30	2	–	3	5	26
Patrick Hager	36	1	1	2	4	6
Noel Guyaz	25	2	1	–	3	6

SC BERN

Name	GP	G	A1	A2	Pt	PIM
Gaetano Orlando	36	24	27	4	55	58
Thomas Vrabec	36	21	18	7	46	61
Patrick Howald	36	14	11	4	29	26
Roberto Triulzi	36	14	7	6	27	36
Trevor Meier	38	11	7	4	22	20
Martin Rauch	36	5	7	8	28	38
Gilles Montandon	24	9	8	1	18	14
Vincent Lechenne	36	8	6	2	16	18
Sven Leuenberger	35	5	7	4	16	34
René Friedli	36	11	3	1	15	25
Mikko Haapakoski	17	2	6	6	14	28
Lars Leuenberger	34	5	4	3	12	34
Régis Fuchs	32	2	9	1	12	24
Gaeton Voisard	36	4	4	2	18	28
Reijo Ruotsalainen	19	3	2	5	18	28
Andreas Beutler	36	3	4	1	8	46
Andy Keller	29	3	1	3	7	24
Patrick Oppliger	25	1	–	–	1	–
Philippe Müller	22	1	–	–	1	–
Jörg Reber	36	–	1	–	1	6

HC LUGANO

Name	GP	G	A1	A2	Pt	PIM
Andy Ton	36	20	18	18	48	18
Tommy Sjödin	36	17	18	9	44	40
Jan Larsson	36	16	19	7	42	20
Marcel Jenni	36	14	12	12	38	40
André Rötheli	36	16	13	6	35	34
Jörg Eberle	34	13	11	1	25	15
Jean-J. Aeschlimann	36	9	8	7	24	10
Sandro Bertaggia	38	8	8	7	23	42
Ruedi Niederöst	36	8	4	6	18	46
Remo Walder	35	7	1	4	12	32
Patrick Sutter	22	4	2	5	12	50
Peter Kobel	13	4	5	1	10	28
Stefano Togni	12	4	2	–	6	2
Mathias Schenkel	22	4	2	–	6	6
Patrick Looser	10	1	3	1	5	12
Pat Schafhauser	36	–	2	1	3	42
Ruben Fontana	28	1	1	–	2	–
Marco Capaul	31	–	2	–	2	10
René Ackermann	22	1	–	–	1	4
Claudio Ghillioni	35	–	1	–	1	–

Goalkeeper Regular Season 1994/95

	Name	Team	MIN	GA	∅
1.	Weibel	Lugano	2083	95	2,7
2.	Pavoni	Kloten	2207	117	3,2
3.	Wieser	Davos	1994	108	3,2
4.	Schöpf	Zug	2127	117	3,3
5.	Tosio	Bern	2177	121	3,3
6.	Meuwly	Gottéron	1177	68	3,5
7.	Bachschmied	Ambri-Piotta	1820	113	3,7
8.	Stecher	Zürcher SC	1362	93	4,1
9.	Liesch	Gottéron	945	65	4,1
10.	Wahl	Biel	872	61	4,2
	Papp	Zürcher SC	814	57	4,2
12.	Bösch	Rapperswil	1574	118	4,5
13.	Crétin	EHC Biel	1306	107	4,9

SC RAPPERSWIL

Name	GP	G	A1	A2	Pt	PIM
Harry Rogenmoser	36	19	9	4	32	22
Tom Bisset	33	12	9	6	27	18
Harijs Vitolinsh	38	6	11	6	23	50
Sergio Soguel	35	9	6	1	16	36
Doug Gilmour	9	2	11	2	15	16
Laurent Stehlin	27	18	2	2	14	2
Arthur Camenzind	34	7	5	2	14	7
Andreas Ritsch	35	5	7	2	14	10
Christian Hofstetter	35	5	4	1	10	10
André Rufener	19	5	3	1	9	8
Marc Haueter	36	2	5	2	9	52
Daniel Bünzli	35	4	2	2	8	34
Marco Werder	36	3	4	1	8	49
Armin Berchtold	36	2	4	1	7	6
Daniel Rutschi	26	4	2	–	6	8
Marc Weber	12	2	1	1	4	16
Michael Meier	26	2	2	–	4	18
Christian Langer	35	1	1	1	3	16
J.-Noel Honegger	35	2	–	–	2	–
Roland Kradolfer	35	–	–	1	1	24

EHC BIEL

Name	GP	G	A1	A2	Pt	PIM
Jan Alston	36	28	19	4	51	48
Alfred Lüthi	35	15	11	6	32	18
Gilles Dubois	24	8	7	1	16	12
Patrick Glanzmann	35	8	6	2	16	16
Axel Heim	36	9	3	3	15	37
Leif Carlsson	31	5	6	4	15	4
Björn Schneider	36	3	4	6	13	38
Martin Steinegger	36	5	4	3	12	44
Cyrill Pasche	21	4	6	1	11	12
Sven Schmid	35	5	2	2	9	68
Eric Bourquin	34	4	4	1	9	26
Thomas Burillo	36	2	4	–	6	14
Yannick Robert	29	3	2	–	5	12
Reynald de Ritz	28	2	2	1	5	6
Stefan Grogg	27	2	2	–	4	8
Beat Cattaruzza	36	–	3	1	4	30
Bernhard Schümperli	35	2	1	–	3	6
Chris Chelios	3	–	2	1	3	4
Sven Dick	33	1	–	1	2	10
Marc Weber	18	–	2	–	2	30
Michael Riesen	12	–	1	1	2	–

TEAMS PLAY-OFF

EHC KLOTEN

Name	GP	G	A1	A2	Pt	PIM
Roman Wäger	12	11	2	3	16	22
Mikael Johansson	12	4	8	1	13	8
Felix Hollenstein	12	6	2	4	12	12
Anders Eldebrink	12	1	6	4	11	10
Manuele Celio	12	3	4	–	7	4
Bruno Erni	12	5	1	–	6	14
Martin Bruderer	12	2	1	2	5	22
Oliver Hoffmann	12	2	3	–	5	8
Marco Bayer	12	–	2	2	4	4
Sacha Ochsner	12	3	–	–	4	4
Mathias Holzer	11	2	–	1	3	4
Martin Kout	12	–	2	1	3	14
Michael Diener	12	1	–	–	1	4
Daniel Sigg	12	–	1	–	1	12
Reto Pavoni	12	–	–	1	1	–
Patrik dells Rossa	12	–	–	1	1	2

EV Zug

Name	GP	G	A1	A2	Pt	PIM
Misko Antisin	11	5	7	6	18	33
Ken Yaremchuk	12	5	11	1	17	24
Tom Fergus	12	3	9	1	13	26
Colin Müller	12	8	1	1	10	12
Thomas Künzi	12	5	3	2	10	12
Dino Kessler	12	2	3	5	10	26
Steve Rebersold	12	5	2	2	9	–
Ph. Neuenschwander	12	4	1	3	8	8
Patrick Fischer	12	2	2	2	6	4
Bill Schafhauser	12	2	–	3	5	14
André Künzi	12	2	3	–	5	6
Fausto Mazzoleni	12	2	2	1	5	8
Franz Steffen	12	2	1	2	5	16
Daniel Meier	11	1	3	1	5	4
Daniel Giger	12	2	–	–	2	–
Patrick Schöpf	12	–	–	2	2	6
Livio Fazio	12	–	–	1	1	2

ZÜRCHER SC

Name	GP	G	A1	A2	Pt	PIM
Patrick Lebeau	5	4	4	2	10	6
Marc Fortier	5	2	3	3	8	2
Claudio Micheli	5	3	1	1	5	–
Adrian Bachofner	5	1	1	3	5	8
Andreas Zehnder	5	3	–	–	3	14
Edgar Salis	5	3	–	–	3	12
Michael Zeiter	5	1	2	–	3	4
Patrick Hager	5	–	2	1	3	12
Bruno Steck	5	1	1	–	2	2
Vjeran Ivankovic	5	1	–	1	2	4
Didier Princi	5	–	2	–	2	2
Roger Thöny	5	–	1	–	1	2

HC AMBRI-PIOTTA

Name	GP	G	A1	A2	Pt	PIM
Nicola Celio	3	3	1	–	4	–
Dimitri Kwartalnov	3	2	–	–	2	2
Keith Fair	3	1	1	–	2	6
Thomas Heldner	3	1	1	–	2	–
Markus Studer	3	1	1	–	2	–
John Fritsche	3	–	2	–	2	2
Luigi Riva	3	–	–	1	1	6
Ivan Bazzaroli	3	–	1	–	1	–
Luca Vigano	3	–	–	1	1	–
Tiziano Gianini	3	–	1	–	1	2
A. Steppanischev	2	–	–	1	1	–
Blair Müller	3	–	–	1	1	2

HC LUGANO

Name	GP	G	A1	A2	Pt	PIM
Jan Larsson	4	1	4	1	6	4
Tommy Sjödin	5	3	2	–	5	2
Marcel Jenni	5	2	2	1	5	12
Andy Ton	5	1	1	3	5	2
Jean-J. Aeschlimann	5	1	2	–	3	4
André Rötheli	5	2	–	–	2	2
Patrick Sutter	5	1	1	–	2	12
Remo Walder	5	1	–	–	1	4
Ruedi Nideröst	5	1	–	–	1	2
Stefano Togni	5	1	–	–	1	2
Ruben Fontana	5	–	1	–	1	–
Janne Ojanen	1	–	1	–	1	–

HC FRIBOURG

Name	GP	G	A1	A2	Pt	PIM
Andrej Khomutov	8	4	6	3	13	4
Slava Bykov	8	6	4	–	10	4
Patrice Brasey	7	1	4	2	7	14
Chad Silver	8	4	–	1	5	–
Pascal Schaller	8	2	2	1	5	–
Doug Honegger	6	–	1	3	4	–
Christophe Brown	8	1	1	1	3	6
Mario Rottaris	8	1	2	–	3	4
Alain Reymond	8	1	1	1	3	2
Christian Hofstetter	8	2	–	–	2	–
Mathias Bächler	8	2	–	–	2	4
Fredy Bobillier	8	–	1	1	2	12
Marc Leuenberger	8	1	–	–	1	4
Bruno Maurer	8	–	1	–	1	6
Antoine Descloux	8	–	1	–	1	6
Olivier Keller	8	–	1	–	1	6

SC Bern

Name	GP	G	A1	A2	Pt	PIM
Gaetano Orlando	6	3	7	–	10	8
Roberto Triulzi	6	4	1	1	6	6
Reijo Ruotsalainen	6	1	2	3	6	4
Trevor Meier	6	2	–	3	5	2
Sven Leuenberger	6	2	1	–	3	2
Gilles Montandon	6	–	2	1	3	2
Thomas Vrabec	6	2	–	–	2	2
Patrick Howald	6	2	–	–	2	2
Régis Fuchs	6	1	1	–	2	–
Gaeton Voisard	6	1	1	–	2	4
Lars Leuenberger	6	–	1	1	2	2
Andreas Beutler	6	–	1	1	2	6
Martin Rauch	6	–	1	1	2	4
René Friedli	6	1	–	–	1	6
Andy Keller	6	–	–	1	1	–

HC DAVOS

Name	GP	G	A	Pt	PIM
Gilles Thibaudeau	5	5	4	9	–
Christian Weber	5	2	3	5	–
Magnus Svensson	5	2	2	4	8
Marc Gianola	5	2	1	3	6
Dan Hodgson	5	2	3	5	4
Martin Brich	5	1	2	3	–
René Müller	5	–	2	2	2
Sami Balmer	5	–	2	2	4
Olivier Roth	5	–	1	1	2
Gian-Marco Crameri	5	1	–	1	4
Roger Sigg	5	–	1	1	4
Reto Stirnimann	5	–	1	1	4
Peter Bärtschi	5	1	1	2	–
Riccardo Signorell	5	–	1	1	–
Beat Equilino	5	–	1	1	–
Andy Egli	5	–	–	–	–
Ivo Röthemann	5	–	–	–	2
Ivo Kleeb	5	–	–	–	–
Mario Schocher	5	–	–	–	–
Andy Näser	5	–	–	–	6

Spain

Federation:
Federación Española
Deportes de Invierno
Infanta Maria Teresa 14
E-28016 Madrid
Spain
Telephone (+34.1) 344 0944
Fax   (+34.1) 344 1826
President: Segismundo Fraile Villegas
Gen. Secretary: Gregorio Sanchez Lopez

Segismundo Fraile Villegas
President

Gregorio Sanchez Lopez
Gen. Secretary

Clubs

F.C. Barcelona
Manuel Cerezo Lopez
Aristides Maillol
08028 Barcelona

Club Hielo Gasteiz
Hortaleza 8
01002 Vitoria

Club Hielo Jaca
Ayuntamiento
Jaca – Huesca

Club Hielo Puigcerda
Apartado 105
Puigcerda
Gerona

Club Hielo Txuri Urdin
Palacio de Hielo
Ciudad Deportiva Anoeta
San Sebastian

National Championships 1994/95

Team	GP	W	T	L	Goals	Pts
1. CHH Txuri Urdin	8	8	0	0	86: 19	16
2. CAI CH Jaca	8	5	0	3	64: 28	10
3. FC Barcelona	8	4	0	4	42: 45	8
4. C. GEL Puigcerda	8	3	0	5	33: 41	6
4. CH Gasteiz	8	0	0	8	17:109	0

Play-off
Txuri Urdin   – GEL Puigcerda   3:6, 5:2, 5:4
CAI Jaca   – FC Barcelona   9:3, 9:3
Final
Txuri Urdin   – CAI Jaca   7:4
3th place
FC Barcelona – GEL Puigcerda   7:10

Champions 1984–1995

1984	CH Jaca	1990	San Sebastian
1985	San Sebastian	1991	CH Jaca
1986	Puigcerda	1992	San Sebastian
1987	No Champion	1993	San Sebastian
1988	No Champion	1994	CH Jaca
1989	Puigcerda	1995	Txuri Urdin

Slovenia

Federation:

Ice Hockey Federation of Slovenia
Celovska 25
61000 Ljubljana
Slovenia
Telephone (+386.61) 313 121
Fax   (+386.61) 313 121
President: Ljubo Jasnic
Secretary: Srdan Kuret

Ljubo Jasnic
President

Srdan Kuret
Gen. Secretary

Slovenia Championships 1994/95

Team	GP	W	T	L	Goals	Pts
1. Olimpija Ljubljana	12	11	0	1	106: 22	22
2. Acroni Jesenice	12	10	0	2	90: 30	10
3. Sportina Bled	12	7	1	4	78: 35	15
4. Inntal Celje	12	7	1	4	68: 36	15
5. Maribor Leljak	12	3	0	9	46: 82	6
6. Triglav	12	3	0	9	45: 60	6
7. Slavija Jata	12	0	0	12	14:182	0

Second part of championships

Pool A

Team	GP	W	T	L	Goals	Pts
1. Olimpija Ljubljana	18	16	0	2	165: 33	35
2. Acroni Jesenice	18	12	1	5	112: 54	27
3. Inntal Celje	18	10	1	7	76: 85	21
4. Sportina Bled	18	8	0	10	78: 85	17

Pool B

Team	GP	W	T	L	Goals	Pts
1. Triglav	28	12	0	16	124:104	25
2. Maribor Leljak	28	7	0	21	93:191	16
3. Slavija Jata	28	0	0	28	39:360	0

Play-off

Semifinals
Olimpija Ljubljana   – Sportina Bled   4:0 (6:2, 3:1, 4:2, 6:2)
Acroni Jesenice   – Inntal Celje   4:0 p. f.

Final
Olimpija Ljubljana   – Acroni Jesenice   4:2 (3:4, 0:1, 5:1, 4:3, 6:4, 5:1)

Slowakia

Federation:
Slovak Ice Hockey Federation
Junacka 6
83280 Bratislava
Slovenska Republika
Telephone (+42.7) 258 381 or 258 398
Fax   (+42.7) 258 344
President: Dr. Jan Mitosinka
Gen. Secretary: Pavol Macko

Dr. Jan Mitosinka
President

Pavol Macko
Gen. Secretary

Clubs

HC Slovan Bratislava
Odbojarov 3
83215 Bratislava

HC Kosice
Nerudova 12
04001 Kosice

SKP PS Poprad
Stefanikova 46
05801 Poprad

Dukla Trencin
Povazska 34
91101 Trencin

HK Dubnica
Zimny Stadion
01841 Dubnica nad Vahom

HC ZT 5 Martin
Gorkeho 2
036001 Martin

Liptovsky Mikulas
Ul. Partizanov 14
03101 Liptovsky Mikulas

AC Nitra
Jesenskeho 2
94901 Nitra

TJZPA Presov
Pod Kalvariou 50
08001 Presov

HK Spisska Nova Ves
Ul. T. Vansovej 1
05201 Spisska Nova Ves

Extraleague 1994/95

Team	GP	W	L	T	Goals	Pts
1. Dukla Trencin	36	27	4	5	188: 82	86
2. HC Kosice	36	26	5	5	188: 96	83
3. Slovan Bratislava	36	23	11	2	167:117	71
4. SKP PS Poprad	36	19	13	4	128:106	61
5. HK Liptovsky Mikulas	36	14	18	4	107:130	46
6. Martimex Martin	36	12	18	6	94:110	42
7. HC Dragon Presov	36	9	16	11	92:131	38
8. Spartak Dubnica	36	9	23	4	83:153	31
9. HC Nitra	36	8	22	6	87:147	30
10. HK Spisska Nova Ves	36	7	24	5	83:145	26

*Three points for a win

Play-off

Quarterfinals
Dukla Trencin	– Spartak Dubnica	11:3, 3:2, 4:2
HC Kosice	– HC Dragon Presov	10:1, 4:3, 6:3
Slovan Bratislava	– Martimex Martin	5:1, 5:2, 2:0
SKP PS Poprad	– HK Liptovsky Mikulas	8:5, 4:1, 4:3

Semifinals
Dukla Trencin	– SKP Poprad	9:5, 5:3, 5:3
HC Kosice	– Slovan Bratislava	11:1, 8:1, 3:1

Finals
HC Kosice	– Dukla Trensin	4:2, 5:3, 7:1

SLOVAN BRATISLAVA

Pos	Name	GP	G	A	P	PM	GP	G	A	P	PM
F	Karol Rusznyak	34	23	29	52	60	9	6	6	12	16
F	Dusan Pohorelec	36	25	21	46	4	9	5	3	8	6
F	Richard Kapus	36	13	20	33	41	9	4	2	6	8
F	Bystrik Scepko	35	12	17	29	18	9	2	2	4	12
F	Radoslav Kropac	35	17	8	25	38	7	1	2	3	4
F	Rudolf Vercik	33	14	9	23	22	0	0	0	0	0
D	Milos Rehak	36	3	19	22	49	9	1	0	1	6
D	Lubomir Visnovsky	36	11	10	21	10	9	1	3	4	2
F	Peter Staron	31	14	5	19	47	9	3	0	3	10
F	Martin Funta	32	9	10	19	12	6	0	2	2	0
F	Jozef Voskar	36	7	12	19	26	9	2	4	6	10
F	Jan Lipiansky	12	8	7	15	4	8	0	2	2	6
D	Ladislav Cierny	31	4	6	10	14	9	0	3	3	4
F	Marcel Sakac	12	4	3	7	6	9	2	0	2	6
D	Roman Veber	21	0	6	6	44	0	0	0	0	0
D	Marek Zrncik	24	1	4	5	18	0	0	0	0	0
D	Marian Bazany	25	1	3	4	4	5	0	0	0	2
D	Martin Strbak	17	0	3	3	0	9	2	1	3	8
F	Michal Stastny	12	1	0	1	12	1	0	0	0	0
D	Patrik Luza	26	0	1	1	8	9	0	0	0	0
D	Mihal Vrabel	9	0	1	1	2	3	0	0	0	0
D	Michal Kudzia	8	0	0	0	2	0	0	0	0	0

SPARTAK DUBNICA

Pos	Name	GP	G	A	P	PM	GP	G	A	P	PM
F	Michal Mravik	35	10	4	14	16	3	0	0	0	0
F	Miroslav Nemcek	30	11	2	13	6	3	2	0	2	2
F	Stefan Zitnansky	33	6	5	11	12	3	0	0	0	30
F	Roman Capek	36	8	3	11	4	3	2	0	2	0
D	Andrej Andrejev	36	8	2	10	4	3	0	0	0	0
F	Miroslav Hantak	23	10	0	10	10	0	0	0	0	0
F	Juraj Jakubik	34	4	6	10	8	3	1	1	2	0
D	Dalibor Laurencik	34	2	6	8	42	3	0	0	0	4
F	Milan Pazitka	32	1	6	7	16	3	0	0	0	0
F	Stanislav Kolar	26	5	1	6	2	1	0	0	0	2
F	Miroslav Ozvalda	22	3	3	6	8	3	1	1	2	0
F	Peter Kotlarik	32	3	3	6	10	3	1	0	1	0
F	Anton Lezo	33	2	3	5	4	3	0	0	0	0
F	Mario Kazda	26	5	0	5	10	1	0	0	0	4
D	Lubomir Valjent	36	2	2	4	32	3	0	1	1	2
D	Milan Zitny	20	2	1	3	6	0	0	0	0	0
F	Jozef Tatar	11	1	2	3	4	3	0	0	0	0
D	Oliver Pastinsky	24	0	3	3	2	1	0	0	0	0
D	Erik Smolka	28	0	2	2	30	3	0	0	0	2
D	Jan Kobezda	33	0	2	2	45	3	0	0	0	0
D	Mikulas Lorinc	22	0	2	2	4	3	0	0	0	0
D	Ropman Chatrnuch	16	0	1	1	29	2	0	0	6	6
G	Vladimir Hladlovsky	23	0	0	0	8	0	0	0	0	0
D	Peter Janik	28	0	0	0	8	3	0	0	0	0

KOSICE

Pos	Name	GP	G	A	P	PM	GP	G	A	P	PM
F	Vlastimil Plavucha	36	35	18	53	24	9	12	6	18	12
F	Lubomir Rybovic	34	21	22	43	6	8	4	13	17	12
F	Pavol Zubek	34	16	24	40	13	6	3	9	12	0
F	Slavomir Ilavsky	36	11	26	37	12	9	4	2	6	8
F	Rene Pucher	34	16	18	34	10	7	4	8	12	2
F	Miroslav Ihnacak	20	13	17	30	16	9	6	14	20	6
F	Peter Zubek	30	14	14	28	4	9	9	6	15	8
D	Jan Varholik	33	12	8	20	48	9	2	2	4	12
F	Martin Mizik	36	10	10	20	6	9	2	2	4	2
F	Richard Sechny	31	9	10	19	33	8	4	2	6	4
F	Miroslav Pazak	18	10	7	17	0	8	0	2	2	2
D	Stanislav Jasecko	36	5	10	15	34	9	0	1	1	8
D	Daniel Sedlak	32	3	10	13	33	9	0	2	2	0
D	Matej Bukna	36	1	11	12	22	8	3	5	8	4
F	Anton Bartanus	27	4	8	12	12	1	0	0	0	0
D	Pavol Valko	33	2	8	10	8	2	1	1	2	0
D	Slavomir Vorobel	21	3	5	8	12	9	3	3	6	4
F	Robert Pohanka	5	1	3	4	0	5	0	0	0	2
F	Peter Bondra	2	1	0	1	0	0	0	0	0	0
D	Martin Lendak	28	0	1	1	10	9	1	0	1	4
F	Juraj Faith	2	0	1	1	2	0	0	0	0	0
F	Juraj Hornak	5	0	1	1	2	0	0	0	0	0
F	Peter Kuzar	4	0	0	0	2	1	0	0	0	0

LIPOVSKY MIKULAS

Pos	Name	GP	G	A	P	PM	GP	G	A	P	PM
F	Anton Kalousek	36	11	15	26	10	3	1	0	1	25
F	Jan Plch	35	17	4	21	8	3	0	2	2	0
F	Juraj Strecok	35	10	9	19	32	3	0	1	1	29
F	Jan Gazo	36	7	10	17	44	3	3	0	3	4
F	Jan Sebo	36	9	6	15	35	3	0	1	1	10
F	Milan Listiak	36	9	5	14	10	3	0	0	0	2
F	Jan Cibula	35	7	5	12	10	3	2	0	2	0
D	Pavol Farkas	35	7	5	12	18	3	0	0	0	0
F	Michal Mravec	36	6	1	7	27	3	0	0	0	2
D	Juraj Kledrowetz	31	4	3	7	53	3	0	0	0	0
F	Dimitri Zajcev	27	2	5	7	6	0	0	0	0	0
F	Martin Ortcykr	33	3	4	7	12	3	0	0	0	2
F	Peter Listiak	33	3	3	6	34	3	1	0	1	0
D	Peter Klepac	32	1	5	6	36	3	1	1	2	4
F	Vladimir Bella	16	5	0	5	27	3	0	1	1	0
D	Peter Zitnik	36	1	3	4	12	3	0	1	1	4
D	Rudolf Zaruba	36	0	3	3	38	3	1	0	1	6
D	Ladislav Baca	17	0	2	2	8	0	0	0	0	0
D	Robert Illencik	16	2	0	2	14	3	0	0	0	2
D	Marian Glut	12	1	1	2	0	2	0	0	0	0
F	Ivan Strecok	32	2	0	2	2	3	0	0	0	0
G	Frantisek Poliacek	13	0	1	1	2	0	0	0	0	0
D	Jan Zimani	10	0	0	0	8	0	0	0	0	0
G	Lubo Babura	28	0	0	0	4	0	0	0	0	0

MARTIMEX MARTIN

		Regular season					Play-offs			
Pos	Name	GP	G	A	P	PM	GP	G	A	P	PM
---	---	---	---	---	---	---	---	---	---	---	---
F	Peter Bartos	34	15	20	35	20	3	0	0	0	0
F	Michal Beran	34	14	6	20	14	3	0	0	0	2
F	Marian Uharcek	26	17	2	19	16	0	0	0	0	0
F	Miroslav Chudy	34	3	16	19	33	3	1	0	1	12
D	Peter Krachac	35	7	7	14	24	3	0	0	0	6
D	Jan Zlocha	28	8	1	9	24	3	1	0	1	0
F	Miroslav Bohme	35	2	7	9	20	3	0	0	0	0
F	Jaroslav Torok	20	3	4	7	34	3	0	0	0	8
D	Daniel Babka	36	5	2	7	40	3	0	0	0	8
D	Miroslav Kluch	36	3	3	6	10	3	0	0	0	4
F	Dimitri Voronzov	11	3	3	6	0	3	0	1	1	0
F	Robert Kral	31	3	2	5	20	1	0	0	0	0
F	Marcel Hanzal	24	3	2	5	14	2	0	0	0	0
F	Martin Opatovsky	12	1	3	4	0	3	0	0	0	0
D	Dimitri Kamysnikov	9	3	1	4	76	2	0	0	0	40
F	Radovan Somik	25	4	0	4	29	3	1	0	1	2
F	Radislav Samik	25	3	0	3	29	0	0	0	0	0
D	Robert Hodon	29	1	2	3	10	2	0	0	0	2
F	Pavol Paukovcek	11	0	2	2	31	3	0	0	0	4
D	Branislav Stolarik	35	1	1	2	32	3	0	1	1	6
D	Slavomir Hrina	6	0	1	1	6	0	0	0	0	0
D	Martin Bizon	28	0	1	1	6	3	0	0	0	0
D	Ratislav Bohme	12	0	0	0	4	0	0	0	0	0
F	Stefan Konecny	22	0	0	0	6	1	0	0	0	0

POPRAD

		Regular season					Play-offs			
Pos	Name	GP	G	A	P	PM	GP	G	A	P	PM
---	---	---	---	---	---	---	---	---	---	---	---
F	Arne Krotak	36	15	20	35	6	9	3	6	9	0
F	Slavomir Pavlicko	36	14	16	30	12	9	4	5	9	2
F	Miroslav Skovira	28	19	10	29	6	9	4	3	7	6
F	Habart Wittlinger	33	12	6	18	6	9	5	4	9	2
F	Igor Rataj	29	6	11	17	36	3	0	0	0	6
F	Martin Frank	30	11	3	14	4	9	5	0	5	0
F	Peter Junas	33	6	7	13	39	9	0	4	4	6
F	Patrik Krisak	33	8	5	13	14	9	7	2	9	4
F	Peter Vascura	25	9	4	13	8	9	4	1	5	6
F	Jan Pleva	33	6	6	12	6	8	3	5	8	2
D	Peter Gapa	34	4	6	10	6	7	1	2	3	12
D	Peter Hrehorcak	33	6	3	9	18	9	1	1	2	4
F	Rudolf Fedor	26	3	5	8	2	0	0	0	0	0
D	Vladimir Turan	35	0	8	8	12	9	0	4	4	4
F	Jozef Regec	17	2	3	5	0	0	0	0	0	0
F	Pavol Svitana	16	1	4	5	4	0	0	0	0	0
D	Miroslav Turan	27	1	4	5	16	9	0	0	0	2
D	Rastislav Bonco	29	2	2	4	14	3	0	0	0	0
D	Rastislav Ondrejcik	11	2	1	3	22	0	0	0	0	0
D	Dusan Brincko	7	0	2	2	0	9	0	3	3	37
F	Dubos Bartecko	3	1	0	1	0	0	0	0	0	0
G	Martin Klempa	34	0	1	1	0	9	0	0	0	10
G	Miro Simonovic	6	0	0	0	0	0	0	0	0	0
D	Maros Sklar	10	0	0	0	4	4	0	0	0	0
F	Branislav Gavalier	6	0	0	0	2	0	0	0	0	0
D	Patrik Scibran	5	0	0	0	2	0	0	0	0	0
D	Jan Smolko	35	0	0	0	16	9	1	1	2	0

PRESOV

		Regular season					Play-offs			
Pos	Name	GP	G	A	P	PM	GP	G	A	P	PM
---	---	---	---	---	---	---	---	---	---	---	---
F	Peter Pucher	36	15	11	26	12	3	3	0	3	2
F	Jaroslav Balaz	36	10	11	21	26	3	0	0	0	4
F	Jaroslav Majer	34	9	10	19	10	0	0	0	0	0
F	Jozef Roman	36	12	6	18	75	3	0	0	0	22
F	Rudolf Orosz	35	6	8	14	10	3	0	0	0	2
F	Eduard Janak	35	5	7	12	20	3	0	0	0	0
F	Igor Salata	33	7	4	11	42	0	0	0	0	0
F	Marcel Pavlovsky	28	5	4	9	10	0	0	0	0	0
D	Michal Segla	34	2	7	9	63	3	0	0	0	0
F	Viliam Belas	9	6	1	7	22	3	0	0	0	0
D	Alexander Bobak	35	2	3	5	10	3	0	0	0	0
D	Rudolf Fabula	35	2	3	5	16	3	0	0	0	2
F	Rastislav Blahut	24	2	2	4	14	3	0	0	0	2
F	Viliam Chovanec	19	4	0	4	2	3	1	0	0	0
D	Igor Griger	18	0	3	3	10	3	0	0	0	2
F	Jaroslav Goffa	18	0	3	3	4	0	0	0	0	0
D	Igor Kinik	35	1	2	3	16	3	0	0	0	0
D	Frantisek Pulscak	22	2	1	3	6	2	0	0	0	0
D	Robert Cop	29	0	1	1	52	2	0	0	0	2
D	Kamil Kuriplach	10	1	0	1	2	0	0	0	0	0
D	Martin Strbak	10	1	0	1	6	0	0	0	0	0
F	Vladimir Stas	7	0	0	0	0	0	0	0	0	0
G	Marek Mily	36	0	0	0	27	3	0	0	0	10

DUKLA TRENCIN

		Regular season					Play-offs			
Pos	Name	GP	G	A	P	PM	GP	G	A	P	PM
---	---	---	---	---	---	---	---	---	---	---	---
F	Lubomir Kolnik	36	31	23	54	24	9	10	3	13	12
F	Zdeno Ciger	34	23	25	48	57	9	2	9	11	2
F	Branislav Janos	34	22	16	38	96	9	3	4	7	8
F	Jozef Dano	35	16	18	34	41	9	5	3	8	8
D	Stanislav Medrik	36	13	20	33	44	9	2	2	4	6
F	Roman Kontsek	31	7	24	31	24	6	1	1	2	8
F	Martin Madovy	34	21	8	29	10	9	2	2	4	4
F	Jan Pardavy	31	19	7	26	8	9	10	2	12	14
D	Lubomir Sekeras	36	11	12	23	26	9	2	7	9	8
F	Marian Horvath	33	3	17	20	37	9	1	2	3	4
D	Vladimir Vik	31	1	15	16	34	9	0	0	0	0
F	Milos Melicherik	30	6	8	14	4	9	2	3	5	0
D	Marian Smerciak	35	4	4	8	73	9	0	1	1	12
D	Richard Pavlikovsky	35	4	3	7	8	7	1	0	1	4
D	Rastislav Pavlikovsky	14	0	7	7	4	6	1	1	2	0
F	Pavol Paukovcek	13	2	3	5	29	2	0	1	1	0
F	Matej Marcinek	10	1	2	3	2	2	0	0	0	0
D	Dalibor Kusovsky	25	3	0	3	8	9	0	1	1	12
F	Radoslav Hecl	13	1	0	1	8	5	1	0	1	4
D	Martin Kivon	15	0	0	0	2	2	0	0	0	0
F	Rastislav Palov	4	0	0	0	4	0	0	0	0	0

SPISSKA NOVA VES
Regular season

Pos	Name	GP	G	A	P	PM
F	Pavol Fedor	31	11	6	17	30
F	Jan Bednar	34	5	11	16	6
F	Peter Filip	33	10	3	13	4
F	Mario Konstantinidis	22	9	4	13	10
F	Vladimir Klinga	29	7	6	13	10
F	Peter Krajnak	33	8	3	11	10
F	Lubomir Valc	20	5	4	9	2
D	Jan Macejko	35	5	4	9	9
D	Roman Gavalier	36	4	4	8	55
F	Robert Cernak	26	4	4	8	6
D	Peter Stubendek	35	2	4	6	47
D	Patrik Scibran	20	1	4	5	16
F	Jozef Petrovic	24	2	3	5	4
D	Dusan Kacvinsky	32	1	4	5	16
D	Michal Chromco	26	1	3	4	18
F	Miroslav Farkasovsky	14	2	1	3	2
F	Jaroslav Zelinsky	28	2	1	3	35
F	Juraj Faith	10	2	0	2	4
F	Rastislav Jurko	26	0	2	2	6
F	Radoslav Maslik	3	1	1	2	0
F	Miroslav Sarga	5	1	1	2	0
F	Marian Cmel	12	0	1	1	4
D	Robert Jurcak	17	0	1	1	33
F	Slavomir Jencak	17	0	0	0	6
D	Jan Novak	5	0	0	0	6
F	Rene Mandelik	9	0	0	0	4
D	Igor Repka	9	0	0	0	2

NITRA
Regular season

Pos	Name	GP	G	A	P	PM
F	Martin Miklik	36	26	8	34	10
F	Igor Bafrnec	33	10	13	23	8
F	Milos Fleischer	35	7	10	17	32
F	Martin Mihola	33	7	7	14	24
D	Dusan Milo	33	5	8	13	10
F	Juraj Stefanka	32	8	4	12	99
D	Peter Kostal	35	3	7	10	28
F	Branislav Okuliar	26	3	5	8	14
F	Ivan Jancek	33	1	5	6	14
F	Norbert Vigh	25	3	2	5	0
F	Peter David	19	2	2	4	4
D	Daniel Socha	32	1	3	4	10
D	Michal Barto	30	1	2	3	10
F	Miroslav Kukla	29	3	0	3	10
D	Tibor Turan	7	1	1	2	6
D	Milan Darula	22	1	1	2	10
F	Peter Konc	16	2	0	2	31
D	Juraj Paucek	13	0	1	1	4
D	Martin Skara	15	0	1	1	8
D	Jozef Drzik	4	1	0	1	4
F	Peter Oremus	7	1	0	1	6
F	Ivan Ciernik	6	1	0	1	2
F	Peter Himler	5	0	1	1	0
D	Miroslav Smidriak	21	0	1	1	14
D	Erik Marinov	7	0	0	0	0
F	Jaroslav Jacko	15	0	0	0	4
F	Jaroslav Kunik	7	0	0	0	41
D	Erik Marinov	7	0	0	0	0

Leading scorers

Name	Team	GP	G	A	P
Lubomir Kolnik	Trencin	35	31	23	54
Vlastimil Plavucha	Kosice	35	35	18	53
Karol Rusznyak	Bratislava	34	23	29	52
Zdeno Ciger	Trencin	34	23	25	48
Dusan Pohorelec	Bratislava	35	25	21	46
Lubomir Rybovic	Kosice	34	21	22	43
Pavol Zubek	Kosice	34	16	24	40
Bratislav Janos	Trencin	34	22	16	38
Slavomir Ilavsky	Kosice	36	11	26	37
Arne Krotak	Poprad	36	15	20	35
Peter Bartos	Martin	34	15	20	35

Slovakia Championship

1994   Dukla Trencin
1995   HC Kosice

Goaltending

Name	Team	GP	MIN	GA	GAA
Roman Mega	Slovan	33	1959	99	3.03
Branislav Fatul	Slovan	1	27	4	8.89
Mark Masztics	Slovan	4	174	13	10.54
Jaromir Dragan	Kosice	34	2033	82	2.42
Jan Rimsky	Kosice	2	71	6	5.07
Lubomir Babura	Mikulas	28	1680	93	3.32
Frantisek Poliacek	Mikulas	9	540	37	4.11
Rastislav Rovnianek	Martin	28	1652	88	3.20
Jaroslav Brno	Martin	9	508	28	3.31
Ivan Karvanek	Nitra	36	2126	143	4.03
Roland Gabas	Nitra	1	34	4	7.06
Martin Klempa	Poprad	33	1925	92	2.87
Miroslav Simonovic	Poprad	5	235	13	3.32
Marek Mily	Presov	35	2089	122	3.50
Mario Luterancik	Presov	1	28	1	2.14
Zdeno Pistej	Presov	1	46	8	10.43
Vladimir Hiadlosvky	Dubnica	23	1348	95	4.23
Jarolim Balas	Dubnica	3	147	17	2.17
Roman Cunderlik	Dubnica	14	640	38	3.56
Patrik Nemcak	Dubnica	1	25	3	7.20
Sanislav Kubus	Spisska	33	1894	118	3.74
Jan Antoni	Spisska	5	232	21	5.43
Martin Richtarcik	Spisska	1	34	4	7.06
Igor Murin	Trencin	14	757	29	2.30
Eduard Hartman	Trencin	24	1403	53	2.27

South Africa

Federation:
South African Ice Hockey Association
P.O. Box 926
Parklands 2121
South Africa
Telephone (+27.11) 918 5534 or 786 5931
Fax   (+27.11) 918 5534 or 786 5931
Chairman: David May
Gen. Secretary: Mrs. Nives Swart

David May
Chairman

Final standing 1994/95

Team	GP	W	T	L	Goals	Pts
1. Flyers Roodenpoort	18	14	1	3	143: 66	29
2. Hawks Johannesburg	18	10	1	7	109: 79	21
3. North Stars Pretoria	18	10	1	7	124:106	21
4. Flames Randburg	18	0	1	17	48:173	1

2nd division

Team	GP	W	T	L	Goals	Pts
1. Flames Randburg 2	12	10	0	2	83: 34	20
2. Hawks Johannesburg 2	12	9	1	2	95: 55	19
3. Sharks Durban	12	7	1	4	87: 64	15
4. Penguins	12	6	0	6	63: 65	12
5. North Stars Pretoria	12	4	0	8	58: 84	8
6. Vikings	12	4	0	8	47: 65	8
7. Flyers Roodenpoort 2	12	1	0	11	37:103	2

Thailand

Federation:
Thailand Ice Skating Association
Admiral Pimol Hatajich
215 Soi Sainamthip 2, Sukhumvit 22, Klongtoey
10110 Bangkok
Thailand
Telephone (+66.2) 259 3073-4
Fax   (+66.2) 258 2192
President: Admiral Pimol Hatayij
Gen. Secretary: Nitaya Kitaphanich

Pimol Hatayij
President

Turkey

Federation:

Turkish Ice Sports Federation
Nuzhet Atav Ishani
Sanayi Cad. No. 28 K. 3
Ulus/Ankara
Turkey
Telephone (+90.312) 310 8167 or 309 0292
Fax (+90.312) 311 2554
President: Ali Aytemiz
Gen. Secretary: Mehmet Koc

Ali Aytemiz
President

Mehmet Koc
Gen. Secretary

Championships 1994/95

Team	GP	W	T	L	Goals	Pts
1. Büyüksehir Ankara	8	8	0	0	159:22	16
2. Emniyet Spor Kulubu	8	6	0	2	80:63	12
3. Kolejlier	8	3	0	5	58:76	6
4. Istambul Paten	8	2	0	6	42:105	4
5. Ankara Paten	8	1	0	7	35:108	2

Most Goals

Name	Team	GP	G
1. Sergej Kislitsyn	Büyüksehir	8	36
2. Bekir Akgül	Emniyet	8	27
3. Ömer Arasan	Büyüksehir	8	26

Most Assists

Name	Team	GP	G
Fahri Pasli	Büyüksehir	8	29

Champion Team
Büyüksehir Ankara

Sergej Kislitsyn
Rejneid Shat
Fahri Pasli
Ömer Arasan
Tuncay Kilic
Süleyman Cici
Celal Bilgin
Serhat Kaytaz
Erkan Ertugrul
Metin Soydas
Reha Intepeli

Cagan Köse
Ömer Alpay
Ahmet Sesigürgil
Coskun Ölcer
Firat Öget
Tufan Kaya
Cenk Sindel
Atil Tokcan
Korkut Parla
Sunday Öget

Ukraine

Federation:
Ukrainian Ice Hockey Federation
11A Sichnevogo
Povstannya Street
252010 Kiev
Ukraine
Telephone (+380.044) 226 3392
           (+380.044) 290 6130
           (+380.044) 290 2044
Fax   (+380.044) 290 7270
President: Anatoli Khorozov
Gen. Secretary: Volodimir Osipchuk

Anatoli Khorozov
President

Volodimir Osipchuk
Gen. Secretary

Ukrainian Championships 1994/95

(1st round)

Team	GP	W	T	L	Goals	Pts
1. Masters Club Kiev	5	4	1	0	36:10	9
2. Atek Kiev	5	3	1	1	21:17	7
3. Politechnik Kiev	5	3	0	2	21:17	6
4. Salamandra Kharkiv	5	1	1	3	17:29	3
5. Ldinka Kiev	5	1	1	3	16:30	3
6. Olympic Reserves Sokol	5	1	0	4	13:33	2

Final round

Sokol Kiev	– Atek Kiev		7:1 (1:0, 2:1, 4:0)
Sokol Kiev	– Masters Club Kiev		5:0 (5:0, 0:0, 0:0)
Atek Kiev	– Masters Club Kiev		1:0 (1:0, 0:0, 0:0)

Final standings

1. Sokol Kiev
2. Atek Kiev
3. Masters Club Kiev

Ukrainian Champions

1992 Sokol Kiev
1993 Sokol Kiev
1994 Masters Club Kiev
1995 Sokol Kiev

USA

Federation:

USA Hockey
4965 North 30th Street
Colorado Springs / CO 80919
USA
Telephone (+1.719) 599 5500
Fax   (+1.719) 599 5994

President: Walter Bush Jr.

Executive Director: Dave Ogrean

Walter Bush Jr.
President

Dave Ogrean
Executive Director

1995 USA Hockey National Champions

12 or under tier I	Chicago Young Americans
14 or under tier I	Compuware Ambassadors
17 or under tier I	Detroit Little Caesars
12 or under tier II	Lincoln Park Kings
14 or under tier II	Grand Forks South
17 or under tier II	Woburn, MA
Women senior A	Needam, MA
Women senior B	Minnesota Northern Lights
Girls 19 or under	Wisconsin Challengers
Girls 15 or under	Connecticut Polar Baers
Junior A	De Moines Buccaneers
Junior B	Minneapolis Kodiaks
Junior C	Binghamton Jr. Rangers
Senior Non-check	Michigan Paddock Pools
Senior Non-check over 30	Tampa Teal Wheel
Senior US	Minneapolis Bucks
Senior Elite	Alaska Gold Kings

WCHA
WESTERN COLLEGIATE Hockey Association
Final standings

	GP	Goals	Pts
1. Colorado College	30	147: 96	44
2. Denver	30	119:107	35
3. Minnesota	30	116: 89	35
4. Wisconsin	30	114:106	34
5. St. Cloud	30	120:108	29
6. North Dakota	30	110:134	27
7. Michigan Tech	30	103:126	27
8. Minnesota-Duluth	30	110:123	26
9. Northern Michigan	30	106:122	23
10. Alaska-Anchorage	30	99:132	20

Play-off
Minnesota – North Dakota	3:2
Wisconsin – Denver	5:4
Colorado College – Minnesota	5:4

Championship game
Wisconsin – Colorado College	4:3

CCHA
Final standings

	GP	Goals	Pts
1. Michigan	27	151: 74	45
2. Bowling Green	27	135:101	38
3. Michigan State	27	123: 79	37
4. Lake Superior	27	114: 78	32
5. Miami-Ohio	27	88: 87	32
6. Ferris State	27	82:111	22
7. Western Michigan	27	87:102	22
8. Illinois-Chicago	27	99:132	19
9. Notre Dame	27	77:126	15
10. Ohio State	27	76:142	8
11. Alaska-Fairbanks	14	–	0

Alaska-Fairbanks
is affiliated with the CCHA

Play-off
Ohio State – Alaska	7:2

First round
Ohio State – Michigan	2:4, 0:4
Bowling – Notre Dame	7:2, 5:4
Michigan State – Illinois	6:4, 4:2
Lake Superior – W. Michigan	7:2, 5:0
Miami – Ferris State	10:2, 4:2

Championship Qualifier
Lake Superior – Miami	5:2

Conference Finals
Lake Superior – Michigan State	5:4
Michigan State – Bowling	4:3

Final
Lake Superior – Michigan State	5:3

CENTRAL
Final standings

	GP	Goals	Pts
1. Wichita	66	320:268	92
2. San Antonio	66	336:281	81
3. Tulsa	66	307:281	78
4. Oklahoma City	66	274:267	77
5. Fort Worth	66	314:288	72
6. Memphis	66	259:327	55
7. Dallas	66	266:364	54

Play-off
First round (best of 7)

Wichita – Oklahoma City
10:3, 4:6, 7:5, 7:3, 8:1

Tulsa – San Antonio
6:5, 1:4, 3:6, 6:3, 3:7, 5:4, 1:6

Championships series

Wichita – San Antonio
7:6, 5:3, 2:5, 4:3, 2:6, 9:4

HOCKEY EAST
COLLEGE LEAGUE
Final standings

	GP	Goals	Pts
1. Maine	24	104: 63	88
2. Boston University	24	131: 82	88
3. New Hampshire	24	113: 85	78
4. Northeastern	24	98: 89	70
5. UMass.-Lowell	24	105:116	58
6. Providence	24	74: 91	48
7. Merrimack	24	74: 91	48
8. Boston College	24	86:119	45
9. UMass.-Amherst	24	64:129	15

Play-off
Providence – Maine	7:3
Boston University – UMass.-Lowell	4:2

Championship game
Boston University – Providence	3:2

ECAC
EASTERN COLLEGE Athletic Association
Final standings

	GP	Goals	Pts
1. Clarkson	22	116: 70	31
2. Brown	22	78: 76	28
3. Harvard	22	79: 68	25
4. Colgate	22	98: 78	25
5. Vermont	22	85: 61	24
6. Rensselear	22	75: 78	23
7. Princeton	22	81: 83	21
8. St. Lawrence	22	83:110	20
9. Cornell	22	72: 76	20
10. Union	22	70: 87	16
11. Dartmouth	22	80:111	16
12. Yale	22	65: 84	15

Play-off
Princeton – Union	5:2
Cornell – St. Lawrence	6:2

First round
Clarkson – Cornell	6:2, 7:2
Princeton – Brown	4:3, 2:3, 3:2
Rensselaer – Harvard	2:2, 3:1
Vermont – Colgate	5:2, 0:2, 1:1

Semi finals
Rensselaer – Colgate	2:1
Princeton – Clarkson	2:1

Championship final
Rensselaer – Princeton	5:1

NCAA
East regionals

Denver (WCHA) –
New Hampshire (H. E.) 9:2

Lake Superior (CCHA) –
Clarkson (ECAC) 5:4

Maine (H. E.) –
Denver (WCHA) 4:2

Boston University (H. E.) and
Maine (H. E.) advance to NCAA Championships

West regionals

Minnesota (WCHA) –
Rensselaer (ECAC) 3:0

Wisconsin (WCHA) –
Michigan State (CCHA) 5:3

Minnesota (WCHA) –
Colorado College (WCHA) 5:2

Michigan State (CCHA) –
Wisconsin (WCHA) 4:3

Michigan State (CCHA) and Minnesota (WCHA) advance to NCAA Championships

Final four

Maine (Hockey East) –
Michigan (CCHA) 3:2

Boston University (H. E.) –
Minnesota (WCHA) 7:3

Championship game

Boston University (H. E.) –
Maine (Hockey East) 6:2

Yugoslavia

Federation:
Yugoslav Ice Hockey Federation
Carli Caplina 39 / Hala Pionir
Y-11000 Beograd
Yugoslavia
Telephone (+381.11) 764 479
Fax   (+381.11) 764 976
President: Momcilo Zivkovic
Gen. Secretary: Milivoje V. Ilic

Momcilo Zivkovic
President

Milivoje V. Ilic
Gen. Secretary

Clubs

HC Partizan-BLP
Humska 1
Y-11000 Beograd
Tel. (+381.11) 647 040
Fax (+381.11) 651 328

**HC Crvena
Zvezda-Eurotrend**
Ljutice Bogdana 1a
Y-11000 Beograd
Tel. (+381.11) 444 1684
Fax (+381.11) 661 520

HC Spartak
Lenjinov park 12 a
Y-24000 Subotica
Tel. (+381.24) 52 017
Fax (+381.24) 51 289

HCVojvodina
Bul. Avnoj-a bb
Y-21000 Novi Sad
Tel. (+381.21) 54 235
Fax (+381.21) 338 833

Final standings 1994/95

Team	GP	W	T	L	Goals	Pts
1. HC Partizan Beograd	12	12	0	0	117: 18	24
2.HC Vojvodina Novi Sad	12	6	0	6	72: 65	12
3. HC Crvena Zvezda Beograd	12	5	0	7	72: 54	9
4. HC Spartak Subotica	12	1	0	11	31:161	2

Play-off
HC Partizan	– HC Spartak	5:0, 22:2
HC Vojvodina	– HC Crevena Zvezda	1:9, 3:9

3rd Place
HC Vojvodina	– HC Spartak	15:3, 14:2, 22:3

Finals
HC Partizan	– HC Crvena Zvezda	10:1, 5:1, 9:3

Yugoslavia Cup

HC Partizan	– HC Vojvodina	12:3
HC Spartak	– HC Crvena Zvezda	5:7

Finals
HC Partizan	– HC Crvena Zvezda	6:3

Top scorer

Name	Team	G	A	P
1. Igor Kalanjin	Partizan Beograd	26	30	56
2. Sergej Hruscov	Partizan Beograd	23	24	47
3. Aleksander Kosic	Crvena Zvezda	23	19	42
4. Vladimir Sajban	Vojvodina Novi Sad	25	12	37
5. Sergej Kuljev	Partizan Beograd	25	12	37

7. Deutschland-Cup 1994
Stuttgart – November 3 – 6, 1994

Pool A

1. Slovakia	4:2	4
2. Canada	4:4	2
3. Germany	1:3	0

Pool B

1. Czech Republic	6:4	4
2. Finland	6:7	1
3. DEL All Stars	6:7	1

3rd Place:

Canada – Finland   4:2

Final:

Czech Republic
    – Slovakia   4:3

Deutschland-Cup 1987 – 1994

	1987	1988	1990	1991	1992	1993	1994
Soviet Union	–	1	–	1	–	–	–
Sweden	–	–	2	2	–	6	–
Germany	2	2	4	3	2	4	6
CSFR	1	–	3	4	3	5	–
Finland	–	–	1	–	–	3	4
Switzerland	–	3	–	–	–	7	–
Poland	3	4	–	–	–	–	–
Russia	–	–	–	–	1	1	–
Canada	–	–	–	–	4	2	3
Czech Republic	–	–	–	–	–	5	1
Slovakia	–	–	–	–	–	–	2
All Stars DEL	–	–	–	–	–	–	5

7. Nissan-Cup 1994
Freiburg/Fribourg – November 4 – 6, 1994

Nissan-Cup 1994/II

1. Sweden	11: 5	5
2. Russia	13: 7	5
3. Finland	7: 8	2
4. Switzerland	4:15	0

SUI	–	SWE	0:5
SUI	–	FIN	2:3
RUS	–	FIN	3:2
SUI	–	RUS	2:7
RUS	–	SWE	3:3
SWE	–	FIN	3:2

Nissan-Cup 1989 – 1994

	1989	1990	1991	1992	1993	1994	1994/II
Sweden	1	–	–	–	–	–	1
Finland	2	1	–	3	4	1	3
Switzerland	3	2	2	1	3	2	4
Germany	–	3	4	4	1	3	–
Soviet Union	–	–	1	–	–	–	–
Canada	–	–	3	–	2	–	–
Russia	–	–	–	2	–	–	2
Latvia	–	–	–	–	–	4	–

National Hockey League (NHL) 1994/95

Eastern-Conference
Regular Season 1994/95 (48 Games Season)

Northeast-Divison

Team	Goals	Pts
1. Quebec Nordiques	185:134	65
2. Pittsburgh Penguins	181:158	61
3. Boston Bruins	150:127	57
4. Buffalo Sabres	130:119	51
5. Hartford Whalers	127:141	43
6. Montreal Canadiens	125:148	43
7. Ottawa Senators	117:174	23

Atlantic-Divison

Team	Goals	Pts
1. Philadelphia Flyers	150:132	60
2. New Jersey Devils	136:121	52
3. Washington Capitals	136:120	52
4. New York Rangers	139:134	47
5. Florida Panthers	115:127	46
6. Tampa Bay Lightning	120:144	37
7. New York Rangers	126:158	35

Western Conference

Central-Divison

Team	Goals	Pts
1. Detroit Red Wings	180:117	70
2. St. Louis Blues	178:135	61
3. Chicago Black Hawks	156:115	53
4. Toronto Maple Leafs	135:146	50
5. Dallas Stars	136:135	42
6. Winnipeg Jets	157:177	39

Pacific-Divison

Team	Goals	Pts
1. Calgary Flames	163:135	55
2. Vancouver Canucks	153:148	48
3. San Jose Sharks	129:161	42
4. Los Angeles Kings	142:174	41
5. Edmonton Oilers	136:183	38
6. Anaheim Mighty Ducks	125:164	37

Play-offs

EASTERN

Quarter Finals

		H	H	A	A	H	A	H
Quebec Nordiques	– New York Rangers	5:4	3:8	3:4	2:3	4:2	2:4	–
Philadelphia Flyers	– Buffalo Sabres	4:3	3:1	1:3	4:2	6:4	–	–
Pittsburgh Penguins	– Washington Capitals	4:5	5:3	2:6	2:6	6:5	7:1	3:0
Boston Bruins	– New Jersey Devils	0:5	0:3	3:2	0:1	2:3	–	–

Semi Finals

Philadelphia Flyers	– New York Rangers	5:4	4:3	5:2	4:1	–	–	–
Pittsburgh Penguins	– New Jersey Devils	3:2	2:4	1:5	1:2	1:4	–	–

Conference Finals

Philadelphia Flyers	– New Jersey Devils	1:4	2:5	3:2	4:2	2:3	2:4	–

WESTERN

Quarter Finals

		H	H	A	A	H	A	H
Detroit Red Wings	– Dallas Stars	4:3	4:1	5:1	1:4	3:1	–	–
Calgary Flames	– San Jose Sharks	4:5	4:5	9:2	6:4	5:0	3:5	4:5
St. Louis Blues	– Vancouver Canucks	3:1	3:5	1:6	5:2	5:6	8:2	3:5
Chicago Black Hawks	– Toronto Maple Leafs	3:5	0:3	3:2	3:1	4:2	4:5	5:2

Semi Finals

Detroit Red Wings	– San Jose Sharks	6:0	6:2	6:2	6:2	–	–	–
Chicago Black Hawks	– Vancouver Canucks	2:1	2:0	3:2	4:3	–	–	–

Conference Finals

Detroit Red Wings	– Chicago Black Hawks	2:1	3:2	4:3	2:5	2:1	–	–

Stanley Cup Finals

Detroit Red Wings	– New Yersey Devils	1:2	2:4	2:5	2:5	–	–	–

Individual Statistic
Regular Season

Top scorers

Name	Team	GP	G	A	P
1. Jaromir Jagr	PIT	48	32	38	70
2. Eric Lindros	PHI	46	29	41	70
3. Alexej Zhamnov	WPG	48	30	35	65
4. Joe Sakic	QUE	47	19	43	62
5. Ron Francis	PIT	44	11	48	59
6. Theo Fleury	CGY	47	29	29	58
7. Paul Coffey (D)	DET	45	14	44	58
8. Mikael Renberg	PHI	47	26	31	57
9. John LeClair	PHI	46	26	28	54
10. Mark Messier	NYR	46	14	39	53

Most goals

Name	Team	GP	G
1. Jaromir Jagr	Pittsburgh	48	32
2. Owen Nolan	Quebec	46	30
3. Alexander Zhamnov	Winnipeg	48	30
4. Eric Lindros	Philadelphia	46	29
5. Theo Fleury	Calgary	47	29
6. Brett Hull	St. Louis	48	29
7. John LeClair	Philadelphia	46	26
8. Mikael Renberg	Philadelphia	47	26
9. Pierre Turgeon	Montreal	48	24
10. Mats Sundin	Toronto	47	23

Top defensemen

Name	Team	GP	G	A	P
1. Paul Coffey	DET	45	14	44	58
2. Ray Bourque	BOS	46	12	31	43
3. Phil Housley	CGY	43	8	35	43
4. Brian Leetch	NYR	48	9	32	41
5. Larry Murphy	PIT	48	13	25	38
6. Steve Duchesne	STL	47	12	26	38
7. Chris Chelios	CHI	48	5	33	38
8. Gary Suter	CHI	48	10	27	37
9. Sergej Zubov	NYR	38	10	26	36
10. Todd Gill	TOR	47	7	25	32

Top rookies

Name	Team	GP	G	A	P
1. Peter Forsberg	QUE	47	15	35	50
2. Paul Kariya	ANA	47	18	21	39
3. David Oliver	EDM	44	16	14	30
4. Ian Laperriere	STL	37	13	14	27
5. Todd Marchant	EDM	45	13	14	27
6. M. Czerkawski	BOS	47	12	14	26
7. Jeff Friesen	S.J.	48	15	10	25
8. Roman Oksiuta	VAN	38	16	6	20
9. Todd Harvey	DAL	40	11	9	20
10. Brian Savage	MTL	37	12	7	19

Play-offs

Top scorers

Name	Team	GP	G	A	P
1. Sergej Fedorov	DET	17	7	17	24
2. Stephan Richer	N.J.	19	6	15	21
3. Neal Broten	N.J.	20	7	12	19
4. Ron Franchis	PIT	12	6	13	19
5. Dennis Savard	CHI	16	7	11	18
6. Paul Coffey (D)	DET	18	6	12	18
7. John McLean	N.J.	20	5	13	18
8. Claude Lemieux	N.J.	20	13	3	16
9. Slava Kozlov	DET	18	9	7	16
10. Niklas Lidström	DET	18	4	12	16

Top defensemen

Name	Team	GP	G	A	P
1. Paul Coffey	DET	18	6	12	18
2. Niklas Lidström	DET	18	4	12	16
3. Larry Murphy	PIT	12	2	13	15
4. Brian Leetch	NYR	10	6	8	14
5. Chris Chelios	CHI	16	4	7	11

Top rookies

Name	Team	GP	G	A	P
1. Denis Chasse	STL	7	1	7	8
2. Peter Forsberg	QUE	6	2	4	6
3. Jeff Friesen	S.J.	11	1	5	6
4. Roman Oksiuta	VAN	10	2	3	5
5. Sergej Gonchar	WSH	7	2	2	4

Goalkeeper (min. 300 MIN)

Name	Team	MIN	GA	GAA
1. Martin Brodeur	N.J.	1222	34	1.67
2. Ed Belfour	CHI	1014	37	2.19
3. Mike Vernon	DET	1063	41	2.31
4. Ron Hextal	PHI	897	42	2.81
5. Felix Potvin	TOR	424	20	2.83
6. Ken Wregget	PIT	661	33	3.00
7. Kirk McLean	VAN	660	36	3.27
8. Dominik Hasek	BUF	309	18	3.50
9. Trevord Kidd	CGY	434	26	3.59
10. Mike Richter	NYR	384	23	3.59
11. Curtis Joseph	STL	392	24	3.67
12. Jim Carey	WSH	358	25	4.19
13. Wade Flathery	S.J.	377	31	4.93
14. Artur Irbe	S.J.	316	27	5.13

Goalkeeper Statistic
Regular Season

Goaltender	GP	MIN	GAA	GA	SV%
Ed Belfour	42	2450	2.28	93	.906
Jeff Hackett	7	328	2.38	13	.913
Jim Waite	2	119	2.52	5	.902
CHI Totals	48	2909	2.37	115	.904
Chris Osgood	19	1087	2.26	41	.917
Mike Vernon	30	1807	2.52	76	.893
DET Totals	48	2900	2.42	117	.903
Dominik Hasek	41	2416	2.11	85	.930
Robb Stauber	6	317	3.79	20	.867
Grant Fuhr	3	180	4.00	12	.859
BUF Totals	48	2920	2.45	119	.918
Jim Carey	28	1604	2.13	57	.913
Rick Tabaracci	8	394	2.44	16	.891
Olaf Kolzig	14	724	2.49	30	.902
Byron Dafoe	4	187	3.53	11	.863
WSH Totals	48	2922	2.46	120	.899
Martin Brodeur	40	2184	2.45	89	.902
Chris Terreri	15	734	2.53	31	.900
NJ Totals	48	2926	2.48	121	.901
J. Vanbiesbrouck	37	2087	2.47	86	.914
Mark Fitzpatrick	15	819	2.64	36	.900
FLA Totals	48	2916	2.61	127	.907
Blaine Lacher	35	1965	2.41	79	.902
Vincent Riendeau	11	565	2.87	27	.878
Craig Billington	8	373	3.06	19	.864
BOS Totals	48	2911	2.62	127	.891
Dominic Roussel	19	1075	2.34	42	.914
Ron Hextall	31	1824	2.89	88	.890
PHI Totals	48	2906	2.73	132	.898
Jocelyn Thibault	18	898	2.34	35	.917
Stephane Fiset	32	1879	2.78	87	.910
Garth Snow	2	119	5.55	11	.825
QUE Totals	48	2908	2.76	134	.908
Jason Muzzatti	1	10	0.00	0	1.000
Rick Tabaracci	5	202	1.49	5	.946
Trevor Kidd	43	2463	2.61	107	.909
Andrei Trefilov	6	236	4.07	16	.877
CGY Totals	48	2922	2.77	135	.904
Andy Moog	31	1770	2.44	72	.915
Manny Fernandez	1	59	3.05	3	.889
Darcy Wakaluk	15	754	3.18	40	.883
Mike Torchia	6	327	3.30	18	.895
DAL Totals	48	2925	2.77	135	.903
Glenn Healy	17	888	2.36	35	.907
Mike Richter	35	1993	2.92	97	.890
NYR Totals	48	2895	2.78	134	.894
Jon Casey	19	872	2.75	40	.900
Curtis Joseph	36	1914	2.79	89	.902
Geoff Sarjeant	4	120	3.00	6	.885
STL Totals	48	2912	2.78	135	.900

Goaltender	GP	MIN	GAA	GA	SV%
Sean Burke	42	2418	2.68	108	.912
Jeff Reese	11	477	3.27	26	.889
HFD Totals	48	2914	2.90	141	.904
Daren Puppa	36	2013	2.68	90	.905
J. C. Bergeron	17	883	3.33	49	.869
TB Totals	48	2906	2.97	144	.891
Damian Rhodes	13	760	2.68	34	.916
Felix Potvin	36	2144	2.91	104	.907
TOR Totals	48	2920	3.00	146	.905
Kirk McLean	40	2374	2.75	109	.904
Kay Whitmore	11	558	3.98	37	.867
VAN Totals	48	2942	3.02	148	.896
Patrick Roy	43	2566	2.97	127	.906
Ron Tugnutt	7	346	3.12	18	.895
MTL Totals	48	2921	3.04	148	.903
Tommy Salo	6	358	3.02	18	.905
Tommy Soderstrom	26	1350	3.11	70	.902
Jamie McLennan	21	1185	3.39	67	.876
NYI Totals	48	2909	3.26	158	.891
P. Derouville	1	60	3.00	3	.889
Ken Wregget	38	2208	3.21	118	.903
Wendell Young	10	497	3.26	27	.894
Tom Barrasso	2	125	3.84	8	.893
PIT Totals	48	2901	3.27	158	.900
Wade Flaherty	18	852	3.10	44	.903
Arturs Irbe	38	2043	3.26	111	.895
SJ Totals	48	2904	3.33	161	.894
Guy Hebert	39	2092	3.13	109	.904
M. Shtalenkov	18	810	3.63	49	.891
ANA Totals	48	2913	3.38	164	.897
Pauli Jaks	1	40	3.00	2	.920
Kelly Hrudey	35	1894	3.14	99	.910
Jamie Storr	5	263	3.88	17	.888
Grant Fuhr	14	689	4.04	47	.876
Robb Stauber	1	16	7.50	2	.667
L.A. Totals	48	2925	3.57	174	.896
Mike Bales	1	3	0.00	0	1.000
Don Beaupre	37	2101	3.37	118	.897
Darrin Madeley	6	315	3.43	18	.895
Craig Billington	9	472	4.07	32	.867
OTT Totals	48	2913	3.58	174	.889
N. Khabibulin	26	1339	3.41	76	.895
Tim Cheveldae	30	1571	3.70	97	.881
WPG Totals	48	2923	3.63	177	.885
Bill Ranford	40	2203	3.62	133	.883
Fred Brathwaite	14	601	3.99	40	.863
Joaquin Gage	2	99	4.24	7	.825
EDM Totals	48	2912	3.77	183	.875

NHL-Awards Trophys 1980-1995

Hart-Trophy

1994	Sergej Fedorov	DET
1993	Marion Lemieux	PIT
1992	Mark Messier	NYR
1991	Bret Hull	STL
1990	Mark Messier	EDM
1989	Wayne Gretzky	L.A.
1988	Mario Lemieux	PIT
1987	Wayne Gretzky	EDM
1986	Wayne Gretzky	EDM
1985	Wayne Gretzky	EDM
1984	Wayne Gretzky	EDM
1983	Wayne Gretzky	EDM
1982	Wayne Gretzky	EDM
1981	Wayne Gretzky	EDM
1980	Wayne Gretzky	EDM

Lady Byng-Trophy

1994	Wayne Gretzky	L.A.
1993	Pierre Turgeon	ISL
1992	Wayne Gretzky	L.A.
1991	Wayne Gretzky	L.A.
1990	Brett Hull	STL
1989	Joe Mullen	CAL
1988	Mats Näslund	MON
1987	Joe Mullen	CAL
1986	Mike Bossy	ISL
1985	Jari Kurri	EDM
1984	Mike Bossy	ISL
1983	Mike Bossy	ISL
1982	Rick Middleton	BOS
1981	Rick Kehoe	PIT
1980	Wayne Gretzky	EDM

Jack Adams-Award

1994	Jacques Lemaire	N.J.
1993	Pat Quinn	VAN
1992	Pat Quinn	VAN
1991	Brian Sutter	STL
1990	Bob Murdoch	WIN
1989	Pat Burns	MON
1988	Jacques Demers	DET
1987	Jacques Demers	DET
1986	Glen Sather	EDM
1985	Mike Keenan	PHI
1984	Bryan Murray	WSH
1983	Orval Tessier	CHI
1982	Tomm Watt	WIN
1981	Red Berensen	STL
1908	Pat Quinn	PHI

James Norris-Trophy

1994	Ray Bourque	BOS
1993	Chris Cheldis	CHI
1992	Brian Leetch	NYR
1991	Ray Bourque	BOS
1990	Ray Bourque	BOS
1989	Chris Chelios	MON
1988	Ray Bourque	BOS
1987	Ray Bourque	BOS
1986	Paul Coffey	EDM
1985	Paul Coffey	EDM
1984	Rod Langway	WSH
1983	Rod Langway	WSH
1982	Doug Wilson	CHI
1981	Randy Carlyle	PIT
1980	Larry Robinson	MON

Art Ross-Trophy

1994	Wayne Gretzky	L.A.
1993	Mario Lemieux	PIT
1992	Mario Lemieux	PIT
1991	Wayne Gretzky	L.A.
1990	Wayne Gretzky	L.A.
1989	Mario Lemieux	PIT
1988	Mario Lemieux	PIT
1987	Wayne Gretzky	EDM
1986	Wayne Gretzky	EDM
1985	Wayne Gretzky	EDM
1984	Wayne Gretzky	EDM
1983	Wayne Gretzky	EDM
1982	Wayne Gretzky	EDM
1981	Wayne Gretzky	EDM
1980	Marcel Dionne	L.A.

Calder-Trophy

1994	Martin Brodeur	N.J.
1993	Teemu Sälänne	WIN
1992	Pavel Bure	VAN
1991	Ed Belfour	CHI
1990	Sergei Makarov	CAL
1989	Brian Leetch	NYR
1988	Joe Nieuwendyk	CAL
1987	Luc Robitaille	L.A.
1986	Gary Suter	CAL
1985	Mario Lemieux	PIT
1984	Tom Barrasso	BUF
1983	Steve Larmer	CHI
1982	Dale Hawerchuk	WIN
1981	Peter Stastny	QUE
1980	Ray Bourque	BOS

Vezina-Trophy

1994	Dominik Hasek	BUF
1993	Ed Belfour	CHI
1992	Patrick Roy	MON
1991	Ed Belfour	CHI
1990	Patrick Roy	MON
1989	Patrick Roy	MON
1988	Grant Fuhr	EDM
1987	Ron Hextall	PHI
1986	J. Vanbiesbrouck	NYR
1985	Pelle Lindbergh	PHI
1984	Tom Barrasso	BUF
1983	Pete Peeters	BOS

1982	Bill Smith	ISL
1981	R. R. Sevigny, D. Heron	
	M. Laroque	
1980	B. Sauve, D. Edwards	

Con Smythe-Trophy

1994	Brian Leetch	NYR
1993	Patrick Roy	MON
1992	Mario Lemieux	PIT
1991	Mario Lemieux	PIT
1990	Mario Lemieux	PIT
1989	Al MacInnis	CAL
1988	Wayne Gretzky	EDM
1987	Ron Hextall	PHI
1986	Patrick Roy	MON
1985	Wayne Gretzky	EDM
1984	Mark Messier	EDM
1983	Bill Smith	ISL
1982	Mike Bossy	ISL
1981	Butch Goring	ISL
1980	Bryan Trottier	ISL

TROPHYS 1995

Hart-Trophy
Eric Lindros   PHI

James Norris-Trophy
Paul Coffey   DET

Art Ross-Trophy
Jaromir Jagr   PIT

Jack Adams-Trophy
Mark Crawford   QUE

Calder-Trophy
Peter Forsberg   QUE

Con Smythe-Trophy
Claude Lemieux   N.J.

Vezina-Trophy
Dominik Hasek   BUF

Lady Byng-Trophy
Ron Francis   Pit

BOSTON BRUINS

Player	GP	G	A	P	+/–	PIM	GP	G	A	P	PIM
Oates	48	12	41	53	11–	8	5	1	0	1	2
Bourque	46	12	31	43	3	20	5	0	3	3	0
Neely	42	27	14	41	7	72	5	2	0	2	2
Smolinski	44	18	13	31	3–	31	5	0	1	1	4
Czerkawski	47	12	14	26	4	31	5	1	0	1	0
Naslund	34	8	14	22	4–	4	5	1	0	1	0
Sweeney	47	3	19	22	6	24	5	0	0	0	4
Donato	47	10	10	20	3	10	5	0	0	0	4
Stumpel	44	5	13	18	4	8	5	0	0	0	0
Heinze	36	7	9	16	0	23	5	0	0	0	0
Kasatonov	44	2	14	16	2–	33	5	0	0	0	2
Hughes	44	6	6	12	6	139	5	0	0	0	4
Leach	35	5	6	11	3–	68	0	0	0	0	0
Rohloff	34	3	8	11	1	39	5	0	0	0	6
Reid	38	5	5	10	8	10	5	0	0	0	0
Moger	18	2	6	8	1–	6	0	0	0	0	0
Murray	35	5	2	7	11–	46	2	0	0	0	2
Shaw	44	3	4	7	9–	36	5	0	1	1	4
Huscroft	34	0	6	6	3–	103	5	0	0	0	11
Gruden	38	0	6	6	3	22	0	0	0	0	0
Knipscheer	16	3	1	4	1	2	4	0	0	0	0
Makela	11	1	2	3	0	0	0	0	0	0	0
Harkins	1	0	1	1	0	0	0	0	0	0	0
Potvin	6	0	1	1	1	4	0	0	0	0	0
Lacher	35	0	1	1	0	4	5	0	0	0	0
Stewart	5	0	0	0	0	2	0	0	0	0	0
Riendeau	11	0	0	0	0	2	0	0	0	0	0
Billington + OTT	17	0	0	0	0	4	1	0	0	0	0

CALGARY FLAMES

Player	GP	G	A	P	+/–	PIM	GP	G	A	P	PIM
Fleury	47	29	29	58	6	112	7	7	7	14	2
Nieuwendyk	46	21	29	50	11	33	5	4	3	7	0
Housley	43	8	35	43	17	18	7	0	9	9	0
Reichel	48	18	17	35	2–	28	7	2	4	6	4
Zalapski	48	4	24	28	9	46	7	0	4	4	4
Chiasson	45	2	23	25	10	39	7	1	2	3	9
Titov	40	12	12	24	6	16	7	5	3	8	10
Otto	47	8	13	21	8	130	7	0	3	3	2
Walz	39	6	12	18	7	11	1	0	0	0	0
Kruse	45	11	5	16	13	141	7	4	2	6	10
Kennedy	30	7	8	15	5	45	7	3	1	4	16
Stern	39	9	4	13	4	163	7	3	1	4	8
Dahl	34	4	8	12	8	38	3	0	0	0	0
Kisio	12	7	4	11	2	6	7	3	2	5	19
Sullivan	38	4	7	11	2–	14	7	3	5	8	2
Borschevsky + TOR	27	0	10	10	10	0	0	0	0	0	0
Patrick	43	0	10	10	3–	14	5	0	1	1	0
McCarthy	37	5	3	8	1	101	6	0	1	1	17
Esau + EDM	15	0	6	6	10–	15	0	0	0	0	0
Keczmer	28	2	3	5	7	10	7	0	1	1	2
May + DAL	34	2	3	5	3	119	0	0	0	0	0
Musil	35	0	5	5	6	61	5	0	1	1	0
Roberts	8	2	2	4	1	43	0	0	0	0	0
Viitakoski	10	1	2	3	1–	6	0	0	0	0	0
Ward	2	1	1	2	2–	2	0	0	0	0	0
Greig	8	1	1	2	1	2	0	0	0	0	0
Stillman	10	0	2	2	1	2	0	0	0	0	0
Tabaracci + WSH	13	0	2	2	0	2	1	0	0	0	0
Yawney	37	0	2	2	4–	108	2	0	0	0	2
Hlushko	2	0	1	1	1	2	1	0	0	0	2
Peplinski	6	0	1	1	2–	11	0	0	0	0	0
Nylander	6	0	1	1	1	2	6	0	6	6	2
Kidd	43	0	1	1	0	2	7	0	0	0	0
Trefilov	6	0	0	0	0	0	0	0	0	0	0

NHL action direct from Canada to your door.
Hockey News – 42 issues per year

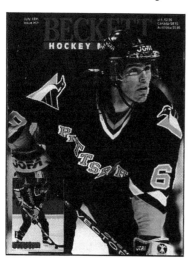 

ALSO AVAILABLE: **Sporting News, New NHL Magazine - Center Ice,**
NHL Match Team Programmes, and Hockey International - European Hockey Monthly,
plus many other North American Sporting Publications. Send for your free list today.

Available from
Barkers Worldwide Publications
155 Maybury Road, Woking, Surrey, UK, GU21 5JR.
Tel: (01483) 776141 Fax: (01483) 776141

EASY PAYMENT BY VISA, MASTERCARD AND EUROCARD

BUFFALO SABRES

Player	GP	G	A	P	+/-	PIM	GP	G	A	P	PIM
								Play-off			
Mogilny	44	19	28	47	0	36	5	3	2	5	2
Audette	46	24	13	37	3–	27	5	1	1	2	4
Galley + PHI	47	3	29	32	4	30	5	0	3	3	4
LaFontaine	22	12	15	27	2	4	5	2	2	4	2
Khmylev	48	8	17	25	8	14	5	0	1	1	8
Plante	47	3	19	22	4–	12	0	0	0	0	0
Bodger	44	3	17	20	3–	47	5	0	4	4	0
Presley	46	14	5	19	5	41	5	3	1	4	8
Hawerchuk	23	5	11	16	2–	2	2	0	0	0	0
Hannan	42	4	12	16	3	32	5	0	2	2	2
Zhitnik + L.A.	32	4	10	14	6–	61	5	0	1	1	14
Dawe	42	7	4	11	6–	19	5	2	1	3	6
Simpson	24	4	7	11	5–	26	0	0	0	0	0
Smehlik	39	4	7	11	5	46	5	0	0	0	2
Sweeney	45	5	4	9	6–	18	5	0	0	0	4
Pearson + EDM	42	3	5	8	14–	74	5	0	0	0	4
Huddy + L.A.	41	2	5	7	7–	42	0	0	0	0	0
May	33	3	3	6	5	87	4	0	0	0	2
Muni	40	0	6	6	4–	36	5	0	1	1	2
Astley	14	2	1	3	2–	12	2	0	0	0	0
Houda	28	1	2	3	1	68	0	0	0	0	0
Holzinger	4	0	3	3	2	0	4	2	1	3	2
Ray	46	0	3	3	4–	173	5	0	0	0	14
Brown	1	1	1	2	2	2	0	0	0	0	0
Barnaby	23	1	1	2	2–	116	0	0	0	0	0
Gordiouk	10	0	2	2	3–	0	0	0	0	0	0
Primeau	1	1	0	1	2–	0	0	0	0	0	0
Ambroziak	12	0	1	1	1–	0	0	0	0	0	0
Melanson	5	0	0	0	1–	4	0	0	0	0	0
Stauber + L.A.	7	0	0	0	0	0	0	0	0	0	0
Hasek	41	0	0	0	0	2	5	0	0	0	0

CHICAGO BLACK HAWKS

Player	GP	G	A	P	+/-	PIM	GP	G	A	P	PIM
								Play-off			
Nicholls	48	22	29	51	4	32	16	1	11	12	8
Murphy	40	23	18	41	7	89	16	9	3	12	29
Chelios	48	5	33	38	17	72	16	4	7	11	12
Suter	48	10	27	37	14	42	12	2	5	7	10
Amonte	48	15	20	35	7	41	16	3	3	6	10
Roenick	33	10	24	34	5	14	8	1	2	3	16
Poulin	45	15	15	30	13	53	16	4	1	5	8
Savard + TB	43	10	15	25	3–	18	16	7	11	18	10
Krivokrasov	41	12	7	19	9	33	10	0	0	0	8
Shantz	45	6	12	18	11	33	16	3	1	4	2
Sutter	47	7	8	15	6	51	16	1	2	3	4
Graham	40	4	9	13	2	42	16	2	3	5	8
Weinrich	48	3	10	13	1	33	16	1	5	6	4
Smith	48	1	12	13	6	128	16	0	1	1	26
Craven	16	4	3	7	2	2	16	5	5	10	4
Grieve	24	1	5	6	2	23	0	0	0	0	0
Cummins + TB	37	4	1	5	6–	158	14	1	1	2	4
Diduck + VAN	35	2	3	5	5–	63	16	1	3	4	22
Russell	33	1	3	4	4	88	16	0	3	3	8
Smyth	22	0	3	3	2	33	0	0	0	0	0
Belfour	42	0	3	3	0	11	16	0	0	0	6
Daze	4	1	1	2	2	2	16	0	1	1	4
Johansson	11	1	0	1	1	6	0	0	0	0	0
Carney	18	1	0	1	1–	11	4	0	1	1	0
Horacek	19	0	1	1	4–	25	0	0	0	0	0
Gauthier	5	0	0	0	0	0	0	0	0	0	0
Hackett	7	0	0	0	0	0	2	0	0	0	0
Kimble	14	0	0	0	5–	30	0	0	0	0	0
Dubinsky	16	0	0	0	5–	8	0	0	0	0	0

DALLAS STARS

Player	GP	G	A	P	+/-	PIM	Play-off GP	G	A	P	PIM
Gagner	48	14	28	42	2	42	5	1	1	2	4
Modano	30	12	17	29	7	8	0	0	0	0	0
K. Hatcher	47	10	19	29	4–	66	5	2	1	3	2
M. Donnelly + L.A.	44	12	15	27	4–	33	0	0	0	0	0
Millen + NJ	45	5	18	23	6	36	5	1	0	1	2
Klatt	47	12	10	22	2–	26	5	1	0	1	0
Adams + VAN	43	8	13	21	3–	16	5	2	0	2	0
Harvey	40	11	9	20	3–	67	5	0	0	0	8
Kennedy	44	6	12	18	4	33	5	0	0	0	10
Ledyard	38	5	13	18	6	20	3	0	0	0	2
Broten	47	7	9	16	7–	36	5	1	2	3	2
D. Hatcher	43	5	11	16	3	105	0	0	0	0	0
Evason	47	8	7	15	3	48	5	1	2	3	12
Gilchrist	32	9	4	13	3–	16	5	0	1	1	2
Cavallini	44	1	11	12	8	28	5	0	2	2	6
Zezel	30	6	5	11	6–	19	3	1	1	0	0
Ludwig	47	2	7	9	6–	61	4	0	1	1	2
Zmolek	42	0	5	5	6–	67	5	0	0	0	10
Churla	27	1	3	4	0	186	5	0	0	0	20
Varvio	5	1	1	2	1	0	0	0	0	0	0
Matvichuk	14	0	2	2	7–	14	5	0	2	2	4
G. Donnelly	16	1	0	1	1	52	5	0	1	1	6
Marshall	2	0	1	1	1	0	0	0	0	0	0
Moog	31	0	1	1	0	14	5	0	0	0	2
Torchia	6	0	0	0	0	0	0	0	0	0	0
Lalor	12	0	0	0	0	9	3	0	0	0	2
Wakaluk	15	0	0	0	0	4	1	0	0	0	0

DETROIT RED WINGS

Player	GP	G	A	P	+/-	PIM	Play-off GP	G	A	P	PIM
Coffey	45	14	44	58	18	72	18	6	12	18	10
Fedorov	42	20	30	50	6	24	17	7	17	24	6
Ciccarelli	42	16	27	43	12	39	16	9	2	11	22
Primeau	45	15	27	42	17	99	17	4	5	9	45
Sheppard	43	30	10	40	11	17	17	4	3	7	5
Yzerman	47	12	26	38	6	40	15	4	8	12	0
Kozlov	46	13	20	33	12	45	18	9	7	16	10
Lidstrom	43	10	16	26	15	6	18	4	12	16	8
Brown	45	9	12	21	14	16	18	4	8	12	2
Errey + SJ	43	8	13	21	13	58	18	1	5	6	30
Fetisov + NJ	18	3	12	15	1	2	18	0	8	8	14
Burr	42	6	8	14	13	60	16	0	2	2	6
Konstantinov	47	3	11	14	10	101	18	1	1	2	22
McCarty	31	5	8	13	5	88	18	3	2	5	14
Lapointe	39	4	6	10	1	73	2	0	1	1	8
Johnson	22	3	5	8	1	14	1	0	0	0	0
Draper	36	2	6	8	1	22	18	4	1	5	12
Rouse	48	1	7	8	14	36	18	0	3	3	8
Howe	18	1	5	6	3–	10	3	0	0	0	0
Krushelnyski	20	2	3	5	3	6	8	0	0	0	0
Taylor	22	0	4	4	1	16	6	0	1	1	12
Carkner	20	1	2	3	7	21	0	0	0	0	0
Ramsey	33	1	2	3	11	23	15	0	1	1	4
Ward	1	0	1	1	1	2	0	0	0	0	0
Ferner + ANA	17	0	1	1	4–	6	0	0	0	0	0
Grimson + ANA	42	0	1	1	11–	147	11	1	0	1	26
McKim	2	0	0	0	0	2	0	0	0	0	0
Osgood	19	0	0	0	0	2	2	0	0	0	0
Vernon	30	0	0	0	0	8	18	0	0	0	0

NEW JERSEY DEVILS

Player	GP	G	A	P	+/-	PIM	GP	G	A	P	PIM
Richer	45	23	16	39	8	10	19	6	15	21	2
N. Broten + DAL	47	8	24	32	1	24	20	7	12	19	13
MacLean	46	17	12	29	13	32	20	5	13	18	14
Guerin	48	12	13	25	6	72	20	3	8	11	30
Stevens	48	2	20	22	4	56	20	1	7	8	24
Chambers + TB	45	4	17	21	2	12	20	4	5	9	2
Holik	48	10	10	20	9	18	20	4	4	8	22
C. Lemieux	45	6	13	19	2	86	20	13	3	16	20
Niedermayer	48	4	15	19	19	18	20	4	7	11	10
Chorske	42	10	8	18	4–	16	17	1	5	6	4
Rolston	40	7	11	18	5	17	6	2	1	3	4
Carpenter	41	5	11	16	1–	19	17	1	4	5	6
Driver	41	4	12	16	1–	18	17	1	6	7	8
Albelin	48	5	10	15	9	20	20	1	7	8	2
Brylin	26	6	8	14	12	8	12	1	2	3	4
McKay	33	5	7	12	10	44	19	8	4	12	11
Peluso	46	2	9	11	5	167	20	1	2	3	8
Cole + TB	38	4	5	9	1–	14	1	0	0	0	0
Dowd	10	1	4	5	5–	0	11	2	1	3	8
Zelepukin	4	1	2	3	3	6	18	1	2	3	12
Daneyko	25	1	2	3	4	54	20	1	0	1	22
McAlpine	24	0	3	3	4	17	0	0	0	0	0
Brodeur	40	0	2	2	0	2	20	0	1	1	6
Emma	6	0	1	1	2–	0	0	0	0	0	0
Dean	17	0	1	1	6	4	3	0	2	2	0
Smith	2	0	0	0	3–	0	0	0	0	0	0
Simpson	9	0	0	0	1–	27	0	0	0	0	0
Modry	11	0	0	0	1–	0	0	0	0	0	0
Terreri	15	0	0	0	0	0	1	0	0	0	0

NEW YORK RANGERS

Player	GP	G	A	P	+/-	PIM	GP	G	A	P	PIM
M. Messier	46	14	39	53	8	40	10	3	10	13	8
Leetch	48	9	32	41	0	18	10	6	8	14	8
Zubov	38	10	26	36	2–	18	10	3	8	11	2
Verbeek + HFD	48	17	16	33	2–	71	10	4	6	10	20
Graves	47	17	14	31	9	51	10	4	4	8	8
Larmer	47	14	15	29	8	16	10	2	2	4	6
Kovalev	48	13	15	28	6–	30	10	4	7	11	10
Noonan	45	14	13	27	3–	26	5	0	0	0	8
Nedved	46	11	12	23	1–	26	10	3	2	5	6
Nemchinov	47	7	6	13	6–	16	10	4	5	9	2
Karpovtsev	47	4	8	12	4–	30	8	1	0	1	0
Loney + NYL	30	5	4	9	2–	23	1	0	0	0	0
Wells	43	2	7	9	0	36	10	0	0	0	8
LaFayette + VAN	39	4	4	8	3	2	8	0	0	0	0
Matteau	41	3	5	8	8–	25	9	0	1	1	10
Lowe	44	1	7	8	2–	58	10	0	1	1	12
Osborne	37	1	3	4	2–	19	7	1	0	1	2
Kypreos	40	1	3	4	0	93	10	0	2	2	6
Beukeboom	44	1	3	4	3	70	9	0	0	0	10
Kocur	48	1	2	3	4–	71	10	0	0	0	8
Norstrom	9	0	3	3	2	2	3	0	0	0	0
Langdon	18	1	1	2	0	62	0	0	0	0	0
J. Messier	10	0	2	2	2	18	0	0	0	0	0
Healy	17	0	2	2	0	2	5	0	0	0	0
Roy	3	1	0	1	1–	2	0	0	0	0	0
McCosh	5	1	0	1	1	2	0	0	0	0	0
Lacroix + BOS	24	1	0	1	2–	38	0	0	0	0	0
Richter	35	0	0	0	0	2	7	0	0	0	0

179

						Play-off				
Player	**GP**	**G**	**A**	**P**	**+/–**	**PIM**	**GP**	**G**	**A**	**P**	**PIM**
Lindros	46	29	41	70	27	60	12	4	11	15	18
Renberg	47	26	31	57	20	20	15	6	7	13	6
LeClair + MTL	46	26	28	54	20	30	15	5	7	12	4
Brind'Amour	48	12	27	39	4–	33	15	6	9	15	8
Desjardins + MTL	43	5	24	29	12	14	15	4	4	8	10
Yushkevich	40	5	9	14	4–	47	15	1	5	6	12
Dineen	40	8	5	13	1–	39	15	6	4	10	18
Therien	48	3	10	13	8	38	15	0	0	0	0
Fedyk	30	8	4	12	2–	14	9	2	2	4	8
Mac Tavish	45	3	9	12	2	23	15	1	4	5	20
Semenov + ANA	41	4	6	10	12–	10	15	2	4	6	0
Podein	44	3	7	10	2–	33	15	1	3	4	0
Haller	36	2	7	9	16	48	15	4	4	8	10
Dionne + MTL	26	0	9	9	4–	4	3	0	0	0	0
Dykhuis	33	2	6	8	7	37	15	4	4	8	14
Svoboda + BUF	37	0	8	8	5–	70	14	0	4	4	0
Juhlin	42	4	3	7	13–	6	13	1	0	1	0
DiMaio	36	3	1	4	8	53	15	2	4	6	4
Brown	28	1	2	3	1–	53	3	0	0	0	0
Montgomery + MTL	13	1	1	2	4–	8	7	1	0	1	0
Hextall	31	0	1	1	0	13	15	0	1	1	0
Zettler	32	0	1	1	3–	34	1	0	0	0	0
Malgunas	4	0	0	0	1–	4	0	0	0	0	0
Bowen	4	0	0	0	2–	0	0	0	0	0	0
Roussel	19	0	0	0	0	6	1	0	0	0	0
Dupre	22	0	0	0	7–	8	0	0	0	0	0
Antoski + VAN	32	0	0	0	4–	107	13	0	1	1	0

PHILA-DELPHIA FLYERS

						Play-off				
Player	**GP**	**G**	**A**	**P**	**+/–**	**PIM**	**GP**	**G**	**A**	**P**	**PIM**
Jagr	48	32	38	70	23	37	12	10	5	15	6
Francis	44	11	48	59	30	18	12	6	13	19	4
Sandstrom	47	21	23	44	1	42	12	3	3	6	16
Robitaille	46	23	19	42	10	37	12	7	4	11	26
Murphy	48	13	25	38	12	18	12	2	13	15	0
Mullen	45	16	21	37	15	6	12	0	3	3	4
Cullen	46	13	24	37	4–	66	9	0	2	2	8
Stevens	27	15	12	27	0	51	12	4	7	11	21
McEachern	44	13	13	26	4	22	11	0	2	2	8
Maciver + OTT	41	4	16	20	2–	16	12	1	4	5	8
Murray + OTT	46	4	12	16	2–	39	12	2	1	3	12
U. Samuelsson	44	1	15	16	11	113	7	0	2	2	8
Joseph	33	5	10	15	3	46	10	1	1	2	12
Barrie	48	3	11	14	4–	66	4	1	0	1	8
Hudson	40	2	9	11	1–	34	11	0	0	0	6
K. Samuelsson	41	1	6	7	8	54	11	0	1	1	32
Hawgood	21	1	4	5	2	25	0	0	0	0	0
Naslund	14	2	2	4	0	2	0	0	0	0	0
Andrusak	7	0	4	4	1–	6	0	0	0	0	0
McKenzie	39	2	1	3	7–	63	5	0	0	0	4
Tamer	36	2	0	2	0	82	4	0	0	0	18
Berehowsky + TOR	29	0	2	2	9–	28	1	0	0	0	0
Leroux	40	0	2	2	7	114	12	0	2	2	14
Fitzgerald	4	1	0	1	2	0	5	0	0	0	4
Park	1	0	1	1	1	2	3	0	0	0	2
Taglianetti	13	0	1	1	1	12	4	0	0	0	2
Barrasso	2	0	0	0	0	0	2	0	0	0	2
Young + TB	10	0	0	0	0	2	0	0	0	0	0
Wregget	38	0	0	0	0	14	11	0	0	0	7

PITTS-BURGH PENGUINS

QUEBEC NORDIQUES

Player	GP	G	A	P	+/–	PIM	GP	G	A	P	PIM
							Play-off				
Sakic	47	19	43	62	7	30	6	4	1	5	0
Forsberg	47	15	35	50	17	16	6	2	4	6	4
Nolan	46	30	19	49	21	46	6	2	3	5	6
Young	48	18	21	39	9	14	6	3	3	6	2
Ricci	48	15	21	36	5	40	6	1	3	4	8
Clark	37	12	18	30	1–	45	6	1	2	3	6
Kamensky	40	10	20	30	3	22	2	1	0	1	0
Bassen	47	12	15	27	14	33	5	2	4	6	0
Kovalenko	45	14	10	24	4–	31	6	0	1	1	2
Krupp	44	6	17	23	14	20	5	0	2	2	2
Deadmarsh	48	9	8	17	16	56	6	0	1	1	0
Leschyshyn	44	2	13	15	29	20	3	0	1	1	4
Lefebvre	48	2	11	13	13	17	6	0	2	2	2
Lapointe	29	4	8	12	5	41	5	0	0	0	8
Simon	29	3	9	12	14	106	6	1	1	2	19
Rucinsky	20	3	6	9	5	14	0	0	0	0	0
Wolanin	40	3	6	9	12	40	6	1	1	2	4
Foote	35	0	7	7	17	52	6	0	1	1	14
Huard + OTT	33	3	3	6	0	77	1	0	0	0	0
MacDermid	14	3	1	4	3	22	3	0	0	0	2
Norris	13	1	2	3	1	2	0	0	0	0	0
Gusarov	14	1	2	3	1–	6	0	0	0	0	0
Corbet	8	0	3	3	3	2	2	0	1	1	0
Miller	9	0	3	3	2	6	0	0	0	0	0
Laukkanen	11	0	3	3	3	4	6	1	0	1	2
Fiset	32	0	3	3	0	2	4	0	0	0	0
Finn	40	0	3	3	1	64	4	0	1	1	2
Klemm	4	1	0	1	3	2	0	0	0	0	0
Thibault	18	0	0	0	0	0	3	0	0	0	0

SAN JOSE SHARKS

Player	GP	G	A	P	+/–	PIM	GP	G	A	P	PIM
							Play-off				
Dahlen	46	11	23	34	2–	11	11	5	4	9	0
Janney + STL	35	7	20	27	1–	10	11	3	4	7	4
Friesen	48	15	10	25	8–	14	11	1	5	6	4
Whitney	39	13	12	25	7–	14	11	4	4	8	2
Ozolinsh	48	9	16	25	6–	30	11	3	2	5	6
Makarov	43	10	14	24	4–	40	11	3	3	6	4
Larionov	33	4	20	24	3–	14	11	1	8	9	2
Miller + STL	36	8	12	20	4	13	6	0	0	0	2
Falloon	46	12	7	19	4–	25	11	3	1	4	0
Pederson	47	5	11	16	14–	31	10	0	5	5	8
Tancill	26	3	11	14	1	10	11	1	1	2	8
Baker	43	7	4	11	7–	22	11	2	2	4	12
Rathje	42	2	7	9	1–	29	11	5	2	7	4
Nazarov	26	3	5	8	1–	94	6	0	0	0	9
Odgers	48	4	3	7	8–	117	11	1	1	2	23
Kyte	18	2	5	7	7–	33	11	0	2	2	14
More	45	0	6	6	7	71	11	0	4	4	6
Byakin	13	0	5	5	9–	14	0	0	0	0	0
Sykora	16	0	4	4	6	10	0	0	0	0	0
Butsayev	6	2	0	2	2–	0	0	0	0	0	0
Kozlov	16	2	0	2	5–	2	0	0	0	0	0
Wood	9	1	1	2	0	29	0	0	0	0	0
Kroupa	14	0	2	2	7–	16	6	0	0	0	4
Cronin	29	0	2	2	0	61	9	0	0	0	5
Flaherty	18	0	1	1	0	0	7	0	0	0	0
Donovan	14	0	0	0	6–	6	7	0	1	1	6
Irbe	38	0	0	0	0	4	6	0	0	0	10

ST. LOUIS BLUES

Player	GP	G	A	P	+/-	PIM	GP	G	A	P	PIM
Hull	48	29	21	50	13	10	7	6	2	8	0
Shanahan	45	20	21	41	7	136	5	4	5	9	14
Duchesne	47	12	26	38	29	36	7	0	4	4	2
Tikkanen	43	12	23	35	13	22	7	2	2	4	20
Creighton	48	14	20	34	17	74	7	2	0	2	16
Norton + SJ	48	3	27	30	22	72	7	1	1	2	11
MacInnis	32	8	20	28	19	43	7	1	5	6	10
Laperriere	37	13	14	27	12	85	7	0	4	4	21
Anderson	36	12	14	26	9	37	6	1	1	2	49
Gilbert	46	11	14	25	22	11	7	0	3	3	6
Elik + SJ	35	9	14	23	8	22	7	4	3	7	2
Houlder	41	5	13	18	16	20	4	1	1	2	0
Chasse	47	7	9	16	12	133	7	1	7	8	23
Carbonneau	42	5	11	16	11	16	7	1	2	3	6
Tardif	27	3	10	13	4	29	0	0	0	0	0
Roberts	19	6	5	11	2	10	6	0	0	0	4
Karamnov	26	3	7	10	7	14	2	0	0	0	2
Lidster	37	2	7	9	9	12	4	0	0	0	0
Johnson	15	3	3	6	4	6	1	0	0	0	2
Zombo	23	1	4	5	7	24	3	0	0	0	2
McRae	21	0	5	5	4	72	7	2	1	3	4
Baron	39	0	5	5	9	93	7	1	1	2	2
Twist	28	3	0	3	0	89	1	0	0	0	6
Dufresne	22	0	3	3	2	10	3	0	0	0	4
Stastny	6	1	1	2	1	0	0	0	0	0	0
Sarjeant	4	0	1	1	0	2	0	0	0	0	0
Joseph	36	0	1	1	0	0	7	0	1	1	0
Hollinger	5	0	0	0	1-	2	0	0	0	0	0
Batters	10	0	0	0	5-	21	0	0	0	0	0
Casey	19	0	0	0	0	0	2	0	0	0	0
Bozon	1	0	0	0	0	0	0	0	0	0	0

Header spanning: Play-off | GP G A P PIM

WASHINGTON CAPITALS

Player	GP	G	A	P	+/-	PIM	GP	G	A	P	PIM
Bondra	47	34	9	43	9	24	7	5	3	8	10
Juneau	44	5	38	43	1-	8	7	2	6	8	2
Pivonka	46	10	23	33	3	50	7	1	4	5	21
Johansson	46	5	26	31	6-	35	7	3	1	4	0
Khristich	48	12	14	26	0	41	7	1	4	5	0
Konowalchuk	46	11	14	25	7	44	7	2	5	7	12
Miller	48	10	13	23	5	6	7	0	3	3	4
Hunter	45	8	15	23	4-	101	7	4	4	8	24
Jones	40	14	6	20	2-	65	7	4	4	8	22
Cote	47	5	14	19	2	53	7	1	3	4	2
Johnson	47	0	13	13	6	43	7	0	2	2	8
Tinordi	42	3	9	12	5-	71	1	0	0	0	2
Poulin	29	4	5	9	2	10	2	0	0	0	0
Eagles + WPG	40	3	4	7	11-	48	7	0	2	2	4
Gonchar	31	2	5	7	4	22	7	2	2	4	2
Reekie	48	1	6	7	10	97	7	0	0	0	2
Berube	43	2	4	6	5-	173	7	0	0	0	29
Pearson	32	0	6	6	6-	96	3	1	0	1	17
Ulanov + WPG	22	1	4	5	1	29	2	0	0	0	4
Klee	23	3	1	4	2	41	7	0	0	0	4
Peake	18	0	4	4	6-	12	0	0	0	0	0
Gendron	8	2	1	3	3	2	0	0	0	0	0
Allison	12	2	1	3	3-	6	0	0	0	0	0
Slaney	16	0	3	3	3-	6	0	0	0	0	0
Kaminski	27	1	1	2	6-	102	5	0	0	0	36
Nelson	10	1	0	1	2-	3	0	0	0	0	0
Dafoe	4	0	0	0	0	0	1	0	0	0	0
Kolzig	14	0	0	0	0	4	2	0	0	0	0
Carey	28	0	0	0	0	0	7	0	0	0	4

TORONTO MAPLE LEAFS

Player	GP	G	A	P	+/-	PIM	GP	G	A	P	PIM
							Play-off				
Sundin	47	23	24	47	5–	14	7	5	4	9	4
Andreychuk	48	22	16	38	7–	34	7	3	2	5	25
Ridley	48	10	27	37	1	14	7	3	1	4	2
Gilmour	44	10	23	33	5–	26	7	0	6	6	6
Gill	47	7	25	32	8–	64	7	0	3	3	6
Wood	48	13	11	24	7	34	7	2	0	2	6
Gartner	38	12	8	20	0	6	5	2	2	4	2
Mironov	33	5	12	17	6	28	6	2	1	3	2
Hogue + NYL	45	9	7	16	0	34	7	0	0	0	6
Ellett	33	5	10	15	6–	26	7	0	2	2	0
Dipietro + MTL	34	5	6	11	9–	10	7	1	1	2	0
Craig	37	5	5	10	21–	12	2	0	1	1	2
Macoun	46	2	8	10	6–	75	7	1	2	3	8
Domi + WPG	40	4	5	9	5–	159	7	1	0	1	0
Jonsson	39	2	7	9	8–	16	4	0	0	0	0
Butcher	45	1	7	8	5–	59	7	0	0	0	8
Rychel + L.A.	33	1	6	7	4–	120	3	0	0	0	0
Berg	32	5	1	6	11–	26	7	0	1	1	4
Jennings + PIT	35	0	6	6	4–	43	4	0	0	0	0
Yake	19	3	2	5	1	2	0	0	0	0	0
Ward	22	0	3	3	4–	31	0	0	0	0	0
Sutter + CHI	37	0	3	3	6–	38	4	0	0	0	2
Hendrickson	8	0	1	1	0	4	0	0	0	0	0
Manderville	36	0	1	1	2–	22	7	0	0	0	6
Warriner	5	0	0	0	3–	0	0	0	0	0	0
Rhodes	13	0	0	0	0	4	0	0	0	0	0
Martin	15	0	0	0	2	13	0	0	0	0	0
Potvin	36	0	0	0	0	4	7	0	0	0	0

VANCOUVER CANUCKS

Player	GP	G	A	P	+/-	PIM	GP	G	A	P	PIM
							Play-off				
Bure	44	20	23	43	8–	47	11	7	6	13	10
Linden	48	18	22	40	5–	40	11	2	6	8	12
R. Courtnall + DAL	45	11	24	35	2	17	11	4	8	12	21
G. Courtnall	45	16	18	34	2	81	11	4	2	6	34
Beranek + PHI	51	13	18	31	7–	30	11	1	1	2	12
Brown	33	8	23	31	2–	16	5	1	3	4	2
Momesso	48	10	15	25	2–	65	11	3	1	4	16
Ronning	41	6	19	25	4–	27	11	3	5	8	2
Gelinas	46	13	10	23	8	36	3	0	1	1	0
Oksiuta + EDM	38	16	4	20	12–	10	10	2	3	5	0
Ruuttu + CHI	45	7	11	18	14	29	9	1	1	2	0
Lumme	36	5	12	17	4	26	11	2	6	8	8
Babych	40	3	11	14	13–	18	11	2	2	4	14
Hedican	45	2	11	13	3–	34	11	0	2	2	6
Peca	33	6	6	12	6–	30	5	0	1	1	8
Odjick	23	4	5	9	3–	109	5	0	0	0	47
Murzyn	40	0	8	8	14	129	8	0	1	1	22
Hunter	34	3	2	5	1	120	11	0	0	0	22
McIntyre	28	0	4	4	3–	37	0	0	0	0	0
Cullimore	34	1	2	3	2–	39	11	0	0	0	12
Namestnikov	16	0	3	3	2	4	1	0	0	0	2
Leemann	10	2	0	2	3–	0	0	0	0	0	0
Aucoin	1	1	0	1	1	0	4	1	0	1	0
Charbonneau	3	1	0	1	0	0	0	0	0	0	0
Jackson	3	1	0	1	0	4	6	0	0	0	10
Whitmore	11	0	1	1	0	7	1	0	0	0	0
Walker	11	0	1	1	0	33	0	0	0	0	0
McLean	40	0	1	1	0	4	11	0	1	1	0
Stojanov	4	0	0	0	2–	13	5	0	0	2	2

ANAHEIM MIGHTY DUCKS

Player	GP	G	A	P	+/-	PIM
Kariya	47	18	21	39	17–	4
van Allen	45	8	21	29	4–	32
Lebeau	38	8	16	24	6	12
Krygier	35	11	11	22	1	10
Douris	46	10	11	21	4	12
Carnback	41	6	15	21	8–	32
Dollas	45	7	13	20	3–	12
Corkum	44	10	9	19	7–	25
Sacco	41	10	8	18	8–	23
Rucchin	43	6	11	17	7	23
Sillinger + DET	28	4	11	15	4	8
Tverdovsky	36	3	9	12	6–	14
Karpov	30	4	7	11	4–	6
Holan	25	2	8	10	4	14
York + DET	24	1	9	10	2	10
Valk	36	3	6	9	4–	34
Kurvers	22	4	3	7	13–	6
Ladouceur	44	2	4	6	2	36
Karpa + QUE	28	1	5	6	1–	91
Lilley	9	2	2	4	2	5
Williams	21	2	2	4	5–	26
Lambert	13	1	3	4	3	4
Dirk	38	1	3	4	3–	56
Sweeney	13	1	1	2	3–	2
Sacco	8	0	2	2	3–	0
Vanimpe	1	0	1	1	0	4
Marshall	2	0	1	1	0	4
McSween	2	0	0	0	0	0
Shtalenkov	18	0	0	0	0	2
Ewen	24	0	0	0	2–	90
Hebert	39	0	0	0	0	5

EDMONTON OILERS

Player	GP	G	A	P	+/-	PIM
Weight	48	7	33	40	17–	69
Arnott	42	15	22	37	14–	128
Corson	48	12	24	36	17–	86
Oliver	44	16	14	30	11–	20
Marchant	45	13	14	27	3–	32
Buchberger	48	7	17	24	0	82
Thornton	47	10	12	22	4–	89
Kravchuk	36	7	11	18	15–	29
Stapleton	46	6	11	17	12–	21
Richardson	46	3	10	13	6–	40
Slegr + VAN	31	2	10	12	5–	46
Maltby	47	8	3	11	11–	49
Kennedy	40	2	8	10	2	25
Olausson	33	0	10	10	4–	20
Mironov	29	1	7	8	9–	40
Sutton + BUF	24	4	3	7	3–	42
White	9	2	4	6	1	0
Marchment	40	1	5	6	11–	184
Ciger	5	2	2	4	1–	0
Fraser + DAL	13	3	0	3	0	0
DeBrusk	34	2	0	2	4–	93
Mark	18	0	2	2	9–	35
Ranford	40	0	2	2	0	2
Bonsignore	1	1	0	1	1–	0
Nilsson	6	1	0	1	5–	0
Wright	6	1	0	1	1	14
Intranuovo	1	0	1	1	1	0
Gage	2	0	1	1	0	0
Aivazoff	21	0	1	1	2–	2
Bonvie	2	0	0	0	0	0
Smyth	3	0	0	0	1–	0
Tuomainen	4	0	0	0	0	0
McAmmond	6	0	0	0	1–	0
Brathwaite	14	0	0	0	0	0
McGill + PHI	20	0	0	0	4–	21

FLORIDA PANTHERS

Player	GP	G	A	P	+/-	PIM
Belanger	47	15	14	29	5–	18
Barnes	41	10	19	29	7	8
Mellanby	48	13	12	25	16–	90
Murphy	46	6	16	22	14–	24
Lowry	45	10	10	20	3–	25
Hull	46	11	8	19	1–	8
Lindsay	48	10	9	19	1	46
Fitzgerald	48	3	13	16	3–	31
Skrudland	47	5	9	14	0	88
Garpenlov + SJ	40	4	10	14	1	2
Hough	48	6	7	13	1	38
Woolley	34	4	9	13	1–	18
Duchesne + SJ	46	3	9	12	3–	16
Niedermayer	48	4	6	10	13–	36
Kudelski	26	6	3	9	2	2
Benning	24	1	7	8	6–	18
Svensson	19	2	5	7	5	10
Lomakin	31	1	6	7	5–	6
Laus	37	0	7	7	12	138
Smith	47	2	4	6	5–	22
Moller	17	0	3	3	5–	16
Svehla	5	1	1	2	3	0
Eakins	17	0	1	1	2	35
Cirella	20	0	1	1	7–	21
Vanbiesbrouck	37	0	1	1	0	6
Richer	1	0	0	0	0	2
Daniels	3	0	0	0	0	0
Linden	4	0	0	0	1–	17
Tomlinson	5	0	0	0	2–	0
Brown	13	0	0	0	1	2
Fitzpatrick	15	0	0	0	0	0

HARTFORD WHALERS

Player	GP	G	A	P	+/-	PIM
Cassels	46	7	30	37	3–	18
Turcotte	47	17	18	35	1	22
Sanderson	46	18	14	32	10–	24
Rice	40	11	10	21	2	61
Ranheim	47	6	14	20	3–	10
Kucera	48	3	17	20	3	30
Carson	38	9	10	19	5	29
Kron	37	10	8	18	3–	10
Nikolishin	39	8	10	18	7	10
Burt	46	7	11	18	0	65
Wesley	48	2	14	16	6–	50
Pronger	43	5	9	14	12–	54
Lemieux	41	6	5	11	7–	32
Drury	34	3	6	9	3–	21
Janssens	46	2	5	7	8–	93
Glynn	43	1	6	7	2–	32
Smyth	16	1	5	6	3–	13
Chibirev	8	3	1	4	1	0
Chase	28	0	4	4	1	141
Featherstone + NYR	19	2	1	3	7–	50
Storm	6	0	3	3	2	0
Daniels	12	0	2	2	1	55
Malik	1	0	1	1	1	0
McCrimmon	33	0	1	1	7	42
Burke	42	0	1	1	0	8
Petrovicky	2	0	0	0	0	0
Reese	11	0	0	0	0	0
Sandlak	13	0	0	0	10–	0
Godynyuk	14	0	0	0	1	8

LOS ANGELES KINGS

Player	GP	G	A	P	+/-	PIM
Gretzky	48	11	37	48	20–	6
Tocchet	36	18	17	35	8–	70
Quinn	44	14	17	31	3–	32
Kurri	38	10	19	29	17–	24
Granato	33	13	11	24	9	68
Sydor	48	4	19	23	2–	36
McSorley	41	3	18	21	14–	83
Druce	43	15	5	20	3–	20
Burridge + WSH	40	4	15	19	4–	10
Petit	40	5	12	17	4	84
Lacroix	45	9	7	16	2	54
Conacher	48	7	9	16	9–	12
Lang	36	4	8	12	7–	4
Blake	24	4	7	11	16–	38
Todd	33	3	8	11	5–	12
Shuchuk	22	3	6	9	2–	6
Snell	32	2	7	9	7–	22
Cowie	32	2	7	9	6–	20
Perreault	26	2	5	7	3	20
Boucher + BUF	15	2	4	6	3	4
Brown	23	2	3	5	7–	18
Crowder	29	1	2	3	0	99
O'Donnell	15	0	2	2	2–	49
Shevalier	1	1	0	1	1	0
Johnson	14	1	0	1	0	102
Blomsten + WPG	5	0	1	1	2	2
Thomlinson	1	0	0	0	1–	0
Watters	1	0	0	0	1	0
Lavigne	1	0	0	0	1–	0
Jaks	1	0	0	0	0	0
Brown	2	0	0	0	2–	0
Storr	5	0	0	0	0	0
Fuhr + BUF	17	0	0	0	0	2
Tsygurov + BUF	25	0	0	0	3–	15
Hrudey	35	0	0	0	0	0

MONTREAL CANADIENS

Player	GP	G	A	P	+/-	PIM
Recchi + PHI	49	16	32	48	9–	28
Turgeon + NYI	49	24	23	47	0	14
Damphousse	48	10	30	40	15	42
Brunet	45	7	18	25	7	16
Malakhov + NYI	40	4	17	21	3–	46
Keane	48	10	10	20	5	15
Savage	37	12	7	19	5	27
Bellows	41	8	8	16	7–	8
Brisebois	35	4	8	12	2–	26
Racine	47	4	7	11	1–	42
Odelein	48	3	7	10	13–	152
Daigneault	45	3	5	8	2	40
Stevenson	41	6	1	7	0	86
Fogarty	21	5	2	7	3–	34
Petrov	12	2	3	5	7–	4
Ronan	30	1	4	5	7–	12
Popovic	33	0	5	5	10–	8
Bure	24	3	1	4	1–	6
Lamb + PHI	47	1	2	3	12–	20
Brashear	20	1	1	2	5–	63
Conroy	6	1	0	1	1–	0
Rivet	5	0	1	1	2	5
Sarault	8	0	1	1	1–	0
Roy	43	0	1	1	0	20
Ferguson	1	0	0	0	0	0
Wilkie	1	0	0	0	0	0
Murray	3	0	0	0	0	4
Fleming	6	0	0	0	1–	17
Tugnutt	7	0	0	0	0	0
Roberge	9	0	0	0	2–	34
Sevigny	19	0	0	0	5–	15

NEW YORK ISLANDERS

Player	GP	G	A	P	+/-	PIM
Ferraro	47	22	21	43	1	30
Schneider + MTL	43	8	21	29	8–	79
Muller + MTL	45	11	16	27	18–	47
Flatley	45	7	20	27	9	12
Thomas	47	11	15	26	14–	60
King	43	10	16	26	5–	41
Palffy	33	10	7	17	3	6
McInnis	41	9	7	16	1–	8
Lachance	26	6	7	13	2	26
Green	42	5	7	12	10–	25
Vaske	41	1	11	12	3	53
Beers	22	2	7	9	8–	6
Severyn + FLA	28	2	4	6	2–	71
Dalgarno	22	3	2	5	8–	14
Marinucci	12	1	4	5	1–	2
Sutter	27	1	4	5	8–	21
Lindros	33	1	3	4	8–	100
Luongo	47	1	3	4	2–	36
Stanton	18	0	4	4	6–	9
Taylor	10	0	3	3	1	2
Kaminsky	2	1	1	2	2	0
Pilon	20	1	1	2	3–	40
Darby + MTL	13	0	2	2	6–	0
Chynoweth	32	0	2	2	9	77
Vukota	40	0	2	2	1	109
Salo	6	0	1	1	0	0
Miller	8	0	1	1	1	0
Kasparaitis	13	0	1	1	11–	22
Widmer	1	0	0	0	1–	0
Tichy	2	0	0	0	1–	2
Vasiliev	2	0	0	0	0	2
Dineen	9	0	0	0	5–	2
Chyzowski	13	0	0	0	2–	11
McLennan	21	0	0	0	0	2
Soderstrom	26	0	0	0	0	2

OTTAWA SENATORS

Player	GP	G	A	P	+/-	PIM
Yashin	47	21	23	44	20–	20
Daigle	47	16	21	37	22–	14
Turgeon	33	11	8	19	1–	29
Straka + PIT	37	5	13	18	1–	16
Larouche	18	8	7	15	5–	6
Hill	45	1	14	15	11–	30
Gaudreau	36	5	9	14	16–	8
Picard	24	5	8	13	1–	14
Levins	24	5	6	11	4	51
McLlwain	43	5	6	11	26–	22
Bonk	42	3	8	11	5–	28
Cunneyworth	48	5	5	10	19–	68
Elynuik	41	3	7	10	11–	51
Mallette	23	3	5	8	6	35
Dahlquist	46	1	7	8	30–	36
Demitra	16	4	3	7	4–	0
Bourque	38	4	3	7	17–	20
Huffman	37	2	4	6	17–	46
Archibald	14	2	2	4	7–	19
Neckar	48	1	3	4	20–	37
Vial	27	0	4	4	0	65
Davydov	3	1	2	3	2	0
Laperriere + STL	17	1	1	2	3–	15
Paek	29	0	2	2	5–	28
Boivin	3	0	1	1	1–	6
Pitlick	15	0	1	1	5–	6
Bales	1	0	0	0	0	0
Shaw	2	0	0	0	3	0
Guerard	2	0	0	0	0	0
Madeley	2	0	0	0	0	0
Bicanek	6	0	0	0	3	0
Beaupre	37	0	0	0	0	10

TAMPA BAY LIGHTNING

Player	GP	G	A	P	+/-	PIM
Bradley	46	13	27	40	6–	42
Ysebaert + CHI	44	12	16	28	3	18
Gratton	46	7	20	27	2–	89
Klima	47	13	13	26	13–	26
Tucker	46	12	13	25	10–	14
Hamrlik	48	12	11	23	18–	86
Semak + NJ	41	7	11	18	7–	25
Selivanov	43	10	6	16	2–	14
Zamuner	43	9	6	15	3–	24
Bureau	48	2	12	14	8–	30
Andersson	36	4	7	11	3–	4
Ciccone	41	2	4	6	3	225
Bergevin	44	2	4	6	6–	51
Cross	43	1	5	6	6–	41
Halkidis + DET	31	1	4	5	10–	46
Wiemer	36	1	4	5	2–	44
Charron	45	1	4	5	1	26
Plavsic + VAN	18	2	2	4	8	8
Myhres	15	2	0	2	2–	81
Poeschek	25	1	1	2	0	92
Hankinson + NJ	26	0	2	2	5–	13
Gretzky	3	0	1	1	2–	0
Puppa	36	0	1	1	0	2
Gallant	1	0	0	0	0	0
LiPuma	1	0	0	0	2	0
Bergeron	17	0	0	0	0	2

WINNIPEG JETS

Player	GP	G	A	P	+/-	PIM
Zhamnov	48	30	35	65	5	20
Tkachuk	48	22	29	51	4–	152
Selanne	45	22	26	48	1	2
Emerson	48	14	23	37	12–	26
Korolev	45	8	22	30	1	10
Drake	43	8	18	26	6–	30
Quintal	43	6	17	23	0	78
Numminen	42	5	16	21	12	16
Eastwood + TOR	49	8	11	19	9–	36
Manson	44	3	15	18	20–	139
Steen	31	5	10	15	13–	14
Shannon	40	5	9	14	1	48
Olczyk + NYR	33	4	9	13	1–	12
Gilhen	44	5	6	11	17–	52
Shannon	19	5	3	8	6–	14
King	48	4	2	6	0	85
Wilkinson	40	1	4	5	26–	75
Grosek	24	2	2	4	3–	21
Brown	9	0	3	3	1	17
Murray	10	0	2	2	1	2
Mikulchik	25	0	2	2	10	12
Martin	20	0	1	1	4–	19
Khabibulin	26	0	1	1	0	4
Cheveldae	30	0	1	1	0	2
Hansen	1	0	0	0	0	0
LeBlanc	2	0	0	0	0	0
Borsato	4	0	0	0	1–	0
Romaniuk	6	0	0	0	3–	0
Thompson	29	0	0	0	17–	78

PLAYER CARDS
ALL MAJOR BRANDS IN STOCK

Available from

**Barkers Worldwide Publications
155 Maybury Road, Woking,
Surrey, UK, GU21 5JR.
Tel: (01483) 776141 Fax: (01483) 776141**

Visa – Mastercard – Eurocard
Accepted

*Baseball - Basketball
American Football
Cards also available*

Stanley Cup 1883-1995

Cup winners prior formation of the NHL 1893-1917

1892/93	Montreal A. A. A.
1893/94	Montreal A. A. A.
1894/95	Montreal Victorias
1895/96	(Feb.) Winnipeg Victorias
	(Dec.) Montreal Victorias
1896/97	Montreal Victorias
1897/98	Montreal Victorias
1898/99	Montreal Shamrocks
1899/1900	Montreal Shamrocks
1900/01	Winnipeg Victorias
1901/02	Montreal A. A. A.
1902/03	Ottawa Silver Seven
1903/04	Ottawa Silver Seven
1904/05	Ottawa Silver Seven
1905/06	Montreal Wanderers
1906/07	(Jan.) Kenors Thistles
	(March) Montreal Wanderers
1907/08	Montreal Wanderers
1908/09	Ottawa Senators
1909/10	Montreal Wanderers
1910/11	Ottawa Senators
1911/12	Quebec Bulldogs
1912/13	Quebec Bulldogs
1913/14	Toronto Blueshirts
1914/15	Vancouver Millionairs
1915/16	Montreal Canadiens
1916/17	Seattle Metropolitans

NHL Cup winners 1918-1993

1917/18	Toronto Arenas
1919/20	Ottawa Senators
1920/21	Ottawa Senators
1921/22	Toronto St. Pats
1922/23	Ottawa Senators
1923/24	Montreal Canadiens
1924/25	Victoria Cougars
1925/26	Montreal Maroons
1926/27	Ottawa Senators
1927/28	New York Rangers
1928/29	Boston Bruins
1929/30	Montreal Canadiens
1930/31	Montreal Canadiens
1931/32	Toronto Maple Leafs
1932/33	New York Rangers
1933/34	Chicago Black Hawks
1934/35	Montreal Maroons
1935/36	Detroit Red Wings
1936/37	Detroit Red Wings
1937/38	Cicago Black Hawks
1938/39	Boston Bruins
1939/40	New York Rangers
1940/41	Boston Bruins
1941/42	Toronto Maple Leafs
1942/43	Detroit Red Wings
1943/44	Montreal Canadiens
1944/45	Toronto Maple Leafs
1945/46	Montreal Canadiens
1946/47	Toronto Maple Leafs
1947/48	Toronto Maple Leafs
1948/49	Toronto Maple Leafs
1949/50	Detroit Red Wings
1950/51	Toronto Maple Leafs
1951/52	Detroit Red Wings
1952/53	Montreal Canadiens
1953/54	Detroit Red Wings
1954/55	Detroit Red Wings
1955/56	Montreal Canadiens
1956/57	Montreal Canadiens
1957/58	Montreal Canadiens
1958/59	Montreal Canadiens
1959/60	Montreal Canadiens
1960/61	Chicago Black Hawks
1961/62	Toronto Maple Leafs
1962/63	Toronto Maple Leafs
1963/64	Toronto Maple Leafs
1964/65	Montreal Canadiens
1965/66	Montreal Canadiens
1966/67	Toronto Maple Leafs
1967/68	Montreal Canadiens
1968/69	Montreal Canadiens
1969/70	Boston Bruins
1970/71	Montreal Canadiens
1971/72	Boston Bruins
1972/73	Montreal Canadiens
1973/74	Philadelphia Flyers
1974/75	Philadelphia Flyers
1975/76	Montreal Canadiens
1976/77	Montreal Canadiens
1977/78	Montreal Canadiens
1978/79	Montreal Canadiens
1979/80	New York Islanders
1980/81	New York Islanders
1981/82	New York Islanders
1982/83	New York Islanders
1983/84	Edmonton Oilers
1984/85	Edmonton Oilers
1985/86	Montreal Canadiens
1986/87	Edmonton Oilers
1987/88	Edmonton Oilers
1988/89	Calgary Flames
1989/90	Edmonton Oilers
1990/91	Pittsburgh Penguins
1991/92	Pittsburgh Penguins
1992/93	Montreal Canadiens
1993/94	New York Rangers
1994/95	New Jersey Devils

How to build an ice stadium without wasting energy, the environment or money?

FinnIce knows how to make ice stadiums flexible and profitable.

Instead of wasting energy, the **FinnIce** method actually converts ice rinks, and stadiums into energy producers!

You can save on construction and operation costs without compromising on quality and usability. The **FinnIce** concept can save up to 50% in operating costs per year compared to a conventional ice rink.

For more information please contact:

FinnIce Europe
Mr Mika Wilska
Stuhlbrudergasse 3 · D-67346 Speyer
Telefon +49- (0)6232-240 13
Fax +49- (0)6232-261 47

NHL-Teams

Mighty Ducks of Anaheim
The Pond of Anaheim
2695 Katelle Ave. P.O. Box 61077
Anaheim CA, 92803

Boston Bruins
Boston Garden
150 Causeway Street
Boston, Massachusetts 02114

Buffalo Sabres
Memorial Auditorium
Buffalo, N. Y. 14202

Calgary Flames
P.O. Box 1540 Station M
Calgary, Alberta T2P 389

Chicago Black Hawks
Chicago Stadium
1800 W. Madison St.
Chicago, IL 60612

Dallas Stars
901 Main Street Suite 2301
Dallas TX 75202

Detroit Red Wings
Joe Louis Sports Arena
600 Civic Center Drive, D
Detroit, Michigan 48226

Edmonton Oilers
Northlands Coliseum
Edmonton, Albarta T5B 4M9

Florida Panthers
100 North East Third Ave. Tenth Floor
Fort Lauderdale FL 33301

Hartford Wheelers
242 Turmbull Street
Hartford, Connecticut 06103

Los Angeles Kings
3900 West Manchester Boulevard
Box 17013
Inglewood, California 90306

Montreal Canadiens
2313 St. Catherine Street West
Montreal, Quebec H3H 1N2

New Yersey Devils
Meadowlands Arena
Box 504
East Rutherford, N. J. 07073

New York Islanders
Nassau Veterans Memorial Coliseum
Uniondale, N. Y. 11553

New York Rangers
Madison Square Garden
4 Pennsylvania Plaza
New York, N. Y. 10001

Ottawa Senators
301 Moodie Drve Suite 200
Nepean, ONT K2H 9C4

Philadelphia Flyers
Zhe Spectrum, Pattison Place
Philadelphia, PA 19148

Pittsburgh Penguins
Civix Arena
Pittsburgh, PA 15219

Quebec to Denver
Colorado/USA

San Jose Sharks
525 West Sta. Clara Street
Box 1240
San Jose, California 95113

St. Louis Blues
5700 Oakland Avenue
St. Louis, Mo 63110

Tampa Bay Lightning
East Kennedy Blvd. Suite 175
Tampa, Florida 33602

Toronto Maple Leafs
Maple Leaf Gardens, 60 Carlton Street
Toronto, Ontario M5B 1L1

Vancouver Canucks
100 North Renfrew Street
Vancouver, B. C. V5K 3N7

Washington Capitals
US Air Arena
1 Warry S. Truman Drive
Landover, Maryland 20785

Winnipeg Jets
10th Floor 161 Portage Ave.
Winnipeg, Manitoba R3J 3T7

EUROPEAN-CUP 1994

Quarter Finals

Pool A (Esbjerg/DEN)
1. VIF Ishockey*   NOR   25: 6   5
2. Esbjerg*   DEN   29:15   4
3. Guards Nijmegen   NED   14:11   3
4. Txuri Urdin   ESP   5:41   0

Pool B (Trencin/SVK)
1. Tivali Minsk*   UKR   20: 1   6
2. Dukla Trencin*   SVK   26: 4   4
3. Narva Kreenholm   EST   6:19   2
4. Slavia Sofia   BUL   4:32   0

Pool C (Jesenice/SLO)
1. Ust Kamenogorsk* KAZ   31: 6   6
2. HK Jesenice*   SLO   19:11   4
3. VSV Villach   AUT   18:12   2
4. HK Zagreb   CRO   5:44   0

Pool D (Riga/LAT)
1. Pardagauva Riga* LAT   32: 6   5
2. Sokol Kiev*   UKR   22: 4   5
3. Devils Cardiff   GBR   15:23   2
4. Elektr. Vilnius   LTU   4:40   0

Pool F (Budapest/HUN)
1. HC Sparta Praha* CZE   44: 7   6
2. Ferencvarosi TC* HUN   64:23   4
3. Steaua Bukarest   ROM   22:20   2
4. Büküks. Ankara   TUR   3:83   0

* Promoted to Semi-Finals

Semifinals

Pool A (Olomouc/CZE)

	TOG	OLO	KAM	BUK	Goals	P
1. Lada Togliatti (RUS)*		4:4	9:1	13:1	26: 6	5
2. HC Olomouc (CZE)*	4:4		7:4	9:0	20: 8	5
3. Ust Kamenogorsk (KAZ)	1:9	4:7		6:4	11:20	2
4. Steaua Bukarest (ROM)	1:13	0:9	4:6		5:28	0

Pool B (München/GER)

	MÜN	KLO	RIG	MAI	Goals	P
1. Maddogs München (GER)*		4:2	5:3	4:3	13: 8	6
2. EHC Kloten (SUI)	2:4		10:1	3:2	15: 7	4
3. Padaugava Riga (LAT)	3:5	1:10		5:3	9:18	2
4. Devils Milano (ITA)	3:4	2:3	3:5		8:12	0

Pool C (Minsk/BLR)

	MIN	TRE	VEU	CAR	Goals	P
1. Tivali Minsk (BLR)*		1:1	5:2	14:0	20: 3	5
2. Dukla Trencin (SVK)*	1:1		4:1	14:2	19: 4	5
3. VEU Feldkirch (AUT)	2:5	1:4		13:1	16:10	2
4. Cardiff Devils (GBR)	0:14	2:14	1:13		3:40	0

Pool D (Malmö/SWE)

	MAL	ROU	JES	POD	Goals	P
1. Malmö IF (SWE)*		4:1	8:2	9:2	21: 5	6
2. HC Rouen (FRA)	1:4		13:0	5:0	19: 4	5
3. HC Jesenice (SLO)	2:8	0:13		7:5	9:26	2
4. Podhale Novy Targ (POL)	2:9	0:5	5:7		7:21	0

* Promoted to Final round

Final Tournament 1994 (Helsinki, Turku/FIN)

Pool A	JOK	OLO	RIG	MIN	Goals	P
1. Jokerit Helsinki (FIN)		6:1	9:4	3:1	18: 6	6
2. HC Olomouc (CZE)	1:6		1:2	3:1	5: 9	2
3. Pardaugava Riga (LAT)*	4:9	2:1		3:4	9:14	2
4. Tivali Minsk (BLR)	1:3	1:3	4:3		6: 9	2

* Riga for München (bankruptcy)

Pool B	TOG	TUR	MAL	TRE	Goals	P
1. Lada Togliatti (RUS)		3:3	3:1	9:2	15: 6	5
2. TPS Turku (FIN)	3:3		4:1	5:0	12: 4	5
3. Malmö IF (SWE)	1:3	1:4		4:2	6: 9	2
4. Dukla Trencin (SVK)	2:9	0:5	2:4		4:18	0

FINAL: Jokerit Helsinki – Lada Togliatti   4:2

EUROPEAN-CUP 1966-1994

Cup winners

1966	ZKL Brünn	TCH	1981	CSKA Moscow	URS
1967	ZKL Brünn	TCH	1982	CSKA Moscow	URS
1968	ZKL Brünn	TCH	1983	CSKA Moscow	URS
1969	CSKA Moscow	URS	1984	CSKA Moscow	URS
1970	CSKA Moscow	URS	1985	CSKA Moscow	URS
1971	CSKA Moscow	URS	1986	CSKA Moscow	URS
1972	CSKA Moscow	URS	1987	CSKA Moscow	URS
1973	CSKA Moscow	URS	1988	CSKA Moscow	URS
1974	CSKA Moscow	URS	1989	CSKA Moscow	URS
1975	Krylija Moscow	URS	1990	CSKA Moscow	URS
1976	CSKA Moscow	URS	1991	Djurgarden Stockholm	SWE
1977	Poli Kladno	TCH	1992	Djurgarden Stockholm	SWE
1978	CSKA Moscow	URS	1993	Malmö IF	SWE
1979	CSKA Moscow	URS	1994	TPS Turku	FIN
1980	CSKA Moscow	URS	1995	Jokerit Helsinki	FIN

Titels

CSKA Moscow	URS	20	Poldi Kladno	TCH	1
ZKL Brünn	TCH	3	Malmö IF	SWE	1
Djurgarden Stockholm	SWE	2	TPS Turku	FIN	1
Krylija Moscow	URS	1	Jokerit Helsinki	FIN	1

FEDERATION CUP 1994

Finals: Ljubljana/Laibach (SLO) · December 28. – 29., 1994

Play-off games	HC Pardubice (CZE)	– Partizan Belgrad (YUG)	6:1
	Olimpia Laibach (SLO)	– Salavat Yulayev Ufa (RUS)	1:7
	Olimpia Laibach (SLO)	– Partizan Belgrad	12:0
	HC Pardubice (CZE)	– Salavat Yulayev Ufa (RUS)	1:4

Final standing	1. Salavat Yulayev Ufa	RUS
	2. HC Pardubice	CZE
	3. Olimpia Laibach	SLO
	4. Partizan Belgrad	YUG

EUROPEAN CUP 1995/96

Quarter Finals (October 6–8)

Group A (in Bulgaria)
Steaua Bucharest (Rumania)
Sokol Kiev (Ukraine)
Partizan Belgrade (Yugoslavia)
Levski Sofia (Bulgaria)

Group B (in Hungary)
Tivali Minsk (Belarus)
Ust-Kamenogorsk (Kazakhstan)
Ferencvarosi (Hungary)
Medvescak (Croatia)

Group C (in Denmark)
Herning (Denmark)
Kreenholm (Estonia)
Energija (Lithuania)

Group D (Netherlands)
Tilburg (Netherlands)
Sheffield (Great Britain)
Olimpija (Slovenia)

The winner between Bat-Yam (Israel) and Ankara (Turkey) will qualify to Group C.

The winner between Txuri-Urdin (Spain) and Tornado (Luxembourg) will qualify to Group D.

Semi Finals (November 10–12)

Group E (in Norway)
HV-71 (Sweden)
Storhamar (Norway)
Kosice (Slovakia)
Winner of Group A

Group F (in Switzerland)
TPS (Finland)
Feldkirch (Austria)
Kloten (Switzerland)
Winner of Group B

Group G (in Italy)
Dynamo Moscow (Russia)
Bolzano (Italy)
Pardaugava (Latvia)
Winner of Group C

Group H (in Czech Republic)
Dadak Vsetin (Czech Republic)
Rouen (France)
Podhale (Poland)
Winner of Group D

The Finals will be played in Cologne, Germany from December 26 till 30. The defending European Champion Jokerit (Finland) automatically has qualified to the finals as well as the hosting Kölner EC. Four other teams will be the winners of the semi final tournaments.

SPENGLER CUP

DAVOS

1994

Final Standing	FÄR	DAV	CAN	TSC	IFK	Goals	Pts.
1. Färjestad Karlstad		8:2	3:2	3:2	5:6	19:13	6
2. Davos Selection	2:8		6:0	4:1	8:3	21:12	6
3. Team Canada	2:3	0:6		2:1	6:5	10:15	4
4. T. Tscheljabinsk	2:3	1:4	1:2		4:2	8:11	2
5. IFK Helsinki	6:5	3:8	5:6	2:4		16:23	2

Final: Färjestad Karlstad - Davos Selection 3:0

All Star-Team

Wieser
(DAV)

Jushkiewitsch   Svensson
(DAV)   (DAV)

Chomutov   Kortelainen   V. Karpov
(DAV)   (IFK)   (TSCH)

Top-Scorers

Name	Team	T	A	P
1. J. Höglund	FÄR	7	2	9
2. Ch. Weber	DAV	2	7	9
3. C. Eriksson	FÄR	2	6	8
4. Kortelainen	IFK	5	1	6
5. D. Hodgson	DAV	3	3	6

Fairplay-Cup: Färjestad Karlstad

Cupsieger 1923-1994

1923	Oxford University
1924	Berliner SC
1925	Oxford University
1926	Berliner SC
1927	HC Davos
1928	Berliner SC
1929/30	LTC Praha
1931	Oxford University
1932	LTC Praha
1933	HC Davos
1934/35	Diavolo Rosso Neri
1936	HC Davos
1937	LTC Praha
1938	HC Davos
1939/40	nicht ausgetragen
1941–1943	HC Davos
1944/45	Zürcher SC
1946–1948	LTC Praha
1949	nicht ausgetragen
1950	Diavolo Rosso Neri
1951	HC Davos
1952	EV Füssen
1953/54	HC Milan Inter
1955	Ruda Hvezda Praha
1956	nicht ausgetragen
1957/58	HC Davos
1959–1961	ACBB Paris
1962/63	Sparta Iglau
1964	EV Füssen
1965/66	Dukla Iglau
1967	Lokomotive Moscow
1968	Dukla Praha
1969	Lokomotive Moscow
1970/71	SKA Leningrad
1972–1974	Slovan Bratislava
1975	CSSR Olympic
1976	CSSR B
1977	SKA Leningrad
1978	Dukla Iglau
1979	Krilija Moscow
1980/81	Spartak Moscow
1982	Dukla Iglau
1983	Dynamo Moscow
1984	Team Canada
1985	Spartak Moscow
1986/87	Team Canada
1988	USA Selects
1989/90	Spartak Moscow
1991	CSKA Moscow
1992	Team Canada
1993/94	Färjestad Karlstad

Eishockey on the Rocks

Spengler Cup Davos
26. bis 31. Dezember 1995
Information und Reservation
Telefon 0041/81/415 21 18
Fax 0041/81/415 21 19

Hauptsponsor:

Sponsoren:

1967–1993
ISVESTIJA-TOURNAMENT

	URS	TCH	SWE	FIN	CAN	POL	DDR	GER	SUI	RUS A	RUS B
1967	1	4	–	–	5	6	–	–	–	–	–
1968	1	–	–	3	4	–	–	–	–	–	–
1969	1	3	4	5	2	–	6	–	–	–	–
1970	2	1	3	4	–	5	–	–	–	–	–
1971	1	2	4	3	–	–	–	–	–	–	–
1972	1	2	3	4	–	5	–	–	–	–	–
1973	1	2	5	3	–	4	–	–	–	–	–
1974	2	1	3	4	–	–	–	–	–	–	–
1975	1	2	3	4	–	–	–	–	–	–	–
1976	1	3	2	5	4	–	–	–	–	–	–
1977	2	1	3	4	5	–	–	–	–	–	–
1978	1	2	4	5	3	–	–	–	–	–	–
1979	1	2	4	3	5	–	–	–	–	–	–
1980	1	2	4	3	–	–	–	–	–	–	–
1981	1	2	4	3	–	–	–	–	–	–	–
1982	1	3	4	2	–	–	–	5	–	–	–
1983	1	2	3	4	5	–	–	–	–	–	–
1984	1	2	4	3	–	–	–	5	–	–	–
1985	2	1	3	5	4	–	–	–	–	–	–
1986	1	4	3	5	2	–	–	–	–	–	–
1987	2	4	3	5	1	–	–	6	–	–	–
1988	1	3	2	5	4	–	–	–	–	–	–
1989	1	2	6	3	4	–	–	5	–	–	–
1990	1	3	2	4	5	–	–	–	–	–	–
1992	–	2	4	5	7	–	–	8	6	3	1

1993	1. RUS A · 2. RUS B · 3. SWE · 4. USA and CZE, FRA, FIN, CAN, NOR, BLR

Tournament 1994

Pool A

1. Russia	17: 5	5
2. Finland	13: 2	5
3. Italy	3:12	1
4. France	4:18	1

Pool B

1. Czech Republic	14: 5	6
2. Sweden	16: 8	4
3. Norway	6:12	2
4. Switzerland	6:17	0

3rd Place: Finland – Sweden 2:1

Final: Russia – Czech Republic 1:0